New Psychotherapy for Men

William S. Pollack
Ronald F. Levant

John Wiley & Sons, Inc.
NewYork • Chichester • Weinheim • Brisbane • Singapore • Toronto

Published by John Wiley & Sons, Inc.

Published simultaneously in Canada.

This publication is designed to provide accurate and authoritative information in regard to the subject matter covered. It is sold with the understanding that the publisher is not engaged in rendering professional services. If legal, accounting, medical, psychological or any other expert assistance is required, the services of a competent professional person should be sought.

Library of Congress Cataloging-in-Publication Data:

New psychotherapy for men / [edited by] William S. Pollack and Ronald
    F. Levant.
        p.   cm.
    Includes bibliographical references and index.
    ISBN 0-471-17772-5 (hardcover : alk. paper)
    1. Men—Mental health. 2. Psychotherapy. I. Pollack, William S.
II. Levant, Ronald F.
RC451.4.M45N49   1998
616.89'14'081—dc21   98-5652

Printed in the United States of America.

10 9 8 7 6 5 4 3 2 1

For Marsha Padwa, Sarah Faye Pollack, my parents and grandparents.

W.S.P.

To Carol Slatter, Caren Levant, Adrian and Jeremy Shanker, and Wilma and Harry Levant.

R.F.L.

Editors and Contributors

William S. Pollack, PhD, is the codirector of the Center for Men and the director of Continuing Education (Psychology) at McLean Hospital, and is assistant clinical professor of psychology in the Department of Psychiatry at Harvard Medical School. He is the past president of the Massachusetts Psychological Association, a Candidate at the Boston Psychoanalytic Institute, a diplomate in Clinical Psychology (ABPP, Board Certified), and a founding member and fellow of the Society for the Psychological Study of Men and Masculinity, a division of the American Psychological Association. Dr. Pollack is coauthor (with Dr. Bill Betcher) of *In a Time of Fallen Heroes: The Re-creation of Masculinity* and coeditor (with Dr. Levant) of *A New Psychology of Men,* and author of *Real Boys.* His articles have appeared in the *New York Times, Wall Street Journal, USA Today,* and numerous other national and international publications.

Ronald F. Levant, EdD, is dean and professor of Psychology, Nova Southeastern University, Ft. Lauderdale, Florida. The founder and former director of the Boston University Fatherhood Project, Dr. Levant has played a major role in the American Psychological Association in setting up organizational structures on the reexamination of masculinity: He is founder and chair of the APA Division of Psychotherapy's Task Force on Men's Roles and Psychotherapy and cofounder and first president of the Society for the Psychological Study of Men and Masculinity (SPSMM). Dr. Levant is the author of sixty refereed articles and book chapters and ten books, including *Men and Sex* (edited with Gary R. Brooks, and also from Wiley), *Between Father and Child* (with John Kelly), *Masculinity Reconstructed* (with Gini Kopecky), and *A New Psychology of Men* (edited with Dr. Pollack).

Gary R. Brooks, PhD, received his doctorate from the University of Texas at Austin. He currently is the chief of psychology service at the Central Texas Veterans' Health Care System in Temple, Texas. He is an associate professor in psychiatry and behavioral sciences with the Texas

A&M University Health Sciences Center, adjunct faculty member at Baylor University, and instructor of men's studies with Texas Women's University. He has been president of the Division of Family Psychology of the American Psychological Association, president of the Society for the Psychological Study of Men and Masculinity, and an executive board member of the National Organization of Men Against Sexism (NOMAS). He has written more than 30 articles and book chapters. He has authored or co-authored four books—*The Centerfold Syndrome* (Jossey-Bass, 1995), *Men and Sex: New Psychological Perspectives* (Wiley, 1997), *Bridging Separate Gender Worlds* (APA Press, 1997), and *A New Psychotherapy for Traditional Men* (Jossey-Bass, 1998). He has traveled nationally to present continuing education workshops on psychotherapy for men. He received the 1996 Distinguished Practitioner Award of The APA Division of Men and Masculinity and the 1997 Texas Distinguished Psychologist Award.

Anderson J. Franklin, PhD, is a professor and past director of the Clinical Psychology Program at The City College and Graduate School of the City University of New York. He is a psychotherapist in private practice working with African American males in individual, group, marital, and family therapy. For many years, he has run therapeutic support groups for African American males.

In 1996, he received the Janet Helms Award for Mentoring and Scholarship in Psychology and Education at the Teachers College, Columbia University, Winter Roundtable in Cross Cultural Psychology and Education as well as honors for Outstanding Contribution from the National Association of Black Social Workers 28th Annual Conference. In 1995, the Association of Black Psychologists gave him the Distinguished Psychologist Award at their 28th Annual Conference. He has also received honors for his contributions to the field from the American Psychological Association, the New York State Board for Psychology, New York Society of Clinical Psychologists, and the New York Association of Black Psychologists.

Dr. Franklin has numerous publications and presentations about the mental health of African Americans. He has lectured and been a consultant on cultural diversity issues at universities and institutions throughout Europe, Africa, and the Caribbean. His publications include "Therapeutic Support Groups for African American Men" in L. Davis book titled *African American Males: A Practice Guide* (Sage Publications) . . . "Importance of Friendship Issues Between African American Men in a Therapeutic Support Group in the *Journal of African American Men,* and . . . "The Invisibility Syndrome" in *The Family Therapy Networker* which is the subject of his forthcoming book.

Judith V. Jordan, PhD, is the director of training at the Stone Center, Wellesley College, where she is also founding scholar of The Jean Baker Miller Institute. She is an attending psychologist at McLean Hospital and assistant professor of Psychology at the Harvard Medical School. She is the recipient of the Massachusetts Psychology Association's Career Achievement Award for Outstanding Contributions to the Advancement of Psychology as a Science and a Profession. Dr. Jordan founded the Women's Studies Program and Women's Treatment Network at McLean Hospital and served as its first director. She works as a psychotherapist, supervisor, teacher, and consultant. She is coauthor of *Women's Growth in Connection,* editor of *Women's Growth in Diversity,* and has published chapters and journal articles. Dr. Jordan has written, lectured, and conducted workshops nationally and internationally on the subjects of women's psychological development, empathy, mutuality, courage, shame, relational resilience, psychotherapy with women, a relational model of self, relational psychotherapy, gender issues in psychotherapy, relationships between women and men, the mother-daughter relationship, women's sexuality, special treatment programs for women, and treating posttraumatic stress.

Steven Krugman, PhD, received his doctorate in clinical psychology from New York University. He is a practicing clinical psychologist in the Boston area, where he also teaches at the Center for Psychoanalytic Studies at Massachusetts General Hospital and at the Trauma Center at the Human Resources Institute. He has a long-standing interest in many aspects of men's development and has written and presented on male violence, the impact of trauma, affect development, and intimate relationships.

Richard F. Lazur, PsyD, has written about the significance of male gender roles to adolescents, men of color, sex offenders, and in relationships. His chapters are included in *The Handbook of Counseling and Psychotherapy with Men* (Sage, 1987), *A New Psychology of Men* (Basic Books, 1995), and *Men in Groups* (APA Press, 1996). A licensed psychologist in the practice of Lazur & Lazur, Ltd., he earned a doctor of psychology degree from the Massachusetts School of Professional Psychology in 1983. Dr. Lazur serves as clinical director, Mental Health of Iliuliuk Family & Health Services on the Aleutian island of Unalaska and is a member of the adjunct faculty of Alaska Pacific University and the University of Alaska-Anchorage. He also serves as secretary of American Psychological Association Division 51 Society for the Psychological Study of Men and Masculinity. Dr. Lazur continues to explore the impact of male gender in his lectures in the United States and Canada.

David Lisak, PhD, is an associate professor of psychology at the University of Massachusetts-Boston and director of the Men's Sexual Trauma Research Project. He conducts and supervises research on the long-term effects of childhood abuse in adult men and on the relationship between early abuse and the later perpetration of interpersonal violence. He has been studying the impact of male gender socialization in the lives of traumatized men. His research has been published in the *Journal of Traumatic Stress,* the *Journal of Interpersonal Violence, Psychotherapy,* and other journals. In addition to his research and teaching, Dr. Lisak maintains a private practice specializing in the treatment of men, and serves as an expert witness in death penalty cases in which child abuse issues are raised.

Carolynn P. Maltas, PhD, earned her doctorate in clinical psychology from Boston University and is an assistant clinical professor in the Department of Psychiatry at Harvard Medical School. She was on the staff of McLean Hospital for 23 years, for the last nine years as founder and co-director of the McLean Institute for Couples and Families. She is currently an attending psychologist at Massachusetts Mental Health Center where she teaches family and couple therapy. She is a co-founder and faculty member of the Psychoanalytic Couple and Family Institute of New England and also a founding member of the Section on Couple and Family Therapy of the Division of Psychoanalysis (Division 39) of the American Psychological Association.

Dr. Maltas' primary clinical and scholarly interests are in the integration of psychoanalytic and family systems theories and the application of an integrated model to various areas of marital and family life. She has authored and co-authored articles on narcissistic couples, marital problems of midlife, the impact of childhood sexual abuse on adult intimate relationships, working with men in couple therapy, and the management of conflicts among therapists in multitherapist systems. She maintains a private practice in Cambridge, Massachusetts.

Thomas F. Mooney received his doctorate in Counseling Psychology at Western Michigan University. He has been on the Psychology faculty at St. Clair County Community College since 1965, receiving the Distinguished Faculty Award in 1994. In addition to his teaching, Dr. Mooney has maintained a private practice in the Port Huron, Michigan area for over 20 years. He is currently the Mens' Task Force Coordinator for the Albert Ellis Institute and has been working on applying cognitive therapy to men's issues. He has lectured on rational emotive behavioral therapy at Trinity College, Dublin, Ireland, Oatar University, Doha, Oatar. He has conducted men's groups in the Port Huron area and teaches an undergraduate class on the psychology of men.

Larry A. Morris, PhD, is a clinical psychologist with a private practice in Tucson, Arizona. He is a specialist in the evaluation and treatment of sexual disorders, childhood sexual abuse victims, adult victims of sexual assault, and sexual perpetrators. Dr. Morris has made presentations at numerous conferences about the impact of male gender roles on male sexuality. He provides workshops nationwide on treating male survivors of sexual victimization. Dr. Morris has served as secretary of the Society for the Psychological Study of Men and Masculinity, Division 51 of the American Psychological Association. He is one of the founding members and a past president of the National Organization on Male Sexual Victimization. Dr. Morris serves on the editorial board of the *Journal of Child Sexual Abuse* and is the author or coauthor of numerous articles, reports, and book chapters. Dr. Morris is also coauthor of *Males at Risk: The Other Side of Child Sexual Abuse* (Sage, 1989) and author of *The Male Heterosexual: Lust in His Loins, Sin in His Soul?* (Sage, 1997).

Marlin S. Potash, PhD, is a licensed psychologist, psychological business consultant, and psychotherapist specializing in financial services and men's issues. She is the author of *Hidden Agendas: What's Really Going on in Your Relationships, in Love, at Work and in Your Family* (Delacorte, 1990; Dell Trade Paper, 1990) and co-author of *Cold Feet: Why Men Don't Commit* (Dutton, 1988; NAL, 1989). She has also authored a variety of articles for professional journals and two book chapters. A Harvard Business School Case Note on partnerships was based on her work comparing entrepreneurial partnerships and family systems theory. A book on adolescents and sexuality is in progress.

Dr. Potash is a frequent speaker for business and educational organizations and was recently named Woman of Distinction of the Year in Canada. Dr. Potash appears regularly on television and has been quoted in numerous publications.

Dr. Potash is a magna cum laude graduate of Jackson College, Tufts University, and received her master's and doctoral degrees from Boston University. She has been on the faculty of Harvard University and assistant professor of Behavioral Science at Boston University School of Dentistry. She has also taught at Lesley College; Emmanuel College; Tufts University; Harvard University Medical School, and Fordham University School of Social Service.

Larry Rosenberg, PhD, is an instructor in psychology, Harvard Medical School and Cambridge Hospital. He is in private practice in Cambridge, Massachusetts. He has presented and written on sexual identity, hypnosis trauma, and integrative psychotherapy.

Steven Schwartzberg, PhD, earned his doctorate in clinical psychology at The University of Massachusetts at Amherst. He is assistant clinical professor of psychology, Department of Psychiatry at Harvard Medical School, and an associate psychologist at McLean Hospital in Belmont, Massachusetts. He is the author of *A Crisis of Meaning: How Gay Men Are Making Sense of AIDS* (Oxford University Press). He maintains a private practice in Cambridge, Massachusetts.

Joseph J. Shay, PhD, is currently director of psychological services at Two Brattle Center in Cambridge, Massachusetts, and also maintains a private practice in Cambridge. He is an instructor in psychology in the Department of Psychiatry at Harvard Medical School and associate attending psychologist at McLean Hospital in Belmont, Massachusetts, where he has practiced and taught for the past 20 years. Dr. Shay has been treating couples with reluctant men for more than two decades and has written and presented nationally on the subject.

Foreword

IT IS an honor to invite readers into this wonderful collection of theoretical and clinically informed papers addressing the dilemmas and strategies involved in the conduct of psychotherapy with male clients. For the past several years, Drs. William Pollack and Ron Levant have been creating exciting new models for the psychologies of men and in this ground-breaking book they have included other innovative clinicians in this expanding dialogue.

Since its inception, psychotherapy has been widely used by women. It has been avoided by most men. As one contributor notes, "Traditional men hate psychotherapy." The typical therapy dyad has been male therapist and female client. While feminists have protested against the gender biases of traditional therapy that have been detrimental to women, little has been written about the difficulty that men have had in entering therapy or making use of it.

Until recently most clinical theories pretended that psychotherapy could or even should be gender-neutral. When gender of therapist was referred to, it was often with the caveat that all therapists can speak to or call forth a maternal or paternal transference. Gender was seen as having relatively little importance. It was felt that most traditional therapy models were equally valid for both men and women. Feminist therapy early suggested that gender as well as other contextual factors needed to be included in our theories and practices. Since the 1970s, there has been an increasing emphasis on different developmental and clinical models for women and men. Psychological theories that spoke to the human condition have increasingly been viewed as limited in their application to both men and women. Thus application of theories of human psychology, without attention to gender, may be not only subtly distorting but destructive for both men and women clients.

This volume provides the practitioner with many valuable applications of the new understanding of mens' psychology that have been emerging in the past decade. It has been suggested that men are not typically allowed to ask for help; indeed they have not been allowed to show "weakness" or vulnerability. Men have not easily embraced traditional treatment models. The very qualities that are called for in psychotherapy (emotional vulnerability and availability, capacity to ask for help, the ability to articulate feelings states, openness to being affected by others) are discouraged in men. Few clinicians or theoreticians have undertaken the task of finding ways to address the specific needs that men have in therapy. Nor have we sought ways of rethinking the obstacles that keep men from getting help with their suffering or participating in psychotherapy.

The authors in this book have taken on the task of increasing the accessibility and usefulness of psychotherapy for men. They have demonstrated poignantly and powerfully that beneath the mask of stoicism and lonely strength that men are encouraged to present to the world, men suffer enormous psychological pain. These chapters detail the experiences of isolation of those who cannot reach out when help is needed, the shame of those seeking to meet impossible standards for masculinity, the stress of those cut off from their own resources for empathy and connection, and the ongoing, often hidden, yearnings of those who want to be close and intimate without sacrificing their sense of competence or masculinity. These authors provide both understanding of these dilemmas and practical clinical suggestions for helping men move out of their isolated pain.

This volume is rich in its appreciation of the special pathways to healing that are growth-enhancing for men. Written by practitioners from many different therapeutic and theoretical persuasions, as well as from diverse personal experiences, the book serves as a much-needed bridge to effective psychotherapeutic work with men. As a society, we cannot afford to neglect the profound psychological suffering that men encounter in their lives. As professionals, we clinicians need to seriously reconsider our approach to male clients. Old models of male development and treatment of men are at best inadequate and at worst lead to treatment failures and unremitting pain for men in therapy. This book offers a comprehensive and compassionate reworking of our understanding of men. It contains solid, exciting new theory and moving clinical case studies and examples. It also provides practical guidance and new ways to think about approaching men's psychological suffering. This comprehensive book brings us a discussion of normative alexithymia in men and ways to bring men into greater awareness of their emotions; the psychotherapy of shame; unrecognized depression in men and how to help men become more empathic with themselves; psychotherapy with gay and bisexual men; working with violent men; men in couples therapy; treating anger in African-American men; using group therapy; working with erectile disorders; adapting psychoanalytic and cognitive behavioral approaches. The chapters are thoughtful, pragmatic, and cutting edge. They offer a pathway for men from a place of hating or fearing psychotherapy to a place of healing possibility.

This is a book filled with wisdom and practical clinical advice but most importantly, it offers hope. We must assist men in their growth and realization of their full potential through acknowledgment of their need for help and the special ways that need manifests itself. We also must assist men in dealing with the ultimate human vulnerability with which we all struggle. In so doing, we offer the possibility of new developmental pathways to all men and women. I believe this book should become required reading for all those who are or will be treating men in psychotherapy. Beyond that, I hope its visions of new models of male development and personal change will impact a broader audience who will be moved to question and challenge the limiting and distorting socialization which we impose on young boys and men.

JUDITH V. JORDAN, PHD

Acknowledgments

WE WOULD like to thank our original editor, Jo Ann Miller, whose peerless knowledge and experience in the field of professional psychology publishing has been of enormous benefit to this book; and our final editors Jennifer Simon and Dorothy Lin for integrating this project at its important final stages. We would also like to thank Nancy Marcus Land and her staff at Publications Development Company for their work during book production.

Dr. Pollack would like to acknowledge the gracious input of his colleagues at Harvard Medical School/ McLean Hospital, and the support of the Department of Continuing Education at McLean, including Carol Brown and Cathy Toon. Patti Brown's aid with the typing of the manuscript is also gratefully recognized, as is the research assistance of the chief librarians at McLean and The Boston Psychoanalytic Institute, respectively, Lynn Dietrich and Ann Menashi. The special empathic and intellectual contribution of Dr. Judith Jordan as colleague friend and "fellow traveler" has had a tremendous positive impact on my thinking in this field. My colleagues and teachers in psychoanalysis have played a shaping role in enhancing my dynamic appreciation of men's inner lives, and members of this group I would like to particulary thank Drs. David Berkowitz, Arnold Modell, Gerald Adler, Dan Buie, Ralph Engle, Tony Kris, Lynn Layton, Paul Lynch, Risa Weinrit, Dianne Fader, Laura Weissberg, Rita Teusch, and Steve Rosenthal. Dr. Shervert Frazier, Psychiatrist in Chief, Emeritus of McLean Hospital has been a mentor, helping to develop, nurture, and support a new intellectual "voice" and a great debt of gratitude is owed to him. Such projects are impossible without the constant patience, love, and understanding of one's family and I am deeply indebted to my wife, Dr. Marsha Padwa, and daughter, Sarah Faye Pollack, for their unflagging support. My special thanks go to my colleague, friend, and co-editor, Dr. Ronald Levant.

Dr. Levant would like to thank his colleagues from whom he has learned much. Joe Pleck's work has been an inspiration for almost two decades. Gary Brooks has been a colleague and friend to whom he could turn in moments of doubt and also share the excitement of discovery. Co-editor Bill Pollack has been a stimulating friend and co-voyager in the exciting field of the new psychology of men. I would also like to express my gratitude to the men who participated in my Fatherhood Courses and Workshops, from whom I have learned an incalculable amount about the psychology of men. Projects like these require enormous understanding, patience, and love from one's family; and for that I am eternally grateful to my wife, Carol Slatter.

We would also like to thank the members of the "Men's Studies Seminar and Play Group," a group which we have both had the pleasure of participating in from 1990. It has been a wonderful environment in which to test new ideas and hear about the experiences of others groping around in this new field: Joel Eichler, Alan Gurwitt, Steve Krugman, David Lisak, Jon Reusser, and Bob Weiss. Finally, we have both learned from many other colleagues in Gender Studies and the Society for the Psychological Study of Men and Masculinity (SPSMM): Mike Andronico, Bill Betcher, Bob Brannon, Adele Cuthbert, Richard Eisler, Jeff Fischer, Marion Gindes, Glenn Good, Corey Habben, Marty Heesacker, Jaime Inclan, Michelle Kelley, Mark Kiselica, Richard Lazur, Richard Majors, Larry Morris, Jim O'Neil, Carol Philpot, Marlin Potash, George Rowan, Jeannette Rossello, Jerry Shapiro, Louise Silverstein, Denise Twohey, Lenore Walker, and many others.

To our patients, who have intrusted their lives to us, and who have taught us so much through their struggles, we extend our personal gratitude and thanks.

W.S.P.
R.F.L.

Contents

Introduction: Treating Men in the 21st Century   1
William S. Pollack and Ronald F. Levant

PART ONE   TREATMENT MODALITIES

1 The Trauma of Oedipus: Toward a New Psychoanalytic
  Psychotherapy for Men   13
  William S. Pollack

2 Desperately Seeking Language: Understanding,
  Assessing, and Treating Normative Male Alexithymia   35
  Ronald F. Levant

3 Cognitive Behavior Therapy for Men   57
  Thomas F. Mooney

4 Group Therapy for Traditional Men   83
  Gary R. Brooks

5 Reluctant Men in Couple Therapy: Corralling the
  Marlboro Man   97
  Joseph J. Shay and Carolynn P. Maltas

6 Men in the Family: A Family System's Approach to
  Treating Men   127
  Richard F. Lazur

PART TWO   ENDURING PROBLEMS, NEW SOLUTIONS

7 Mourning, Melancholia, and Masculinity: Recognizing
  and Treating Depression in Men   147
  William S. Pollack

8 Men's Shame and Trauma in Therapy   167
  Steven Krugman

9 Gender Role Stress and Male Erectile Disorder   191
  Larry A. Morris

10 Confronting and Treating Empathic Disconnection in
    Violent Men   214
    David Lisak

PART THREE BROADENING THE SPECTRUM

11 Treating Anger in African American Men   239
    Anderson J. Franklin
12 Being Gay and Being Male: Psychotherapy with
    Gay and Bisexual Men   259
    Steven Schwartzberg and Lawrence G. Rosenberg
13 When Women Treat Men: Female Therapists/
    Male Patients   282
    Marlin S. Potash

Index   309

Introduction: Treating Men in the 21st Century

William S. Pollack and Ronald F. Levant

B ECOMING AND being a man in today's world is as hard as it has ever been. The rigid codes of masculine behavior that women have deftly decried have taken a toll on men as well. Indeed, masculinity itself may be hazardous to males' physical and/or mental health (Harrison, 1978). Like lemmings to the sea, modern, postindustrialized men are dropping in droves: as the victims of the physiological sequelae of gender-role strain (Pleck, 1995)—succumbing to early cardiac events and stress-induced gastrointestinal diseases—and as the silent sufferers of severe psychological and emotional pain.

From childhood onward, men appear to be at risk. Infant males are more likely to undergo complications during labor and delivery and to have more birth defects. Boys often manifest behavioral difficulties and learning disabilities in elementary school. By eighth grade, boys are only half as likely as girls to aspire to be a professional or career person; boys are nine times more likely to suffer from hyperactivity and more than twice as likely to be suspended from school. Men are less likely to attend college and/or graduate school than women. Compared to young women, young men are four times more likely to be victims of homicide and are five times more likely to kill themselves (Pollack, 1998).

Men suffer under a code of masculinity that requires them to be: aggressive, dominant, achievement-oriented, competitive, rigidly self-sufficient, adventure-seeking, willing to take risks, emotionally restricted, and constituted to avoid all things, actions, and reactions that are potentially "feminine" (Levant & Pollack, 1995). Such a code is bound to take a toll on men's longevity. The average life expectancy for males in the United States is seven years shorter than that for women. Traditional male role traits inhibit men from seeking medical help in the early stages of disease and from being sufficiently attuned to their own internal processes to detect early warnings of illness (Waldron & Johnson, 1976).

While more women than men currently report psychological distress and attempt suicide, the gap appears to be closing in both arenas (Kessler & McRae, 1983). A National Institute of Mental Health (NIMH) catchment area study found that although women show higher rates of affective, anxiety, and somatic disorders, men continue to have higher rates of substance abuse and antisocial personality disorders (Landers, 1989). A Rand study has demonstrated that depression is not only denied by the men themselves but goes chronically underdetected. Over 60% of the time, healthcare professionals fail to diagnose and treat male patients' depressive disorders (Potts, Burnam, & Wells, 1991).

Men who are in dire need of psychological treatment and psychotherapy, however, do not utilize it readily. Six factors appear to stand in the way:

1. Difficulty in admitting the existence of a problem, which stems from what David and Brannon (1976) describe as the "sturdy oak" trait—a man feels he must conceal weakness even from himself. Dave Barry (1995, p. 120) captures this quality with his inimitable humor in the following dialogue, taken from his chapter "Special Medical Concerns of the Guy, or 'It's Just a Sprain' ":

   DOCTOR: So what seems to be the problem?
   PATIENT: Well . . . I keep coughing up blood. Plus I have these open sores all over my body. Also I have severe chest pains and double vision, and from time to time little worms burrow out of my skin.
   DOCTOR: It's just a sprain.
   PATIENT: That's what I thought.

2. Difficulty in asking for help (linked to the requirement for rigid self-sufficiency) and inability to tolerate *dependency* on others. Pollack (1995) has dubbed these traits defensive autonomy.
3. Difficulty in identifying and processing vulnerable and caring emotions—a form of gender-based alexithymia that leads to deficits of emotional intelligence in men (Levant & Kopecky, 1995).
4. Fear of intimacy or the interdependent sharing of vulnerable feelings—often resulting from the traumatic effects of early socialization experiences in boyhood (Pollack, 1995).
5. Sexualization of encounters with female therapists, and homophobic barriers in encounters with male therapists.

6. Lack of appropriate psychological and psychotherapeutic treatments designed from a perspective that is empathic to men's needs, struggles, and conflicts (Levant, 1990).

Given the gender-bifurcated nature of American society, one may conceptualize the designing of psychological interventions and psychotherapy for men as a *cross-cultural* process. The culture of traditional psychotherapy has required the expression of feelings and behaviors that often conflict with both conscious and unconscious aspects of the traditional male role. Traditional psychological therapies were historically designed by *male* doctors in order to treat *female* patients. In the past two decades, feminist scholars have pointed out the phallocentric flaws underlying these assumptions. However, this traditional treatment arrangement that has proven unworkable for women is equally unmanageable for men. At one time, it may have supported the power base of male doctors, but it has never taken into account the experience of *male patients,* and it entirely breaks down when women clinicians treat men. Our task is clear: to create and study psychological interventions and psychotherapies designed specifically and empathically for men.

As a field of professional study, the psychology of men and masculinity is still in its infancy. We have begun to recognize, however, from a gender-aware perspective (and aided by feminist-inspired scholarship), the unique socializing and developmental influences that shape the personalities of men and how these influences affect men's life experiences. Levant and Pollack (1995) have previously summarized this nascent field of the new psychology of men.

With specific reference to men and psychotherapy, much has begun to be accomplished. Beginning a decade ago, the Task Force on Men's Roles and Psychotherapy of the Division of Psychotherapy of the American Psychological Association sponsored numerous symposia at the annual conventions of the American Psychological Association (APA) and published a special series on men and psychotherapy in the journal *Psychotherapy* (Levant, 1990). Growing out of this effort, a new division of the APA was formed—Division 51, the Society for the Psychological Study of Men and Masculinity. From this and other quarters, a new body of work on the treatment of men has emerged (e.g., Andronico, 1996; Meth & Pasick, 1990; Scher, Stevens, Good, & Eichenfield, 1987).

New literature is taking the next steps and is evolving, for men, new psychotherapeutic approaches based on a more accurate understanding of male personality development and the male experience. Examples are:

Brooks's (1993, 1995) group therapy for traditional men; Levant's (1997; Levant & Kopecky, 1995) psychoeducational therapy; and Pollack's (1993, 1995; Betcher & Pollack, 1993) empathic psychoanalytic psychotherapy. The present volume brings together state-of-the-art psychotherapeutic models and applied psychological interventions that are specifically designed and/or creatively modified for men.

OVERVIEW OF THE CHAPTERS

Judith Jordan in her thoughtful Foreword points up the need for all therapists—male and female—to reconsider their treatment techniques. For Jordan this is not merely a choice but a necessity.

William Pollack, in his redefinition of psychoanalytic psychotherapy for men, "The Trauma of Oedipus: Toward a New Psychoanalytic Psychotherapy for Men," posits that much of men's unconscious pain is linked to a repressed trauma of abandonment or premature separation caused by male-role socialization processes. Consequently, men seeking treatment require the provision of an empathic holding environment in which that early pain can be assuaged without confronting their dependency needs before they are ready to acknowledge them. Therapy should not exacerbate men's sense of shame concerning the need for others, and therapists must tolerate their own narcissistic depletion in accepting many patients' need to deny the efficacy of therapy, even in the midst of process. Healing is conceptualized as both a relational and an interpretive process; it reaffirms the vibrancy of the hidden core self through the empathic self-object functions of the therapist.

Ronald Levant, in his chapter, "Desperately Seeking Language: Understanding, Assessing, and Treating Normative Male Alexithymia," focuses on his construct of normative male alexithymia, which he views as a central result of traditional masculinity ideology informing the male gender-role socialization process. He discusses the empirical literature on the emotion socialization of boys and shows how the combined influences of mothers, fathers, and peer groups result in a crossover in emotionality. As newborns, boys are much more emotional than girls—a difference that continues until at least six months of age. However, by the age of two years, the dampening effects of the socialization of emotions are seen in verbal expression; by six years, they are evident in facial expression. Levant presents a model for assessment of men's unique limitations in being able to experience and express aspects of their emotional life. He then presents a five-step psychoeducational model for increasing the emotional self-awareness of male psychotherapy patients, which helps them overcome their normative alexithymia and enables their deeper engagement in psychotherapy. He presents the case of Raymond, a "numb expectant father" with whom he has conducted the psychoeducational program, enabling the patient to grieve the loss of a sense of connection with his father, which has kept him from fully embracing his own imminent fatherhood.

Tom Mooney, in "Cognitive Behavior Therapy for Men," redefines traditional models of cognitive behavioral treatment and attempts to articulate the cognitive dimension to unhealthy masculinity. Mooney focuses specifically on those cognitive schemas that underlay Pleck's concept of gender role strain and he provides a cognitive therapy framework for clinically changing these unhealthy masculine schemas. Utilizing the concept of *internalized gender-role expectations,* Mooney adapts central concepts of Rational Emotive Behavior Therapy to the gender-specific treatment of men. Replete with individual cases, as well as examples applied to couples, Mooney's chapter deftly integrates modern cognitive techniques, pragmatic advice to the psychotherapist, personal disclosure/illustration, and the new psychology of men.

Gary Brooks, in "Group Therapy for Traditional Men," presents a model for therapy with working-class men that he has developed in his practice at the Veterans Administration Hospital in Temple, Texas. Group therapy can be especially helpful to men when it emphasizes the following key elements: (a) offering noble ascriptions for traditional male behavior; (b) accommodating men's communication styles; (c) framing men's problems in a larger gender context; (d) decreasing men's isolation from other men, and promoting the universality of their experiences; (e) instilling hope; (f) evoking and catharting men's psychological pain; (g) generating self-disclosure; and (h) lessening overdependence on women. He sees his group work as the foundation for an ambitious "therapy journey" comprised of several stages:

1. Initial therapy contact, where change-resistant forces are neutralized
2. Intense involvement in a men's group where change-enhancing forces are discovered and nourished, and personal growth is realized
3. Transition to marital and family therapy, where changes are translated into higher levels of relationship functioning
4. Social activism, where men encourage other men to consider new role potentials

In presenting the case of Luis, a 38-year-old, divorced Mexican-American bricklayer and Vietnam War combat veteran, Brooks describes his experiences in group therapy—from initial resistance to preparation for participation in a meaningful course of couples therapy.

Carolynn Maltas and Joseph Shay, in "Reluctant Men in Couple Therapy: Corralling the Marlboro Man," describe their work with a middle-aged couple whom they call Robert and Betty Marlboro. The authors place their work with this couple in the larger context of the difficulties men and women have in intimate cross-gender relationships in our era of gender-role strain, change, and confusion. The authors paint a portrait of the Marlboro man and discuss the special considerations that are required to successfully engage such a man in therapy. After reviewing the major approaches to addressing men's intimacy problems, the authors spell out the dilemmas of couples therapy when the male is reluctant. Interestingly, couples initiate therapy because of what appears to be a betrayal. In this case, the wife discovered a note in which a female associate of her husband stated how much she had enjoyed his company at dinner the previous night. The reader comes to realize, as the case artfully unfolds, that this is but the tip of the iceberg. The authors provide a nicely detailed and quite helpful example of how to successfully engage and hold reluctant male patients in a fairly deep process of couples therapy.

Richard F. Lazur, in "Men in the Family: A Family System's Approach to Treating Men," focuses on the manifestations of gender-role strain in the context of the family system. He first reviews the elements of family systems theory and shows how gender issues may be interlaced in the structure, functions, and processes of the family system. He then provides two case examples. In the first case, a 13-year-old son has been caught stealing. A pattern of sibling rivalry surfaces when the 8-year-old daughter complains that her brother occupies a privileged position in the family while she is burdened with chores. Later, in therapy, it becomes clear that the children's roles mirror those of their parents. The father occupies a distant role with minimal familial expectations; the mother occupies a central role and feels overburdened. The second, more detailed case involves a soon-to-be-blended family: Scott, a blue-collar worker and a divorced custodial father of four children, who deals with his stress by exhibiting explosive bursts of anger; Beth; and Beth's 12-year-old daughter. The treatment of this family hinged on helping Scott become more emotionally self-aware and hence more capable of managing the stress in his life.

In his second contribution to this volume, William Pollack extends his theory of men's false self development due to abandonment to aid as an intervention in and an explanation of male-type depressions. In his chapter, "Mourning, Melancholia, and Masculinity: Recognizing and Treating Depression in Men," after showing definitively that major depression is underdiagnosed in males, he presents a new diagnostic rubric of Major Depression—Male Type. Utilizing the case history of an older and apparently "angry" man, Pollack demonstrates an empathic intervention into the underlying sadness in his patient's lifelong rage and makes suggestions for integrating psychotherapy and psychopharmacology in the treatment of men's depressions.

Steven Krugman, in a continuation of his groundbreaking work on shame as a central component in the therapy of men, has contributed "Men's Shame and Trauma in Therapy." Utilizing as an illustrative model the case history of a man traumatically abused in his family of origin, Krugman explains the formative nature of shame affects in human experience and the prominent but unspoken role of shame in men's lives. Women are likely to reveal their shameful hurt; men attempt to mask equivalent feelings, giving shame a greater potential for emotional fragmentation in males. One of the great contributions of Krugman's chapter is that it recognizes and identifies shame elements in the gender-sensitive treatment of most men, and it offers technical, practical, clinical suggestions for dealing with such sensitive issues in an empathic way that avoids therapeutic impasse and transforms shameful experience into healthy, prideful hopefulness.

Larry Morris, in his clear and forthright chapter, "Gender Role Stress and Male Erectile Disorder," faces a reality that most men (and many therapists) find it only too easy to avoid: male impotence. Differentiating between medically generated illness and psychologically mediated disorders of male erectile functioning, Morris proposes a treatment approach which recognizes that a major component in the development of sexual disorders in men emanates from the uniquely traumatic male socialization process in our society. He focuses particularly on comprehensive evaluation and incisive treatment and offers excellent and multiple case examples. Several useful reference tables provide an intensive but quick review of instruments for assessing sexual adjustment and of models for gender-role-sensitive evaluation and treatment of erectile disorders in men.

Dave Lisak takes up a treatment issue that is vital to the new psychotherapy of men—violence—in his insightful chapter, "Confronting and Treating Empathic Disconnection in Violent Men." The ubiquity of this pressing problem, revealed through a thoughtful analysis of the roots of male violence and a succinct summary of the author's groundbreaking research on this subject, serves as a backdrop to a clinically fascinating treatment of a violent male patient and its creative application to violent issues within the psychotherapy of a broad range of male patients. Aimed at both specialists and generalists in the field, this chapter fills an important void in finding practical and empathic means to address men's aggression in psychotherapy.

Anderson Franklin, in "Treating Anger in African American Men," addresses a central dilemma in the lives of African American men: the anger and stress that result from their experiences with racial discrimination. In Franklin's conceptualization, the "Invisibility Syndrome" is a model for understanding the inner struggle for personhood and identity among African Americans. They must confront a racist pressure that seeks to make Black people invisible. Their response may take the form of feeling that one's true self *is* invisible, making it harder to find criteria for self-validation and self-esteem. The Invisibility Syndrome is also used to assess the degree to which individuals internalize the anger and stress that result from this confrontation between self and racism. The anger and stress may thus be viewed as ethnospecific risk factors that have major implications for the physical and mental health of African Americans. Franklin illustrates his argument with a therapeutic support group for young Black men.

Steven Schwartzberg and Lawrence Rosenberg, in "Being Gay and Being Male: Psychotherapy with Gay and Bisexual Men," turn our attention to a specialized population of men whose needs reflect an important admixture of traditional male socialization and the experience of being gay. The authors provide a model for a gay affirmative psychotherapy that emphasizes this interwoven process of male enculturation and gay identity formation. They argue convincingly that this framework, besides enhancing clinical work with gay and bisexual patients, broadens our understanding of modern psychotherapy for *all* men because, in our society cultural attitudes and struggles about homosexuality are inextricably tied to maleness and to each man's sense of his masculinity. This rich and informative chapter centers around an extensive psychotherapy with a gay man. Issues of maleness are interwoven with a host of other complex psychological issues.

Marlin Potash, in "When Women Treat Men: Female Therapists/Male Patients," offers a perspective that is unique in this volume—and in the field. A female psychotherapist approaches the treatment of men from a gender-informed perspective. Strategically situated to provide an outstanding view of the issues facing successful men, her practice serves investment bankers, media executives, attorneys, and fund managers in midtown Manhattan. She describes her model patient as an alexithymic, stressed man who confuses sex with intimacy—a man who is unable to bring major parts of his emotional life into awareness and assertively pursues sex as a goal in and of itself. She details the case of a patient whom she calls Mike, who initiated therapy shortly after his 40th birthday. Mike was a polygamist who had filled his life with an accumulating succession of affairs while his marriage steadily declined. The therapeutic turning point occurred when Mike learned to be alone and at ease with himself.

Taken as a whole this volume redefines the day-to-day pragmatic treatment modalities for men in our society.

REFERENCES

Andronico, M. (Ed.). (1996). *Men in groups.* Washington, DC: APA Books.

Barry, D. (1995). Special medical concerns of the guy, or "it's just a sprain." In D. Barry (Ed.), *Dave Barry's complete guide to guys* (pp. 99–120). New York: Random House.

Betcher, W., & Pollack, W. S. (1993). *In a time of fallen heroes: The recreation of masculinity.* New York: Atheneum.

Brooks, G. R. (1993). *Men treating men: Group therapy for traditional men.* Paper presented at the annual convention of the American Psychological Association, Toronto, Canada.

Brooks, G. R. (1995). *The centerfold syndrome.* San Francisco: Jossey-Bass.

David, D., & Brannon, R. (Eds.). (1976). *The forty-nine percent majority: The male sex role.* Reading, MA: Addison-Wesley.

Harrison, J. (1978). Warning: The male sex role may be dangerous to your health. *Journal of Social Issues, 34*(1), 65–86.

Kessler, R., & McRae, J. (1981). Trends in the relationship between sex and psychological distress: 1957–1976. *American Sociological Review, 46,* 443–452.

Kessler, R., & McRae, J. (1983). Trends in the relationship between sex and attempted suicide. *Journal of Health and Social Behavior, 24,* 98–110.

Landers, S. (1989, January). In U.S., mental disorders affect 15 percent of adults. *APA Monitor,* 16.

Levant, R. F. (1990). Special series on men's roles and psychotherapy. *Psychotherapy, 27,* 307–308.

Levant, R. F. (1997). *Men and emotions: A psychoeducational approach* (The Assessment and Treatment of Psychological Disorders Video Series). New York: Newbridge Communications.

Levant, R. F., & Kopecky, G. (1995). *Masculinity reconstructed: Changing the rules of manhood.* New York: Dutton/Plume.

Levant, R. F., & Pollack, W. S. (Eds.). (1995). *A new psychology of men.* New York: Basic Books.

Meth, R. L., & Pasick, R. S. (1990). *Men in therapy: The challenge of change.* New York: Guilford Press.

Pleck, J. (1995). The gender role strain paradigm: An update. In R. Levant & W. S. Pollack (Eds.), *A new psychology of men.* New York: Basic Books.

Pollack, W. S. (1993). *Treating the fallen hero: Empathic psychoanalytic psychotherapy designed for men.* Paper presented at the annual convention of the American Psychological Association, Toronto, Canada.

Pollack, W. S. (1995). No man is an island: Toward a new psychoanalytic psychology of men. In R. Levant & W. Pollack (Eds.), *A new psychology of men.* New York: Basic Books.

Pollack, W. S. (1998). *Real boys: Rescuing our sons from the myths of boyhood.* New York: Random House.

Potts, M. K., Burnam, M. A., & Wells, K. B. (1991). Gender differences in depressive detection: A comparison of clinician diagnosis and standardized assessment. *Psychological Assessment, 3*(4), 60–65.

Scher, M., Stevens, M., Good, G., & Eichenfield, G. A. (Eds.). (1987). *Handbook of counseling and psychotherapy with men* (pp. 30–38). Newbury Park, CA: Sage.

Waldron, I., & Johnson, S. (1976). Why do women live longer than men? *Journal of Social Stress, 2,* 19–29.

PART ONE

TREATMENT MODALITIES

The Trauma of Oedipus: Toward a New Psychoanalytic Psychotherapy for Men

William S. Pollack

LMOST A century ago, Freud (1912/1957b) described a painful dilemma in many men's lives—a neurotic conflict so universal as to be understood as a paradigm for derailment of the boy's journey toward healthy manhood: The unconscious split between an idealized image of the female (as mother substitute) and the symbol of degraded femininity (as prostitute)—The *Madonna* and *Whore* dichotomy. He summarized that for these men (and, I believe, to some extent, he meant *everyman*), "Where they love they do not desire and where they desire they cannot love" (p. 183, vol. XI, 1957b). Freud understood this degradation of men's lives to be a direct consequence of the burdens of the Oedipal struggles of desire and aggression in boyhood. To a large extent (whether openly or unwittingly), our psychology of men and the dynamic psychotherapies that emanate from it have accepted either this aggression and desire/conflict-based model or, alternatively, a paradigm of separation/autonomy for understanding and for attempting to treat men's pain.

This chapter attempts to forge an empathic foundation for a *new psychotherapy for men*, from a modern psychoanalytic (developmental/self-psychology) perspective. Listening to male patients reveals a fissure in many men's self-systems, one beginning well before the Oedipal period. This chapter is organized to support the theory that historical, cultural, and economic forces affect parenting styles so as to make it likely that as boys, men will suffer a traumatic disruption of their early holding environment, a premature psychic separation from both maternal and paternal caregivers. This is a normative male gender linked, loss, a *trauma of abandonment* for boys which may appear later in adult men, through symptomatic behavior and characterological defense.

Because of the unconscious sense of shame accompanying this frightening sense of deficit, many men seek treatment only reluctantly and under pressure from significant others. Often they enter the treatment setting with: empathic disruptions in their relationships (love/desire splits in romance or an inability to commit) as an attempt to unconsciously protect against further loss, limited emotionality with an intolerance of feelings of vulnerability, or to express and bear sadness; which consequently, hinders their ability to grieve—to mourn, and to change. These defenses are often incorporated into a syntonic character armor blocking a man's overt expression of all strong feelings, except anger, and may be maintained consciously, and valued, as a (false) self-sufficiency—a process I previously described as defensive autonomy (Pollack, 1990).

Clinical insights derived from modern psychoanalysis, including the need to address men's harsh self-criticism, alertness to the painful affect of shame as well as guilt, awareness of the deprivation-entitlement divergent conflict, and the provision of a self-object holding environment—with uncritical acceptance (for extended periods) of men's illusion of self-sufficiency—will illustrate how psychoanalytic psychotherapy can cure. The myth of Oedipus—so central to our received wisdom about masculinity—will be deconstructed to reveal unempathic parenting, intergenerational trauma, premature separation and loss, the overarching dynamic of shame-driven aggression, and a shame-phobic character style in men. Two case studies follow.

CASE STUDY: ALAN

Alan, a successful attorney in mid-life, sought treatment under pressure from his fiancée when he continued to put off setting a date for their wedding. Somewhat shamefully, he recounted his worry that monogamy was perhaps not "in man's nature," at least not in his. No matter how much he loved his fiancée, the thought of "hitching" himself to one woman for the rest of his life was an anathema to him. He worried that he might be "addicted to sex," requiring an unending number of new female conquests; and he felt too disturbed to marry.

Alan had previously undergone a trial of psychotherapy after college, but broke off the treatment when the psychologist encouraged him to stay attached to his, then, girlfriend—even though he was "feeling bored"—in order to see what feelings might emerge. He remembered leaving both the therapist and his girlfriend, simultaneously.

While remaining empathic to his patient's pain as a result of his psychic split between erotic desire and sex, on the one hand, and love or intimacy on the other, the current therapist maintained an open mind as to whether this was a problem of so-called addictive sexuality or a sexual issue at all. What finally emerged, slowly and painfully over time, were a series of memories of early childhood separations from his family which Alan experienced as painful. These left him in later childhood with terrifying anxiety culminating in attacks of panic. Adding to his distress were his caretakers' unempathic injunctions to "act like a man," not "like a baby" and accept the necessary and rational reasons for what was a tremendously hurtful disruption of his holding environment. In adolescence, these anxieties were driven underground when Alan rediscovered masturbation as both a stimulating and self-soothing device. During his college years, masturbation gave way to serial sexual affairs. Later, Alan came to understand that his intermittently intense sexual drive and activities were often an attempt to create, what he called, a "sense of safety"—to self-soothe overwhelming internal tension states when separation anxiety threatened to engulf him.

During this patient's long and successful analytically oriented therapy, he reported the following fantasy:

> It's like I'm an astronaut all alone in space . . . very exciting and not burdened by commitments. I'm connected by a cord, like an umbilicus which keeps me connected, but free to roam. When I have the desire, I can land on base, either eat or fuck, be satisfied again—refuel—and then go back out into space.

Alan was struggling to integrate intimacy and individuation without falling prey to a terrifying sense of loss.

Like Alan, many men's normative traumatic experience of premature separation, though often not consciously remembered, forever cast a pall on their relationships. Men are constantly seeking, yearning to be connected. However, they are terribly frightened of the shameful dependency such connections may bring forth. Too often the focus in the psychology of men has been the suppression of anxieties and depressive defenses these connections elicit and to replace experience-near fear with a model of sexually-based conflict. Men are not merely independent aggressive competitors, autonomously disconnected from others. They are frightened searchers, looking to connect, but wary should the bond once more be tragically broken. *To help men become more empathic to themselves, as well as to others, we must provide a psychotherapy that is more empathic to men.*

DECONSTRUCTING OEDIPUS: BOYS' TRAUMAS

For Freud and generations of psychoanalysts who followed, the myth of Oedipus became the central paradigm of unconscious forces at work in self and gender identity formation—especially for little boys. The story came to represent boys' unconscious sexual wishes for their mothers, fears of retributive castration by their fathers, and finally, the renunciation of this wish—leading to a more stable sense of self through the boy's identification with his father's masculine role. Freud believed the great power of this myth rests in our fearful recognition that all men harbor the same wishes that Oedipus lived out, and that such unconscious conflicts make up men's neurosis. Freud felt: ". . . (that) the poet, as he unravels the past, brings to light the guilt of Oedipus, . . . compelling us to recognize our own inner minds, in which those same impulses, though suppressed, are still to be found. . . . Like Oedipus, we live in ignorance of these wishes, . . . (and) seek to close our eyes to the scenes of our childhood" (Freud, 1900/1957a).

Yet, it appears to be Freud who closed his eyes to two central components of the myth he analyzed. First, the tragedy is set in motion *not* by a child's fantasies, but by an adult's hurtful actions. Laius, Oedipus's father, was so frightened that his son's birth would lead to his power on the throne being usurped that he hired a herdsman to murder the child. One rendering of the myth goes even further and suggests that it was not Laius alone, but also Oedipus's mother Jocasta who attempted to sacrifice the infant to appease the gods.

Oedipus survived, was adopted into another family, and on his return to Thebes, inadvertently murdered his father. He was soon to marry the queen, whom he did not consciously know to be his mother. Oedipus was worried, however, by dark prophesies and tried to reflect upon his action of marriage, contemplating withdrawal. Again he was betrayed by one of his parents, this time Jocasta (his mother, soon to be wife) who mocked the dire predictions and urged Oedipus to marry her without any further delay.

Freud chose to ignore Oedipus's earliest trauma, blaming the fantasies of the unconscious. But, in fact, the story of Oedipus is indeed a tale of a young boy betrayed and abandoned to die by his own mother and father. It is not Oedipus' unconscious lust for his mother or jealousy of his father that sets the stage for downfall, but his parents' hurtful rejection of him. I have no argument with Freud's pivotal belief in unconscious fantasy as the nidus of neurosis. Yet, I believe that boys also deserve an empathic under- standing of what may be a gender-specific trauma for males. The point is not to villainize Jocasta, or cast aspersions on Laius—to condemn mothers or fathers—but rather to highlight that men may either feel, or uncon- sciously experience a sense of having been prematurely and traumatically abandoned, betrayed, or hurtfully separated from their primary love ob- jects. Like Oedipus, most men may have no conscious memory of this ear- lier trauma, though their vulnerabilities (especially to shame) in adult life may be the evidence of the unhealed wound. I believe that this normative traumatic abrogation of the holding environment, for boys, comes about due to a complex combination of factors.

THEORY

I choose to read this myth and its modern deconstruction as illustrative of the pain many boys have suffered—not due to vicious sadism or economic neglect—but normatively and repetitively as a result of unconscious soci- etal demands for a separation model of male growth and development.

Almost 30 years ago, Ralph Greenson coined the term *dis-identify*, to de- note what he considered to be a "special vicissitude in the normal psycho- logical development of the boy which occurs in the pre-Oedipal years" (Greenson, 1968, p. 370). His model, based primarily on his clinical work with and research studies of transsexuals (and bolstered by his interpreta- tion of the underlying dysfunctions that gave way to his male neurotic pa- tient's conflicts), led him to opine "that the male child, in order to attain a healthy sense of maleness, must *replace* the primary object of his identifica- tion, the mother, and must identify *instead* with the father" (p. 370, italics mine). He went on to state categorically that the boy "must dis-identify from mother and identify with a male figure if he is to develop a male gen- der identity" (p. 372). Although he felt that all infants emerged into younger childhood from a "primitive symbiotic-identification with a mothering person" (p. 372), boys appeared to have a more fragile and special problem in maintaining a healthy sense of gender identity. This, Greenson believed, was because boys required an additional develop- mental step: They needed to dis-identify from mother and form what he called a *counter identification* or *contra-identification* as a way to counteract the early identifictory basis with a primary female figure. Girls, it seems, had it easier, theoretically, because they could remain identified with their mothers; but boys had a more rocky course for two reasons: (1) the need to renounce their love for their mothers, and (2) the often less available alternative identificatory figure of father.

> This a special problem because the boy must attempt to renounce the plea-sure and security-giving closeness that identification with the mothering person affords, and he must form an identification with the less accessible father. (Greenson, 1968 p. 373)

Make no mistake about it, Greenson saw this need to dis-identify as essential to the young boy's capacity to internalize a healthy male gen-der identity (equally as salient as anatomical or biological differences) and saw the consequences for any disruption of such a process of separa-tion as dire. The example of his 5-year-old patient, Lance, leaves little doubt that if this little boy's identification with mother and play with his "Barbie" doll were not interrupted by Greenson's active attempts to push for dis-identification, he would become "either a full-fledged trans-sexual or a transvestite" (Greenson, 1968 p. 371).

Much as this model of dis-identification may seem impossibly simplistic to us today, when it was combined historically with an object-relations model that conceptualized separation (Mahler, Pine, & Bergman, 1975) as the hallmark of mental health, the push for intrapsychic and intrapersonal separation from the mother became a central normative developmental focus in the early growth and development of boys—a focus still embraced in some quarters. As we move to deconstruct the essentially *masculine*, re-placing it with a societally constructed model of gender—in which women are primarily responsible for the early caretaking of children, and fathers have historically been emotionally unavailable—we may begin to see that the need for male dis-identification is not just a clumsy and cumbersome model of normal human development. It is an unwitting justification for the normative traumatization of boys, and later adult men.

Chodorow (1978, 1989), in her thoughtful critique of Freud's theories of early development, pointed her finger at the emperor's new clothes. Girls did not come to motherhood as second-class citizens in relinquishing their hope for a penis, turning away from their mothers and toward their fathers with the wish to provide them with a baby. Since women are still largely responsible for caretaking in the early years of a child's life, identity for-mation for females occurred through the integration of and identification with an ongoing relational attachment to their mothers. This "sense of continuity and similarity to their mother" led to a healthy sense of mutuality in relationship, and identification with the caretaking and maternal feminine role from early childhood onward. What, then, for boys?

If one accepts Chodorow's argument, one must basically agree with her that in society, historically, "because women mother the sense of maleness in men differs from the sense of femaleness in women and masculinity (or maleness) becomes more conflictual and more problematic, than femaleness" (Chodorow, 1989, p. 109). What becomes clear from this perspective is that little boys and grown men, unconsciously, fend off an earlier sense of oneness with their mother that tends to threaten their gender identity, and/or independent sense of self. Not as a normal developmental pathway based upon a biological bedrock, but, rather, as a result of a fault in our child-rearing systems. Both because of the current child-rearing practices which create the significance of the mother, and the consequent "absence of concrete, real, available male figures of identification and love who are [equally] salient" for the boy, "learning what it is to be masculine comes to mean learning to be not womanly." As a result, separateness becomes more salient, for boys. Boys, and later men, come to eschew "feminine" identifications and experiences, such as: dependency, the expression of strong feelings (with the exception of anger), and relational bonding.

A NORMATIVE (GENDER-LINKED) DEVELOPMENTAL TRAUMA

Yet, deep in the adult male's psyche lies the formative experience of a little boy, struggling to maintain a sense of a masculine self, vis-à-vis his attachment to his mother. He is also struggling with the very real loss of an earlier affiliative oneness, which can never be regained—within this system—without a threat to masculine identity.

While Chodorow's discussion of gender identity development is insightful, it does not adequately capture what this experience of development must feel like for a little boy. Nowhere do we get a sense of the loss associated with the boy's definition of his own masculine identity and core gender self: an experiential process that requires (according to this model) a separation from the most cherished, admired, and loved object in his life—at what would be a phase inappropriate time from the point of view of girls' development. Equally significant, this broken maternal connection or *dis-identification* (Greenson, 1968) occurs within a social context of child rearing: (a) in which girl siblings are allowed to remain connected; and, (b) in which the father often remains absent or emotionally unavailable to his young son, as an alternate nurturing figure for the "lost" mother.

Chodorow (1978) makes the suggestion that the intrapsychic developmental events so significant to the young boy may actually be played out *reciprocally,* and *interpersonally* between mother and son: "Though children of both sexes are originally part of her self, a mother unconsciously and often consciously experiences her son as more of an *other* than her daughter. By contrast, mothers experience their sons as a male *opposite.* Boys are more likely to have been pushed out of the pre-Oedipal relationship and to have had to curtail their primary love and sense of empathic tie with their mother" (p. 166, italics mine).

As a consequence, males may be more vulnerable to traumatic and premature actual separations—disruptions that may later be experienced by the child as loss or abandonment—than females are.

I have argued (Pollack, 1992) that we may be seeing a developmental basis for a gender-specific *vulnerability to a traumatic abrogation of the early holding environment* (Winnicott, 1974), an impingement in boys' development—a normative life-cycle loss—which may later in life leave many adult men at risk for fears of intimate connection. This traumatic experience of abandonment occurs so early in the life course that the shameful memory of the loss would likely be deeply repressed.

Boys have a problematic course toward gender identity. They also have a continuing need to defend against urges toward affiliation and intimacy because of the repressed trauma of shameful and premature separation. This is a loss that may have been unassuaged by their father's inability to assume an alternative nurturant role. Having experienced a sense of hurt in the real connection to their mothers (as a result of her societally constructed role to make gender differentiation clear), and the subsequent loss of finding no equally salient alternative in their fathers, many boys, and later men, are left at risk for empathic disruptions in their affiliative connections—searching endlessly and yet fending others off in order to avoid the fear of retraumatization.

Later cross-gender relationships may revive the deeply repressed and ambivalent yearnings toward the early mother. The result may be the creation of *transitional* or *self-object* relationships with women who function unconsciously as mother substitutes meant to both repair and assuage the unspeakable hurt of premature traumatic separation; while allowing men to simultaneously deny the loss of the earlier relational bond. In their unconscious yearning for closeness, men may seek out women who meet these repressed needs, only to deny such women any mutually empathic response. This occurs not because these men are immature or bad or fear symbiotic reunion. Rather, they need to protect themselves from the danger of reexperiencing the repressed pain, sadness, or depression which the new affiliation threatens to evoke and which they feel unable to mourn or tolerate. Such men maintain that they are self-sufficient while they are in the midst of a deeply dependent or interdependent connection. Elsewhere I have called this phenomenon in men *defensive autonomy* (Pollack, 1990).

This paradoxical situation may lead to the misunderstanding that we see in traditional, intimate relationships between men and women, and perhaps may account for much of the pain experienced by the two genders as they attempt to listen to and interpret each other's "voice." It may also begin to explain the apparent resistance that men show in unmodified forms of dynamic psychotherapy, and the preponderance of the diagnosis of *narcissistic personality disorder* among males. Following Modell (1976), I believe that dynamic treatment must pay close attention to the requirement for creating a symbolic recreation of the early holding environment in the treatment of narcissistic issues. Kohut's (1971, 1977) understanding of the need for facilitating and maintaining (for long periods of time) an experience-near, nonjudgmental, stabilizing self-object transference arrangement—either of a mirroring or idealizing type—may broaden our capacity for empathic connection with patients so conflicted about relationship itself, patients who often are men.

NATURE AND NURTURE

In addition to my argument for powerful unconscious sequelae in the functioning of adult men—as a result of our gender differentiation processes in the parenting of young boys—are two additional influences on the developmental psychology of men. First, the historically insidious, psychoeducationally oriented, skill-based, gender-tracked role socialization models in schools and homes (see Levant, this volume); and second, the biological predispositions to male fragility and expressivity in infancy and its psychosocial consequences throughout the life cycle of men.

GENDER-BIFURCATED ROLE SOCIALIZATION

The very systems of gender-bifurcated role socialization that have been strongly criticized by feminist scholars as stifling girls' voice and for tracking them into doll play, sibling care, and away from assertion and mathematics skills have been equally devastating and limiting for young boys, in their developmental pathways. David and Brannon (1976) have delineated four stereotyped male ideals or admonitions through which we have historically socialized boys into manhood. The injunction to become a "Sturdy Oak" refers to men's stoicism and our teaching boys not to share pain or to openly grieve. The "Give 'em Hell" stance of our athletic coaches creates the false self of daring, bravado, and love for violence; while the ideal of being a "Big Wheel" stresses the need to achieve status and power at any cost. But perhaps the most traumatizing, straitjacketing social role training is that of "No Sissy Stuff"—the condemnation of the expression of any strong, dependent, or warm feelings or urges which are seen as feminine and therefore, totally unexceptable or taboo. The mommy track for women and its equally destructive counterpart, the daddy without feeling, work-'til-you-drop track for men, begins long before the work/career ladder is in view. It is the fruition of our early, rigid gender-bifurcated socialization systems—systems internalized into early models of boys' intrapsychic, engendered ideal selves.

Pleck (1981, 1995) has argued that men are ground down trying to live up to such inhuman standards of masculinity or what he calls *gender role strain*. The Fox Indians of Iowa refer to the ritualized achievement of manhood status as "The Big Impossible" (Gilmore, 1990). Levant and Kopecky (1995) have pointed cogently to the skill deficits resulting in adult men due to these gender-based training experiences in boyhood. They note a severe inability of men to identify, express, and describe their own feeling states, particularly those of warmth, caring, sadness, or pain. This Levant links to the psychological disorder of *alexithymia*—the inability to connect words with feelings, leaving men with a vague "buzz" feeling of undifferentiated affect, rather than a clear or articulate emotional message of caring and love to convey to their loved ones (Levant & Kopecky, 1995).

The Biological Imperatives

Although it is difficult to parse out the distinct contributions of nature versus nurture in gender differentiation, some infancy research data is helpful in this process. A critical review of the developmental and biological data concerning the differences between female and male babies supports the claim that girl infants are generally more calm and less irritable while male infants are more expressive and emotive (Haviland & Malatesta, 1981). As a result, some researchers (Silverman, 1987) argue:

> The less stable state system of the male infant leads to decreased social interaction. Not only is it difficult to establish social interchange during fussy irritable states, but the parents' task during these states becomes one of soothing and calming rather than socializing. . . . This then produces

diminished social interchange between mother and infant, and, as does not happen with female infants, provides increasing separation with mothers and sons. (p. 328)

Brody (1993, 1996) takes a different route to a strikingly similar conclusion: Gender dimorphic, biologically based temperamental predispositions in infants, in combination with specific caretaker interactions, lead to radically different affective socialization for boy and girl babies. Following from Cunningham and Shapiro (1984) and Weinberg (1992), Brody opines that, "Infant boys are more emotionally expressive than are infant girls, and hence their expressions are *easier* for . . . parents to read" (Brody, 1996, italics mine).

Supported by her interpretation of the findings by Tronick and his research laboratory (Tronick, 1989; Tronick & Cohn, 1989) that mothers and their infant sons have an easier time matching their emotional interactive states, Brody suggests that, "Both mothers and daughters may have to work harder to read each others' emotional signals than do mothers and sons" (1996). The result may be the beginning of a long journey toward affective bonding for mothers and their daughters and an increasing emotional inexpressiveness and disconnection for parents and their young sons:

> Working harder may translate into talking more to daughters about feelings, as well as in displaying a wider range of feelings to daughters. . . . For females, this may eventually result in both amplified facial expressiveness in order to communicate more clearly, as well as in better emotional recognition abilities. In contrast, in adapting to their sons' higher emotional intensity, parents may respond with more constraint and a de-emphasis on emotional expressiveness. These types of socialization patterns also represent the conformity to the cultured gender role stereotype that girls should be more emotionally expressive and that boys should be more emotionally constrained. (Brody, 1996)

The empirical findings on differential socialization of emotion language for young boys and girls do not disappoint us in this regard. Mothers appear to use more words about emotions when they speak to their young daughters than their sons (Dunn, Bretherton, & Munn, 1987); mothers tend to speak more about sadness with girls and anger with boys (Fivush, 1989). By the time they are of school age, young girls expect more positive reaction from mothers for the expression of sadness than for anger, while young boys expect negative reactions from both parents if they express sadness (Fuchs & Thelen, 1988).

Fathers have been especially active in promulgating such gender-bifurcated socialization models of the expression of emotion. They use more emotion-laden words with their daughters than with their sons and engage in more negative teasing or aggressive verbal jousting with their sons than with their daughters (Gleason & Greif, 1983; Schell & Gleason, 1989).

We are gaining a better developmental understanding of why anger has been the more accepted emotion for men. Through anger—the *final common pathway* for all their other strongly repressed affects—boys, and later men, express their vulnerability, powerlessness, and their pain in their search for safety. Anger is the stepchild of men's repression of their vulnerability in their search for legitimate authority. Its true parentage remains too shameful to face—the earlier trauma of abandonment—hence, the poorly defined responses of violence and rage, by which men hope to achieve what is in essence the unachievable.

Biological predisposition combines with cultural and social patterns to foster an earlier and potentially more hurtful separation paradigm between boys and their parents. Added to the thesis arguing for the unconscious trauma of loss, such an integrated biopsychosocial model becomes a powerful hermeneutic for a new psychoanalytic psychology of men.

What would a man, who as a boy sustained such gender-bifurcated socialization and early unconscious psychological hurt, look like? In all likelihood, he would be obsessionally concerned about maintaining a rigidly independent self and have a matrix of intrapsychic defenses, something like: unconscious anger or rage toward women, defensive condescension of anyone in a care-taking role, overvaluation of independence (defensive autonomy), devaluation of the need for connectedness or interdependence, stoic denial of sadness or pain with an inability to grieve loss or to mourn, a walling off of a vulnerable but hidden core self, a proclivity to externalize inner conflict, a relative incapacity to put feelings into words (alexithymia), and the need to take refuge in impulsive action to avoid anxiety. This is remarkably similar to the description of a prototypic *narcissistic* character structure.

In addition, you would expect that any overt sense of dependency—especially upon women—would be quite frightening for men; since this would threaten a repetition of the *undependable* earlier tie, which had been disrupted. Simultaneously, however, there would be the conflicted need to be mirrored and to connect with an idealizable soothing object, side-by-side with the terror of sustaining such a connection, for fear of its disruption. If this is indeed men's dilemma, from whence comes the resolution?

Healthy traditional masculine gender identity (replete with rigid differentiation from femininity) is an element of the *false self* construction in men and is founded in two faulty biopsychic constructs:

1. An identification with the absent aggressor "bogey man" father (Mitscherlish, 1963) creating a self-critical and perfectionistic super-ego that demands never ending reaffirmation through workaholic production-oriented successes to fend off rageful states of depressed self-esteem, and

2. A self shaming need to hide the prematurely disrupted sense of needing to be held, which manifests itself in angry defiance and pseudoindependence. Consequences of such a faulty construct is a susceptibility to a gender-specific type of disorder of the self, listed in Table 1.1 (see also Pollack, 1998, this volume, Chapter 7).

TREATMENT

To help men become more empathic, we must become more empathic to men. In psychotherapy we see many men who are frightened about some aspect of their work or love life that they cannot master. These men are most afraid of the very fact that they are *afraid*. They have been brought up to believe that a man must not seek help at a time when he needs it most. So they deny their dependence on the therapy or the therapist. If pushed prematurely to face the truth, they will resort to more drastic protection of their fragile self, their independence—they will flee from treatment or devalue the therapy or the therapist. If the therapist remains calm and does not criticize in return, if he or she recognizes and supports men's need to save face when receiving help, then internal changes of great consequence may occur. We must be sensitive to men's shame and not further shame them in psychotherapy.

Table 1.1
Disorder of the Self: Male Type

- Partial affective/intellectual split
- Anger prominence or "repression" personality
- Walling off of vulnerable core self
- Phobic avoidance/denial of interdependent object relations: sexualized self-object yearnings
- Shame sensitive/shame phobic
- Action blunting of empathic recognition
- Incapacity to translate feelings into language: alexithymia
- Harsh unconscious self-criticism: sometimes projected onto others
- Perfectionistic need to master: workaholism
- Inability to grieve/mourn
- Vulnerability to substance abuse and depression (male type)

Winnicott wrote that one should never ask "Did you conceive of this or was it presented to you from without?" If we can sustain the process of change without putting demands upon men before they can accept them, transformation can occur. This is not very different from the theory of how to get a good idea accepted by an organization. Consultants know that the best way to help others is to enable them to feel they have come to the good idea themselves. They can then own it and empower its implementation.

In Alan's case, it was necessary to modify psychoanalytic psychotherapy—not so much in its frequency (intensity), duration, or self-reflective associative model—but rather in the arena of supporting the patient's need to believe, for long periods of time and without interpretation or challenge to his denial, that both the therapy and therapist are almost unimportant to him. In this way, my approach is similar to Modell's (1976) understanding of the cocoon transference necessary for the maintenance of what he calls the illusion of self-sufficiency within the early holding environment of a psychoanalysis—a background of safety that is required for mutative change in the treatment of narcissistic personality disorder. It differs, however, in that it does not require a confrontation of the reality of separateness, and thereby falls closer to Kohut's (1977) concept of the creation of a stabilizing, idealizing *self object* transference.

Heinz Kohut (1971, 1977) argued that the appropriate treatment response in narcissistic development is an empathic or "experience-near" understanding of the individual's needs to take in and utilize the other, that is, the selfobject, in a manner that silently performs missing functions within the self—without necessarily acknowledging these significant external contributions. Kohut accepted that certain people may need to be highly dependent on others to fulfill deficits or tolerate conflicts and traumas in their earlier lines of self-development, while never consciously acknowledging such dependency. Consequently, he advised against disrupting such a stable transference constellation until it could be interpreted from within the patient's own perspective—rather than imposing our own external "maturity morality," due to the therapists countertransference needs for recognition and authority. I find such advice invaluable in the depth of psychological treatment of men.

Sometimes, as in Alan's case, the early phase of the treatment may be conceptualized—by patient and therapist alike—along the lines of an *extended consultation* in which the patient's defensive independence and fear of connection is neither interpreted nor confronted. Rather, in this case, as in many others, the associations often begin in the work arena with discussions of disappointments in competitive expectations and interpersonal conflicts with coworkers, without requiring any acknowledgement of the patient's need for support for extended periods.

The more extensive case vignette of Jim will be utilized to illustrate this new psychoanytic psychotherapy designed for men.

CASE STUDY: JIM

Jim, a single man in his late thirties, came for intensive psychoanalytic therapy because of struggles with colleagues at work and the inability to maintain an emotional commitment with a woman. In the initial sessions, Jim described his family as a 1950s American classic—somewhere between "Leave It to Beaver" and "Ozzie and Harriet." Past therapies had failed to deal with his overly rigid self-requirements for success and his painful sense of failure in heterosexual romantic relationships. His past experiences with former therapists were unhelpful, leaving him feeling "misunderstood." Later it emerged that Jim had experienced an intense sense of dread in trying to depend upon these treaters, and eventually a terrifying experience of *shame* or humiliation in being unable to utilize the treatment offered to him.

Over the course of our intensive psychodynamically oriented treatments, it also became clear that Jim's parents—although well-intentioned and caring—had substituted rigid rules for living for a more empathic understanding of their child's specific psychic needs. Jim's father would often pull away from his son when he was upset; and his mother would preach to Jim about what he *should* be doing or how silly it was for a boy to be so emotional.

Given such a childhood background, Jim had developed a classic combination of psychodynamic defenses and deficits woven into a character structure common to many men in our society. First, he unconsciously split off and/or repressed most of his deep core feelings (especially vulnerable emotions of sadness or loss)—except those of anger. Consequently, he was "angry" much of the time. Next, he eschewed any overt dependent relationship with another person out of the likelihood that they might disappoint and abandon him—leading to a dangerous sense of embarrassment or shame. He created and lived out what I have described elsewhere (Pollack, 1990) as a gender-based model of defensive autonomy or pseudo-self-sufficiency. He devalued empathic insights or language-based self-reflections ("What difference do they make?") and searched, instead, for *actions* he should engage in to change things. Jim engaged in perfectionistic attempts at work-based mastery, and consequently fell victim to harsh self-criticism punctuated with episodic projections onto others during rage release attacks. And, finally, he clung to this defensive character structure consciously as a type of syntonic armor to protect himself.

Kohut, the pioneer of self-psychological, experience-near psychoanalytic treatment, often commented that such an approach—from within the patient's needs, and perspective—can often put extreme strain on the therapists' narcissistic need to be valued. So, we are all likely to slip. In Jim's case, this occurred toward the end of the first year of the psychotherapy: prior to a planned interruption in our treatment due to my upcoming vacation. Although Jim was in the midst of discussing some very painful issues concerning his sense of "failure" and "shame" at work and was bitterly deriding me for not "doing enough" or "really being there" to help him, he remained steadfastly silent about the upcoming interruption—one quite ill-timed from the perspective of *his* needs. When finally, I could no longer avoid what appeared to be a series of associations to the important issue of *abandonment,* I somewhat meekly raised the concern that the upcoming interruption due to my vacation might be affecting Jim and his feelings. He remained silent for quite a while and then finally said, "You're just like all the rest of them, then! You think you're all so important, to tell the truth I really don't think at all about your going and it doesn't matter to me!"

This derailment from the empathic understanding of Jim's need to keep his sense of dependence upon the therapy and therapist out of awareness was not without potential benefit. Once I realized what Jim had experienced in my interpretation—that he would be forced to recognize his "inferiority" through his reliance upon me—I responded, "You know, I think you're right. I don't think it's so much that you'll miss me or you have to miss me. That's where others have misunderstood you. I do think though that you're working very hard and we're working very hard together, and . . . all things being equal . . . it's not completely fair to you to have to interrupt at this time . . . so you might have some thoughts or feelings about that."

Jim responded immediately, "You're absolutely right! I wish I could come here during those few weeks and keep working on this. But you'll be away, so what's the use of talking about all this, anyway." To which I replied, "The use is that you have a need right now to keep working on this very actively and your needs *count,* and my plans are getting in the way of your needs!" Jim replied, "I didn't think it would be all right to say that I wouldn't miss you very much, but I'd miss doing our work." "It's perfectly all right, because that's what you feel," I replied. "Here we should feel free to talk about whatever you think and feel."

Over time, Jim became trusting enough to share an unconscious fantasy. Reviewing his sense of failure and the feeling of being doomed to boring work, he tentatively shared the memory that when feeling scorned, incompetent, or ashamed as a child—all alone without support of parents or friends—Jim used to retreat to his room and fantasize about the future: A house would be burning down and no one would know how to save the occupants. Out of the blue Jim would arrive and without a glimmer of fear or hesitation thrust himself into the burning building, carrying out the women and children into complete safety. Then he would be hailed as a hero and the "limelight" (as he described it) would be on him. Finally, he would be "important," receive a medal, and everyone would recognize his courage. This *reparative* fantasy (or *curative* fantasy/Ornstein)—a pastiche of boyhood Superhero comics and Jim's father's wartime exploit stories—was the heroic and grandiose alternative to a real life filled with an endless sense of the shame of "never measuring up."

Jim's rich unconscious fantasy life guided our creation of the unique nature of the holding environment (Modell, 1976) required in this man's therapy. There needed to be a sense of safety, continuity, and responsiveness—that the therapist would be available, nonjudgemental, and responsive: Shining the spotlight when necessary. Yet, this had to be juxtaposed with a respect for Jim's need for distance, safety, and (for a long period of time) denial of any dependent urges or wishes vis-à-vis his therapist. Jim required the use of the therapist as—what Kohut has described as—a *self-object*: A part self/part other to be manipulated by the patient into the approximately responsive and supportive stance—without the therapist's complaint, expectation of recognition, or premature interpretation of this function (Kohut, 1971, 1977).

Although Jim continued to complain that no one—including and *especially*, his therapist—understood or cared about him, with the aid of this experience-near, gender-sensitive, uncritical holding environment of psychotherapy, he gradually became able to meet and, then to sustain relationships with women whom he liked; and one whom he grew to love. Ambivalent all the while, he felt increasingly confident that he wished to make a permanent commitment, and married.

A crystalizing moment in the treatment emerged when Jim's father took ill and was dying. Jim debated about whether or not he should return to make one last attempt at contact with this man who, "was never there for me," and, "so I'm not really losing anyone, anyway." Together, during this period, we worked through how painful it had felt for Jim—over and over again—when his father abandoned him emotionally as he attempted to find support as a growing child. Due to his own perfectionism and isolation of affect, Jim's father, "always had to get things right"; and couldn't be bothered "with children interfering." Consequently, if Jim and his dad were building models together (one positive activity Jim remembers) and if they didn't work, his father would vociferously and angrily blame the manufacturer, and literally leave Jim holding the pieces. Perhaps, most painful, was Jim's realization that these stereotypically masculine defensive traits—the avoidance of vulnerable feelings and workaholic perfectionism—were the only male role models available to him in his predominantly female world. And that, therefore, to his horror in retrospect, he had identified with them, internalized them, and made them his own. As Jim said, almost in tears, "I've become just like my dad."

Jim journeyed home and saw his father for what turned out to be the last time. Upon his return, after his father's death, and with tears in his eyes, Jim recounted the last discussion: a warm and friendly chat, but still devoid of the deeper meaning and connection that Jim had always longed for. Yet, for the first time, Jim acknowledged the fact that they both had done the best they could—and this recognition of the limitations of the human condition was a new and relieving experience for Jim.

Now, the depth psychological work on the intrapsychic defenses against relationships, the defensive autonomy, took place. We learned together that it had become better for Jim, "not to ask for help, than to ask and not receive it" due to the devastating shame and frightening vulnerability that such a rebuff would generate. Jim revealed that all his life he had "wanted somebody by his side" (an older brother figure); yet often he felt in the treatment like telling the therapist to "Go away," so that his need for a soothing, guiding object would not show in this interpersonal context; and thereby lead to further embarrassment or an intolerable sense of loss. Jim was not really so often *mad* as he was *sad* and frightened. We unearthed an unconscious belief (that was once available to him in childhood) that shame came from feeling feelings and that, therefore, if he could achieve a state of "having no feelings," or the next best thing, not experiencing any, he could avoid all pain. The pain of depending upon a potentially helpful, later abandoning significant other (male or female) was almost annihilatory: "Needing someone like that is like being part of someone else's dream. . . . They wake up and you disappear." It was only Jim's own childhood dream or fantasy of the invulnerable heroes that could soothe such deep anxieties and maintain connections. In fact, when the therapist commented that Jim had legitimate reasons to continue to attempt to defend against deeper connection, and consequently potential further *hurt,* Jim returned to the next session uncharacteristically positive in his attitude. He commented how important that clarification had been, "You said *hurt*, and that was . . . (a revelation). I never realized that it was hurt and . . . (not anger), I was struggling with."

Returning to this issue, Jim spoke about his struggle with *trust,* "It's not really that I don't trust you . . . I've known you for quite a while now and you have really helped me . . . it's that I feel too vulnerable to have needs, to really show my needs, and maybe . . . to show that *I need you*. It makes me feel weak and very scared." I then replied, "Yes it's frightening, but it's part of the human condition to depend on each other, isn't it?" Jim, said, "Is it? You know when they talk about those homeless people sleeping alone out in the cold and how can they do it . . . I sort of know how they can do it. It's their way of keeping themselves private, of not having to let anyone in." He went on to say, "You know it's not just letting someone in once, it's needing them, and then feeling they won't be there, or they're expecting that they can come in again . . . It leaves you with no private sense, no sense of your self."

Soon, Jim began to speak about how he had fantasized for several years about having children, but felt it impossible. How could he risk being like his own father and emotionally abandoning his child in his time of need? "You really have to be dedicated to them all the time," he said. And Jim wasn't sure he'd have the emotional stamina and self-esteem security to achieve this seemingly daunting task. Most of all he worried that, " I won't be able to take their hand, help them stand up for themselves, and let them know that they're important, too."

Jim was afraid that what was now becoming his wife's pressing need— to address childbearing—would bully him into just doing, "what looks like the right thing," repeating the earlier traumatic interaction with his mother and father, to his detriment. He felt certain that the therapist also would have expectations of "mature behavior" and shame him into becoming a father. When it was clarified that no normative expectations were being held by the therapist, but that perhaps Jim was selling himself short in thinking that he *had to fail* at parenting, as his own father had, Jim began to cry, and then said:

> I see myself like in the picture of the student uprisings in Communist China, in Tiananmen Square. . . . Standing tall with my son by my side, facing the tanks and armies of totalitarianism. I am holding my son's hand and telling him, *"This is important, you're important!"*

Jim began to play with his nephews when they visited and spoke of the joy it triggered. Stopping himself somewhat, he acknowledged, "Parenting won't just be fun!" The therapist agreed but suggested that it needn't be seen as an unbearable burden, either. Jim began to talk about the kind of father he'd like to be. (The work continues.)

SUMMARY

Jim's dilemma, although personally tied to his own early developmental experience is a paradigm for the pain that many men feel in all relationships—including psychotherapy. Men are constantly seeking and yearning to be connected, often with women, but also with their fellow men. However, they are terribly frightened of the shameful vulnerability of memory of past hurt and trauma that such connection will bring. Too often, the psychology of men has been only a means to suppress the anxiety and fear that such connections elicit and to replace them with a defensive withdrawal of angry frustration that tends to cloud the real issues. Men are not narcissistic, self-sufficient loners, who care for no one else. They, we, are frightened searchers looking to connect, but very unsure of what unconscious "insurance" we need, should the connection go awry.

I would like to provide a poetic metaphor of what the balance within the healing process needs to be like for men and for the people who love them or treat them as we deconstruct the traumatic effects of dis-identification:

West African Ballad

Do not seek too much fame,
but do not seek obscurity.
Be proud.
But do not remind the world of your deeds.
Excel when you must,
but do not excel the world.
Many heroes are not yet born,
many have already died.
To be alive to hear this song is a victory.

We must rethink our psychoanalytic and psychodynamic treatment models as they pertain to men, across the life cycle: Questioning whether our conceptualization of both healthy resolution of conflict and remediation of deficit are truly experience-near to many men's unconscious experience of father and mother hunger (Herzog, 1978)—to their early, pre-Oedipal struggles with a separation trauma, which only too often can be neither named nor mourned.

REFERENCES

Betcher, R. W., & Pollack, W. S. (1993). *In a time of fallen heroes: The re-creation of masculinity.* New York: Atheneum.

Brody, L. R. (1993). On understanding gender differences in the expression of emotion. In S. Ablon, D. Brown, J. Mack, & E. Khantazian (Eds.), *Human feelings: Explorations in affect development and meaning* (pp. 87–121). Hillsdale, NJ: Analytic Press.

Brody, L. R. (1996). Gender, emotional expression and the family. In R. Kavanaugh, B. Zimmerberg-Glick, & S. Fein (Eds.), *Emotion: Interdisciplinary perspectives.* Hillsdale, NJ: Erlbaum.

Chodorow, N. (1978). *The reproduction of mothering.* Berkeley: University of California Press.

Chodorow, N. (1989). *Feminism and psychoanalytic theory.* New Haven, CT: Yale University Press.

Cunningham, J., & Shapiro, L. (1984). *Infant affective expression as a function of infant and adult gender.* Unpublished manuscript, Brandeis University, Waltham, MA.

David, D., & Brannon, R. (1976). *The forty-nine percent majority: The male sex role.* Reading, MA: Addison-Wesley.

Dunn, J., Bretherton, I., & Munn, P. (1987). Conversations about feeling states between mothers and their children. *Developmental Psychology, 23,* 132–139.

Fivush, R. (1989). Exploring sex differences in the emotional content of mother-child conversations about the past. *Sex Roles, 20,* 675–691.

Freud, S. (1957a). The interpretation of dreams. In J. Strachey (Ed. & Trans.), *The standard edition of the complete psychological works of Sigmund Freud* (Vol. IV). London: Hogarth Press. (Original work published 1912)

Freud, S. (1957b). On the universal tendency to debasement in the sphere of love. In J. Strachey (Ed. & Trans.), *The standard edition of the complete psychological works of Sigmund Freud* (Vol. XI, pp. 177–190). London: Hogarth Press. (Original work published 1912)

Fuchs, D., & Thelen, M. (1988). Children's expected interpersonal consequences of communicating their affective state and reported likelihood of expression. *Child Development, 59,* 1314–1322.

Gilmore, D. D. (1990). *Manhood in the making.* New Haven, CT: Yale University Press.

Gleason, J. B., & Greif, E. G. (1983). Men's speech to young children. In B. Thorne, C. Kramarae, & N. Henley (Eds.), *Language, gender and society* (pp. 140–150). London: Newbury House.

Greenson, R. (1968). Disidentifying from mother. *International Journal of Psychoanalysis, 49,* 370–374.

Haviland, J. J., & Malatesta, C. Z. (1981). The development of sex differences in nonverbal signals: Fallacies, facts, and fantasies. In C. Mayo & N. M. Henly (Eds.), *Gender and non-verbal behavior.* New York: Springer-Verlag.

Herzog, J. (1982). On father hunger. In S. Cath, A. Gurwitt, & J. Ross (Eds.), *Father and child* (pp. 163–174). Boston: Little, Brown.

Kohut, H. (1971). *The analysis of the self.* New York: International Universities Press.

Kohut, H. (1977). *The restoration of the self.* New York: International Universities Press.

Levant, R., & Kopecky, G. (1995). *Masculinity reconstructed.* New York: Dutton.

Mahler, M., Pine, F., & Bergman, A. (1975). *The psychological birth of the human infant.* New York: Basic Books.

Mitscherlich, A. (1963). *Society without the father.* New York: Harcourt.

Modell, A. H. (1976). The "holding environment" and the therapeutic action of psychoanalysis. *Journal of the American Psychoanalytic Association, 24,* 285–308.

Pleck, J. (1981). *The myth of masculinity.* Cambridge, MA: MIT Press.

Pleck, J. (1995). The gender role strain paradigm: An update. In R. Levant & W. S. Pollack (Eds.), *A new psychology of men.* New York: Basic Books.

Pollack, W. S. (1990). Men's development and psychotherapy: A psychoanalytic perspective. *Psychotherapy, 27*(3), 316–321.

Pollack, W. S. (1992). Should men treat women? Dilemmas for the male psychotherapist: Psychoanalytic and developmental perspectives. *Ethics and Behavior, 2,* 39–49.

Pollack, W. S. (1994). Engendered psychotherapy: Listening to the male and female voice. *Voices, 30*(3), 43–47.

Pollack, W. S. (1995). No man is an island: Toward a new psychoanalytic psychology of men. In R. Levant & W. Pollack (Eds.), *A new psychology of men.* New York: Basic Books.

Ross, J. M. (1982). Oedipus revisited: Laius and the "Laius Complex." *Psychoanalytic Study of the Child, 37,* 169–200.

Schell, A., & Gleason, J. B. (1989, December). *Gender differences in the acquisition of the vocabulary of emotion.* Paper presented at the annual meeting of the American Association of Applied Linguistics, Washington, DC.

Silverman, D. K. (1987). What are little girls made of? *Psychoanalytic Psychology, 4,* 315–334.

Tronick, E. (1989). Emotions and emotional communication in infants. *American Psychology, 44,* 112–119.

Tronick, E., & Cohn, J. (1989). Infant-mother face-to-face interaction: Age and gender differences in coordination and the occurrence of miscoordination. *Child Development, 60,* 85–92.

Weinberg, M. K. (1992). Boys and girls: Sex differences in emotional expressivity and self-regulation during early infancy. In L. J. Bridges (chair), *Early emotional self-regulation: New approaches to understanding developmental change and individual differences.* Symposium conducted at the International Conference on infant studies, Miami, FL.

Winnicott, D. W. (1974). *The maturational processes and the facilitating environment.* New York: International Universities Press.

CHAPTER 2

Desperately Seeking Language: Understanding, Assessing, and Treating Normative Male Alexithymia

Ronald F. Levant

NORMATIVE MALE ALEXITHYMIA

THIS CHAPTER is focused on a specific aspect of psychotherapy for men; one that has general significance—namely the understanding, assessment, and treatment of normative male alexithymia.

Alexithymia literally means the inability to put emotions into words. The term has Greek roots: A (without)–LEXUS (words)–THYMOS (emotions) or without words for emotions. This condition was originally described by Sifneos (1967) and Krystal (1982) to characterize the severe emotional constriction that they encountered in their (primarily male) psychosomatic, drug-dependent, PTSD patients (see also Sifneos, 1988). They were dealing with cases of severe alexithymia, which is at the far end of the continuum of this disorder. Through my work in the Boston University Fatherhood Project (Levant & Kelly, 1989) and in my subsequent research and

---

An earlier version of this chapter was presented in a symposium, "Treating the Reluctant Male: Psychotherapy with the Marlboro Man," at the 102nd Annual Convention of the American Psychological Association, August 1994, Los Angeles, CA.

clinical practice (Levant & Kopecky, 1995), I have found that alexithymia also occurs in mild-to-moderate forms. These forms, are very common and widespread among men and I call this condition "normative male alexithymia."

As a result of the male role socialization ordeal, boys grow up to be men who are genuinely unaware of their emotions, and sometimes even their body sensations, as is illustrated in the following clinical vignette:

> George, 53, a self-made multimillionaire, collapsed one day in his office. He was rushed to the emergency room, where a complete examination revealed no medical illness. He was simply out of touch with the cues that his body was sending him—in this case exhaustion from a trip to the west coast, and running a sales meeting after only 2 hours sleep. His hobby was competing in car races, and he complained in the first interview that he had a better idea of what was going on with his car, as he put it through its paces, than he did with himself. He wanted a set of dials and gauges that would allow him to know what was going on inside himself.

When men are required to give an account of their emotions and are unable to identify them directly, they tend to rely on their cognition to deduce logically what they should feel under the circumstances. As is illustrated in the following anecdote, they cannot do what is easy and almost automatic for most women—simply direct their senses inward, feel the feeling, and let the verbal description come to mind.

> I once asked a father, "What were your feelings, Don, when your son stood you up for the father-son hockey game?" Don's response, "He shouldn't have done it!" "No, Don," I said, "I didn't ask you what you thought he should have done. I asked you what you felt." Don's response, "Oh. Let me think . . . I guess I felt, I think I felt, I must have felt . . . upset."

> In contrast, ask a woman what she felt when her daughter stood her up for an afternoon of shopping at the mall, and listen as she peels off layer after layer of her feelings, "At first I was angry. Then I got worried, because I didn't know what happened to her. Then I was really disappointed, because I was really looking forward to spending this time with her before she left for college."

This widespread inability among men to identify emotions and put them into words has enormous consequences. It blocks men who suffer from it from utilizing the most effective means known for dealing with life's stresses and traumas—namely, identifying, thinking about, and discussing one's emotional responses to a stressor or trauma with a friend, family member, or therapist. Consequently, it predisposes such men to deal with stress in ways that make certain forms of pathology more likely, such as substance abuse, violent behavior, sexual compulsions, stress-related illnesses, and early death. It also makes it less likely that such men will be able to benefit from psychotherapy as traditionally practiced.

I hasten to point out that by characterizing men's traditional inability to put emotions into words as a mild form of alexithymia I do not mean to pathologize men. Rather, I hope to engage the reader in a consideration of the idea that this aspect of traditional masculinity does not serve men well in *today's* world, and is therefore dysfunctional, although it did serve a purpose in earlier historical eras (Grunebaum, 1996). I also hope to point out that normative alexithymia, like the more severe forms, is a result of trauma—in this case, the trauma of the male role socialization process, a trauma that is so normative that we do not think of it as trauma at all (see also Betcher & Pollack, 1993; Pollack 1995, 1998a, 1998b).

THE MALE ROLE SOCIALIZATION PROCESS

THE GENDER ROLE STRAIN PARADIGM

The Gender Role Strain Paradigm (Pleck, 1981, 1995) is the best developed representative of the social constructionist perspective on gender in the new psychology of men. In contrast to the older Gender Role Identity Paradigm, the Strain Paradigm does not assume that masculinity and femininity are the same thing as, nor are they essential to, being male or female, respectively. Rather it sees these definitions of gender as historically relative and socially constructed. Further, the Strain Paradigm proposes that, to the extent that parents, teachers, and peers subscribe to a particular gender role ideology extant in a society or historical era, children will be socialized accordingly. Prior to the late-1960s in the United States, what has been termed *traditional gender role ideologies* prevailed (Thompson & Pleck, 1995). Hence, male children brought up in the postwar era were reared to conform to traditional norms of masculinity, of which Levant et al. (1992) identified seven:

1. Avoiding all things feminine
2. Restrictive emotionality
3. Toughness and aggression
4. Self-reliance
5. Achievement and status
6. Nonrelational attitudes toward sexuality
7. Fear and hatred of homosexuals

Traditional masculinity ideology fit better with harsh social conditions, such as occurred in this country from the period of industrialization through the Great Depression and the two World Wars (Gilmore, 1990; Rotundo, 1990). In such conditions, certain male traits such as toughness, self-reliance, and lack of awareness of emotions are likely to be more adaptive.

The Strain Paradigm also proposes that gender roles do not fit individual personalities particularly well, resulting in gender-role strain. Of the several types of gender role strain that have been described, the most relevant in this context is *trauma-strain,* the notion that the processes required to develop this role are traumatic (Pleck, 1995). The concept of trauma-strain has been applied to certain groups of men whose experiences with gender role strain are thought to be particularly harsh, such as professional athletes (Messner, 1992), war veterans (Brooks, 1990), survivors of child abuse (Lisak, 1995), men of color (Lazur & Majors, 1995), and gay and bisexual men (Harrison, 1995). But above and beyond the recognition that certain classes of men may experience trauma-strain, a perspective on the male role socialization process has emerged that views socialization under traditional masculinity ideology as *inherently* traumatic (Levant, 1996). The traumatic aspects are seen most clearly in the emotion socialization process, through which boys' natural emotional expressivity is suppressed and channeled.

THE EMOTION SOCIALIZATION ORDEAL FOR BOYS

Due to what seem to be biologically based differences, males start out life more emotionally expressive than females. Haviland and Malatesta (1981), reviewing data from 12 studies (11 of which were of neonates), concluded that male infants are more emotionally reactive and expressive than their female counterparts—that they startle more easily, become excited more quickly, have a lower tolerance for tension and frustration, become distressed more quickly, cry sooner and more often, and fluctuate more rapidly between emotional states. Furthermore, Cunningham and Shapiro (1984, cited in Brody & Hall, 1993) found that infant boys were judged to be more emotionally expressive than were infant girls, even when the judges were misinformed about the infant's actual sex, thus controlling for the effects of gender-role stereotyping on the part of judges. Finally, boys remain more emotional than girls at least until six months of age. Weinberg (1992, vii) found that six-month-old boys exhibited "significantly more joy and anger, more positive vocalizations, fussiness, and crying, [and] more gestural signals directed toward the mother . . . than girls."

Despite this initial advantage in emotional expressivity, males learn to tune out, suppress, and channel their emotions, whereas the emotion socialization of females encourages their expressivity. These effects become evident with respect to verbal expression by 2 years of age, and facial expression by 6 years. Dunn, Bretherton, and Munn (1987) found that 2-year-old females refer to feeling states more frequently than do 2-year-old males. Buck (1977) assessed the ability of mothers of 4- to 6-year-old boys and girls to accurately identify their child's emotional responses to a series of slides by observing their child's facial expressions on a television monitor. The older the boy, the less expressive his face, and the harder it was for his mother to tell what he was feeling. Buck found no such correlation among the girls: Their mothers were able to identify their emotions no matter what their age. Buck concluded that between the ages of 4 and 6 "boys apparently inhibit and mask their overt response to emotion to an increasing extent, while girls continue to respond relatively freely." (See also Allen & Haccoun, 1976; Balswick & Avertt, 1977; Brody & Hall, 1993; Stapley & Haviland, 1989.)

What are the socialization processes that would account for this "crossover in emotional expression" (Haviland & Malatesta, 1981, p. 16), such that boys start out more emotional than girls, and wind up much less so? Levant and Kopecky (1995) proposed that the socialization influences of mother, father, and peer group combine to result in the suppression and channeling of male emotionality and the encouragement of female emotionality. The mechanisms of emotion socialization include selective reinforcement, direct teaching, differential life experiences, and punishment:

1. Mothers work harder to manage their more excitable and emotional male infants: They "employ more contingent responding (and particularly contingent smiling) in playing with their sons. Mothers may go to special lengths to ensure that their sons are contented" (Haviland & Malatesta, 1981, p. 202). Mothers also control their own expressivity to "preclude upsetting their [sons'] more fragile emotional equilibria" (p. 202). In contrast, mothers expose their infant daughters to a wider range of emotions than they do their sons (Malatesta, Culver, Tesman, & Shephard, 1989).

2. Fathers take an active interest in their children after the thirteenth month of life (Lamb, 1977), and from that point on socialize their toddler sons and daughters along gender-stereotyped lines (Lamb, Owen, & Chase-Lansdale, 1979; Siegal, 1987). Fathers interact more

with infant sons than they do with daughters (Lamb, 1977). With older children, fathers engage in more verbal rough-housing with sons, and tend to speak more about emotions with daughters (Grief, Alvarez, & Ulman, 1981; Schell & Gleason, 1989). Fathers also express more disapproval to sons who engage in gender inappropriate play (Langlois & Downs, 1980). Many adult men that I have counseled recall experiences where their fathers made them feel deeply ashamed of expressing either vulnerable (i.e., sadness or fear) or caring/ connection emotions (i.e., warmth or affection).

3. Both parents participate in the gender-differentiated *development of language* for emotions. Parents discourage their son's learning to express vulnerable emotions; and, while they encourage their daughters to learn to express their vulnerable and caring/connection emotions, they discourage their expression of anger and aggression. Female language superiority also plays a role in their greater ability to express emotions verbally (Brody & Hall, 1993). Dunn et al. (1987) found that mothers used more emotion words when speaking with daughters than they did with sons. Fivush (1989) found that mothers spoke more about sadness with daughters than with sons, and only spoke about anger with sons. With daughters, mothers discussed the experience of the emotion, whereas with sons they discussed the "causes and consequences of emotions," which would serve to help sons learn to control their emotions. Greif et al. (1981) had parents "read" stories to their children using wordless books, and videotaped and transcribed their conversations. Mothers talked about anger twice as frequently with sons as compared to daughters. Finally, Fuchs and Thelen (1988) found that school-aged sons expected their parents to react negatively to the expression of sadness, whereas school-aged daughters expected their mothers to react more positively to the expression of sadness than they would to anger.

4. Sex-segregated *peer groups* complete the job. Young girls typically play with one or two other girls and their play consists of maintaining the relationship (by minimizing conflict and hostility, and maximizing agreement and cooperation) and telling each other secrets, thus fostering their learning skills of empathy, emotional self-awareness, and emotional expressivity. In contrast, young boys typically play in larger groups in structured games, in which skills such as learning to play by the rules, teamwork, stoicism, toughness, and competition are learned (Lever, 1976; Maccoby, 1990; Paley, 1984). A recent study (Crombie & DesJardins, 1993, cited in Brody, 1994) found that boys

experience direct competition in their play half of the time, whereas girls experience it very infrequently (less than 1% of the time). Boy culture is also notoriously cruel to boys who violate male role norms, such as expressing vulnerable emotions, showing affection, or being unwilling to fight (Krugman, 1995).

The suppression and channeling of male emotionality by mothers, fathers, and peer groups has four major consequences: The development of "action empathy," normative alexithymia, the overdevelopment of anger, and the channeling of caring emotions into sexuality.

ACTION EMPATHY

Empathy can be defined in cognitive-developmental terms as "interpersonal understanding" (Selman, 1980), which puts the emphasis on the ability to "de-center" from one's own frame of reference, and take another person's perspective. In this view, many men develop a form of empathy which I call "action empathy," which can be defined as the ability to see things from another person's point of view, and predict what they will, or should, *do* (Brody & Hall, 1993; Eisenberg & Lennon, 1983; Hall, 1978; Levant & Kopecky, 1995). This is in contrast to emotional empathy—taking another person's perspective and being able to know how they *feel*. Action empathy also differs from emotional empathy in terms of its aim: emotional empathy is usually employed to help another person, and is thus prosocial; whereas action empathy is usually (though not always) employed in the service of the self. Action empathy is usually learned in the gymnasiums and on the playing fields, from gym teachers and sports coaches, who put a premium on learning an opponent's general approach, strengths, weaknesses, and body language in order to be able to figure out how he might react in a given situation.

NORMATIVE ALEXITHYMIA

Normative alexithymia is a predictable result of the male gender role socialization process. Specifically, it is a result of boys being socialized to restrict the expression of their vulnerable and caring/connection emotions and to be emotionally stoic. This socialization process includes both the creation of skill deficits (by not teaching boys emotional skills nor allowing them to have experiences that would facilitate their learning these skills) and trauma (including prohibitions against boys' natural emotional expressivity, and punishment, often in the form of making the boy feel deeply ashamed of himself for violating these prohibitions).

Emotions consist of three components (Taylor, 1994):

1. The neurophysiological substrate, which includes both autonomic and endocrinological components. For example, in the fight/flight response the sympathetic nervous system is activated, and the adrenal glands release epinephrine.
2. The motor/behavioral response, which involves the activation of the skeletal-muscular system in facial expression, tone of voice, and body language, or in direct action, such as a physical attack or an embrace.
3. The cognitive/affective component, which includes the subjective awareness of the emotion and the ability to put it into words. Men who suffer from normative alexithymia typically lack the third component, and some also lack the second.

Some men report that their wives know what they are feeling when they themselves do not. This might be accounted for by the men lacking the third component of the emotion but having the second component, from which their wives can read their emotions in their facial expression and tone of voice.

Men who are having an emotion that they cannot bring into awareness often experience it in one of two ways: (a) As a bodily sensation, which may be the result of the neuroendocrinological and/or the skeletal-muscular components of the emotion, examples include tightness in the throat, constriction in the chest, clenching of the gut, antsy feeling in the legs, constriction in the face, difficulty concentrating, and gritting of teeth. This particular way of experiencing emotions as bodily sensations has been described by Buck (1984) as "internalizing," which he defines as physiological arousal coupled with facial inexpressiveness, and by Gottman and Levenson (1988) as the way that men in conflicted marriages experience marital conflict. (b) Second, men may experience external pressure and feel "stressed out," "overloaded," "zapped," or have the need to "just veg out."

The Overdevelopment of Anger and Aggression

An important corollary of normative alexithymia is the overdevelopment of anger and aggression. Boys are allowed to feel and become aware of emotions in the anger and rage part of the spectrum, as prescribed in the toughness dimension also known as the "Give 'em Hell" injunction of the male code (David & Brannon, 1976). As a result, men express anger more aggressively (as a motor/behavioral response) than do women (Brody & Hall, 1993; Campbell, 1993; Eagly & Steffen, 1986; Frodi, Macaulay, & Thome, 1977). The aggressive expression of anger is, in fact, one of the few ways boys are encouraged to express emotion, and as a consequence, the outlawed vulnerable emotions, such as hurt, disappointment, fear, and shame, get funneled into the anger channel. Long (1987) refers to this as "the male emotional funnel system," the final common pathway for all those shameful vulnerable emotions which it is too unmanly to express directly (see also Keltikangas-Jarvinen, 1982).

For some men the process is more active; the vulnerable emotions are actively *transformed* into anger, a process learned on the playing fields, as when a boy is pushed down on the ground and he knows that his job is to come back up with a fistful of gravel rather than a faceful of tears.

In addition, due to the general lack of sensitivity to emotional states that characterizes alexithymia, many men do not recognize anger in its mild forms, such as irritation or annoyance, but only detect it when they are very angry. Consequently, angry outbursts often come too readily in men. Such men are victims of what Levant and Kelly (1989) call the "rubber band syndrome."

THE SUPPRESSION AND CHANNELING OF TENDER FEELINGS INTO SEXUALITY

Boys experience sharp limitations on the expression of caring/connection emotions. This message often comes from the father, as illustrated in the following anecdote:

> The father drove into the driveway and his children bounded out to greet him. He first hugged and kissed one little daughter, and then hugged and kissed the second daughter. His 4-year-old son stood waiting to be hugged and kissed. The father said, "No, Timmy, men don't hug and kiss." Slowly, Timmy got reorganized and offered a stiff manly little hand for a handshake.

Boys also get the message from their peers that it is not socially acceptable for boys to express affection either to girls (a peer might taunt, singsong fashion, "Johnny loves Susie"), or boys (lest they be called a faggot). Socialization experiences of this type, often accompanied by enormous feelings of shame, set up powerful barriers to the overt expression of caring/connection emotions. Later, in adolescence, the pent-up caring/

connection emotions get channeled into sexuality. Fueled by the hormonal changes that accompany puberty, and fused with the adolescent boy's need to prove himself, this often takes the form of nonrelational sexuality or unconnected lust (Brooks, 1995; Hudson & Jacot, 1991; Levant & Kopecky, 1995).

Zilbergeld (1992) describes how teenage boys learn about sex. An absence of realistic, compassionate portrayals of sexuality combined with ubiquitous fantasy images of the woman as sex-object, fosters the development of unconnected lust:

> The message is clear: For men sex doesn't have to be connected to anything except lust, and it doesn't matter much toward whom it's directed. . . . The female in his fantasies is simply a tool to gain release. And then to do it again, and again, and again. Next time it will probably be with a different female. And he certainly doesn't have to like the girl to have sex with her. . . . Sex is a thing unto itself for adolescent boys, cut off from the rest of their life and centered on their desire for physical release and the need to prove themselves. (pp. 34–35)

Hence, the male role socialization ordeal, through the combined influences of mothers, fathers, and peer groups, suppresses and channels natural male emotionality to such an extent that boys grow up to be men who develop an action-oriented variant of empathy, who cannot readily sense their feelings and put them into words, and who tend to channel or transform their vulnerable feelings into anger, and their caring feelings into sexuality.

I began working with men to help them identify and process their emotions in a preventive program that I ran in the 1980s, the Boston University Fatherhood Project (Levant & Kelly, 1989). Since then I have experimented with the treatment of normative alexithymic men individually and in groups. My approach integrates cognitive-behavioral, psychoeducational, skills-training, and family systems components. The program that I have developed is an active, problem-solving approach, which relies on the use of homework assignments. I have found that many men find such an approach very congenial, because it is congruent with aspects of the male code. In addition, men who are demoralized for one reason or another may find that it restores their sense of agency, by giving them something that they can *do* to improve their situation.

Helping men overcome normative alexithymia is useful at the beginning stages of therapy for many men, because it enables them to develop the skills of emotional self-awareness and emotional expressivity that will empower them to wrestle with the deeper issues. Such was the case with Raymond.

CASE STUDY: A NUMB EXPECTANT FATHER

Raymond, a 41-year-old successful software designer currently racing to bring a new, preemptive telecommunications product to market, called for an appointment because he "felt nothing" about the fact that he and his wife of 20 years were expecting their first child. He and his wife had met in high school and had postponed having a child because Raymond's work required many moves over the years. Raymond was a hard-driving guy, who met or exceeded most of the requirements of the male code. The first-born son of a rural family, responsibility was his middle name. He took care of various members of his family of origin and his extended family.

Apart from the fact that his wife was pregnant and he thought he "should" feel something about that, Raymond did not find it particularly odd that he "felt nothing." He usually felt nothing. The last time he cried was when his dog was hit by a car. That was 10 years ago.

ASSESSMENT: SESSION 1

During the first interview, in addition to taking a standard history, I also assess the man's ability to become aware of his emotions and put them into words. Here is the format I typically follow:

1. To what extent is the patient aware of discrete emotions, as contrasted with either the neuroendocrinological and skeletal-muscular components of emotions (i.e., tension in the forehead, tightness in the gut) or signs of stress (i.e., feeling overloaded or zapped)? Some specific questions: Do you have feelings that you can't quite identify? Is it easy for you to find the right words for your feelings? Are you often confused by the emotion you are feeling? Do you find yourself puzzled by sensations in your body? (Questions borrowed or adapted from the TAS-20, Bagby, Taylor, & Parker, 1994.)
2. What emotions does the patient become aware of? Is he aware of his emotions in the vulnerable part of the spectrum—that is, emotions that make us feel vulnerable, such as worry, fear, anxiety, sadness, hurt, dejection, disappointment, rejection, or abandonment? ("When you are upset do you know if you are sad, frightened, or angry?" Question adapted from the TAS-20, Bagby et al., 1994.) If he

is not aware of his vulnerable emotions, are these emotions transformed into anger and expressed as anger, rage, or violence?

3. Is the patient aware of his emotions in the caring/connection part of the spectrum, such as caring, concern, warmth, affection, appreciation, love, neediness/dependency, closeness, or attachment? Is he limited in his ability to express caring/connection emotions? Does he express them primarily through the channel of sexuality?

4. Is the patient aware of his emotions in the anger part of the spectrum? Does he become aware of an emotion, such as anger, only where it is very intense?

5. At what intensities does the patient experience his emotions? Some specific questions: Would "cool, calm, and collected" describe you? When you are angry is it easy for you to still be rational and not overreact? Does your heart race at the anticipation of an exciting event? Do sad movies deeply touch you? When you do something wrong do you have strong feelings of shame and guilt? (Questions borrowed or adapted from the AIM, Larsen & Diener, 1987.)

Raymond was not aware of discrete emotions, but instead experienced them as signs of stress. He did not tend to transform vulnerable emotions into anger, and in fact was not often aware of his anger. He felt most connected to his wife during sex.

ALEXITHYMIA TREATMENT: SESSIONS 2–4

The program for the treatment of alexithymia that I have developed has five steps.

Step One: Psychoeducation about Normative Alexithymia

In order for the patient to be able to make sense of his experience and utilize the treatment techniques, he needs to know what his limitations are in his ability to know and express his emotions, and how these limitations came about. An important part of this is helping the patient develop his ability to tolerate certain emotions (such as fear or sadness) which he may regard as unmanly and therefore shameful (Krugman, 1995). I tailor this step to the individual patient, drawing on the material in the first two sections of this chapter (see also Krystal, 1979).

Step Two: Develop a Vocabulary for Emotions

Since men tend not to be aware of emotions, they usually do not have a very good vocabulary for emotions. The next step, then, is to help the man develop a vocabulary for the full spectrum of emotions, particularly the vulnerable and caring/connection emotions. I asked Raymond to record as many words for feelings that he could several times during the week.

Step Three: Learn to Read the Emotions of Others

The third step involves learning to apply emotional words to feeling states. Since it is often less threatening to do this with other people than with oneself, and since men can readily build on their action-empathy skills to learn emotional empathy, I recommend focusing on other people at this stage. I taught Raymond to read facial gestures, tone of voice, and other types of body language in other people. I encouraged him to learn to identify the emotions of other people in conversations, while observing other people, or while watching movies. I instructed him to ask himself questions during this process such as: What is he feeling? What does this feel like from her perspective?

Step Four: Keep an Emotional Response Log

The next step involved teaching Raymond to apply emotional words to his own experience. To do this, I asked him to keep an Emotional Response Log, noting when he experienced a feeling that he could identify, or a bodily sensation or sign of stress that he became aware of, and what the circumstances were that led up to it. The instructions for keeping an Emotional Response Log are as follows:

- Record the bodily sensation or sign of stress (or feelings, if you notice them) that you become aware of, and when you first started to experience them.
- Describe the social or relational context within which the emotion was aroused: Who was doing what to whom? How did that affect you?
- Go though your emotional vocabulary list and pick out the words that seem to best describe the emotion that you were experiencing.

Raymond was pretty good at recording the emotions or sensations and the context within which they occurred. But, as with many other men, the third task required discussion in the session in order to develop the connections between his emotional experiences and language.

Step Five: Practice

The fifth and final step involves practice. Emotional self-awareness is a skill, and like any other skill it requires practice to become an automatic part of one's functioning. In the Fatherhood Project (and the Fatherhood Course that I currently teach), we use role-plays, videotaped for immediate feedback, to practice the skill. Fathers are taught to tune in to their feelings through watching and discussing immediate playbacks of role-plays in which feelings were engendered. By pointing out the nonverbal cues and asking questions such as "What were your feelings, Tom, when you grimaced in that last segment?" fathers learn how to access the ongoing flow of emotions within. The video playback is often so effective that we refer to it as the "mirror to a man's soul."

Although working on these matters in a group context with video feedback is obviously advantageous, one can also practice this skill without such arrangements. By systematically keeping an Emotional Response Log and discussing the results in therapy, one can gradually build up the ability to recognize feelings as they occur and put them into words.

Men can learn this skill fairly easily. What we are teaching the men is a skill that young girls learn as a matter of course, and that they might have learned themselves had they not been shunted onto the male emotion socialization track. When men learn this skill, they feel very empowered. One man said that it was as though he had been living in a black-and-white television set that had suddenly gone to color.

During sessions 2 through 4 Raymond worked on increasing his capacity to recognize his emotions, using the five-step program, with an emphasis on the Emotional Response Log. Raymond was a quick study, and although he did not feel vulnerable emotions very intensely, and he certainly could not yet let his feelings pour out, he was able to discern quite subtle differences in his emotional states by the fourth session.

Fatherhood Issues: Sessions 2–5

Raymond said at the outset that he thought a lot of his problems had to do with his father. His father was 11 years older than his mother, was 38 when Raymond was born, and had died 13 years ago. Raymond believed that his father had a great and adventurous life as an air force officer during World War II—a life that he had to leave behind when he married and started a family, and one that he seemed to miss greatly throughout Raymond's childhood. Because of the age difference and his father's detachment, Raymond never felt that he knew his father. And yet, he admired him greatly, and yearned to know him. For example, Raymond's life-long hobby was participating in Scottish rites and learning about his Scottish ancestry, an activity in which he had earlier hoped he could involve his father. The first time I saw Raymond display emotions openly was in an unguarded moment when he spoke of how he had always wanted to see his dad in a kilt, carrying a set of pipes.

Raymond's father was a hard-driving publisher of a local newspaper who, even when he was home for an evening or weekend instead of traveling or working late, was usually closeted in his den with paperwork or tied up in meetings with community leaders who were always paying late evening calls. He had had a heart attack three years before he died and had to drastically curtail his activities. At that time, Raymond was in the service stationed in the northwestern part of the United States and didn't have time for a visit home. In fact he didn't visit at all during the last three years of his father's life.

During the fifth session, Raymond's tone had shifted from detachment to curiosity. As we explored it, he found he had many questions about his father. Utilizing this curiosity, we constructed a therapeutic ritual during the fifth session, in which he would spend 30 minutes in the evening, two evenings a week, writing down the questions that he had for his father on index cards. Using his newly developed emotional self-awareness, he also described the emotions that accompanied the questions and represented them with colors, using pens with different colors to represent different emotions, and indicating the intensity of the emotion by the amount of color. I also asked him to try to locate some family photos from when he was child.

SESSION 6: SADNESS EMERGES

Raymond came in with a thick sheaf of photos and an equally thick folder of questions. The questions he came up with: Did his father not feel anything toward him and was that why he was so distant? Is there a "family curse" of nonfeeling fathers? Was the family (Raymond, mother, and younger identical twin sisters) a burden on his father? And did his father resent the family for this burden? Was that why he was so detached? Raymond said that he could have written more, except that he ran out of cards. He said it doesn't matter because he realized that if you take all of his questions and roll them into one, what you come up with is that "I don't know a damn thing about my father."

The photos provided an epiphany of sorts. He could find no pictures of him and his dad together. At first he thought his mother had kept them but he called her to ask if she could send him a couple and she didn't have any either. He shook his head and laughed a hard-edged laugh, "It fits, see?"

"What does?"

"The photos, the questions." His face was flushed now. "Of course I don't know anything about my dad. He was never there! He was always too busy with more important things, except spending time with his own son. And later, after his heart attack, when he did have time it was like, 'Fuck you, I can be busy too. And then—,'" his voice cracked. He gazed out the window, tears welled in his eyes, lifted a hand to his face, and began to cry. He didn't cry long, but long enough to feel a sense of relief (as well as some of the predictable embarrassment).

Session 7: Visit to His Aunt

Raymond had an opportunity between the sixth and seventh sessions (three weeks apart) to get some of his questions answered. He had a business trip that would take him to the city where his aunt lived.

Settling in for our first session after his return, Raymond reached inside his jacket pocket, pulled out what looked like an old snapshot, placed it gently on the table in front of him, and stared at it for a moment before starting to speak. He'd seen his Aunt Millie and had dinner at her house.

They'd been sitting around the table having an after-dinner coffee when Raymond had casually mentioned that he'd been thinking about his dad lately, realizing he'd never really known him all that well.

His aunt's eyes had lit up. Then she got up, left the room, and came back with photo albums and boxes of old letters. He wanted to know about his dad, her beloved older brother? "It was almost like she'd been waiting for me to ask." They'd spent the rest of the night sifting through his aunt's trove of memorabilia and talking. "She talked. I listened." He shook his head. "All this stuff—all this stuff I never knew."

He'd known his father's own father had died when he was six and his father and his aunt had been raised by a stepfather. He hadn't known the stepfather had been a drinker who beat his wife and stepchildren until, at age 12, his father had put a stop to the beatings by shoving the man against a wall and threatening to kill him if he laid a hand on them again. He'd known this stepfather had died when his dad was 15. He hadn't known his dad had quit school then to get a job to help support the family, and that he'd finished high school and put himself through college by working days and taking classes at night. He'd known that his dad had always managed money wisely. He hadn't know that, when his parents married, his dad had put the money his in-laws had given him toward a downpayment on a house into college savings bonds for his future children instead. He'd known his dad as an aloof, unavailable, taciturn man who never showed emotion. He hadn't known that his dad actually had shed tears once—the first time he held his newborn son in his arms.

And the snapshot? A present from his aunt—of his father at age 2. He picked it up, held it cupped in one hand. "I'd never seen a picture of him as a baby before." Smiling, he passed it to me. "It's uncanny, really. Even my wife says so. If I didn't know better, I'd think it was me."

SESSION 8: VISIT TO THE GRAVE

The denouement to the therapy occurred during a trip to see his mother, during which he visited his father's grave. He described the experience as "raw emotion." His grief poured out of him, as he stood alone at his father's headstone, reading though his color-coded cards filled with unanswered questions.

SESSIONS 9 AND 10: FEAR EMERGES AND TURNS TO EXCITEMENT

Having broken through the walls that protected him from his grief, Raymond began to experience some strong feelings about his expectant fatherhood, specifically fear, worry, and anxiety. He began to worry about whether the baby was going to be all right, given his wife's age (41 also). He also investigated some obscure genetic diseases that ran in families of Scottish descent. I encouraged him to address his worries directly, by attending one of his wife's visits to the obstetrician. He did so and was reassured about the baby's health, and also heard the baby's heartbeat. His fear then turned to joy and excitement. We terminated after the tenth visit, one month before the baby was due. I got a postcard two months later:

> Ron, the baby was 2 weeks late. But he's a big guy, 8 lbs. 13 oz. And he definitely looks Scottish!
>
> Raymond

DISCUSSION

We considered the problem of normative male alexithymia. After a brief introduction to the Gender Role Strain Paradigm, we examined in depth the male emotion socialization process and saw how, guided by traditional masculinity ideology, mothers, fathers, and peer groups conspire to channel and suppress natural male emotional expressivity to such an extent that males come to be normatively alexithymic. We further saw the traumatic nature of that process, not only in its resultant deformation of men's ability to experience and express the full range of their emotions, but also in the process, where fathers and peer groups in particular dole out shame-based forms of punishment for violations of the male code.

A method to assess the degree to which male patients suffer from normative male alexithymia was presented, as was a five-step psychoeducational program that is useful at the beginning stages of treatment.

The case of Raymond was presented—an expectant father whose chief complaint was that he felt nothing about his future baby. Raymond was assessed to be normatively alexithymic and was treated with the psychoeducational program. As is typical of many of the men I treat, an action-oriented approach to therapy in which the patient is asked to do something to get better, was well received, and Raymond willingly did the homework that was assigned. As a result of psychoeducational treatment, long-buried issues about his own father started to surface by the fifth session. Utilizing his emerging curiosity, a therapeutic ritual was constructed in which he was asked to identify the questions he had about his father. In addition, he was asked to identify both his emotional response to the questions verbally, and to color code them. I used this latter suggestion, which draws on right-brain processes, to bypass any defensive equivocation that might have come into play. Finally, I used family photo reconnaissance to stimulate memories and additional questions. The combined effect of these interventions was to bring the patient face-to-face with his bitterness about his father's psychological absence, which initiated a long-delayed grieving process.

Fortuitously, the patient had an opportunity to visit his aunt (his father's younger sister) at a time when he was receptive to learning more about his father and was treated to a wealth of information about his father. This helped him begin to see his father as a whole man, far from perfect, but doing the best he could with what he had. But it was not until a visit to his father's grave that he was able to fully grieve the father he never knew.

Having done a brief but significant piece of grief work, the patient found his feelings about becoming a father had come unblocked. The first set of feelings he had were on the anxious end of the spectrum. After a visit to his wife's doctor, he not only was able to get his worries addressed, but also to hear the direct evidence of his baby's heart beat. At that point his anxiety turned into excitement, and the therapy ended.

Is this therapy useful for all types of male patients? I certainly don't have enough experience to answer that question, but I can say that it does seem to work best with those normatively alexithymic male patients motivated to comply with treatment, that is, those who are willing and motivated to follow a directive, homework-based therapy. It seems to be less useful to patients who tend to defy treatment, for whom resistance is a much larger matter.

REFERENCES

Allen, J. G., & Haccoun, D. M. (1976). Sex differences in emotionality: A multidimensional approach. *Human Relations, 29*(8), 71–722.

Bagby, R. M., Taylor, G. J., & Parker, J. D. A. (1994). The twenty-item Toronto Alexithymia Scale—II. Convergent, discriminant, and concurrent validity. *Journal of Psychosomatic Research, 38,* 33–40

Balswick, J., & Avertt, C. P. (1977). Differences in expressiveness: Gender, interpersonal orientation, and perceived parental expressiveness as contributing factors. *Journal of Marriage and the Family, 39,* 121–127.

Betcher, W., & Pollack, W. S. (1993). *In a time of fallen heroes: The recreation of masculinity.* New York: Atheneum.

Brody, L. (1994). Gender, emotional expression, and parent-child boundaries. In R. Kavanaugh, B. Zimmerberg-Glick, & S. Fein (Eds.), *Emotion: Interdisciplinary perspectives.* New Jersey: Erlbaum.

Brody, L., & Hall, J. (1993). Gender and emotion. In M. Lewis & J. M. Haviland (Eds.), *Handbook of emotions.* New York: Guilford Press.

Brooks, G. R. (1990). Post-Vietnam gender role strain: A needed concept? *Professional Psychology: Research and Practice, 21*(1), 18–25.

Brooks, G. R. (1995). *The centerfold syndrome.* San Francisco: Jossey-Bass.

Buck, R. (1977). Non-verbal communication of affect in preschool children: Relationships with personality and skin conductance. *Journal of Personality and Social Psychology, 35*(4), 225–236.

Buck, R. (1984). *The communication of emotion.* New York: Guilford Press.

Campbell, A. (1993). *Men, women and aggression.* New York: Basic Books.

David, D., & Brannon, R. (Eds.). (1976). *The forty-nine percent majority: The male sex role.* Reading, MA: Addison-Wesley.

Dunn, J., Bretherton, I., & Munn, P. (1987). Conversations about feeling states between mothers and their children. *Developmental Psychology, 23,* 132–139.

Eagly, A. H., & Steffen, V. J. (1986). Gender and aggressive behavior: A meta-analytic review of the social psychological literature. *Psychological Bulletin, 100*(3), 309–330.

Eisenberg, N., & Lennon, R. (1983). Sex differences in empathy and related capacities. *Psychological Bulletin, 94*(1), 100–131.

Fivush, R. (1989). Exploring sex differences in the emotional content of mother child conversations about the past. *Sex Roles, 20,* 675–691.

Frodi, A., Macaulay, J., & Thome, P. R. (1977). Are women always less aggressive than men: A review of the experimental literature. *Psychological Bulletin, 84*(4), 634–660.

Fuchs, D., & Thelen, M. (1988). Children's expected interpersonal consequences of communicating their affective state and reported likelihood of expression. *Child Development, 59*, 1314–1322.

Gilmore, D. (1990). *Manhood in the making: Cultural concepts of masculinity.* New Haven, CT: Yale University Press.

Gottman, J., & Levenson, R. (1988). The social psychophysiology of marriage. In P. Noller & M. A. Fitzpatrick (Eds.), *Perspectives on marital interaction* (pp. 182–200). Clevedon, England: Multilingual Matters.

Greif, E. B., Alvarez, M., & Ulman, K. (1981, April). *Recognizing emotions in other people: Sex differences in socialization.* Paper presented at meeting of the Society for Research in Child Development, Boston.

Grunebaum, H. (1996, May).Treating the reluctant male, Discussion, in symposium, presented at the annual meeting of the American Orthopsychiatric Association, Boston.

Hall, J. A. (1978). Gender effects in decoding nonverbal cues. *Psychological Bulletin, 85*(40), 845–857.

Harrison, J. (1995). Roles, identities, and sexual orientation: Homosexuality, heterosexuality, and bisexuality. In R. F. Levant & W. S. Pollack (Eds.), *A new psychology of men.* New York: Basic Books.

Haviland, J. J., & Malatesta, C. Z. (1981). The development of sex differences in nonverbal signals: Fallacies, facts, and fantasies. In C. Mayo & N. M. Henly (Eds.), *Gender and non-verbal behavior.* New York: Springer-Verlag.

Hudson, L., & Jacot, B. (1991). *The way men think: Intellect, intimacy, and the erotic imagination.* New Haven, CT: Yale University Press.

Keltikangas-Jarvinen, L. (1982). Alexithymia in violent offenders. *Journal of Personality Assessment, 46*, 462–467.

Krugman, S. (1995). Male development and the transformation of shame. In R. F. Levant & W. S. Pollack (Eds.), *A new psychology of men.* New York: Basic Books.

Krystal, H. (1979). Alexithymia and psychotherapy. *American Journal of Psychotherapy, 33*, 17–30.

Krystal, H. (1982). Alexithymia and the effectiveness of psychoanalytic treatment. *International Journal of Psychoanalytic Psychotherapy, 9*, 353–378.

Lamb, M. E. (1977). The development of parental preferences in the first two years of life. *Sex Roles, 3*, 475–497.

Lamb, M. E., Owen, M. J., & Chase-Lansdale, L. (1979). The father daughter relationship: Past, present, and future. In C. B. Knopp & M. Kirkpatrick (Eds.), *Becoming female.* New York: Plenum Press.

Langlois, J. H., & Downs, A. C. (1980). Mother, fathers, and peers as socialization agents of sex-typed play behaviors in young children. *Child Development, 51*, 1217–1247.

Larsen, R. J., & Diener, E. (1987). Affect intensity as an individual difference characteristic: A review. *Journal of Research in Personality, 21*, 1–39.

Lazur, R. F., & Majors, R. (1995). Men of color: Ethnocultural variations of male gender role strain. In R. F. Levant & W. S. Pollack (Eds.), *A new psychology of men.* New York: Basic Books.

Levant, R. F. (1996). The new psychology of men. *Professional Psychology, 27*, 259–265.

Levant, R. F., Hirsch, L., Celentano, E., Cozza, T., Hill, S., MacEachern, M., Marty, N., & Schnedeker, J. (1992). The male role: An investigation of norms and stereotypes. *Journal of Mental Health Counseling, 14*(3), 325–337.

Levant, R. F., & Kelly, J. (1989). *Between father and child.* New York: Viking.

Levant, R. F., & Kopecky, G. (1995). *Masculinity reconstructed.* New York: Dutton.

Lever, J. (1976). Sex differences in the games children play. *Social Work, 23*(4), 78–87.

Lisak, D. (1995). *Integrating gender analysis in psychotherapy with male survivors of abuse.* Paper presented at the annual convention of the American Psychological Association, New York.

Long, D. (1987). Working with men who batter. In M. Scher, M. Stevens, G. Good, & G. A. Eichenfield (Eds.), *Handbook of counseling and psychotherapy with men.* Newbury Park, CA: Sage.

Maccoby, E. E. (1990). Gender and relationships: A developmental account. *American Psychologist, 45,* 513–520.

Malatesta, C. Z., Culver, C., Tesman, J., & Shephard, B. (1989). The development of emotion expression during the first two years of life. *Monographs of the Society for Research in Child Development, 50*(1/2, Serial No. 219).

Messner, M. A. (1992). *Power at play: Sports and the problem of masculinity.* Boston: Beacon Press.

Paley, V. G. (1984). *Boys and girls: Superheroes in the doll corner.* Chicago: University of Chicago Press.

Pleck, J. H. (1981). *The myth of masculinity.* Cambridge, MA: MIT Press.

Pleck, J. H. (1995). The gender role strain paradigm: An update. In R. F. Levant & W. S. Pollack (Eds.), *A new psychology of men.* New York: Basic Books.

Pollack, W. S. (1995). No man is an island: Toward a new psychoanalytic psychology of men. In R. F. Levant & W. S. Pollack (Eds.), *A new psychology of men.* New York: Basic Books.

Pollack, W. S. (1998a). Hollow men/stuffed men: Recognizing and treating depression in men. In W. S. Pollack & R. F. Levant (Eds.), *New psychotherapy for men: Case studies.* New York: Wiley.

Pollack, W. S. (1998b). Men's desires, men's dread and the trauma of Oedipus: Toward a new psychoanalytic psychotherapy for men. In W. S. Pollack & R. F. Levant (Eds.), *New psychotherapy for men: Case studies.* New York: Wiley.

Rotundo, E. A. (1990). *American manhood: Transformations in masculinity from the revolution to the modern era.* New York: Basic Books.

Schell, A., & Gleason, J. B. (1989). *Gender differences in the acquisition of the vocabulary of emotion.* Paper presented at the annual meeting of the American Association of Applied Linguistics, Washington, DC.

Selman, R. L. (1980). *The growth of interpersonal understanding: Developmental and clinical analyses.* New York: Academic Press.

Siegal, M. (1987). Are sons and daughters treated more differently by fathers than by mothers? *Developmental Review, 7,* 183–209.

Sifneos, P. E. (1967). *Clinical observations on some patients suffering from a variety of psychosomatic diseases.* Proceedings of the seventh European conference on Psychosomatic Research, Basel, Switzerland.

Sifneos, P. E. (1988). Alexithymia and its relationship to hemispheric specialization, affect, and creativity. *Psychiatric Clinics of North America, 11,* 287–292.

Stapley, J. C., & Haviland, J. M. (1989). Beyond depression: Gender differences in normal adolescents' emotional experiences. *Sex Roles, 20*(5/6), 295–308.

Taylor, G. J. (1994). The alexithymia construct: Conceptualization, validation, and relationship with basic dimensions of personality. *New Trends in Experimental and Clinical Psychiatry, 10,* 61–74.

Thompson, E. H., & Pleck, J. H. (1995). Masculinity ideology: A review of research instrumentation on men and masculinities. In R. F. Levant & W. S. Pollack (Eds.), *A new psychology of men.* New York: Basic Books.

Weinberg, M. K. (1992). *Sex differences in 6-month-old infants' affect and behavior: Impact on maternal caregiving.* Doctoral dissertation, University of Massachusetts.

Zilbergeld, B. (1992). *The new male sexuality.* New York: Bantam Books.

CHAPTER 3

Cognitive Behavior
Therapy for Men

Thomas F. Mooney

THE LAST two decades of the 20th century may well go down in history as the time that mental health professionals started to question (even if in a limited way) what it means to be masculine. Traditional masculinity has been taken for granted, unquestioned, unchallenged, promulgated, and encouraged over the centuries and throughout most societies of the world. Until now, traditional masculinity has been considered a normative referent, "boys will be boys," with little or no serious attempt at challenging the basic philosophical and socializational dimensions underlying masculinity (Levant & Pollack, 1995). Scholarly research delineating and differentiating healthy and unhealthy aspects of masculinity is in its infancy. It would be nice if men could take credit for this emerging movement, but, unfortunately, this is not the case. The feminist movement and feminist scholarship have been primarily responsible for the enlightenment of gender differentiations and the overall inequities women have experienced in relationship to men (Levant, 1996). The dark side to traditional masculinity has been emerging slowly over the past 15 to 20 years, revealing unhealthy aspects of traditional masculinity that are detrimental to the individual male's physical and emotional health, as well as detrimental to his relationships—especially the relationships in his personal life.

These dark-side behaviors of traditional masculinity include alexithymia (without words to describe feelings), fear and avoidance of femininity, restrictive affectionate and sexual behavior, lack of emotional intimacy, obsession with status and success, violence and aggression, sexual domination and exploitive behaviors, homophobia, detached parenting, misogyny and devaluation of women, sex disconnected from intimacy, inadequate emotional partnering, and avoidance of health care issues (Brooks & Silverstein 1995; Levant & Kopecky 1995; O'Neil, Good, & Holmes, 1995).

It seems that a collective denial has existed within the masculine world preventing men from developing a healthier skepticism and critical attitudes toward traditional masculinity which would allow them to differentiate healthy from unhealthy elements of masculinity, giving up the unhealthy while retaining and broadening the healthier elements of masculinity. This chapter attempts to articulate the cognitive dimension to unhealthy masculinity, more specifically those cognitive schemas underlying what Joseph Pleck (1981, 1995) has described as "gender role strain," and provides a cognitive therapy framework for changing these unhealthy masculine schemas. Psychotherapy that is oriented toward reducing this gender role strain not only helps the individual male, freeing him to enjoy more of life, but also helps to have a more positive effect on his interpersonal relationships.

Some of the basic principles of cognitive behavior therapy offer individuals a unique form of therapy that places *relative* emphasis on past relationships and past traumas, versus traditional dynamically based, insight-oriented forms of treatment that place a *great deal* of emphasis on the past. Cognitive behavior therapy places more emphasis on current thoughts, feelings, and behaviors, but accepts fully the idea of historical antecedents, early traumatizations, and the importance of early relationships, especially in infancy and childhood.

One of the basic assumptions of cognitive behavior therapy centers around the notion of a nonblaming sense of responsibility for self which includes one's thoughts, feelings, and behaviors. Cognitive behavior therapy accepts the notion that individuals are not always conscious of their cognitions, affects, and behaviors. Ellis (1962, 1994) believes that these issues operate on what Freud called the pre-conscious. Beck (1967; Beck, Rush, Shaw, & Emery, 1979) takes the position that disturbing ideas occur within a process that he calls "automatic thinking."

Cognitive behavior therapy has been evolving over the past 40 years, providing clients with strategies and procedures that by their very nature are empowering and facilitating, leading to quicker cognitive, emotive, and behavioral changes. Aaron Beck and Albert Ellis are generally considered to be the cofounders of cognitive therapy (Freeman, Simon,

Beutler, & Arkowitz, 1989). The proponents of cognitive behavior accept fully the role that biological predispositions and biochemistry undoubtedly play in the cognitive, affective, and behavioral chain. While exciting research is going on in these fields, there has yet to be developed a medication to help men overcome their dark-side behaviors.

This chapter will discuss how cognitive therapy principles can be utilized to help men search for an alternative to traditional dynamically based therapy. Cognitive behavior therapy can help men gain better access to their unhealthy codes of masculinity and help them free themselves of the effects of this rigid code.

COGNITIVE BEHAVIORIST VIEWPOINT OF MALE ISSUES

A cognitive behavioral viewpoint of the previously cited male issues would emphasize both the biological predispositions and learning of these thoughts, feelings, and behaviors; the encoded learning of these issues being located within cognitive schemas. Ellis, more so than other cognitive theoreticians, emphasizes the issue of demandingness as a primary process in human disturbance (Yankura & Dryden, 1994). In revising his original list of 10 irrational ideas, Ellis (1988) now lists three main irrational ideas:

1. Demands on self with lowered self-esteem being the result of failing to meet these demands
2. Expectations and demands on others with consequential blaming, damning, and vilifying of others when they don't meet one's demands and expectations
3. Demands that the world be different than it is with consequential feelings of depression, anger, discouragement, and despair when the world doesn't meet one's expectations

Joseph Pleck's male gender role strain model (1981, 1995) addresses the issue of male role expectations that are central to his model. Pleck takes the view that a significant proportion of males fail to fulfill male role expectations. As a result of failing to meet these expectations, men suffer lowered self-esteem as well as other negative consequences. Pleck calls this dynamic gender role discrepancy and expands his thesis to include the eventuality that if a man does fulfill socialized male role expectations, this fulfillment can have traumatic, long-term negative side effects. He calls this gender role trauma. Pleck cites another notion of successful fulfillment of male role expectations whereby one of the negative resultants would be a low level of family participation—being distant and emotionally aloof within the family dynamics. He calls this gender role dysfunction (1995, p. 12).

A conceptual tool that would help bridge Ellis' concept of demandingness and Pleck's model of gender role strain would be the term *internalized gender role expectations* (Mooney, 1994). This schematic construct can be useful in examining the cognitive framework or cognitive dimension to unhealthy beliefs associated with traditional masculinity, the effects of which Pleck so articulately describes. The principles of cognitive therapy can then be utilized to isolate what these specific beliefs are and which cognitive behavioral strategies can be employed to reduce the unhealthy aspects of traditional masculinity and the learning of more adaptive, less constricting, thoughts, feelings, and behaviors.

One of the central tenets with cognitive therapy is the fostering of awareness within the individual of not only behavioral patterns, but also an awareness of emotions and the associated cognitions or belief systems. One of the areas of therapeutic exploration utilizing Pleck's gender role strain model would be to foster an awareness of unhealthy masculine beliefs that the individual male has internalized, thereby programming his emotions and behaviors. If the Ellisonian taxonomy is true, most, if not all, men have internalized beliefs and expectations of how a man *should* be. If these expectations have evolved into an inner idealization that in effect sets up a masculine ego ideal within the individual, this idealization could easily set into motion the programming of unhealthy and self-defeating emotions and behaviors. This unhealthy process takes from the male a more enjoyable existence both intra- and interpersonally. Pasick (1992) captures the essence of internalized expectations with his concept of the 10 central mandates of manhood that are virtually impossible to attain. As men:

1. We must be self-reliant.
2. We should be competitive in all endeavors.
3. We should not reveal our fears.
4. We should be in control of ourselves at all times.
5. We need to be cautious about getting too close to anyone because intimacy weakens self-reliance and control.
6. We should focus on achieving power and success.
7. When we encounter a problem, we should be able to fix it through action.

8. We should keep score and always know where we stand relative to others.
9. We should remember that we are superior to females and not have to depend on them.
10. We should never allow ourselves to be weak or to act like a girl.

Mooney (1996) drawing on the emerging body of masculine literature, delineates a parallel set of internalized expectations accounting for this unhealthy masculine code. Men:

1. Should be superior to women in all things not feminine
2. Should be the powerful, dominant, and controlling one in the relationship in order to prove their masculinity
3. Should not be feminine—warm, soft, nurturing, caring, and empathic
4. Should strive to be respected for successful achievement and for being the primary breadwinner
5. Should be the adventurer and risk taker, even accepting violence, if necessary
6. Should be the dominant sexual partner and expect sex at his whim
7. Shouldn't be warm and intimate with other men; it might imply homosexuality or effeminacy
8. Should not have to communicate on a feeling level; feelings are for women, sissies, and wusses
9. Should be nurtured, succored, doted upon, worshiped, and adored by his mate, even more than his mother did
10. Should be sexually magnificent

These internalized demands and expectations are of a theoretical nature at this time but show great promise for empirical validation.

DEMANDS VERSUS PREFERENCES

Central to Ellis's theory of rational emotive behavior therapy is the irrationality of the absolutistic rigid, nonflexible, black-and-white nature of the demand. The result of the unfulfilled demand is human misery. Men, putting demands on themselves in attempting to live up to this masculine code, put incredible pressures on themselves that in turn drives them, resulting in a sense of being out of control, as well as setting into motion a whole host of self-defeating behaviors—behaviors that are maladaptive and that interfere with healthier, more adaptive behaviors. Behaviors such as procrastination, avoidance, reliance on drugs and alcohol, overeating, over-sleeping, driving recklessly, irresponsible sexual behaviors, irresponsible spending proclivities, illegal, and unethical behaviors are a few examples of self-defeating behaviors. Out of a deep sense of shame and emasculation, one male client avoided getting help for his sexual dysfunction for 12 years. These demands and the pressures they create cause a state of discomfort. Once more the masculine code prevents the man from talking about his feelings and dealing with them in healthier ways. The masculine code does allow him to reduce these pressures and anxieties by means of alcohol and drugs. Ellis views a healthier cognitive process as a form of nonabsolutistic, relativistic, preferential thinking that allows the individual to experience a healthier sense of control and choices. One goal of cognitive therapy is to help the client move from a belief of absolutistic *should* to a belief of rela-tiveness that includes *desire, want, preference,* and *it would be nice if.* Prefer-ential thinking, also known as *reflective thinking,* allows a calmer thought and problem-solving process. This type of thinking does not have the emo-tional consequences that absolutistic thinking has and allows the individ-ual to make decisions and choices in a healthier manner.

DISPUTATION OF IRRATIONAL BELIEFS

Another main tenet of cognitive behavior therapy is the type of treatment intervention utilized to change these beliefs and their consequential emo-tions and behaviors. Once the irrational belief system has been brought to a higher level of awareness and the individual has a good grasp of the be-liefs, the next intervention is to develop disputational strategies to basi-cally give the irrational beliefs up, ideally ridding them from the cognitive schema (Walen, DiGuiseppe, & Dryden, 1992). DiGuiseppe (1991) has de-veloped a conceptual theory and intervening strategies of disputation. The use of logic, reality testing, heuristics, didactic, and Socratic disputes are employed as well as metaphorical disputing and humor. Disputes are uti-lized to help the client give up the irrational belief. Once the client has begun making gains disputing his irrational beliefs, the process of refram-ing begins whereby the client learns healthier ways of perceiving and in-terpreting his previous irrational beliefs. Reframing means finding different ways to view the situation that are less upsetting, yet allows the individual to perceive more realistically, but with healthier coping mecha-nisms. This certainly is one of the more empowering aspects of cognitive behavior therapy. One of the main goals of cognitive therapy is to help the individual dispute any form of demandingness, thus getting it down to a preferential level for personal control and choice issues.

Cognitive therapy enables men, who are serious about looking at their sense of masculinity, a different avenue of change. Cognitive therapy helps men by allowing them to get in touch with their feelings, their thoughts or the sentences they tell themselves, as well as their behaviors, instead of going off into the woods to get in touch with "deep masculinity" by beating tom-toms. This process increases awareness of these psychological processes leading to the eventual changing of inappropriate and unhealthy thoughts, feelings, and behaviors. I have heard of instances where men have attended "deep masculinity" workshops, gotten in touch with their feelings only to become angrier than usual when they arrived home. Cognitive therapy helps men to get in touch not only with their anger, but then to take it to their own grandiose demands and expectations. Once they have a sufficient level of awareness of the thought/feeling process, skills of disputation are then applied to the irrational thought and the reframing process begins, thereby either reducing or eliminating anger.

A hypothetical example can help explain this process. Steven's anger at his wife has left her frightened and distanced. Steven realizes that his anger is having a destructive effect on his marriage. A cognitive therapist would work with Steven to help him verbalize and become more aware of his angry feelings toward his wife. The next step would be to help Steven see the "sentences he tells himself"—or the demands and expectations he has on his wife that result in his anger. The sentences usually take the form of a *should, ought,* or *must* thought. She should have dinner on time, she shouldn't hassle him, she should be sexually available when he desires.

Homework assignments are generally part of cognitive therapy whereby the client engages in therapeutic assignments outside of the session. With this particular example, Steven would be asked to start keeping track by logging his angry feelings and demanding thoughts that he has toward his wife. To help Steven give up his demanding thoughts, disputational interventions are employed. A common dispute is where is the evidence for this demand, where is it written that she *should, ought, must be.* Helping Steven see the consequences of his anger is another therapeutic tool. "And Steven, when you get angry at her, what's the effect on her? Does this anger help her to love you more? Does this anger help her self-esteem?" By persisting at disputing the demands he makes on his wife, Steven would be able to reframe these demands to preferences—it would be nice if she . . . . Steven can then learn to accept her the way she is or, at most, express his preferences as to what he would like or not like—but without anger.

OBSESSION WITH STATUS AND SUCCESS

So much of the masculine code associates the worth of the man by the amount of money he makes, the kind of life achievements he has accomplished and the risks he has taken for the rewards he has earned. These value systems can be easily translated into internalized gender role expectations that dictate the belief that in order to be successful as a man *I must* work hard, and *I must* do what's expected of me. Even if this means working 70 to 80 hours or more per week, *I must* achieve. The underlying schema is that if a man is to be successful and worthwhile, he *must* work hard, *must* do what's expected, *must* achieve, and *must* work long hours. If he does not fulfill these masculine musts, he's not doing what's expected; therefore, he's less than a real man. He *must* prove himself by achievement, success, sexual performance, and physical strength. Cognitive behavior therapy has no issue with the concepts of success and achievement. Isn't this what humanists have talked about as development of the self and self-actualization? What cognitive behavior therapy would raise issue with is in the level of drive. Does the drive turn into a *must* or a *have to?* Therein lies the cognitive dimension for obsession and compulsion concerning work and achievement. The demand of the *must* creates pressures, leads to a sense of being out of control, and puts blinders on to the negative effects on others. The calmer more effective reflective thinking of the *want to,* and *choose to,* can be very successful and lead to more enjoyment of the process. Friedman and Rosenman's (1959) concept of the Type A and Type B Personality fits here. Most males get scripted early to associate self-worth with some form of *winning, achieving,* and being *successful.* This dimension to the masculine code puts incredible pressures on men to live up to the internalized gender role expectations of masculine *shoulds* and *musts.* Through socialization, biological predispositions, or both, many men create unhealthy pressures on themselves.

Having worked with many sexually dysfunctional males, I continue to probe for and discover the pressure themes with the accompanying demands men place on themselves for sexual performance and the paradoxical effects. The more pressure they put on themselves to perform, the more their performance deteriorates. A sense of worthlessness develops because the man had failed in one of the most important endeavors of masculinity, thus diminishing his sense of self dramatically. Feelings of shame and worthlessness are common emotions experienced when men fail to live up to their masculine expectations.

CASE OF JOHN

John's case captures the theme of overemphasis on achievement and other cognitive issues. John, age 46, began therapy approximately two years ago for depression and alcoholism. He had been unemployed from a full-time job for approximately 18 months and had a series of temporary jobs at various factories and gas stations. He would maintain sobriety for up to two weeks, get triggered with various depressive themes, retreat to his room at his brother's house, and proceed to drink himself into a drunken stupor— sometimes it lasted for weeks. He would also call his current employer to terminate his employment, usually with some fabricated excuse, such as he had just had a heart attack.

In taking John's history, it became obvious that alcoholism was prevalent in John's family: Both his deceased father, an automobile executive, and his uncle, an executive with a national organization, were severe alcoholics. As John began disclosing his history, it also became obvious that his self-doubts and low tolerance to frustration were critical features in his adolescent years and have continued throughout his adult years. Because of his low grade-point average in high school and college, he had developed a sense of academic inferiority that eventually led to his dropping out of college in his sophomore year. His low grade point was certainly not due to lack of intelligence, as both his parents and various aunts and uncles had achieved both undergraduate and graduate degrees. He would get bored easily with scholastics and do minimum work, if any work at all, and then get poor grades.

John began a career in his early 20s in sales, eventually ending up in an advanced position in an insurance agency. Because of his feelings of inadequacy, John would put tremendous pressures on himself to achieve and succeed. He was able to succeed because he was quite intelligent. John had begun using alcohol in his midteens, initially to be accepted by his peers. As he struggled with low self-esteem and pressures to prove himself, he grew more dependent on alcohol as a coping mechanism. His first marriage ended when his wife could no longer tolerate his drunken episodes. His second marriage ended for the same reason; on this occasion after fifteen years of marriage and two children.

John had made many attempts at sobriety, including a 30-day hospitalization, half-hearted attempts at AA, and a prescription for Prozac from his medical doctor. In the language of AA, John had bottomed out when he began treatment with me. He finally realized that all of his denials, rationalizations, and excuses were hurting him, not helping him.

As our sessions progressed, it became clear to both John and me that the main theme was pressure to achieve that had put an incredible and painful strain on his existence. We were able to identify three other themes. One was an urgency of now theme. John would be prone to the irrational ideation that he must have things now—job, money, family, and most of all, success. Not getting what he needed, *now*, resulted in a low tolerance to frustration, merely adding to John's depression. Another theme that was isolated was John's sense of helplessness and hopelessness. The internalized sentences associated with this theme were "It's too hard, I just can't do it, I'll never do it." When this theme was activated, John would just give up. At times like this, he had no motivation for change and just felt that there was no hope for him. The last theme that was identified was self-pity. After John would experience a sense of hopelessness, he would then start to feel sorry for himself, adding to his total state of depression. As this progression of depressive thinking evolved, John would become conscious of two things, how depressed he was, and how alcohol would help anaesthetize his pain.

As therapy began, John had no conscious idea of these themes; had a very difficult time differentiating his feelings; and had no idea of his cognitions nor the internalized sentences he was telling himself. As the sessions progressed, John slowly began seeing these themes more clearly, including the sentences he was telling himself. The most powerful sentence John was telling himself was, "Because I failed to live up to parental expectations of collegiate achievement, I have failed my parents and let them down. Therefore, I must succeed in the world of work not only to prove myself to me, but also to my deceased father, as a means to compensate for my early failings."

John had a hard time disputing this and other irrational sentences outside of the sessions. He was frightened that logging and disputing would cause a backslide to occur. He knew that logging and keeping track of his feelings, thoughts, and the four identified themes would ultimately help him. He could dispute his irrational ideas, as well as reframe his thinking, in sessions, but simply couldn't do this outside of sessions yet. As the sessions progressed, John was better able to articulate these themes. He was eventually able to see that the demands he put on himself for success, and the need to have it immediately, caused so much of his pressure. His instant discouragement would be triggered by the thought that "it's too hard and I can't." He was eventually able to see how self-defeating and untrue this belief was and is currently persistently disputing this belief and reframing with "it's really too hard not to give up my drinking and I can, I really can." Realizing how feeling sorry for himself was only adding to his depression and alcoholism, John was eventually able to make gains disputing his "poor me" thoughts.

Throughout the course of treatment, John would make gains and would insist that he could make it by himself. He was highly resistant to attending AA meetings but read what he could on Rational Recovery, an alternative to AA, utilizing rational emotive principles (Trimpey, 1989). At the writing of this chapter, John is back in treatment. His last hiatus lasted six months. What is interesting at this time is that he is able to call up these themes rather quickly and is able to relate them to his recent backslides. He is able to distinguish more clearly the notion of demand-ingness versus desires and preferences and has a clearer insight into the egotistical demands he has placed on himself. One of his side demands is "I must get better now so that I can financially provide for my children." This noble demand and its paradoxical effect has triggered much depression and alcoholic stupors for John.

Despite the six-month hiatus from therapy, John and I were able to pick up where we left off. His level of self-acceptance is improving. He continues to make gains, separating his sense of personal worth from his behavior. His sense of failure and shame have lessened considerably as he has gained skills in condemning his self-defeating behavior while firming up his sense of self-acceptance. Our current goals are to focus on his emotional health issues, continue to dispute and reframe his irrational beliefs, and help him see that future success—helping his children financially and his own self-actualization process—will be by-products of his emotional health. He has made considerable gains in reducing his demands for success, money, helping his children, which only had paradoxical effects anyway. He can now see more clearly that success, money, and helping his children will be by-products of overcoming his depression and alcoholism.

MISOGYNY AND DOMINATION

With issues of misogyny and domination, the probable belief is that a man should be superior and should be the powerful, dominant, and controlling one in the relationship. There is much historical precedence for this belief. The old notions that the man is king of the castle, ruler of the household, and father knows best have been common euphemisms (Doty, 1993). Patriarchy, where power resides in the male, has long been practiced in many societies around the world.

One of the unfortunate side effects of patriarchy is the idea that women are inferior to men, creating a differential power base, with men assuming more power and often creating a sense of powerlessness within the woman. *DSM-IV* (American Psychiatric Association, 1994) estimates that dysthymia is two to three times more prevalent among women. Epidemiological studies indicate that this phenomenon is not limited to the United States. The American Psychological Association's task force on women and depression (McGrath, Keita, Strickland, & Russo, 1990) suggests strongly that depression in women has strong socialization factors. Patriarchy implies that the man is right, therefore, making the woman wrong. This creates a power differential where the woman often ends up in a powerless position. In strong misogynist relationships, it's quite common to find the woman being very compliant to the will of the man. She learned a long time ago to silence her own self (Jack, 1987) and to keep peace at any cost—two well-established depresogenic issues. It seems clear that if men are going to look seriously at themselves and start questioning unhealthy masculinity, the introspective process needs to address any form of beliefs that have a misogynist domination and controlling theme.

In practicing cognitive therapy for over 20 years, one of the most challenging processes has been trying to help clients increase their awareness to get more in touch with not only the feeling but also the associated cognition. I've observed that clients can learn the language of cognitive therapy and use it in an intellectualizing sense, but, unless they're bullseying or centering on specific feelings and thoughts, little change takes place.

The anger, despair, frustration, resentment, rage, and put-downs that many men feel toward women is based on grandiose schemas of "I am superior—you are inferior," that you "should," "you ought," "you must obey me," "be subservient to me," and "do my will." Perhaps the old transactional analysis (TA) life script of "I'm OK—you're not OK" would be another way of describing this position (Harris, 1967). If men could give up these grandiose notions of superiority, domination, and misogyny, maybe then they could be part of what Martin Buber (1984) calls the "I-Thou Relationship."

It's been my opinion that men have a collective denial when it comes to a willingness to examine their own masculine beliefs and attitudes. Examining masculinity under the scope of scientific inquiry is only recently being carried on by men's studies scholars (Levant & Pollack, 1995). There seems to be a great deal of ego investment for many men, making it difficult, if not impossible, to do the kind of introspection necessary to become aware of their own masculine dark-side behaviors. Peer group pressures to maintain the status quo have a profound effect in reinforcing these dark-side behaviors.

RESULTS OF MISOGYNY AND DOMINATION

Power-based relationships and the imbalance they create have many unhealthy consequences. For the dominant male, it creates an anger based on the aforementioned expectations. When his demands and expectations are engaged, he loses what probably is a better mood, thereby creating misery in himself, resulting in a bad mood. Anger has many undesirable effects on the recipient. When a male acts on anger, he often engages in verbal and/or physical forms of behavior that are blaming, damning, and invalidating, putting women down, while threatening the psychological and/or physical self and creating in the recipient an attack on the sense of self. To paraphrase Janet Wolfe, "this type of behavior is not an aphrodisiac" (Wolfe, 1992).

CASE STUDY: JERRY

Jerry was referred to therapy for work-related issues of anger that resulted in more than one physical fight and many verbal explosions. Jerry was first referred to the employee assistance program. In making the referral, the employee assistance counselor was able to help Jerry see that his anger was very destructive not only to himself but also to his relationships, and, if this continued, would probably result in his getting fired, charged with assault, or both.

When Jerry began treatment, he was aware that his anger was destructive but he knew of no other way of coping. Jerry's anger not only affected him at work but also at home. His short fuse left him vulnerable for angry abusive attacks at home. Jerry had heard the term misogyny and somewhat shamefully admitted that he had been very abusive to his wife throughout the years. The O. J. Simpson murder trial was underway at this time, and Jerry admitted that he and other misogynist men at work were freely using the term "OJ'd" to refer to this kind of treatment and women who deserved it.

While there were certainly personality disordered elements to Jerry's personality, he was able to persist in therapy and deal with many of his issues. He could eventually see that his grandiose sense of self, his need to be superior, and his need to dominate resulted in nothing more than being angry and hurting others. Jerry worked hard at logging and disputing these grandiose misogynist beliefs, and was able to make considerable gains with these issues.

At the time Jerry entered therapy, his wife was giving serious thought to divorcing him. For years, she had lived with the hope that one day he would change. This hope had diminished over the past few years. With Jerry now working on his issues, he was not the abusive, mean husband that he had been. She apparently had not lost her feelings for him, just her hope that the relationship could improve. It's been over a year since therapy has ended. Last year, Jerry's wife sent me a Christmas card informing me that Jerry's gains have continued and that she is realistically hopeful of spending the rest of her life with him.

DEVALUATION OF WOMEN AND LACK OF INTIMACY

Objectification and lack of emotional intimacy are other unfortunate side effects of the masculine code. All too often, men are socialized to sexualize and objectify women (Brooks, 1995). This tendency to sexualize and objectify women is supposedly for the pleasure of the male. The effect of this process diminishes the woman's sense of personhood and the emotional intimacy of the relationship. Pornography has long been the fulfillment of male fantasy. The idea of a young, beautiful, nubile woman engaged in various provocative behaviors for the sexual satisfaction of the male has long been the theme of pornography. It can be argued that some pornography can be an enhancement to erotic stimulation and thereby helpful to sexual fulfillment, but the dark side to pornography is that it reinforces the notion that women and their bodies are to service men and give them pleasure. Many men have internalized this notion and have translated it to an expectation on their female partner. Their irrational idea is some form of "she should be," "I demand her to be." If their female partner fails to fulfill this expectation, they are then prone to devalue her with their derogatory behavior. The truly sad part of this whole misogynist objectification is its effect on intimacy. Men are certainly not socialized to be skilled at intimate behavior nor to be concerned with personhood or the feelings of others. These behaviors are not part of the masculine code. Emotional intimacy, with a high degree of empathic understanding, is too often associated with femininity and thereby rejected by traditional masculinity. If intimacy was the goal, sexual fulfillment might be an easier by-product. Many men have been brought up to evaluate female breasts and buttocks and not have any clue as to the person, how she feels, what she values. Those of us who have practiced psychotherapy for some time have heard often from women how degraded and invalidated they feel when their husband gropes and pinches their breasts or buttocks. Men think it's cute and a turn-on. Most women find this behavior insulting and a turnoff.

Milder forms of misogyny show themselves in the put-downs and teasing that men are prone to direct toward women. These derogatory comments usually deal with assumed inadequacies, mostly revolving around intellectual and body parts issues. Men have traditionally put women down to fuel their own irrational need for superiority. Putting women down reduces women to objects—nonfeeling persons—thereby licensing hurtful comments of a derogatory nature. Epithets like the "stupid bitch" and "fucking cunt" are prime examples of such misogynist behavior.

Men are blinded by their misogynist attitudes, and they are prone not to see the hurtful effects of their behavior. Instead of nurturing a woman's love by respecting and apprising her, the misogynist male, with his insults and derogatory behavior, engenders a sense of resentment, defensiveness, and distance within his partner, as well as diminishing her sense of worth. This misogynist behavior can also result in passive-aggressive behaviors on the part of his partner (Walker, 1994). Many men view this behavior as "cute" and when their partner gets upset, they have a difficult time seeing the harmful effect of their behavior and often accuse their partners of being too sensitive and stating that they "just can't take a joke."

FEAR OF FEMININITY AND HOMOPHOBIA

One of the truly sad effects of the unhealthy masculine code is the negative view that traditional masculinity historically has taken toward femininity. So much of traditional masculinity is antifeminine and therefore femininity is to be avoided, shunned, and rejected at all costs. Femininity is often associated with warmth, softness, emotional expression, and sensitivity.

Homophobia is the irrational fear and intolerance of homosexuality and homosexual persons (Kilmartin, 1994). Fear of femininity and homophobia result in most males rejecting any notions of softness, warmth, caring, and sensitive and emotional expressiveness. The power of the masculine code resides in the cognitive *must*: I *must* be strong; I *mustn't* be weak; I *mustn't* be soft. This will mean I'm not a man!

The iatrogenic effect of this demand is to severely restrict the pleasure that is inherent with being warm, sensitive, caring, in touch with feelings, and having the ability to express feelings. There is much pleasure to be associated with many aspects of femininity. The healthier male who has rid himself of the irrational demands of traditional masculinity is better able to engage in pleasurable behaviors. In true androgyny, the male has the ability to choose healthy behaviors that free him from the restricting effects of traditional masculinity.

AWFULIZING—THE COGNITIVE DIMENSION OF FEAR

As cited previously, Ellis views human irrationality as originating from the predisposition to think in terms of *shoulds, oughts,* and *musts.* Another cognitive process associated with anxiety and fear is *awfulizing* or thinking in terms of catastrophic expectations. The origins of the fear of femininity and homophobia reside in the cognitive process of awfulizing about not meeting the demands of the masculine code.

Expanding our cognitive explanation of unhealthy traditional masculinity now includes those internalized gender role expectations incorporated into the cognitive schemas and the catastrophic expectations associated with failing to meet demands and expectations. *Demandingness* is found in specific sentences of *shoulds, oughts,* and *musts.* Catastrophic expectations are to be found in the rhetorical, catastrophic questions of "what if," "wouldn't it be horrible, terrible, awful if . . . ." By awfulizing, horribilizing, and terriblizing, an individual takes the molehill of an event and elevates it to a mountain of panic, terror, dread, worry, and anxiety. Men's fear of femininity and homophobia is to be found in the process of awfulizing about not living up to "the masculine code." Fear usually does lead to avoidant behavior.

Neurotic fears, such as fears of disapproval and rejection, have long been noted as being mythical fears. No realistic harm would befall us— we wouldn't die! Neurotic fears have more to do with our perception of ourselves in relation to others and the awfulization of what others would think of us if we didn't live up to these idealized expectations, usually of perfection. The concept of living up to what we assume others expect of us is not new in psychological literature. The concept of significant others/dominant others is discussed cogently in the works of Arieti and Bemporad (1978).

The cognitive core of this issue lies in the internalized egotistic demand that *I should* be—and wouldn't it be horrible, terrible, awful, if others judged me, thought less of me, because I didn't live up to what I think they expected or what I expected of me? Demandingness and awfulization are usually associated with egotistical thinking of "I" and "me" semantics: "*I* must be perfect, what if *I* fail, what will others think of *me* or what will *I* think of *me* if *I* don't do what *I* should," are common cognitions of emotional disturbance. The traditional male, trying to live up to the masculine code and awfulizing about failing to meet these expectations, lives a very constricted life, a very controlled life, a life of limited choices and options regarding thoughts, feelings, and behavior.

Cognitive therapy's strategies for the treatment of fear and anxiety issues reside in helping individuals increase awareness and the ability to identify whatever fears and anxieties they are experiencing. As the individual's awareness and skill level increases in identifying anxious and fearful feelings, the focus can now be shifted to the sentences he tells himself of awfulization and catastrophe.

The crux or essence of overcoming fear and anxiety with cognitive therapy lies in the ability to dispute and reframe the concept of awfulization and to gradually engage in what Ellis (1988) has called *shame attacking exercises* to not only conquer the fear but to begin a new repertoire of behaviors that may have been previously feared but are basically healthy. In shame attacking exercises, a person will forthrightly attack a mythical fear (rejection) and do the very thing that he is afraid of. The student who is afraid of asking a dumb question in class purposely asks a not very intelligent question for the purpose of facing up to and conquering his fear. Chances are the teacher and students will not ostracize him and the student can gain skills in overcoming mythical fears, and if they did laugh or make some negative comment, it still wouldn't be awful.

A Jungian approach would suggest that men get more in touch with their feminine side or anima. A cognitive approach would suggest that men overcome their irrational gender fears and start engaging in what has previously been considered feminine behaviors. Overcoming fear of femininity and realizing that many aspects of femininity are really androgynous and healthy, such as warmth, caring, and a true sense of empathy for what another feels can be very rewarding. Overcoming fears of femininity does not imply that a male will lose his masculinity. Rather it allows him to be discriminating about what thoughts, feelings, and behaviors he can engage in and reject previous notions that anything to do with femininity is bad and should be avoided.

The notion of overcoming homophobia, no doubt, requires a delicate explanation. Does overcoming homophobia imply that one will eventually become homosexual? Hardly! The idea of homophobia is that it is an irrational fear that ties into previously discussed masculinized demands and expectations. For a man to be freed from homophobia simply means that he has overcome his fear of looking nonmasculine to others. He is no longer worried that others may think of him as gay, effeminate, and a sissy if he should choose to engage in a traditionally feminine behavior pattern.

Specific techniques in overcoming fear and anxiety initially lie in the introspective ability to see the process of awfulizing. As the individual gains better awareness and skills in the awfulization process, he begins to de-awfulize by answering the rhetorical question of "what if." It is questioning about the situation that causes the panic and anxiety. By answering the rhetorical question and reframing, one pushes the mountain of anxiety back into a mole hill of concern.

Perhaps two disclosures would help explain this better. For years I had been a white knuckle flyer, suffering intense fears while flying. Like many individuals, I coped with this by denial, diversion, and distraction. This fear continued until one flight from Phoenix to Detroit, I finally decided to ask myself what was I telling myself that made me afraid. At 30,000 feet over Chicago, the insight came instantly—the panic and fear seemed like it just evaporated. In that moment, I was able to get in touch with my own awfulization. "Wouldn't it be awful if this plane exploded and I died." Seeing the sentence, finally, I was able to answer the rhetorical question and accept the fact that if the plane exploded and I died, I would be dead— it would be over. I was able to accept the inevitability of death and at 30,000 feet conquered my fear. This insightful moment took place many years ago. Since then, every time I fly I ask myself "What if this plane crashes and I die or get severely maimed?" The answer I give myself is that it would be bad but not awful. I no longer become afraid and have enjoyed flying ever since—including some rocky flights.

Like most males brought up in this American culture, I must plead guilty to having been affected by many of the masculine *shoulds, oughts, musts,* and *wouldn't it be awfuls* of traditional masculinity. I can see the constricting nature that these beliefs put on me. The many pressures that I felt, the many fears that I've had, did not bode well for a healthier, happier young adulthood. In addressing my own homophobia, I could see the horrific effect on my selfhood if I didn't live up to my own code of masculinization. To help me overcome, or at least significantly reduce, my own homophobia, I have given myself assignments where I would purposely approach people—especially strangers—and ask them if they knew of the location of a gay bar. The purpose of this assignment was not to find a gay bar but to fight against my own homophobia that I could see was emotionally too constricting. As with most mythical fears, nothing bad happened to me, nobody attacked me. I did find out where some gay bars were in various cities, but, more importantly, I reduced my own homophobia.

ALEXITHYMIA

One of the really destructive effects of traditional masculinity is alexithymia, a state of being without words to describe feelings (Sifneos, 1967). Traditional masculinization typically excludes men from being highly aware of their affective world. Women are socialized to be more communicative on a feeling level than are their male counterparts. One of the real joys of intimacy is the ability to be in touch with feelings coupled with the ability to express them in a communicative verbalization. Alexithymic males have not developed these skills and are more prone to act out anger in various forms of aggressive acts. The alexithymic male doesn't realize that he is missing out on an important part of life—real intimacy—and the ability to be aware of the wide gamut of human emotion and the ability to express feelings verbally. Ron Levant (Levant & Kopecky, 1995) discusses overcoming the emotional numbness of normative alexithymia by utilizing various strategies and homework assignments.

CASE STUDY: PETER AND JANETTE

Peter and his wife Janette had requested marriage counseling for what they had thought was a communication problem. During the intake it became obvious that Peter, in his late 20s, was mostly frustrated because his wife was not more sexual. Peter was very sexual and had assumed that marriage would naturally meet all of his dreams and expectations for sexual fulfillment. Peter had been an ardent reader of *Playboy* magazine and considered himself a "normal guy" expecting sex frequently.

Janette complained that Peter was obsessed with sex and that he would talk frequently about her breasts and buttocks in what she described as "gutter" terms. She found it very offensive that Peter would often make catcalls, whistle, and make suggestive remarks when she would come out of the shower. Janette felt that Peter was concerned mostly with her as a sex object whom he expected to be his "playmate of the month." Janette had her own issues that played an important role in the dynamics of the relationship. She had developed an attitude that sex was mostly for procreation, not for pleasure. Her early religious indoctrination regarding

sexuality had left her with an extraordinary highly developed level of vir-
tousness resulting in the inhibition of her own natural sexuality. Her conflict was further enhanced by her feminine socialization that she please her
husband and not complain.

As our sessions progressed, Janette eventually learned to access her
virtuous inhibitive beliefs about sexuality and the constricting effects on
her sexual pleasure. She eventually learned to dispute and reframe her
sexual beliefs, allowing her to relax and enjoy sexual pleasure more so
than she ever had previously. She also learned to be more assertive with
Peter in how offensive she found his objectification of her. She was eventually able to express to him that, when he talked to her in those terms
and when he would whistle and make his cat calls, she would cringe, feel
dirty, and feel like a slut. She was able to convey to Peter that when he
does these demeaning behaviors, they are nothing more than a turn off—
not a turn on.

Peter was eventually able to see that his male socialization and his expectations on sexual fulfillment were having a paradoxical effect. Peter
was very persistent at working on his "male issues." Because of his ability
to look inward and see what negative effect his behavior was having on
Janette, he was able to work on behavioral issues as well as his own sense
of objectification. When Peter began therapy, he had no idea that his treatment of Janette was sexist, invalidating, or objectifying. His early assumptions were that she had some sexual hang-ups and that if she read a
book and had some therapeutic sessions, she would get fixed and be the
sex partner he had fantasized about. Remember, they had initially assumed that they had a communication problem.

Peter was amazed to discover these male sexist attitudes inside of himself. Initially he was vaguely aware that his behavior may have been somewhat inappropriate. He was able to trace these sexist and objectifying
attitudes more to his socialization in adolescence and his adherence to
Playboy magazine. As Peter became more aware of these dark-side behaviors of his own masculinity, he also began to realize that there was a big
part of him that loved the feminine object at the cost of not knowing and
respecting the person. Both Peter and Janette were able to do the homework that is an essential part of cognitive therapy. Janette's homework con-
sisted of becoming more aware of what issues he had that prevented her
from being more assertive. These issues were faulty feminine beliefs that a
woman should be subservient to the man and that, if she did express herself, Peter might get angry with her, so that it was better to keep the peace
and not rock the boat. Janette had to force herself at first to make assertive

statements to Peter. Peter's assignment was to listen with empathy when Janette asked him to listen to her.

The therapeutic sessions were spent exploring both partners thoughts, feelings, and behaviors. Both of these individuals were able to log their issues outside of sessions, thus helping their levels of insight. Peter was eventually able to see his less-than-healthy beliefs about what a wife should be and the effect of his inappropriate behaviors. He was able to learn new behaviors as a result of learning a healthier attitude based on respect for Janette's personhood. He was also able to learn a better sense of empathy for her feeling world. Janette was able to learn to express her feelings, thoughts, desires, and preferences in a healthier sense of assertiveness. As a result, both Peter and Janette were able to move into a more emotionally intimate relationship that they both found very rewarding and satisfying. Janette found that she had a true friend in Peter, and that, when she needed to express her feelings and confusions, more often than not, Peter was able to engage in empathic understanding. Peter was able to work on his alexithymia and get more in touch with his sensitive feelings and communicate them to Janette more often. Overcoming his expectations, he experienced less frustration and anger which made him an easier man to love.

As the two worked on their own issues, the relationship moved into a warmer, more respectful mode. Levels of trust, vulnerability, and intimacy increased. Their sex life gradually improved to a more satisfying intimate level, more as a by-product of their individual growth than as a therapeutic goal.

The case of Peter and Janette is certainly an exceptional one. Their gains were a real testament to their love and commitment and the ability to work on their own issues.

FATHER WOUND AND FATHER HUNGER

The concepts of father wound and father hunger have received a considerable amount of attention in the psychological press (Bly, 1990; Herzog, 1982; Kilmartin, 1994; Lee, 1991; Osherson, 1986). As men are becoming more aware of emotional needs, they realize that their fathers were either too busy or just not knowledgeable or skilled in being responsive to their son's emotional needs. For these men, there is a realization of being shortchanged in childhood by an emotionally distant father.

This is an excellent example of Ellis' concept of the absolute nature of the demand versus the relative nature of the preference (Ellis, 1988). What is implied with the concept of father wound and father hunger is that the young boy did not get what he needed—his father's love and affection. Because he did not get his father's love, there is a void and therefore a feeling of not being a whole person because of this void. The issue for the cognitive therapist is the notion of need. A need in an extreme sense is really a demand. The father wound results not so much because the father was not more demonstrative but because of the assumption that the son did not get what he needed, his father's love—his father *should* have been more loving; he *should* not have been as emotionally distant as he was. This wound is really the demand for love and whatever assumptions of self are associated with the unfulfilled need. A healthier frame would be that love is a preference or a desire, but not a need. "It would have been nice if my father would have been more emotionally demonstrative—we would have had a closer relationship and I would have felt better about me. As an adult, now I can see that it was my demand, my need for affection from my father. As I dispute my need for love from my father and reframe it as a preference, I can see where it really would have been nice if my father was more demonstrative. I can accept that my father may not have been skilled in demonstrating affection but showed his affection by working hard, often long hours, so that he could financially support the family" (Farrell, 1993). It's important that men be in touch with their father wounds and work through them. It's also important that men not repeat the mistakes of their fathers. A genuine hug, various messages of "I love you" and "I'm proud of you," and allowing ourselves to remove the barriers of the masculine code that distance us from our sons, help us fill the hunger our sons feel.

Proponents of behavior therapy have long recognized the need to alter, modify, and change inappropriate, self-defeating behaviors. Cognitive therapy has emphasized the thought/feeling connection to the behavioral issue. In engaging in comprehensive cognitive behavior therapy, there is a need to increase awareness of behaviors, emotions, and cognitions—or the sentences we tell ourselves. This awareness is achieved by two prominent modalities:

1. Talking and exploring these issues in a therapeutic setting
2. Taking time, ideally on a daily basis, to log, review, and report these issues to one's self

Logging and its productive effects is not an easy task for most clients. For many clients, the issue of logging (keeping track of thoughts and feelings) is perceived as hard work and the client simply does not have the time nor inclination. Other clients find it difficult because logging forces them to deal with their issues which may be currently too threatening. Other clients just seem to have a built-in resistance to change. As the literature suggests, and as I have observed often, some interesting things happen when the client gains introspection into his thought/feeling/behavioral connection. The client first of all moves from a sense of feeling out of control about himself to a sense of being in control, especially of his thoughts, feelings, and behaviors. The client moves from a sense of wallowing, feeling sorry for himself, and general misery, to a sense of taking charge and feeling confident because he is choosing to behave in healthier, more productive ways.

A SENSE OF VISION FOR THE FUTURE

A hypothetical situation comes to mind. The husband comes home from a hard day at work, in a good mood, focusing on what he can do to help the family that evening. He is eager to help the children with their homework and engage in dialogue with them about their day as well as share some of his day. He is then eager to be helpful regarding household duties. He gladly, willingly, does various household jobs, such as cleaning the toilets, because these tasks give him as much pleasure under these circumstances as the more masculine jobs, such as cutting the grass. In addition to his own satisfaction derived from completing these tasks, he also takes pleasure in knowing that by doing these tasks he helps to reduce the tasks that his wife has to do. His sensitivities are more to his wife's day and how she is feeling.

This hypothetical situation implies that he has worked through his arrogant, self-centered, king of the castle, I'm home dear, please wait on me, I'll be watching TV with my Bud Lite syndrome.

This modern hypothetical male is more concerned about the well-being of others and what he can do to be helpful. He is aware of how others feel and is responsive to his family's needs. He is a true friend to his wife and because he is responsive to her needs, she does not feel that he is one more of the children who needs her nurturing and demands her time and energies.

This hypothetical male is this way because he was able to look inward and gain access to his faulty masculine code. He was able to log and dispute his faulty masculine *shoulds, oughts,* and *musts.* He was able to overcome his homophobia and fear of femininity that kept him from being more in touch with his softer, more tender side. He has been able to overcome his dark-side behaviors because he has been able to reprogram his faulty demands that he has placed on himself and others. He has learned to overcome his fears and has been able to learn healthier, more adaptive behaviors that are not only rewarding to himself but to people that he has relationships with.

The need to redefine and restructure masculinity has begun. Levant and Kopecky (1995), and Levant and Pollack (1995), and Levant (1996) articulate a strong case for reconstruction. So much of the masculine code is dysfunctional, outdated, and just plain useless. The model of the healthier, in touch with feelings, less angry and aggressive, more empathic male is having a more positive attraction for males. The increased number of books on men found in bookstores, and the various gatherings of men and men's groups, of various persuasions, are a testament of this growing movement.

There has been little written applying cognitive therapy to men's issues. This chapter is a beginning contribution of cognitive behavior concepts and strategies that can be helpful in overcoming the bondage that many men still feel to an outdated, miserable, and self-defeating code of behavior. A therapist with cognitive behavior skills can effectively help the male client with those unhealthy masculine schemas for awareness issues, disputation, and reframing issues. These therapy skills can help empower that male client to make those changes that will allow him to lead a healthier, more satisfying life.

REFERENCES

American Psychiatric Association. (1994). *Diagnostic and statistical manual of mental disorders* (4th ed.). Washington, DC: Author.

Arieti, S., & Bemporad, J. (1978). *Severe and mild depression.* New York: Basic Books.

Beck, A. T. (1967). *Depression: Clinical, experimental, and theoretical aspects.* Philadelphia: University of Pennsylvania Press.

Beck, A. T., Rush, A. J., Shaw, B. F., & Emery, G. (1979). *Cognitive therapy of depression.* New York: Guilford Press.

Bly, R. (1990). *Iron John: A book about men.* Reading, MA: Addison-Wesley.

Brooks, G. R., (1995). *The centerfold syndrome.* San Francisco: Jossey-Bass.

Brooks, G. R., & Silverstein, L. B. (1995). Understanding the dark side of masculinity. In R. F. Levant & W. S. Pollack (Eds.), *A new psychology of men* (pp. 280–333). New York: Basic Books.

Buber, M. (1984). *I and thou.* New York: Scribner.

DiGuiseppe, R. (1991). Comprehensive cognitive disputing in RET. In M. Bernard (Ed.), *Using rational emotive therapy effectively: A practitioner's guide* (pp. 173–195). New York: Plenum Press.

Doty, W. G. (1993). *Myths of masculinity.* New York: Crossroad.

Ellis, A. (1962). *Reason and emotion in psychotherapy.* New York: Lyle Stuart.

Ellis, A. (1988). *How to stubbornly refuse to make yourself miserable about anything, yes anything.* New York: Lyle Stuart.

Ellis, A. (1994). *Reason and emotion in psychotherapy* (Revised and updated). New York: Birch Lane Press.

Farrell, W. (1993). *The myth of male power.* New York: Simon & Schuster.

Freeman, A., Simon, K. M., Beutler, L. E., & Arkowitz, H. (Eds.). (1989). *Comprehensive handbook of cognitive therapy.* New York: Plenum Press.

Friedman, M., & Rosenman, R. (1959). Association of specific overt behavior pattern and cardiovascular findings. *Journal of the American Medical Association, 169,* 1286.

Harris, T. (1967). *I'm OK—your OK.* New York: Harper & Row.

Herzog, J. M. (1982). On father hunger: The father's role in the modulation of aggressive drive and fantasy. In S. H. Cath, A. R. Gurwitt, & J. Munder Ross (Eds.), *Father and child.* Boston: Little, Brown.

Jack, D. (1987). Silencing the self: The power of social imperatives in female depression. In R. Formanek & A. Gurian (Eds.), *Women and depression* (pp. 41–45). New York: Springer.

Kilmartin, C. (1994). *The masculine self.* New York: Macmillan.

Lee, J. (1991). *At my father's wedding: Reclaiming true masculinity.* New York: Bantam Books.

Levant, R. F. (1996). The new psychology of men. *Professional Psychology: Research and Practice, 27,* 259–265.

Levant, R. F., & Kopecky, G. (1995). *Masculinity reconstructed: Changing the rules of manhood—at work, in relationships and in family life.* New York: Dutton.

Levant, R. F., & Pollack, W. S. (Eds.). (1995). *A new psychology of men.* New York: Basic Books.

McGrath, E., Keita, G. P., Strickland, B. R., & Russo, N. F. (1990). *Women and depression: Risk factors and treatment issues.* Washington, DC: American Psychological Association.

Mooney, T. F. (1994). Internalized masculine gender role expectations—an approach to men's issues. *Psychotherapy Bulletin, 29,* 53–54.

Mooney, T. F. (1996, August). *Cognitive psychotherapy with men's issues.* Paper presented at 104th annual convention of the American Psychological Association, Toronto, Canada.

O'Neil, J. M., Good, G. E., & Holmes, S. (1995). Fifteen years of theory and research on men's gender role conflict. In R. F. Levant & W. S. Pollack (Eds.), *A new psychology of men* (pp. 164–206). New York: Basic Books.

Osherson, S. (1986). *"Finding our fathers." The unfinished business of manhood.* New York: Free Press.

Pasick, R. S. (1992). *Awakening from the deep sleep: A powerful guide for courageous men.* San Francisco: Hardon.

Pleck, J. (1981). *The myth of masculinity.* Cambridge, MA: MIT Press.

Pleck, J. (1995). The gender role strain paradigm: An update. In R. F. Levant & W. S. Pollack (Eds.), *A new psychology of men* (pp. 11–32). New York: Basic Books.

Sifneos, P. E. (1967). *Clinical observations on some patients suffering from a variety of psychosomatic diseases.* Proceedings of the seventh European conference on Psychosomatic Research, Basel, Switzerland.

Trimpey, J. (1989). *The small book: Rational recovery from alcoholism.* Lotus, CA: Lotus Press.

Walen, S., DiGuiseppe, R., & Dryden, W. (1992). *A practitioner's guide to rational emotive therapy.* New York: Oxford University Press.

Walker, L. (1994). *Abused women and survivor therapy.* Washington, DC: American Psychological Association.

Wolfe (1992). *What to do when he has a headache: Creating renewed desire in your man.* New York: Hyperion.

Yankura, J., & Dryden, W. (1994). *Albert Ellis.* London: Sage.

CHAPTER 4

Group Therapy for Traditional Men

Gary R. Brooks

P SYCHOTHERAPISTS NO longer have the luxury of ignoring the powerful organizing role of gender. Over the past three decades of gender studies research, three vitally important points have gained acceptance. First, we have begun to realize that, in many significant ways, women and men behave differently in the therapy room (Maracek & Johnson, 1980; Mintz & O'Neil, 1990). Second, we have learned that inattention to gender differences impairs therapy and, in some cases, harms clients. Third, on a more positive note, we have seen how therapy enriched by gender awareness is far more relevant to clients and more rewarding to therapists.

GENDER AND PSYCHOTHERAPY

For many years, the dominant psychotherapy dyad has been a female client and a male therapist. Even though increasing numbers of men are finding their way into therapists' offices, women seeking psychotherapy still outnumber men by a two-to-one ratio (Vessey & Howard, 1993). Feminist critics have established that conventional cultural values and therapy practices have harmed women in many ways; for example, women tend toward self-blame, oversubscription to treatment, and identification

of women's "difference" as pathology. It has been appropriate and necessary to look at the way that traditional psychotherapy, an institution
heavily shaped by sexist culture, has harmed women clients.

Gender blindness is also harmful to men, but we have been slow to recognize its bad effects. To see how psychotherapy has shortchanged men,
we need to look at the same facts from a slightly altered perspective: we
need to look at men who are not clients. How have we raised men to hate
therapy, and how have we failed to make psychotherapy more compatible
with traditional masculinity?

MEN'S AVERSION TO THERAPY

Traditional men hate psychotherapy and will do almost anything to avoid
a therapist's office. Scher (1990) has long held that men enter therapy only
when they are desperate.

> The man who comes into the consulting room is usually there because he
> believes there is no alternative. Very few men come for therapy because they
> subscribe to its life-enhancing qualities. Even if they did they would likely
> not see it as something for them anyway. Men are in therapy because some-
> thing, internal or external, has driven them to it. (p. 323)

There is a fairly well articulated view that the dictates of the male role
and the dictates of therapy are contradictory. A prominent theme in the
recent men's studies literature has been the poor match between the dictates of the male gender role and those of the patient role (Brooks, 1997,
1998; Ipsaro, 1986; Levant, 1990; Ragle, 1993; Scher, 1990; Silverberg, 1986;
K. Solomon, 1982; H. Solomon & Levy, 1982).

Levant (1990) noted that "the male role requires that men be independent, strong, self-reliant, competitive, achievement-oriented, powerful,
adventurous, and emotionally restrained. These characteristics . . . make
it difficult for men to seek and use psychological services" (p. 309).

Scher (1990) observed that because male gender roles have two foci—to
be in control and to be unlike women—a man who enters a therapy room
does so because he believes "there is no alternative." Furthermore, "the
typical qualities of men which are contrary to the qualities necessary for
therapy . . . openness and willingness to examine oneself . . . with the aid of
another person . . . [and] Accepting one's vulnerability . . ." (p. 323).

Osherson and Krugman (1990) cited emotional restrictiveness, ego
boundedness, and emphasis on rationality in men as explanations of why
"male utilization of psychotherapy lags behind that of women" (p. 327).

THE MEN'S GROUP—A KEY COMPONENT IN THE PSYCHOTHERAPY JOURNEY OF RESISTANT MEN

Because of the sharp disparity between the norms of the ideal psychotherapy client and the dictates of the traditional male role, I have previously argued for special attention to the "therapy journey of traditional men" and for men's groups as an especially helpful therapy format (Brooks, 1997, 1998). In general, I envision the therapy journey of resistant men as comprising (a) the initial therapy contact, where change-resistant forces are neutralized; (b) intense involvement in a men's group, where change-enhancing forces are discovered and nourished, and personal growth is realized; (c) transition to marital and family therapy, where changes are translated into higher levels of relationship functioning; and (d) social activism, where men encourage other men to consider new role potentials.

The men's group is especially helpful to men when it emphasizes: (a) offering noble ascriptions; (b) accommodating to men's communication style; (c) framing men's problems in gender context; (d) decreasing men's isolation from other men and thereby promoting universality; (e) instilling hope; (f) evoking men's psychic pain; (g) generating participative self-disclosure; and (h) lessening overdependence on women.

Threaded through this chapter is a case history that illustrates how each of these key elements facilitates the therapy journey of traditional men.

CASE STUDY: LUIS

Luis, a 38-year-old divorced Mexican American, was an unemployed bricklayer. As a former Vietnam War combat veteran, he was eligible for services at the Temple (Texas) VA Hospital. Prior to admission, he had been suicidal and homicidal in reaction to separation from his wife Rose (age 35). Rose had broken off the relationship after becoming impatient with Luis's moodiness and temper outbursts, usually directed toward her and her three children from an earlier marriage.

In the initial triage meeting with the psychiatry inpatient staff, Luis was noted to be deeply unhappy and frustrated, though not overtly depressed. He was highly troubled by the breakup of the relationship, but bitterness and anger were the most prominent affects. Dressed in blue jeans and a denim shirt, he was observed to be a neat, clean-shaven, impeccably groomed man. He was short and muscular, with a dark complexion and thick black hair. In addition to several military-theme tattoos on his arms, he had, on his knuckles, "L-O-V-E" on his left hand and "H-A-T-E" on his right hand. His general demeanor was marked by emotional intensity.

Luis seemed to be a deadly serious man of powerful emotions. Obviously bitter and hypervigilant, he was also fearful and desperate. He very much wanted help, yet was confused by the help-seeking process, defensive about self-revelation, and suspicious of the helping community.

Collection of background information did not lessen the treatment team's discomfort with Luis. Following a military career that had included two Vietnam combat tours, Luis had entered a period of heroin abuse, street fighting, antisocial behavior, and, eventually, a prison sentence of several years' duration. During his incarceration, Luis was divorced by his first wife and estranged from his two children.

After leaving prison, Luis resolved to "go straight." He did not resume drug and alcohol use, and he began work with his father as an apprentice bricklayer. In the early 1980s, he met Rose, a divorced mother of three. Luis saw Rose as a "good" woman—loving, supportive, and moral. He was intrigued, but also troubled, that she seemed to be from a higher social class, and that she was bright, educated, socially competent, and politically active as barrio organizer of a Latino political action group.

An impassioned and conflictual relationship developed. Rose was drawn to Luis's strength and loyalty, yet was fearful of his intensity and moodiness. Luis was drawn to Rose as someone who could exorcise his demons, understand him, soothe him, and make him feel manly. She also was the only person who could tease and joke in a fashion that gave him access to a playful side. Unfortunately, these very characteristics made Luis dependent on Rose and fearful of even the most minimal hint of threat to their relationship.

LUIS IN THE MEN'S GROUP—EARLY SESSIONS

At the time of Luis's entry into the group, there were six other participants, three of whom were Vietnam veterans. As is my custom, I spent a great deal of time introducing him to the group, and the other group members to him. Some group leaders prefer this to be a generally free-form activity, as in "Why don't you tell the group about yourself?" Instead, I was very careful to follow a highly structured format. I asked Luis to tell us very little—name, age, current relationship status, preferred line of work, and "one or two sentences about what led to your being in the hospital."

Luis was quite wary and offered only the most minimal information. I supplemented it (with his permission) by telling the group that Luis was a Vietnam combat veteran who had been struggling to accommodate to life back in the States. I noted that he was a very hardworking bricklayer, who was having trouble adjusting to the seasonal nature of the work. I also mentioned that he was in a long-term relationship and, like most of us, was working on trust and communication issues. At that point, we went around the group to introduce the other members. Partly in response to my encouragement, each group member emphasized the areas of commonality between himself and Luis. I wrapped it up by noting that the group had become tight and effective; all members seemed to go out of their way to support each other.

Taking their cue, other members began relating both humorous and poignant moments from the group's past, including some good-natured jabs at the "primary head shrink" (me). "Sometimes he likes to dig in there with a rusty shovel—but, usually, he's pretty much okay." I groaned in mock distress, inciting further stories of past group experiences and leader outrageousness. The more they teased, the more I played along. For the next several minutes, the group remained at that level of good-natured joking and poking fun.

Toward the end of the session, I turned to Luis and said, tongue-in-cheek, "As you can clearly see, these turkeys have nothing but the highest regard for their fearless leader." Everyone smiled, including Luis, who seemed more at ease with such banter.

"But seriously," I added, "I want to talk about that for a second. Please don't think I'm fooled for a minute. It's very clear to me that these guys are not playing. They take these matters very seriously. Every man in here knows firsthand that the world out there isn't real easy for men. We're expected to work our butts off, provide for our families, and watch out for the other guy who might be after what we want or need. It's no picnic. In fact, that's sorta what this group is about—what it takes to survive in this world as a man. In many, many ways, we all have very similar problems. We play, sometimes, because it's a little easier. They joke with me; but if I screw up, they tell me. Am I off base on that, guys?"

The final few minutes of the group were spent in testimonials about each member's attachment to the group, commitment to the exploration of common struggles, and belief in the overall therapy process. Luis was welcomed and assured that he'd be accepted. "Hell," said George, in a half-serious manner, "you're all screwed up, just like us!"

Offering Noble Ascriptions

Luis, like most traditional men, was humiliated to find himself in the psychotherapy environment. To lessen his shame, I placed far less emphasis on pointing out Luis's role failures than on identifying and celebrating

instances of his loyalty to the traditional masculine code. These "noble ascriptions" are designed neither to encourage denial of problems nor to
allow refusal to take responsibility for improper behavior. They are seen
as initial steps in the building of therapeutic relationships. The approach
helped. Luis relaxed noticeably as he realized that he would be treated
with respect and dignity.

Accommodating Men's Communication Style

Over their lifetimes, traditional men learn to adopt a distinctive style
when interacting in groups of men—a style that is frequently antago-
nistic to the most desirable norms of psychotherapy groups. Story-
telling, joking, and avoidance of intimacy are common; expressing
empathic support, showing sincere concern, and admitting vulnerability are rare. Faced with the dilemma of trying to conduct group therapy
with men who have been accustomed to behaving contrary to therapeutic norms, the therapist can either fight directly, using a frontal assault
on men's "sorry" group behavior, or work more indirectly, getting "behind the lines" as an ally. As illustrated above, my strong preference is
to adapt to the "good old boy" style so familiar to most traditional men,
while making it clear that I have not abdicated the serious business of
the group.

Framing Men's Problems in a Gender Context

A special emphasis of this men's group was *gender role psychotherapy*—examining the members' problems through a gender lens and elucidating the
manner in which rigid role definitions contribute to situational problems.
Repeatedly, I defined the group as one that would examine the stresses we
all shared as men.

With Luis, this therapy focused on his obsession with work performance
as the only meaningful evidence of masculine worth. As a blue-collar male,
he was realistic about the survival value of work, but he had additionally
incorporated unrealistic aspects of the work ethic. For example, his rigid
work ethos allowed for no possibility that he could be assisted by Rose's
work, because that would be interpreted as further evidence of his failure
as a male breadwinner. His capacity for providing Rose with practical help
and emotional support was negated as unworthy of a man. Ironically, one
of Luis's traditional ideas about male-female relationships—that women
are drawn to the highest performing male—was a basic source of his insecurity with Rose.

Over the course of the therapy group meetings, Luis was able to grasp what had formerly been in the background: his strong ideas about proper male conduct. Although that new awareness alone did not produce answers to his situational problems, it provided a measure of subjective comfort. What had formerly been regarded as a complete personal failure could now be seen, in part, as a product of a changing culture, with its revolutionary ideas about what is suitable for women and men.

Recognizing Universality and Addressing Men's Isolation from Other Men

As alluded to above, Luis had lost touch with a male reference group. Although he shared the common gender role problems of most traditional men, and carried around the omnipresent and invisible psychic "male chorus" (Pittman, 1990), he had become socially and emotionally isolated from other men. He fully experienced the negative aspects of the male chorus in that he was always evaluating himself negatively against other men who seemed to be problem-free. At some deep level, he truly felt that he alone was experiencing the common problems and failures of contemporary men.

Once he realized he was not alone, Luis experienced a rush of relief and enthusiasm. In George's words, "You're just like us." The new excitement of shared struggles allowed Luis entrée into the most positive and healing aspects of the male community through loyalty, supportive interactions, and a sense of belonging. Within a brief period of time, Luis became a central figure in the group, a status that elevated his personal morale and injected new energy into the group milieu.

Instilling Hope

In his description of the curative group environment, Yalom (1975) emphasized "installation of hope." Luis—demoralized by his seemingly vulnerable position and confused by the vagaries of the psychotherapy process—was buoyed by the testimonials of more experienced group members. Group oldtimers extolled the benefits of the group environment, describing it as a psychological haven that had enabled them to regain a sense of control over their lives. These testimonials, though overblown at times, were particularly helpful in defusing Luis's fear about the shameful or "feminizing" effects of psychotherapy. He was able to discard his long-held warning to himself, "It's for losers and it will make you soft and overly sensitive."

Luis in the Men's Group—Later Sessions

Over several days, Luis warmed to the task. In a particularly intense group session, he tearfully, and haltingly, told the group of his loss of a "normal boyhood." "I didn't have no childhood, man . . . they needed me . . . somebody had to be the man of the family!" With anguish, he related his efforts, as a 12-year-old boy, to provide food for his mother and siblings after the father had abandoned them. He described both his humiliation and his pride at searching through garbage cans to assure family survival. From that reverie, Luis moved to his painful memories of Vietnam—of his failure to save a comrade who had run across a field of fire to reach a departing chopper. Luis had reached down and caught the bloodied wrist of the panicked man, but had lost the grip as the chopper ascended. Luis needed over 30 minutes to describe his years of self-recrimination and the vivid nightmares in which he would reexperience the images and screams of a man about to face death or torture.

The support of the other group members allowed Luis to gain access to deep and painful emotions. Likewise, Luis's explorations and evocative stories catalyzed the group. There was a long silence before George was able to share the feelings kindled by Luis's story. With great difficulty, he told the group of his intense sorrow over the friends he lost in Vietnam. When the group discussed "The Wall" (the Vietnam War Memorial, in Washington, DC), George admitted that he could never visit there, for fear that he would follow through on his 22-year plan to "off" himself—commit suicide to rejoin his buddies "on the other side." He had distanced himself from affectionate relationships, noting that any love or pleasure is a disloyalty to Vietnam comrades who will never return. When under severe stress, he would isolate himself, repeatedly watching *Platoon*, a movie that he felt helped him reexperience closeness with those he'd lost.

Before long, Buck, a 64-year-old retired county sheriff, who had heart problems and severe chronic obstructive pulmonary disease, talked of his rage and bitterness at being forced to leave his life's work. Feeling worthless as a civilian, he would repeatedly reminisce about the camaraderie and closeness he felt with fellow officers. After hearing that one close friend had been killed in the line of duty, Buck castigated himself, "This wouldn't have happened if I'd been where I should have been." With tremulous voice and wet eyes, he vowed, "I'd crawl five miles to get a guy out of trouble!"

Evoking Men's Psychic Pain

Traditional working-class men are subject to intense emotional states that they poorly comprehend and rarely express directly and appropriately. Luis was no exception. His therapy "took off" when the therapist was able to evoke expression of Luis's considerable psychic pain.

Anger, Bitterness, Frustration. In many ways, the legacy of traditional males—minority and working-class men, in particular—seems to be continual susceptibility to the powerful negative emotions of anger, rage, frustration, and bitterness. Commonly, these emotions are engendered by inequities in social class, recent shifts in gender politics, and distinctive aspects of male socialization regarding emotional experience.

It has long been observed that the psychic costs of membership in the lower echelons of a social class system are anger and bitterness—emotions often displaced onto others (Rubin, 1976). Luis was deeply patriotic and loyal to his country, yet he had a disquieting sense of having been "cheated." Worsening his distress was his status as a Vietnam veteran. Returning combat veterans have always been susceptible to feeling resentful (Waller, 1980), but the situation has been worse for Vietnam veterans who have commonly felt that Americans, in general, despised the Vietnam War and its combatants (Brooks, 1990). Group sessions easily became energized when I tapped group members' feelings about Vietnam or other similarly bitter topics.

Accompanying their anger as unappreciated veterans was a strong negative reaction to the changing role of women in American culture. Whatever the underlying discomfort—fear, insecurity, or confusion—the prominent public emotions for these men were anger and hostility toward women for what they viewed as betrayal of fundamental rules of nature.

Luis was an affective leader of the group; his bitterness about Vietnam and women's lib touched responsive chords in the other men. Like most traditional men, Luis gained emotional access through his anger. He had an abundance of emotions, but all were locked behind his rage. This "anger-only" aspect of male emotion has been described both as an aspect of "normative male alexithymia" (Levant & Kopecky, 1995) and as the "emotional funnel system" in men (Long, 1987).

Guilt and Grief. Like most traditional men, Luis was susceptible to formidable feelings of guilt and grief. Guilt seems to be a common outgrowth of men's preoccupation with masculine duties as provider and protector. Grief seems to be partially a by-product of the many relationships and experiences sacrificed in the execution of masculine role mandates. The group allowed Luis to ventilate (and, to some extent, expiate) his residue of profound guilt from his Vietnam experiences. Much to his surprise, he also uncovered a sizable store of previously unrecognized grief about his lost childhood.

Generating Participative Self-Disclosure

A private and proud man, Luis was deeply anguished, ashamed, and humiliated over his "failures." Agreeing to psychiatric admission, which meant exposing himself to the cross-examination of a psychiatric treatment team, was especially painful and further exacerbated his sense of shame. His capacity for relating his distress was impaired by his inflexible ideas about men and masculinity: Ideal men "don't need to go run crying for help." Further, because he viewed the world as divided between real men and "losers," he was prone to guard closely against admissions of vulnerability. A corollary to his growing sense of being a "loser" was his overestimation and idealization of "successful" men, "They've got the world by the balls."

Because of his deficient understanding of all men's private sense of vulnerability and personal failure, Luis was particularly responsive to participative self-disclosure—hearing other men describe identical fears and insecurities. Realizing the universality of his distress, and noting the group's nurturance of each other, he was emboldened to reveal things he had formerly kept deeply private. The traditional male environment, usually replete with competitive "dick-wagging," had been replaced by one that encouraged personal revelation and emotional support.

CONTINUING THE PSYCHOTHERAPY JOURNEY

Luis was making immense progress through his work in the men's group. For the first time in years, he was able to function without the constant support and emotional validation he had demanded from Rose. A crisis generated a brief relapse, which was followed by a major spurt of relational growth.

Rose was due to come to the hospital to pick up Luis for a weekend pass. One day earlier, she had called with most unsettling news. To her horror, she'd learned that, many years before, her oldest daughter Marie (now 22), had been sexually assaulted by her stepfather (Rose's second husband). Rose was tormented by the pain she saw in Marie, but was also terrified to tell Luis. "He'll go crazy," she said. "He'll either kill the bastard or fall all to pieces." I agreed to try to help Rose talk with Luis.

Our conjoint session was superficial and uneventful, as Rose stayed clear of the troubling issue. As the hour neared an end, I suggested that we needed to prepare to stop. Rose became frantic. "No! We can't stop yet." Luis was shocked and perplexed.

I asked her to go on, but she couldn't. I asked her to keep trying. As the silence wore on, Luis became increasingly unnerved. "What the hell is it?" he demanded.

Rose tried, but still couldn't speak.

That was it for Luis. "Well, to hell with this, let me get the hell outta here. You've met a man, haven't you. Don't bother telling me . . . I can see it . . . let's get a goddamn divorce!"

Rose became even more distraught when she saw Luis totally missing her messages. She looked to me in near panic, "Can you help?"

I turned to Luis. "Luis, relax. You are way off the mark. Rose needs to tell you something . . . but it's very hard for her . . . she needs your help and support."

Luis couldn't let it go. "Support! I'll give her support . . . she can pack her damn bags and hit the road . . . let that other dude give her support!"

I continued to try to reach him. "Luis. It's not about divorce . . . it's about something entirely different." That calmed him. He turned to Rose and asked, in a far more tender voice, "What is it?"

Eventually, Rose was able to tell him. Luis, taken completely by surprise, was awkward in trying to comfort Rose. I coached him to sit beside her. He began to get it. Slowly, he put his arm around Rose, who then began wailing. Luis nearly panicked and ran to get her water. He returned and began pacing the floor. I urged him to move back beside Rose. For several minutes, he held and rocked her.

Countering Men's Overdependence on Women

Luis was so preoccupied with losing Rose that he could imagine only one reason for Rose to be upset. Lacking any other substantive relationships or sources of emotional support, he had become obsessed with Rose's nurturance and reassurances. He had been intensely overreactive to any interruptions in her attentions, and was often paralyzed by fear that she might abandon him for a worthier man.

Fortunately, in the group environment, Luis began to broaden his circle of emotional support. He became more confident of his personal assets and less needy of Rose's constant comforting. At times, he was better able to recognize the irrational aspects of his abandonment fears. Yet, in a crisis, his first response was to panic. At this vignette illustrates, the men's group is a critical step in helping a traditional man counter overdependence on a lover. However, it is frequently useful to move to the next step—gender-informed couples therapy.

Preparing for Family Interventions

It is my belief that the men's group is only one step in the therapy journey of traditional men. As a family systems therapist, I believe that families and larger social systems are "rule-governed." Therefore, any attempt to change the beliefs, attitudes, and behaviors of one family member will be met with a "change-back" reaction—homeostatic pressures to return to more customary patterns. For this reason, I commonly envision the group as a critical step toward eventual family therapy.

Not long after Luis had entered therapy, I had made contact with Rose to lay the groundwork for couples therapy and family therapy. Rose had been in therapy herself, and had been impatient for Luis to become more psychologically minded. The session described above provided a marvelous springboard to family therapy, which continued for the next two years.

One might ask why family therapy is not the initial intervention, given my claimed preference for systems therapy. Primarily, I prefer to see the traditional man initially in a men's group because I have found that, for many traditional men, marital and family therapies are premature (Brooks, 1991). Many of these men cannot yet articulate their issues and concerns without exposure to the supportive environment of the all-male group. In that group, however, the therapist is challenged to help men be continually aware of the family systems forces that are impinging on them. If the male group member is encouraged to speculate about the perspectives of other family members, and about how his actions are construed by them, he should become curious enough to view couples therapy and family therapy as a natural outgrowth of the men's group.

The Challenge to Change

Luis received considerable benefit from the men's therapy group. An environment was created where he was able to interact meaningfully with other traditional men in similar straits, and together they constituted a male healing group. He became less distrustful of psychotherapy, and gained markedly in self-respect, once he recognized that his problems were common among other men. He realized tension reduction through the cathartic expression of intensely painful feelings. However, this was not enough. When leaving the group, he would reenter a world undergoing major cultural changes. To maximize Luis's ability to cope with this world, and to facilitate more flexible role functioning in his marital and family life, further work was necessary. Luis had been made more comfortable in therapy because he had been both understood and validated. The discovery of other struggling men made him more comfortable. Ultimate progress, however, is dependent on the therapist's ability to challenge Luis to make still further changes. The central challenge here is for the therapist to convey to traditional men that, whatever their negative feelings about the changing culture, it is their responsibility to make appropriate accommodations within themselves. The seemingly idyllic world of childhood will not return. They may consider it more masculine to be the "ram that keeps buttin' that dam," but they can be assured that, in most cases, that effort produces only dented dams and dead rams.

Men learn to become men in groups, and are forever subject to the pulls and stresses of the male chorus. Some men find communities of other men and are lucky enough to experience the most positive features of the male healing group and of male bonding. However, far too many men either lose touch with male healing communities, or function in male collectives laden with hierarchical rituals, hostile competition, and emotional distancing or alienation. But those alternatives do not have to be exclusive. It is possible to have both supportive benefits of the all-male group, without the psychologically damaging aspects of many all-male environments. With skillful leadership, the male group can nurture and encourage men in a manner not possible in any other therapy format.

REFERENCES

Brooks, G. R. (1990). Post-Vietnam gender role strain: A needed concept? *Professional Psychology: Research and Practice, 21,* 18–25.

Brooks, G. R. (1991). Traditional men in marital and family therapy. In M. Bograd (Ed.), *Feminist approaches for men in family therapy.* New York: Haworth Press.

Brooks, G. R. (1997). Treatment for therapy-resistant men. In M. P. Andronico (Ed.), *Men in groups: Insights, interventions, and psychoeducational work* (pp. 7–20). Washington, DC: American Psychological Association Press.

Brooks, G. R. (1998). *A new psychotherapy for traditional men.* San Francisco: Jossey-Bass.

Ipsaro, A. (1986). Male client-male therapist: Issues in a therapeutic alliance. *Psychotherapy, 23,* 257–266.

Levant, R. F. (1990). Psychological services designed for men: A psychoeducational approach. *Psychotherapy, 27,* 309–315.

Levant, R. F., & Kopecky, G. (1995). *Masculinity reconstructed: Changing the rules of manhood—at work, in relationships, and in family life.* New York: Dutton.

Long, D. (1987). Working with men who batter. In M. Scher, M. Stevens, G. Good, & G. Eichenfield (Eds.), *Handbook of counseling and psychotherapy with men* (pp. 305–320). Newbury Park, CA: Sage.

Maracek, J., & Johnson, M. (1980). Gender and the process of therapy. In A. M. Brodsky & R. Hare-Mustin (Eds.), *Women and psychotherapy: An assessment of research and practice* (pp. 67–93). New York: Guilford Press.

Mintz, L. B., & O'Neil, J. M. (1990). Gender roles, sex, and the process of psychotherapy: Many questions and few answers. *Journal of Counseling and Development, 68,* 381–387.

Osherson, S., & Krugman, S. (1990). Men, shame, and psychotherapy. *Psychotherapy, 27,* 327–339.

Pittman, F. (1990). The masculine mystique. *Family Therapy Networker, 14*(3), 40–52.

Ragle, J. D. (1993). *Gender role related behavior of male psychotherapy patients.* Unpublished doctoral dissertation, University of Texas at Austin.

Rubin, L. B. (1976). *Worlds of pain: Life in the working-class family.* New York: Basic Books.

Scher, M. (1990). Effect of gender-role incongruities on men's experience as clients in psychotherapy. *Psychotherapy, 27,* 322–326.

Silverberg, R. (1986). *Psychotherapy for men: Transcending the masculine mystique.* Springfield, IL: Thomas.

Solomon, H., & Levy, N. (Eds.). (1982). *Men in transition: Theory and therapy* (pp. 247–274). New York: Plenum Press.

Solomon, K. (1982). Individual psychotherapy and changing masculine roles: Dimensions of gender-role psychotherapy. In K. Solomon & N. B. Levy (Eds.), *Men in transition: Theory and therapy* (pp. 247–273). New York: Plenum Press.

Vessey, J. T., & Howard, K. I. (1993). Who seeks psychotherapy? *Psychotherapy, 30,* 546–533.

Waller, W. (1980). The victors and the vanquished. In C. R. Figley & S. Leventman (Eds.), *Strangers at home* (pp. 35–54). New York: Praeger.

Yalom, I. D. (1975). *The theory and practice of group psychotherapy.* New York: Basic Books.

CHAPTER 5

Reluctant Men in Couple Therapy: Corralling The Marlboro Man

Joseph J. Shay & Carolynn P. Maltas

ROBERT AND Betty, each 45, the parents of two children, arrived for couple therapy after Betty had discovered in her husband's suit-coat pocket a note from his female associate at work. The note said simply that the associate enjoyed Robert's company at dinner the night before and hoped they could share such "uproarious" times again. Confused and hurt, Betty asked about the note, but Robert minimized its meaning and refused to discuss it further, arguing that it was just a dinner and he could hardly help it if the woman thought he was funny. Furious, Betty stewed for two days and then, after discussing the situation with her individual therapist, insisted that Robert either go to couple therapy with her or move out of the house. Reluctantly, Robert agreed but only to a single session, since he felt she was blowing out of proportion an innocent situation and demanding they solve relationship problems he didn't think existed. Betty obtained the name of a male therapist, hoping to increase Robert's comfort, and called to arrange the first appointment, mentioning to the therapist on the phone that Robert was barely willing to come for the session. Their marriage and the events that led to the arrival at the couple therapist's office of an angry and frightened Betty and a perplexed and irritated Robert typify one pattern of unhappiness in intimate heterosexual relationships today that this chapter explores.

Many men are in trouble in their intimate relationships and, like Freud almost 100 years ago, wonder what women want from them. Frequently, women bring their reluctant male partners to couple therapists, lamenting the men's difficulties in communicating or understanding feelings, their seemingly inability to listen without leaping to action or advice. Many of the women complain that men desire sex that seems disconnected from feelings of intimacy, pursue achievement at the expense of family ties, and do not share the burden of family responsibilities. In turn, the men frequently feel misunderstood and unappreciated for their contributions to the relationship and criticized for demonstrating the kinds of traits that lead to their succeeding professionally and being good providers. They are frequently unhappy with the couple's sex life or frustrated by their partners' constant dissatisfaction.

The pervasive dissatisfaction with what each gender gets from the other and the lack of mutual understanding seem at times an inevitable by-product of current socialization practices. Whether complaints are about men's over-involvement in work, the division of labor in the family, or the role and meaning of sexuality in their relationship, the central complaint usually is that there are "communication problems," that is, "you just don't understand" (Tannen, 1990). It is a paradox that the very expectation for deep understanding and intimate communication is directed toward someone whose gender socialization is so different as to require skills in a kind of cross-cultural communication.

This chapter explores men's relationship difficulties in the context of a broader understanding of the paradoxes for both men and women in intimate heterosexual dyads today. These relationships are seen as microcosms of the gender dilemmas of our time, where society's ambivalence about changing gender roles are played out each day as couples quarrel over conflicts between family responsibilities and personal needs. Also to be explored is the potential of couple therapy to help men (and their female partners) become more aware of the cultural forces, mediated through their families, which shape their gender ideologies and relationship behaviors. Such heightened awareness makes possible a more conscious evaluation of the implicit choices they have made about their behavior in intimate relationships and an exploration of the costs and benefits of continuing on in the same fashion. Couple therapy can provide a setting for conversations across the gender gap that can temper anger, disappointment, and misunderstanding into empathy, compassion, and tolerance. But first, the partners must feel they can be understood by the couple therapist, and that such understanding can be conveyed to the other partner, in translation if need be. Unfortunately many of the very aspects of male socialization that create problems for men in intimate relationships may make them reluctant participants in couple therapy.

MEN AND PSYCHOTHERAPY

In addressing both the dilemmas in conducting couple therapy with men, and also certain unique opportunities for changing relationship patterns through conjoint treatment, we draw on prior work relating to characteristic problems many men experience with traditional psychotherapy (Gornick, 1986; Levant, 1990, 1995; Maltas, 1997; Pollack, 1990, 1995; Scher, 1990; Shay, 1996; Toomer, 1978). Psychotherapy is an undertaking that relies heavily on verbal communication, exposure of vulnerabilities, and the sharing of intimate feelings, just those factors whose limited currency in the lives of many of the men contribute heavily to relationship problems in the first place. While women's socialization makes the language of psychotherapy and the therapy relationship relatively familiar and comfortable, Shay (1996) notes that "the language of therapy is not the language of men." It is a challenge for the therapist to engage men in therapy by speaking a language they can understand so that their own unhappiness and that of their partners can be addressed. This means weaving the man's own language and metaphors into the fabric of the therapy and engaging him in discussions of topics in which he will not feel at a relative disadvantage (as he may when discussing vulnerable feelings). Engaging men in what has been seen sometimes as the "feminized" discourse of therapy can also be aided by the therapist's respecting the man's reluctance to participate (Shay, 1996) and normalizing it as an understandable outcome of socialization into the male gender role.

The therapist's effort to listen to and understand the perspective of the two partners parallels the central task of couple therapy to facilitate such understanding between the two partners. In learning to speak the languages of both partners, the therapist may function initially as a translator, who furthermore includes both partners' perspectives when formulating the relational problems and resolving them. This initial joining process, or alliance building, is particularly critical in engaging men who are reluctant participants in therapy, because psychotherapy seems to them to be, by its very nature, "the antithesis of masculinity" (Meth & Pasick, 1990).

In addressing the possibilities and dilemmas in the treatment of men's relationship problems through couple therapy, we focus on a particular type of man who, like Robert, epitomizes certain generally agreed upon aspects of the traditional masculine gender role and who we call "the Marlboro man" (Shay, 1994). This icon of one familiar kind of masculine ideal, similar to the star athlete, the business tycoon, or Han Solo, permeates the culture and the subconscious of individual men, even those who consciously reject such models of manhood for themselves. In focusing on this stereotype, we hope to highlight issues that are present in more subtle forms in many men.

The Marlboro Man in Intimate Relationships

The Marlboro man, in the popular view, is the man who is from Mars whose "masculine focused awareness" (Gray, 1992, p. 92) means that he looks for solutions that will efficiently achieve goals and who withdraws into detachment when stressed (Gottman, 1994; Gottman & Levenson, 1988; Levant, 1995). According to Tannen, such men talk "report talk," a language of independence and status, while his female partner is described as speaking "rapport talk" a language "of intimacy and connection" (Tannen, 1990, p. 42). He is the man commonly portrayed in much psychological literature, as he is in the mass media, as unable to love, fearing intimacy, and avoiding commitment, unless forced into it by relationship-starved women (Gray, 1992; Jordan, Kaplan, Miller, Stiver, & Surrey, 1991; Pollack, 1995; Shay, 1996). He is the product of traditional male socialization toward autonomy, self-sufficiency, and aggression who is poorly prepared for close relationships. Richman (1982) is describing this kind of man when he recites as the first commandment of masculinity: *Thou shalt not cry or expose feelings of emotion, fear, weakness, symptoms, empathy, or involvement before thy neighbor* (p. 103). Such men are commonly seen as overinvested in work, emotionally unavailable to their families, and heedless of the costs of this lifestyle to their partners and offspring, and to their own physical and emotional health (Brooks, 1992; Pleck, 1995).

We recognize that this stereotype does not reflect the diversity of men's experiences and overstates the differences between men and women (Aries, 1996; Goldner, 1985; Hare-Mustin, 1987), yet male socialization at the end of the 20th century still does primarily prepare men for the roles of breadwinner and warrior with far less attention to relationship skills (Balswick, 1988; Bergman, 1995; Jordan et al., 1991; Levant, 1995; Pollack, 1995). Most adult men are still rewarded for competing successfully in the workplace, on the playing field, and in the battlefield, places where control over emotions, aggressiveness, and self-assertion pay off while expressing feelings of weakness and vulnerability does not (Brooks & Silverstein, 1995; Levant & Kopecky, 1995; O'Neil, Good, & Holmes, 1995; Pleck, 1995). In sex-segregated peer groups which stress teamwork, toughness, and competition (Levant, 1995; Maccoby, 1990), boys are still taught to ignore their emotional states and "soldier on," often inhibiting the development of a language for feelings which Levant describes as "normative male alexithymia" (Levant, 1995).

Despite the growing acceptance of more fluid and flexible gender roles over the past 20 years, many men still harbor within themselves features of the Marlboro man. Young boys still risk ridicule for showing signs of vulnerability or softness, are in dread of the epithet "girl," and actively suppress the very skills that could prepare them to participate more fully in adult intimate relationships and better care for their own emotional and physical needs. They commonly deny to themselves and hide from others their dependency needs, despite considerable covert reliance on women for nurturance, emotional expressiveness, and physical care (Brooks, 1992; Pollack, 1995). Dependent longings are frequently channeled into sexuality which may be disconnected from intimacy. Boys still think of sex in terms of their performance and "scoring," as ways of proving masculine adequacy (Levant & Kopecky, 1995; Pleck, 1995; Seppa, 1997; Zilbergeld, 1992), while later intimate partners will expect them to be sensitive to the differences in female sexual functioning and desire. In both positive and negative ways, sexuality is frequently far more central to men's satisfaction within intimate relationships than it is to women's and is one of the most frequent reasons for men to initiate couple therapy.

THEORETICAL APPROACHES TO MEN'S INTIMACY PROBLEMS

To help men's relationship problems through couple therapy, therapists must understand the ways traditional male socialization poorly prepares men to have their own needs for intimacy met while simultaneously frustrating and disappointing the women with whom they wish to be intimate. In examining how gender socialization creates problems for heterosexual intimate relationships, certain ideas from psychoanalytic, feminist, and postmodern theories are helpful.

Psychoanalytic Approaches

Psychoanalytic thinkers generally attribute gender-linked characteristics to unconscious internal representations of self and other, as well as beliefs about gender and intimate relations, that are carried forward from early childhood relationships in the family. For many men, the fact that women are primary caretakers centrally shapes traditional masculinity (Benjamin, 1988; Chodorow, 1978; Dinnerstein, 1976) because of the need for the male child to ultimately renounce identification with the mother. The cultural pattern of pushing young boys to separate from their dependent ties to their mothers, and the subsequent repudiation of things that are feminine, is viewed as necessary for masculine development, seen as occurring through disidentification with their mothers and all that is feminine (Chodorow, 1978; Dinnerstein, 1976). Subsequent shame over dependency (Krugman, 1995; Lansky, 1992), and fear of attachment and commitment (Pollack, 1995) is linked to this widespread family pattern (Jordan et al., 1991; Krugman, 1995; Osherson & Krugman, 1990) making closeness to women highly conflictual.

Theorists of the new psychology of men have questioned whether our normative socialization practices are in themselves traumatic and hence produce males whose modal personality is pathological, in that it requires the use of immature defenses like projection, denial, splitting, and projective identification, to rid the self of unbearable shame over dependency and vulnerability. Pollack (1995), for example, observes that this modal male personality, who maintains the pretense of self-sufficiency while covertly relying heavily on intimate others, overlaps remarkably with the common diagnosis of narcissistic personality disorder in men. Krugman (1995) notes that shaming responses to the manifestation of personal doubts or fears have always been central to socialization into the warrior-role. He observes that the development of narcissistic defenses and "character styles associated with self-involvement, self-importance and emotional distance" (p. 29) is a predictable outcome of the suppression of all vulnerabilities and the desperate, but unconscious, need for a close person to function as a self-object who supports and restores a fragile self.

These same traits that protect against the experience of shame and hide vulnerable self-esteem and a fragile sense of self, interfere with men's participating in intimate relationships that require emotional openness and a recognition of and empathy for the other's needs. Psychotherapies that do not address the way the intimate other is used by certain men to shore up a diminished sense of self and/or be the repository of shameful parts of self that are denied and projected, may falter if these interactional defenses are not addressed directly. Men with these characteristic ways of coping with their psychological vulnerabilities often pair up with women with mirror-image vulnerabilities, who, for example, may define themselves primarily through their intimate relationships at the expense of their own self-development. Such interlocking dynamics in the couple relationships, illustrated later with the case of Betty and Robert, are often only apparent when the partners are seen together and therefore may best be addressed through couple therapy (Maltas, 1991, 1996, 1997).

Our couple therapy model is also shaped by contemporary feminist and postmodern theories that both challenge and supplement psychoanalytic understanding of masculine development, offering ideas of fluid and multiple identifications. Writers from these perspectives, for example, note that characteristics such as men's difficulties with emotionality and empathy do not represent some bedrock of psychic experience, but are social constructions (Goldner, Penn, Sheinberg, & Walker, 1990; Hare-Mustin, 1987). Furthermore, they note that various "essentialist" views of gender differences, that have at times been uncritically accepted by family therapists as much as by psychoanalysts, have also been used to rationalize as "natural" the unequal distribution of power in the family and in the larger society (Goldner, 1985; Goldner et al., 1990; Hare-Mustin & Marecek, 1986; James & McIntyre, 1983; Leupnitz, 1988). This may inadvertently reinforce inequality when the celebration of women's relational focus leads women to consistently subordinate their own needs and independent strivings to accommodate men and preserve relationships (Betcher & Pollack 1993; Jordan et al., 1991).

The Postmodern View of Gender

Male and female children, in all cultures and historical periods, have been socialized into very different gender roles, but this has not always created the "war between the sexes" that exists today. The particular dilemmas men and women experience in intimate relationships stem from our social constructions of gender and of intimacy at one particular moment in history in a specific locale. They are not universal nor do they inevitably derive from irreducible biological differences (Aries, 1996; Goldner, 1985; Goldner et al., 1990).

Until fairly recently, models of intimate relationships, especially marriage, were constructed on the foundation of a general acceptance of substantial "natural" differences between men and women (Cancian, 1987). During and after the Industrial Revolution, as men's work moved out of the home, gender roles were more sharply differentiated to fit the need for complementary spheres of a masculine workplace and a feminized home. Men were seen as ideally fitted for work due to their innate characteristics of competitiveness, independence, materialism, and emotional restraint. Women's work, no longer seen as an economic contribution, was understood as the expression of women's "love" and innate nurturing abilities (Cancian, 1987; Mintz & Kellogg, 1988). These shifts were accompanied by new expectations for more companionship between husband and wife, who were now more isolated from other relationships in the larger community and extended family. Paradoxically, the exaggeration of sex role differences made those expectations for a much broader kind of companionship and compatibility more difficult to achieve.

In the 20th century, women's greater access to education, freedom from constant childbearing, and related ability to work outside the family developed in women a taste for the advantages reserved for men. Women have pushed for social changes at home and in the larger society, including men's greater participation in family life and women's further self-development outside of the family. The rapidly climbing divorce rate throughout most of the 20th century in part reflected women's greater financial security but also their raised expectations for marriage. Women now expect greater equality, in addition to companionship, psychological and emotional support, meaningful communication, and mutual sexual enjoyment. Prior to the 20th century, most women expected that their most intense relationships would be with their children and their most emotionally intimate and reciprocal relationships would be with other women (Cott, 1978). Few expected sexual satisfaction for women in general and men frequently sought sexual satisfaction outside of marriage (Cancian, 1987; Cott, 1978; Mintz & Kellogg, 1988). It would have been a rare wife who demanded that her husband curb his work commitments to spend time with her or the children since economic security for the family was the greatest contribution he could make.

The Social Construction of Intimacy

Changing constructions of gender roles naturally accompany shifting constructions of love and intimacy. Current views emphasize verbal self-disclosure and expression of vulnerable feelings as the sine qua non of intimacy (Cancian, 1987; Jordan et al., 1991; Maltas, 1997). These elements which to us seem so natural and obvious, were never before in history seen as essential parts of committed intimate relationships. This construction of intimacy valorizes feminine traits while devaluing or overlooking men's contributions to intimacy such as offering practical help, sharing activities, and sex (Cancian, 1987; Peplau, Rubin, & Hill, 1977;

Weingarten, 1991). Women seem more interested in and more capable of love when measures of love are based on feminine styles of loving, which can also obscure women's difficulties in intimate relationships and underrate men's ways of showing love, attachment, or dependency. Just as Gilligan (1982) noted that women construct morality differently than men, so too men construct intimacy differently and should not be seen as deficient by a model that leaves out significant aspects of male experience. Talking about feelings is not an adequate definition of love or intimacy within a committed relationship, since it leaves out many other elements such as devotion to the other's well-being, physical affection and sexual intimacy, expression of positive feelings, sharing tasks of daily living, and practical assistance (Sternberg & Barnes, 1988).

Positive aspects of men's ways of being intimate need to be acknowledged, while simultaneously recognizing that both men and women will benefit if men are able to become more emotionally aware and expressive within their most intimate relationships. Men learning to identify uncomfortable feeling states and learning to tolerate and regulate them will lessen projection of vulnerable emotional states onto the women and decrease men's overreliance on their women partners to regulate emotional states for them. Women will understand that a more complex person exists below the surface picture that is distorted by the man's defensive suppression of vulnerable emotions.

Just such a reconstruction of gender roles is occurring in our society, with stereotypic views of gender shifting to permit greater self-development for women and the development of more relational skills and emotional awareness in men (Cancian, 1987; Levant, 1995). These societal changes are potentially enormously liberating for men and yet profoundly unsettling as early gender socialization, deeply embedded in the individual psyche and in the structure and beliefs of the family (Goldner et al., 1990; Hare-Mustin, 1987; Maltas, 1997) lags behind changes in societal ideals. Living up to the traditional standards of masculine success (i.e., the Marlboro man) is criticized; at the same time, many men are not prepared to fulfill the expectations for roles as much more involved parents and emotionally available partners (West & Zimmerman, 1987). Zilbergeld (1992) speaks for many men when he observes that a man "who has followed the precepts taught by his parents, the mass media, teachers, coaches, and other authorities now is in the very strange position of hearing that everything he learned was wrong" (p. 11).

While the generation currently entering young adulthood has less traditional expectations regarding things such as women working and men caring for children, it is less clear that social and psychological conditions actually support these changes. Many women are still economically dependent on men, and there frequently is a lack of acknowledgment in the work place that workers have family responsibilities. The culture of the work place is still largely masculine, as though each worker has a wife at home (Thompson & Pleck, 1995). Each couple struggles on their own to construct, in their day-to-day interactions, workable gender roles and responsibilities, and frequently experiences their conflicts in these areas as personal failures or dysfunctions. Feeling disadvantaged in certain realms and over-burdened in others, men and women bring this unhappiness to couple therapists for individual solutions to societal problems.

Feminist and social constructionist theorists challenge therapists to look beyond their own constructs of individual pathology or systemic dysfunction, to see the larger picture of social, cultural, and historical forces at work in creating male and female roles that continue to be problematic for both sexes. The larger view is particularly important when designing treatments that hope to facilitate change in intimate relationships. A couple therapy that is grounded in an awareness of the social construction of gender roles and of views about intimate relationships and can consciously use that awareness to help free men to choose to be different from the men they were taught to be, reconstructing roles and relationships to cause less pain and isolation in men. The social constructionist view also serves as a check against the reification of newer theories about men and women, that run the risk of again promoting *essentialist* views of masculinity, femininity, and intimate relationships.

A Gender-Sensitive Couple Therapy

Couple therapy can offer men the opportunity to become more emotionally aware, acknowledge vulnerability and interdependence, develop sensitivity to their partner's needs, and be able to tolerate and work with relational conflict. A gender-sensitive couple therapy for reluctant males helps these patients examine their gendered beliefs and discover how they impact on their day-to-day relational expectations and behaviors. Historically situating those beliefs about gender and the related views about intimacy in heterosexual relationships further aids patients to make conscious choices about matters they may have unconsciously accepted as both natural and essential, even when they are personally constraining or problematic for the relationship.

Certain changes that might at first glance seem to reduce a man's power and prestige in the eyes of others could, from a different perspective, be seen as both liberating and empowering. To do so, the therapist will have to engage the man sufficiently for him to experience the therapy process as having something to offer him other than shame over ineptness and exposure of his faults. The therapist must truly value the man's contributions to the couple relationship and to the family and affirm his positive motive to fulfill the masculine role as he learned it in his family and sees it continually reinforced by his culture. Only with a strong alliance between male client and therapist will the defensive aspects of the man's behavior ultimately be addressable.

DILEMMAS OF COUPLE THERAPY WITH THE RELUCTANT MALE

Before returning to the story of Robert and Betty which illustrates many of the important difficulties in intimate relationships, we would like to address certain dilemmas of couple therapy. These dilemmas stem from several factors. First, couple therapy commonly begins with complaints, a desire to assign blame, and a wish for judgment. Each partner may be hoping the therapist will see the other as the root of the problem, but when the man is a reluctant participant, he typically expects the judgment to be against him. However, the woman, as initiator of treatment, may be quite resistant to a therapist's questions about her contribution to the relationship problems. The therapist must tread very carefully in the beginning, not accepting either story of the relationship as the whole picture and shifting the focus about the "problem" from the individual to the interaction.

For many men, therapy is identified more with feminine traits of open communication, exposure, vulnerability, and intimate sharing which may seem to further disadvantage the man. A simple request like "Tell me how you feel about that" asks the man to look inward for a feeling which he either may not be able to find or name (Levant, 1995) or which he may be too ashamed to reveal (Osherson & Krugman, 1990). As noted earlier, speaking in a language familiar to the man and demonstrating respect for instrumental actions as well as emotional expression can reassure the man that the deck is not stacked against him. The therapist can consciously employ the words and images of each partner in turn or embed aspects of both manners of speaking in developing shared language for therapy. To acculturate the reluctant male, the therapist can draw from metaphors the man uses, or employ images from familiar areas of his work life or recreation to bridge the familiar and the less familiar world addressed in the therapy.

The central dilemma of the first stage of couple therapy is to develop an empathic connection with each partner despite the differences between them and despite their inability to be empathic toward each other. Demonstrating that both perspectives can be valid and both partners seen as valuable human beings is in itself a healing process. However, a persistent problem in couple therapy is that empathy for one member of the couple is sometimes experienced as invalidating, or at least very insensitive, to the other (Shay, 1990). For example, the man may feel that the therapist's empathy for his wife's pain is tantamount to blaming him, and he may fear the therapist's comments will be used by his wife as a weapon against him at a later date.

Balancing empathy is complicated by the gender imbalance in couple therapy since the therapist is the same gender as one and not the other (Bernadez, 1982; Bograd, 1990; Maltas, 1997; Shay, 1993). This situation can create various fears and fantasies about same-gender bonding or rivalry or cross-gender estrangement of affiliation, the latter sometimes sexually tinged. Male and female therapists may resonate differentially with the difficulties of the male. For example, a male therapist who may initially have been expected to sympathetically understand the reluctant male, may turn out to be a significant threat to the man when the woman starts idealizing the therapist as precisely the kind of empathic and sensitive man she needs. Therapists need to be sensitive to gender-linked transferences and also aware of their own unique, and socioculturally influenced, internalized gender messages that will appear in the countertransference. Gender-linked transferences and countertransferences can be problematic and impede therapy, but they can also highlight expectations, fantasies, and fears about gender roles that contribute to the creation of "warring factions at the very heart of the family" (Goldner et al., 1990).

Resistance to change during couple therapy may derive from conflicts at many levels, from the individual unconscious to the societal. In couple therapy, the most powerful resistance to change sometimes occurs at the level of the couple system. One partner's shifts in one direction may run into countermoves from the other partner, unconsciously re-establishing a familiar, if unsatisfying, equilibrium. In couple therapy, the therapist can directly observe and intervene in the re-equilibrating interactions between the pair that function as resistances to change.

Despite these dilemmas, and sometimes because of them, couple therapy is a powerful intervention for improving the relationship problems of men. The couple therapist can directly block negative interactional patterns between the partners and facilitate new ways of interacting, as will be seen in the case material. Furthermore, the therapist can model new relationship behaviors and the couple can experiment with less stereo-typed ways of relating than were possible in the past. As the projectively distorted perceptions of the partners shift and previously disavowed and projected parts of the self are acknowledged and integrated into an expanded view of self, new levels of relational satisfaction become possible. For example, the man who has felt too depleted to give to his family can discover the rewards in giving as well as getting, in learning to be empathic as well as receiving empathy.

CASE STUDY: THE MARLBOROS

In the following sections a case history and treatment illustrate many of the points discussed previously about men's characteristic difficulties in intimate relationships as well as the particular advantages and dilemmas of couple therapy as a treatment for them.

THE MARLBORO COUPLE'S STORY

The Marlboro couple arrives for the first session. Sensitive to the presence of a reluctant Robert and wishing to promote Robert's comfort while simultaneously supporting Betty, the male therapist (J. S.) carefully begins, "I appreciate your coming today. I know just a little about your situation from my conversation with Betty on the phone. I'd like to begin by asking you to tell me what brings you here today, and then we'll discuss that and other issues that come up, and at the end of the session I'll share some of my thoughts with you and we can decide what the next step should be. If you're like a number of other men who come to this office, Robert, this is probably not your first choice for spending this evening. I wanted you to know I respect that. So, if either of you could tell me what led to your making this appointment?"

Robert turns to Betty and says, with a half smile, "This was your idea so you go first." Betty details the following story while Robert listens. Now married for 20 years, with a 10-year-old daughter and a 15-year-old son, they have grown apart during the past five years. Robert, an architect and a principal in his successful firm, has been working 60 to 70 hours per week for several years now and has little interest in talking with Betty at the end of the day or on weekends, and even less interest in going out for social events. He is, however, interested in connecting with her sexually which irritates Betty, since she is usually too tired when he asks or is "not in the mood."

Betty, busy raising the children and working part-time as a substitute teacher in the high school, has been unhappy for some time, and recently initiated her own psychotherapy to deal with her general malaise. Out of this has come a greater awareness of her dissatisfaction for the past several years with their lack of time together or of meaningful communication when they are together, as well as Robert's limited time with the children. Robert's typical reply is that they need his income for daily living and for retirement. He states that he'll work fewer hours at some point in the near future when the company becomes more successful, and then will spend as much time with Betty as she wants. Betty no longer believes these promises and sees nothing but more of the same for many years ahead. She's not going to continue to wait for a rosier future that will never come, as she had watched her mother wait unsuccessfully for Betty's father to be a better partner to her only to have him die of a coronary when he was 55. She mentions at this point that Robert has two drinks at dinner every night, and this also worries her.

Robert, listening attentively while rustling intermittently in his chair, breaks in. "Wait a minute! This kind of talk does more harm than good— it's not like we've got big problems. I didn't come here to be attacked. What does my drinking have to do with anything? I never get drunk, do I? And I don't work 70 hours a week. Three weeks ago, I came home at noon on a Friday when the office closed early. And, if we're getting things off our chest, why don't you tell the doctor how you push me away in the bed." Robert and Betty glare at each other, and then wait for a comment from the therapist who is momentarily silent, contemplating all the dilemmas: Robert's reluctance to be in therapy; his feeling blackmailed into coming in to discuss his wife's upset over the note, not to review their whole marriage; his fear that naming problems makes them worse. Furthermore, the therapist is aware that his own view of the situation is closer to that of Betty.

Very sensitive to avoiding comments that might be construed by either partner as allying with the other and accepting that person's view as the whole story, he also wants to convey a sense of understanding and acceptance of each view. The therapist is aware that asking questions about Robert's drinking early on could alienate Robert by seeming to accept Betty's definition of the problem situation as including his drinking. If the therapist tries to remain neutral and objective, Betty, expecting an ally, may feel less hopeful about being understood and helped by the therapist than she had when she initially called. If, in an attempt to persuade Robert that the therapist is fair-minded, the therapist suggests that

Robert may have certain dissatisfactions himself, Betty may feel the therapist has misunderstood what she was here for. Before presenting the therapist's response, it is useful to learn more about Robert and Betty.

ROBERT'S STORY

Robert, the oldest of two children, was born in New York City, to Italian immigrant parents. During his early years, Robert's father, described as "uneducated but hard-working," owned a small candy store in the Bronx and when shopping for merchandise for the store, occasionally took Robert along with him. Of this experience, Robert writes, "At times he held my hand very tight to make sure I didn't get lost. It always seemed very confusing and I couldn't understand why he never got lost since he never asked for directions. Dad seemed to me a remote, eccentric person and we never had a single serious conversation that I can remember." Robert's mother worked alongside his father but complained frequently about her husband's lack of initiative at making the business more successful. Mother also took Robert into her confidence about her dissatisfactions with his father and often urged Robert to focus on growing up to become "somebody important." Robert felt "increasingly claustrophobic in the house during adolescence" and began to wander the streets of his neighborhood.

Spending a lot of time on his own, Robert says, "I grew up bored, anxious, and smart in a working class neighborhood. I was probably the smartest kid in my public school but was always a terrible student—constantly talking out of turn, fidgeting, asking smart-ass questions." Apart from his behavior problems, Robert couldn't spell well and developed a reputation for being "slow" which angered him. His parents periodically criticized him for his underperformance at school, and he began to doubt his abilities. One incident from this period stands out for Robert: "In those years, I was bigger than my peers and also mild tempered. As a result they occasionally made fun of me. I remember one incident in which one of my friend's older brother would get close to me and then punch me in the arm. I would move further away but he would get closer while I was involved in something else and he would punch me again, which caused the other kids to laugh. Since he was much older than me, I felt helpless and I eventually just walked away."

In high school, for the first time he began to come into his own. He developed a close relationship with a guidance counselor who told him he was very smart but had some mild learning problems that could be helped. He got involved in the antiwar activities of the 1960s for reasons he still doesn't understand except to say he was probably rebelling against his parents' support for the war. While rarely a leader of these activities, through his diligent perseverance and impressive organizational abilities, he was able to assume a position of stature and to receive acclaim to which he had been unaccustomed.

College was a time of great excitement and new experiences for Robert. He attended an excellent college on a partial scholarship, achieved decent grades, and worked part-time. Politically visible on campus as a member of a high-prestige group, he attracted women and felt popular. While dating frequently, he was unable to develop lasting relationship with a female until his senior year when he met Betty whom he describes as "a great looking woman, smart, self-confident, and generous with affection, attention, and humor. She admired me a great deal and I liked that. We became friends, then lovers—sex was great in those days—and then began living together. We used to talk nonstop for hours and once missed our exit on the highway because we were so busy talking about something or other."

Since the focus of this chapter is treating the reluctant male, Betty's history is limited to those aspects that are essential to understanding the couple's interaction and problems and her dissatisfaction with Robert which was the impetus for treatment. Betty's father had died at age 55 of a coronary, having suffered from alcoholism which he had persistently denied until it was too late. This understanding illuminates her worries that Robert's drinks at dinner are not harmless, even though from his perspective they are insignificant. In addition, Betty's mother, resolutely unable to persuade her husband to get treatment for his drinking, had seemed to Betty throughout her earlier and teen years to be a carping witch. Betty had vowed never to become like her critical mother. Only very recently, in her individual therapy, was she beginning to understand that her mother had her own story to tell.

Having come from a lower-middle-class family and been given the explicit message from her parents to "marry up," Betty felt unequal to her peers, carried herself with a shameful bearing, and was depressed in college until she was swept off her feet by a married professor with whom she had a brief sexual relationship. Energized by this relationship, with its boost to her esteem, she soon found herself courted by several college men. She was attracted to Robert's popularity and stature in college and to his perseverance and drive, appreciating the security this could provide. Matched as well in the sexual arena, enjoying conversation with him, and having great fun together, when Robert proposed, Betty accepted immediately. Beyond settling down with the "right man," she had no clear vision of her own future.

The Marital Story

Upon graduating from college, Robert and Betty married, and Robert began working in a small architectural firm while Betty worked in a nursery school as a teacher. Within a year of their marriage "the first real confrontation in our relationship occurred. I was in the basement of the apartment late into the night working on a design for a dream house I've always wanted to build. When I came up to bed, Betty let me know she was very angry. This registered with me because I had never seen her show anger before and it seemed to me that our whole relationship might evaporate right there." He was too frightened by her anger to really address the problem and Betty seemed willing to let it drop as long as he was contrite.

The two evolved a repetitive pattern of Robert "doing something I should have known was not acceptable, Betty getting angry and criticizing me, and both of us blowing off steam. These fights made me feel very small, so I would try to avoid repeating whatever I had done wrong, even if I wasn't really wrong, and after a while we stopped confronting each other at all. It just seemed easier that way, and certainly more pleasant around the house. Plus, we had the two kids and they occupied a lot of our time, and I began to increase my hours at work because I could see that I could become a principal in the firm and hopefully be on Easy Street one day."

Raising the children, working at their jobs, and maintaining just a few social contacts with neighborhood parents became their lives. As they traveled through these lives, they grew increasingly distant from one another, with Robert deeply engrossed in his work, where he felt appreciated and rewarded, and experiencing minimal conflict with Betty but minimal emotional or physical intimacy as well. Betty became more dissatisfied with the relationship as the years passed and tried to point out to Robert the distance and lack of intimate communication. However, when Robert flatly disagreed and minimized any problems she let it drop, determined not to nag as her mother had. And then she discovered the note.

Couple Therapy with Robert and Betty

Turning now to the treatment of Robert and Betty, our hope is to illustrate a gender-sensitive couple therapy model for working with a reluctant male. We try to demonstrate the integration of a broad sociocultural perspective alongside technical attention to the use of gender-attuned verbal and nonverbal communication which promote the alliance and balance the partners' experiences of being empathically understood by the therapist, while helping each of them develop greater empathy for the other.

In response to Betty's initial phone call to the male therapist detailing the problems and Robert's reluctance to come, the therapist had responded, "It's good you called for the appointment. Robert's position is fairly common among men, and you might want to let him know that he's got lots of company and he can tell me as little as he's comfortable with. We've got to start somewhere." Embedded in this intervention by the therapist is a protective message to the husband through the wife, an empathic message to the wife counseling patience and an unfolding process, and an implicit message about the therapist's sense of competence in dealing with such presentations.

The following summary of the first session gives a picture of their typical presentation. As noted earlier, the therapist reaffirms his understanding that Robert is a reluctant participant and tries respectfully to validate this posture as normative (Shay, 1996). Betty then details the couple's story, emphasizing Robert's extensive work hours, limited interest in talking with Betty or engaging in social activities as a couple, reflecting their increasing distance from one another over the past several years. She also implies a concern about Robert's drinking behavior that rouses him to defend himself, and then, perhaps in retaliation and to redress the developing unfavorable balance in the room, he accuses her of rejecting him in the bedroom. Neither mentions the note.

The therapist's interventions try to balance multiple intents: building an alliance with each partner, respecting their differing treatment-entry positions, anticipating shifting alliances with each of them, acknowledging the gender imbalance in the room, and demonstrating that, despite the gathering tension, which if unchecked can destroy a fragile treatment, the therapy office can be a safe environment for both partners (Shay, 1997). (For the sake of this chapter, the following lengthy therapist comment is made as a single intervention early in this first session, though in practice it is usually broken into segments, and introduced where appropriate at other points in treatment.)

THERAPIST: Now, let me slow you down for a moment and make a few points. As the two of you tell me your story, it's not unusual for a couple to see things differently, for tension to develop, for comments to feel like accusations, and so on. Robert, this may be part of the reason you weren't a big fan of therapy. But, as we review how each of you see your relationship, I trust that each of you will find that your point of view gets airtime in here.

Now, let me put something on the table here. Often in couple therapy, especially when the two people don't feel equally comfortable in being here, one or the other suddenly feels like they're not getting a fair shake in my eyes. You may each feel like this or think this is happening from time to time. In fact, I'm actually not the kind of therapist who never takes sides. I try to be as objective as I can, but I don't always land in the middle when the two of you see something differently. If one of you says the sun rises in the east and the other says it rises in the west, I'm not going to say "the truth lies somewhere in the middle." But I am fairly confident that by the time we get to the end of our time together, you'll each see me as understanding your point of view and as having been even in the way I hear you. For a while, Robert, I'm asking for your patience especially since this may seem rougher on you with Betty having initiated treatment but you probably wouldn't have come along unless you were also worried about the relationship. I don't know if your concerns are the same as or different from Betty's, but it will be very important for you to be able to talk about them as they become clearer to you.

Let me say one more thing here. It's obvious to both of you that I'm the same gender as only one of you. I don't know yet how this will affect our work together, but it may mean that one of you will feel more comfortable with that than the other.

> For example, Betty, may see me as understanding Robert better because we're men, or Robert may see me as siding with Betty because she's been in therapy for a while and talks therapy-talk like I do. I'll keep an eye on this and I hope both of you will as well, and it will help us all a lot if you let me know if you notice anything significant on this score.

At some point early on in the first session, the therapist may strive to promote an alliance with Robert trading on a currency with which Robert is familiar and comfortable. The therapist asks, "So, what kind of work do you do, Robert?" recognizing that men socialized in this culture in general, and hard-working Robert in particular, take pride in their work, derive esteem from it, and are often glad to talk about it because they can do so concretely, with expertise, and in whatever language they feel comfortable rather than in the language of therapy which may put them at a disadvantage. Hearing that Robert is an architect, the therapist playfully insults his own office arrangement, asking Robert to be patient with his primitive taste. This intervention metacommunicates that the therapist respects Robert's skills which are different from his own, and also that humor has a place in therapy. The therapist must monitor the alliance with Betty and might, for example, show appreciation of something from which she derives satisfaction, whether her own work, her childrearing, her friendships, and so on.

At the end of the first session, the therapist asks each member of the couple if they'd be willing to write an autobiographical account for him, presenting this as a suggestion rather than a request or an assignment, "It might really be helpful to us, and you might even remember some things you'd forgotten for a while. If you'd rather not, that's okay too. You can write a page—once someone wrote 30 pages, but that's not necessary—or send me an e-mail or send me your resume. I'm interested in both a chronology of your life and also in moments that were turning points for you, for example, when you were in fifth grade and you were shamed by a teacher who humiliated you in front of the class. Whatever. Don't give me all the details, but focus on what you may have learned about relationships, for instance, messages you got about how to be a man or a woman, a husband or wife, father or mother, for example, from observing how your father treated your mother?"

Within days of the first session, Robert e-mailed the therapist his autobiography and his resume. Betty had hers in hand at the second session, and in it the note from the other woman is finally mentioned. In the second session, and in subsequent sessions, Betty begins each session by detailing a recent situation in which she perceived Robert as neglectful or critical. The couple's typical in-session pattern is then to argue for the correctness of their differing recollections of each event. Intermittently, Betty cries and seems to be more open and vulnerable which makes empathy easier for the therapist than it is with the more constricted and defensive Robert. However, the therapist acknowledges that each is in distress even though they may express it in very different ways.

Central to Robert and Betty's conflict is their differential view of the meaning and effect of Robert's working such long hours. Emphatic statements by Robert that he will simply work less hard alternate with anxious statements that the family will have no retirement income if he slows down. Resigned statements by Betty that she will try to accept Robert as he is alternate with distressed statements that she is growing older and feels lonely much of the time. The therapist comments that while each is trying to create a different marriage than their parents had, they find themselves repeating many of the same patterns. To minimize blame, the therapist also highlights the powerful messages from their families and from the larger culture that encourage Robert to work so hard and be a professional success and for Betty to need him to be very successful professionally and also to be disappointed that he cannot simultaneously be much more available to her emotionally.

As with other couples, treatment with Robert and Betty moves through stages. Using Shay's (1997) model, the therapist weaves back and forth as the treatment progresses from the alliance building stage to assessment and formulation, goal setting, damage reduction, working interaction, closeness, and intimacy. The therapist alternates between trying to help the couple to improve their communication and problem-solving skills and noticing the barriers to such improvement. Supporting each partner to articulate openly their varying perspectives, and the affects which underlie them, predominantly frustration and anxiety for Robert, and hopelessness and concern for Betty, the therapist gently invites the couple to address the profound barriers to change (Shay, 1997). The therapist points to barriers at the familial and societal level, in addition to the individual level, which sometimes illuminate why a conscious shift in personal values about how to live their lives together may still be impeded by conflicting messages or shaming responses from others. For example, Robert talks with great fear about how he would be seen by his colleagues if he began cutting back at work. If viewed as on the "Daddy track" at work, and thus taken less seriously, he would also worry that ultimately he would earn his wife's scorn, as his father did his mother's.

The therapist is aware of an easy and comfortable connection with Betty to which she responds with appreciative smiles. At one point, she even shouts at Robert, "If he can understand me, why is it so hard for you?" The therapist comments, striving for empathic balance, "I'm glad you feel understood. You present yourself very openly making that easier to do. I can see that Robert is also working to be able to understand you, but it's complicated for him. It may be easier for me to do it because I'm not directly involved in your issues so I have the distance that allows me to understand."

Additionally the therapist, as a man who also works long hours, can identify with Robert, and makes clear to Robert his valuing of hard work while also validating Betty's experience of feeling abandoned, "You've got a lot to be proud of, Robert. Your success is a testament to your commitment to your work and to providing well for your family, and I admire that. You can see by our meeting at 8 P.M. that I have respect for long working hours. Betty's admiration of you is clear as well, although her wish to have you more available to her is very understandable, and, ironically, it's something you have always valued as well." Experienced couple therapists will recognize that it is very common for couples in couple therapy initially to adopt polarized positions around issues which, in fact, they have marked underlying agreement. This early feeling of agreement, and the later processes that obscure it, are often worth noting and examining.

As therapy progresses, when the therapist is engaged in the more instrumental task of communication training, Robert seems most satisfied, relieved by the therapist's focus on communication as a two-person process with some clear rules. Addressing the lack of emotional closeness between them and the pain this causes Betty is received more favorably by her. But, when focusing on underlying historical patterns which are repeated by the couple in the present, Betty, initially more open and responsive in such discussions, becomes increasingly defensive when attention to her history implies that she too brings certain maladaptive expectations or behaviors to the relationship. Conversely, when addressing Betty's emotional distress as a consequence of Robert's common empathic lapses, Robert becomes defensive as though he is being accused. Sensing a fragile situation, the therapist makes several universalizing comments about the socialization processes and cultural pressures that contribute to men and women adopting particular postures and communication styles in close relationships. Particularizing those trends, he observes that Betty's experiences in her family of origin led her to need to have a successful, admired husband about whom she could worry and fret over the high costs of that success, to him personally and to them as a couple. Similar paradoxes came out of Robert's upbringing as a male trained to constantly prove to a woman that he was capable and competent in order to win her love, yet needing simultaneously to keep at a safe distance from Betty and her potentially engulfing needs.

Gradually, Robert and Betty become more comfortable in the office. Much of the therapy is specifically focused on the couple's marital issues, now including Betty's worries about Robert's possible infidelity and Robert's concerns about Betty's lack of interest in sex. While Robert, in early discussions, has flatly denied that he is having an affair with his female colleague, the therapist supports Betty's repeated articulation of her fears as evidence in itself of a genuine problem between them, regardless of the facts. The therapist accepts both Betty's concerns and Robert's denial of any basis for them, without trying to ferret out the truth, since the only truth the therapist is sure of is that their conflict over the meaning of Robert's suspicious behavior is key.

Mindful of the centrality of maintaining the therapeutic alliance with both, and that this concern about the possible affair, and the very nature of the therapeutic expectations for emotional vulnerability, openness and exposure, are threatening to Robert, the therapist often supports, and even introduces, discussions of seemingly tangential asides that may engage Robert in less threatening ways. For example, the therapeutic conversation includes reviews of recent movies seen, restaurants visited, sporting events, business successes for Robert, and humorous interactions at Betty's work. Such asides lead often to recall of historical precursors for the couple, to times when Robert and Betty derived greater enjoyment from their relationship. These discussions lead then back to even earlier times.

In this context, almost without knowing that he is now deeply involved in psychotherapy (Shay, 1996), Robert, over many sessions, shares a space with Betty in which they can safely explore the deeper meaning of many of their interactions. While beginning factually to speak about his relationship with his father, for example, Robert finds himself, to his surprise, talking sadly about his confusion about this relationship. His father's hard work was surely proof that he loved Robert and his mother, but why did he never talk to Robert? "He held my hand but he forgot my heart" Robert says, his eyes filling with tears. Betty too begins to cry.

In this absence of emotional contact with his father, Robert remained attached to his mother, identifying with her critical posture toward his father. Robert, however, did not criticize his father's work ethic, which Robert admired, but rather his father's failure to save enough money for retirement before he died. Moreover, growing increasingly uncomfortable with this attachment to his mother, Robert's claustrophobic experience pushed him to yearn for time outside the house. As Robert reviews his history, recalling his fear of being seen as unintelligent, his physical awkwardness, and his vulnerability to being teased with the accompanying shame, Betty grows closer to him during the sessions and feels less critical. Suddenly, Robert and Betty can see Robert's hard work in a new light, partly as a way to emulate his father, partly as a well-worn masculine path to stature and esteem, partly to avoid failure, and partly to protect himself against the kind of smothering intimacy he fled from in his mother and he feared in Betty. Robert is able to see that becoming the kind of man his father would have been proud of, and that society rewards, has had a consequence of not being the kind of husband his wife needed and his children longed for. Hearing Robert's story and his efforts to understand his behavior is moving for Betty, who now seems more deeply empathic.

Concomitantly, as Robert begins to take responsibility for this, Betty speaks more freely about her previously unacknowledged fears that if

Robert worked less hard, they might actually have trouble paying future college bills, let alone have enough for retirement. Yet memories of her father's early death, which she associated with overwork, and her feelings of loneliness and boredom made her angry, fearful, and inconsistent in her reactions to Robert's long hours. Moreover, his working less might mean her needing to work more or find another occupation that paid better. While more involvement in work might be an antidote to her isolation and boredom, it reactivates in Betty a childhood sense of shame, inadequacy, and failure about which Robert knows little. This was an issue she had been struggling to face in her own therapy. She was coming to see that she hid her own fears about her competence under her role as traditional homemaker with only very part-time work, where she felt comfortable, but which did not any longer challenge her intellectually or further her own development. In fact, she is beginning to realize how much her life had come to resemble that of her critical, unhappy mother, overly dependent on her husband's successes or attention.

Now less critical about Robert, Betty is able in individual and couple therapy to explore other aspects of her life that impact on their marital situation. She speaks initially of her father's untreated alcoholism, then of her mother's initially repugnant judgmental posture, and finally of her own fears of becoming her critical mother.

As the couple reviews the history of their relationship, their ability to listen empathically to one another increases in direct relation to the ability of the therapist to attend empathically to each while supporting the other. By the fourth month of therapy, perceiving that Robert feels Betty's renewed respect for his work habits and the forces that shaped them, the therapist, hoping for an opportunity to invite Robert to speak more openly about the issue of the other woman, finds one. In a conversation about a recent movie seen by the couple, *The Natural,* which features a passionate affair, the therapist elects to pursue the issue. He begins by talking with Robert about baseball in general and Robert's love for the game ever since childhood. The two joke about the rivalry between Brooklyn Dodgers fans and Yankee fans, and the therapist asks Betty if she minds if he continues discussing baseball for just another moment with Robert, recognizing it's not an interest of hers. Betty is very supportive about this. The therapist asks Robert, playfully, whether he knows what famous baseball event occurred in 1956, and in a split second, Robert says, "Don Larsen pitched a perfect game in the 6th game of the World Series!" Responding with genuine enthusiasm and admiration, the therapist says, "Wow. I knew it was a perfect game by Larsen, but I would never have remembered which game it was!" The three laugh together, and then the therapist asks them to share with him the plot of *The Natural*, something he has done before with other movies.

In this sharing, with Robert describing the baseball end and Betty the relationship end, they become noticeably more tense with the unspoken obvious to both of them. The therapist intervenes, striving to ally with each and to hold the relationship as the patient, "We've been talking together for several months now, and the two of you have done a wonderful job of trying to put yourself in the other person's shoes, to see the world from the other's perspective. Particularly, the perspective of being a man or a woman, growing up in your particular families, and taking in their views about how to be a husband or a wife. You might recall that I believe this is the single most important feature of successful relationships, to have empathy for where your partner is coming from. Now here we are, with this situation right here right now. I don't know for sure whether the two of you can maintain the good feeling you've developed toward the other enough to take a hard look at the situation—and we're talking about the note; you both know that. But here it is. It's where you're stuck, and it's an opportunity to move forward, one way or the other. Robert, you don't have to pitch a perfect game with this one. You just need to throw pitches down the middle and we'll see what happens."

Feeling a sense of trust, if not deep comfort, Robert reveals that he had indeed been attracted to the other woman, had spent several dinners with her, and had contemplated having an affair with her, but had done nothing more than kiss her once the night she wrote the note. Betty begins to cry, Robert sags, the therapist says softly, "This is very hard for both of you but it's so important to be at this place." The therapy is ready to enter a new phase.

SUMMARY AND IMPLICATIONS FOR TREATMENT

The new psychotherapy of men, as articulated in this book, addresses the high cost to men and their families of male gender socialization, as the feminist critique has illuminated the high cost to women of traditional gender roles. Current socialization poorly prepares many men for intimate relationships, especially relationships that require the verbal expression of feelings and acknowledgment of dependence, rather than emphasizing skills that prepare them to do battle in the outside world. Similarly, women's socialization can be shown to inadequately prepare many of them for independent functioning or to fully appreciate men's positive contributions to intimate relationships. Couple therapy cannot alter social, cultural, and political realities as they impinge on individual men and couples, but it can create an awareness of the social context of relationship problems. The couple can be helped to see how traditional socialization into polarized gender roles almost inevitably leads to dissatisfaction with what each gender gets from the other and to a lack of mutual understanding and empathy. In becoming more aware of their family's messages and cultural forces, partners can more consciously evaluate the implicit choices they have made and explore the costs and benefits of continuing on in the same fashion.

As seen in this clinical case, couple therapy can build on an understanding of gender socialization to address the two partners in a manner that is respectful of their differences, while also highlighting underlying similarities and the common unhappiness which brings them to therapy. The couple therapist's empathic understanding of the pressures and constraints on men from society's and the family's constructions of "appropriate" masculine or feminine characteristics, can help moderate the male patient's feelings of guilt and shame over personal failures and make therapy less threatening than anticipated. The therapist's awareness of cultural and familial forces, with respect to how they create and define interactions, must also include the therapist's active attention to his or her own en-gendered understanding of men, women, and relationships, and the ways in which men and women respond to him or her, as helper, as rival, as guide, as someone from the past, as model for future relationships.

The therapist's central task, to develop an empathic connection with each despite their differences from one another and from the therapist, is complicated by the presence of the two partners in the room, each of whom expects the therapist to see the other as the source of the difficulties. Being the same gender as one partner, and more naturally allied with the partner who seeks out treatment, are further complications. Every intervention by the couple therapist occurs within the dialectic space of simultaneously trying to understand and respect two people who may not understand or respect each other. The couple therapist's balancing act necessary to accomplish this task is worthy of the Wallenda family. More realistically, the therapist can only strive to be sensitively attuned to each, if by turns, model an empathic way of exploring painful issues, and engage at as deep a level of interaction as the couple permits.

There are costs for men associated with changing their roles within intimate relationships. If men choose to become more expressive and vulnerable they put themselves in conflict with certain societal definitions of appropriate male behavior or with specific messages in their families of origin and risk experiencing shame. While the Marlboro man experiences frustration and disappointment within his most intimate relationships, the sanctions against his changing in ways that are more "feminized" are great, far greater than those against women who embrace traditionally masculine behaviors. Furthermore, Weingarten (1991) notes that if men show themselves to be openly dependent on women, it increases women's power over them. She suggests that many men may be equally capable of behaving intimately in the ways that women define intimacy but they may not be desirous of relinquishing aspects of traditional male privilege.

Confronted in couple therapy with the costs and benefits of their often unconscious acceptance of cultural and family-based constructions of masculinity, men can have the choice to reconstruct masculine roles that are less limiting. Couple therapy can create opportunities to further develop both autonomy and connection in both men and women (Goldner, 1985; Maltas, 1997; Sheinberg & Penn, 1991). Specific interactions can be fostered where men can become more aware of, and able to express in words, their doubts, fears, insecurities, and dependence on others (Lansky, 1992; Levant, 1990, 1995; Levant & Kopecky, 1995). Both men and women will benefit if men are more emotionally aware, sensitive to other's needs and comfortable with acknowledging vulnerability and interdependence and able to tolerate and work with relational conflict. This may lessen their disavowed over-reliance on women to regulate their emotional states and buffer their experiences in the world and at the same time it will allow the women to see beneath the men's defensive suppression of vulnerable emotions a more complex human being, more like her than otherwise.

REFERENCES

Aries, E. (1996). *Men and women in interaction: Reconsidering the differences.* New York: Oxford University Press.

Balswick, J. O. (1988). *The inexpressive male.* Lexington, MA: Lexington Books.

Benjamin, J. (1988). *The bonds of love.* New York: Pantheon Books.

Bergman, S. J. (1995). Men's psychological development: A relational perspective. In R. F. Levant & W. S. Pollack (Eds.), *A new psychology of men* (p. 90). New York: Basic Books.

Bernadez, T. (1982). The female therapist in relation to male roles. In K. Solomon & N. B. Levy (Eds.), *Men in transition: Theory and therapy.* New York: Plenum Press.

Betcher, R. W., & Pollack, W. S. (1993). *In a time of fallen heroes: The re-creation of masculinity.* New York: Athenium.

Bograd, M. (1990). Women treating men. *Family Therapy Networker, 15,* 54–58.

Brooks, G. R. (1992). Gender-sensitive family therapy in a violent culture. *Topics in Family Psychology and Counseling, 1,* 24–36.

Brooks, G. R., & Silverstein, L. B. (1995). Understanding the dark side of masculinity: An interactive systems model. In R. F. Levant & W. S. Pollack (Eds.), *A new psychology of men* (pp. 280–333). New York: Basic Books.

Cancian, F. (1987). *Love in America.* Cambridge, England: University of Cambridge Press.

Chodorow, N. (1978). *The reproduction of mothering: Psychoanalysis and the sociology of gender.* Berkeley: University of California Press.

Cott, N., (1978). Divorce and the changing status of women in eighteenth-century Massachusetts. In M. Gordon (Ed.), *The American family in social-historical perspective* (2nd ed., pp. 115–139). New York: St. Martin's Press.

Dinnerstein, D. (1976). *The mermaid and the minotaur: Sexual arrangements and human malaise.* New York: Harper & Row.

Gilligan, C. (1982). *In a different voice.* Cambridge, MA: Harvard University Press.

Goldner, V. (1985). Feminism and family therapy. *Family Process, 24,* 31–47.

Goldner, V., Penn, P., Sheinberg, M., & Walker, G. (1990). Love and violence: Gender paradoxes in volatile attachments. *Family Process, 29,* 343–363.

Gornick, L. K. (1986). Developing a new narrative: The woman therapist and the male patient. *Psychoanalytic Psychology, 3,* 299–325.

Gottman, J. (1994). *Why marriages succeed or fail.* New York: Fireside.

Gottman, J., & Levenson, R. (1988). The social psychophysiology of marriage. In P. Noller & M. A. Fitzpatrick (Eds.), *Perspectives on marital interaction* (pp. 182–200). Clevedon, England: Multilingual Matters.

Gray, J. (1992). *Men are from Mars, women are from Venus.* New York: HarperCollins.

Hare-Mustin, R. T. (1987). The problem of gender in family therapy theory. *Family Process, 26,* 15–27.

Hare-Mustin, R. T., & Marecek, J. (1986). Autonomy and gender: Some questions for therapists. *Psychotherapy, 23,* 205–212.

James , K., & McIntyre, D. (1983). The reproduction of families: The social role of psychotherapy. *Journal of Marital and Family Therapy, 9,* 119–129.

Jordan, J., Kaplan, S., Miller, J., Stiver, I., & Surrey, J. (1991). *Women's growth in connection.* New York: Guilford Press.

Krugman, S. (1995). Male development and the transformation of shame. In R. F. Levant & W. S. Pollack (Eds.), *A new psychology of men* (pp. 91–126). New York: Basic Books.

Lansky, M. R. (1992). *Fathers who fail: Shame and psychopathology in the family.* Hillsdale, NJ: Analytic Press.

Leupnitz, D. A. (1988). *The family interpreted: Feminist theory in clinical practice.* New York: Basic Books.

Levant, R. F. (1990). Psychological services designed for men: A psychoeducational approach. *Psychotherapy, 27,* 309-315.

Levant, R. F. (1995). Toward the reconstruction of masculinity. In R. F. Levant & W. S. Pollack (Eds.), *A new psychology of men* (pp. 229–251). New York: Basic Books.

Levant, R. F., & Kopecky, G. (1995). *Masculinity reconstructed.* New York: Dutton.

Levant, R. F., & Pollack, W. S. (Eds.). (1995). *A new psychology of men.* New York: Basic Books.

Maccoby, E. E. (1990). Gender and relationships: A developmental account. *American Psychologist, 45,* 513–520.

Maltas, C. P. (1991). The dynamics of narcissism in marriage. *Psychoanalytic Review, 78,* 567-581.

Maltas, C. P. (1996). Reenactment and repair: Couple therapy with survivors of childhood sexual abuse. *Harvard Review of Psychiatry, 3,* 351–355.

Maltas, C. P. (1997, March). *Men in intimate relationships: Pain, puzzlement and paradox.* Paper presented at McLean Hospital conference "Treating Men," Belmont, MA.

Meth, R., & Pasick, R. (1990). *Men in therapy: The challenge of change.* New York: Guilford Press.

Mintz, S., & Kellogg, S. (1988). *Domestic revolutions: A social history of American family life.* New York: Free Press.

O'Neil, J. M., Good, G. E., & Holmes, S. (1995). Fifteen years of theory and research on men's gender role conflict: New paradigms for empirical research. In R. F. Levant & W. S. Pollack (Eds.), *A new psychology of men* (pp. 164–206). New York: Basic Books.

Osherson, S., & Krugman, S. (1990). Men, shame, and psychotherapy. *Psychotherapy, 27,* 327-339.

Peplau, L. A., Rubin, Z., & Hill, C. T. (1977). Sexual intimacy in dating relationships. *Journal of Social Issues, 33,* 86-109.

Pleck, J. H. (1995). The gender role strain paradigm: An update. In R. F. Levant & W. S. Pollack (Eds.), *A new psychology of men.* New York: Basic Books.

Pollack, W. S. (1990). Men's development and psychotherapy: A psychoanalytic perspective. *Psychotherapy, 27,* 316–321.

Pollack, W. S. (1995). No man is an island: Toward a new psychoanalytic psychology of men. In R. F. Levant & W. S. Pollack (Eds.), *A new psychology of men* (pp. 33–67). New York: Basic Books.

Richman, J. (1982). Men's experience of pregnancy and childbirth. In L. McKee & M. O'Brien (Eds.), *The father figure.* London: Tavistock.

Scher, M. (1990). Effect of gender role incongruities on men's experience as clients in psychotherapy. *Psychotherapy, 27,* 322–326.

Seppa, N., (1997). What defines a man today? *APA Monitor, 28*(3).

Shay, J. J. (1990). Rules of thumb for the all-thumbs therapist: Weathering the marital storm. *Journal of Integrative and Eclectic Psychotherapy, 9,* 21–35.

Shay, J. J. (1993). Should men treat couples? Transference, countertransference, and sociopolitical considerations. *Psychotherapy, 30,* 93–102.

Shay, J. J. (1994). *Treating the reluctant male: Psychotherapy with the Marlboro man.* Chair and discussant symposium presented at the 102nd American Psychological Association Convention, Los Angeles.

Shay, J. J. (1996). "Okay, I'm here, but I'm not talking!" Psychotherapy with the reluctant male. *Psychotherapy, 33,* 503–513.

Shay, J. J. (1997). *Stages of couples therapy: Do you know where your couple is right now.* Submitted for review.

Sheinberg, M., & Penn, P. (1991). Gender dilemmas, gender questions, and the gender mantra. *Journal of Marital and Family Therapy, 17,* 33–44.

Sternberg, J. S., & Barnes, M. L. (1988). *The psychology of love.* New Haven: Yale University Press.

Tannen, D. (1990). *You just don't understand: Women and men in conversation.* New York: Morrow.

Thompson, E. H., & Pleck, J. H. (1995). Masculinity ideologies: A review of research instrumentation of men and masculinities. In R. F. Levant & W. S. Pollack (Eds.), *A new psychology of men* (pp. 129–163). New York: Basic Books.

Toomer, J. E. (1978). Males in psychotherapy. *Counseling Psychologist, 7,* 22–25.

Weingarten, K. (1991). The discourses of intimacy: Adding a social constructionist and feminist view. *Family Process, 30,* 285–305.

West, C., & Zimmerman, D. (1987). Doing gender. *Gender and Society, 1,* 125–151.

Zilbergeld, B. (1992). *The new male sexuality.* New York: Bantam Books.

CHAPTER 6

Men in the Family: A Family System's Approach to Treating Men

Richard F. Lazur

GENDER ROLE STRAIN AND FAMILY THERAPY

ENDER ROLES may not be the first thing a clinician thinks about when a new referral calls. There are all kinds of things the clinician wants to know: what is the problem, its duration and intensity, precautions necessary to guard the safety of those involved, level of expertise needed to manage the case, personal feelings likely to be stirred-up, and ability to pay. Gender roles usually are not an initial consideration.

But they are there. Whether addressed or not, every clinician encounters gender roles in the course of treatment. Whether it's the male client who has issues with female authority figures, the female client victimized by males, the female client who tries to seduce the male therapist, or the male client who believes "men don't need help," gender roles are an integral part of treatment (Brown, 1986; Good, Gilbert, & Scher, 1990).

In more therapies than not, the client is able to identify areas of distress and, with some work, make changes to remedy the situation. The client may complete a course of therapy and leave satisfied without ever knowing he has not addressed a key area: gender roles.

Cultural expectations exert pressure—albeit subtle and often unexpressed—upon people to conform to prescribed gender behaviors. By not addressing gender roles, the clinician underestimates the power and effect of proscribed gender expectations upon the client. Gender roles must be an integral consideration when doing therapy.

Gender sensitive issues can probably be seen most easily in family therapy where participants' roles are readily determined. Whether relationships are traditional, redefined, or evolving, the interplay between the genders tends to heighten awareness of stereotypes, societal expectations, inconsistencies, and violations of gender roles. The goal of this chapter is to look at male gender role strain within the paradigm of systems theory and address how the gender sensitive therapist can identify and intervene in male gender role strain issues. By looking at how gender role expectations are an integral part of the system, we can see their impact in the family's patterns of interaction. Two case examples will illustrate the integration of gender roles in the assessment and intervention in family therapy.

In everyday life, gender roles are defined by stereotypes and "widely shared beliefs about what the sexes should be like" (Pleck, 1981, p. 135), even when contradictory, inconsistent, and possibly damaging. Violating gender role norms produces negative consequences, for men more than women, so people often try to overconform to avoid social condemnation. Even so, a high proportion of people violate gender role norms and both genders experience strain in their work and family roles (Pleck, 1981).

Many therapists are aware that gender role strain, especially for men, occurs in the dark-side behaviors (Brooks & Silverstein, 1995) of dysfunctional relationships, violence, sexual excess, drug abuse, alcoholism, and other socially irresponsible behaviors. However, these behaviors may be an exaggeration of traditional male gender role socialization and are "directly related to the degree of difficulty involved in performing the male role in a given society" (p. 305). The effects of gender role strain can be seen wherever there are men and women. (For this chapter, the author will limit the scope of application to the Western culture, the population with whom he has worked most extensively mindful that within that broad spectrum, cultural variances occur. For a cross-cultural survey of male gender role strain, see D. Gilmore (1990). *Manhood in the making: Cultural concepts of masculinity.* New Haven: Yale University Press.) The interaction among and between the genders in the domestic, work, and social strata are fertile breeding grounds for both interpersonal and intrapsychic conflicts, the very substance of psychotherapy. Expression of gender role strain is often subtle and such an integral part of the person and/or interaction that it can easily be overlooked by even the most gender-sensitive therapist. Nowhere is gender role strain more evident than in the family. Through the close knit interactions of a couple, parent(s) with children, and children with children, each person's definition and expectation of own and opposite gender are played-out through the most mundane tasks. Whether it be economic contributions to the well-being of the family, daily tasks required for maintenance, or the privileges and responsibilities of the unit within the community, each person takes on an assigned task that goes with his or her age and status within the social system of the family.

A system operates within a bounded space through the constant communication of interdependent members (Von Bertalanffy, 1968). Like a waterbed where pressure exerted in one spot sends ripples to another site when one member moves, it affects the others and the whole changes. To correct for deviance, members attempt to maintain balance in their relationships. Family therapy pioneer Don Jackson (1957) labeled this stability "family homeostasis." (See L. Hoffman, 1981.)

The family therapist (or team) intervenes in the system by introducing ways to alter interpersonal interactions (Stanton, 1988). The intent of any therapy is change. Change, however, is not easy for people to accept and requires that the therapist be able to move in and out of the system without becoming part of it. By building a therapeutic alliance, the therapist is able to gain acceptance, identify problem areas, and effect remedies to alter the maladaptive process.

In the alliance, the therapist is able to address gender role concerns. In the assessment, the therapist becomes aware of each individual's and the unit's belief system about gender. Just as the system's significant triangles, sequence analysis, developmental themes, communication, and intergenerational patterns are determined, the therapist ascertains gender role strain by observing how individuals think and act. Gender role strain holds potential negative consequences for any individual(s) through personal restriction, devaluation, or violation of self or other (O'Neil, Good, & Holmes, 1995). The family therapist can detect personal restrictions by the repercussion it has within the system:

> During a family session, 8-year-old Debby complains that her 13-year-old brother, Todd, "doesn't do nothin'," yet she is expected to clear the table and do the dishes while he goes off and plays with friends. Her father scoffs at her complaint; her mother looks away. Gender role tasks parallel their parents': The father is absent while the mother is responsible for household chores as well as her full-time job.

Clearly defined gender roles are evident as articulated by the system's youngest member. The problem is not just the boy's behavior and the presenting complaint of his stealing but the distribution of work and rewards within the system:

> The therapist talks with Todd about how great it must feel to have time to go off with his friends and not have to worry about mundane tasks like food preparation and clean-up. Todd agrees. The therapist asks mother where she gets her energy to keep the house and a demanding job. She recites a litany of resentments focused on her husband's unavailability due to his work that culminates with her complaint of being tired of "bailing-out" her son. Overwhelmed, she is surprised by Todd's behavior; up until now she and he had a close relationship.

The therapist gets a flavor of family interactions: Mother and son had a close relationship until recently when the pubescent boy started to pull away and assert his autonomy. A generational boundary is crossed: Mother and both children appear to be in coalition against father who is absent due to work. Mother and father are in conflict and everyone in the family feels like he or she is not getting a fair portion. Members of this family feel disconnected:

> The therapist tries to bring the father back into the family by asking about his work, its long hours, and how he sacrifices his time with the family for economic security and a middle-class lifestyle. The father who initially appeared cool to therapy is able to say that he realizes his long hours are hard on everyone but he believes it necessary if "we are to get ahead."

This is an opportunity to identify some of the constraints of gender role expectations. The father believes it is *his* duty to provide for the family. It is also the belief of the family even though mother also works full-time. (She said it was better when she "didn't have to work.") The therapist identifies the myth that men are supposed to be the primary breadwinner even though the reality is 61% of women in two-parent families labor outside the home (U.S. Bureau of the Census, 1996). The therapist identifies the strain this puts on everyone in the family.

Through a series of meetings, the therapist tries to re-align generational boundaries. At one point, he has a session with just the parents to address their marital conflicts, disappointments, and lack of connection, and to help both parents redefine chores and expectations of the children:

> The therapist asks the mother to consider the kind of husband she is creating for her son's wife, and asks her what kind of attitude and know-how she

would like to see the boy have in order to make his family's (of origin and creation) life more comfortable. She never considered it that way. With some guidance, she and her husband move back into a parental role with authority. And by including the son in family chores, he has less free time to wander the malls and get in trouble.

By identifying gender role constraints, the therapist raises the level of awareness of long-held, often unquestioned beliefs regarding gender role expectations and performance. The therapist points out the restrictions in both male and female experience and asks the members to examine the effects such constraints have in how they interact. The therapist suggests the family may want to do something different to ease their conflicts at home. Change in attitude comes about from change in behavior (Ajzen & Fishbein, 1972). Knowledge in and of itself is not enough, behaviors must be altered if family members are to resonate with the desired changes.

As good therapists know, intervention requires more than acknowledgment of a behavior. Confronting gender role strain takes more than pointing out its deleterious effects. Family therapy puts less emphasis on feelings than on change in transactional patterns. Although feelings are acknowledged, the focus is on changing the patterns of interaction that foster gender role strain. In family therapy, this is done by intervening in the structure (how the family is organized), function (roles of members), and/or processes (the rule and policies that govern) (Ginsberg, 1997).

In assessing the family dynamics, the therapist observes interactional patterns starting with relational coalitions in how people position themselves and the flow of conversation (Haley, 1973), sequence of events (Minuchin & Fishman, 1981), and developmental tasks and generational alliances (Bowen, 1978). This assessment reveals abundant information about gender roles. Who is in coalition with whom? If alignments cross the generational boundaries, are gender politics part of the alliance? Whom does the coalition primarily benefit? What status is assigned to members? Does it fit that person's role? Are males valued differently than females? For what reasons and at what costs? What is the family's cultural context for gender roles? Does this family ascribe to those cultural beliefs?

Through observation, the therapist learns not only the reason for this current consultation but also the way members interact with each other, even when a person is not physically present. The therapist's task is to intervene in the system, destabilize the homeostasis, and effect change.

In watching Debby and Todd's parents interact, the therapist started to generate hypotheses about the family's coalitions and gender politics. The mother made the initial call for the appointment, she sat between the two children across from her husband, and she started her list of complaints only after looking at her husband, who said, "Why don't you start? You're the one who thought this would help." Even though he gives her permission to start, he was the first one to speak, in effect launching the session.

At first blush, the words would suggest the parents might be in coalition dealing with an untoward child. The boy sat still, his head bowed, uttering monosyllabic responses to his parents' questioning. It was only when the therapist asked each member what he or she saw as the problem in the family that Debby named the inequality in parity of family members. Often, the youngest member or the identified patient is able to distill the essence of the system; his or her powers of observation detect the system's flaws.

An alliance exists: mother and children against father whose absences due to work distance him from the members' interactions. Mother is enmeshed with *her* children; Todd's developmental transition and his need for more autonomy precipitate the family conflict. Mother is disgruntled that her son is moving away from her, not very different from what her husband does. Loyal to his family, Todd starts to act-out thereby bringing father back into the system.

Children often carry the behavioral family symptom sparing parents the discomfort of disharmony and conflict (Vogel & Bell, 1960). In this family, the father's belief that he needs to be the good provider (Bernard, 1981) is woven into the fabric of how members interact. Money, work, and competition are valued and awarded higher status while feelings, relationships, and household chores have been deemed less important (O'Neil, 1981). Even though the mother works, her contribution to the family is valued less and the expectation that she manage the household and children as well is high (Robinson, 1977).

MALE ROLE STRAIN

Levant (1995) identifies the crisis of masculinity for many men of the baby-boom generation:

> Society no longer seems to value or even recognize the traditional male way of demonstrating care: through *taking care* of his family and friends, looking out for them, solving their problems, and being one who can be counted on when needed. In its place, men are being asked to take on roles and show care in ways that violate the traditional male code and require skills they do not have, such as nurturing children, revealing weakness, and expressing

their most intimate feelings. The net result of this for many men is a loss of self-esteem and an unnerving sense of uncertainty about what it means to be a man. (p. 230)

While celebrating the positive attributes of male gender role socialization, Levant labels its four major negative consequences: action empathy; normative male alexithymia; the overdevelopment of anger and aggression; and the suppression and channeling of tender feelings into sexuality. He defines action empathy as "the ability to see things from another person's point of view and predict what they will do. . . . [It] is usually (though not always) employed in services of the self" (p. 238). Normative male alexithymia is the inability to express feelings in words. Anger is the one emotion most men are allowed to express openly but often without awareness of "its mild forms, such as irritation or annoyance. . . . Consequently, angry outbursts often come too readily in men" (p. 240). Caring feelings are confused with sex and as a result, many relationships suffer because of the man's inability to express his caring in nonsexual terms. These negative consequences take their toll on a man and his family as illustrated by Scott:

> Scott's girlfriend Beth made the appointment for him and the two oldest of his three children because "he's losing it at home." During his divorce two years ago Scott's estranged wife abducted their then 4-year-old daughter. Despite this, Scott, a street maintenance worker, maintains a close relationship with his ex-wife, citing the children as the reasons for his almost daily contact. His 15-year-old son, David, complains about Scott's inconsistency and demandingness which is collaborated by the 14-year-old daughter, Lisa. She has taken over the role of housekeeper, caring for Scott, her brother, and younger sister. When Beth and her 12-year-old daughter, Jennifer, move in, Lisa threatens to return to her mother even though Scott has physical and legal custody. Both children are annoyed with Jennifer and their father's plans to marry. When the children voice their complaints, Scott blows his stack, "going on rampages—yelling and screaming for hours."

Scott's anger is explosive. Often without identifiable precipitant, he erupts and the family suffers from the impact of his emotional discharge. Although his stress is palpable, he doesn't know why he acts as he does. He realizes his family is falling apart and, in his desperation, is willing to try therapy.

The stresses of divorce, abduction of his youngest daughter, continued enmeshment with his ex-wife, single-parenting, job and financial concerns, and the relationship with his girlfriend and her daughter overwhelm this man who tries to do the best he can, doesn't want to hurt anyone but is taxed beyond his limits. Not able to express his irritation and annoyance at simple things, he overreacts when a child says or does something outside his acceptable bounds.

Loyalties, generational boundaries, individual members' developmental needs, and the system's definition create tension within the family. Negative consequences of gender roles exacerbate the already volatile conditions. Willing to continue to take care of her, Scott stays emotionally enmeshed with his ex-wife. He is bitter about the divorce, his financial obligations, and the abduction of his youngest child. Unable to break the affective ties, he maintains daily contact, in effect remaining emotionally married thus robbing his current relationship of intimacy and nurturance. About to create another family with his upcoming marriage, his loyalties are torn.

Generational boundaries are crossed with Lisa assuming care-giving responsibilities for the family. Territorial issues are evident when Beth and Jennifer move into the house. Lisa tries to take on authority that is not hers and resents not only the interlopers but the limits set by Scott. Lisa and Beth compete for Scott's attention, complicated by their derivative names which he sometimes confuses. Beth often feels left out which neither reduces Scott's stress nor adds to a successful relationship.

Lisa and David are moving into adolescence and increased autonomy; Scott wants them to be independent yet do things his way. Whenever the children express their views, Scott blows up. The children see this as inconsistency. He wants to have absolute authority yet his daughter runs the house. The two oldest children create a coalition against Scott and his girlfriend.

The system is unstable. There are conflicting messages: Scott wants to maintain a closed system and protect the family members yet he introduces outsiders, his girlfriend and her daughter, and then reinforces their outside status by not allowing them into therapy saying, "They aren't a part of this." Beth sees what's going on with Scott, is genuinely concerned about his welfare, and tries to draw some boundaries.

In addition to the individual and system's dynamics, many of Scott's issues derive from traditional male gender roles. He wants to be *the* authority. He expresses his anger but not his grief, worry, or feelings of closeness for his children, girlfriend, and even his ex-wife. When others tell him their feelings, he doesn't understand. He believes he has to do something to make the feeling (theirs and his) go away. He wonders how they will respond to him and his actions. He is in crisis.

In joining with Scott and the family system, the therapist acknowledges Scott's concern for his family and his difficulty holding everything together. Knowing that men identify their worth in their work, I learn something about what he does and who he is, his divorce, and his emotional connection with his ex-wife. I start to generate hypotheses: He harbors strong resentments which he never voiced. He remains strongly attached, loyal, to his ex-wife; however, this is a feeling he cannot voice and would deny if spoken. For now, we leave those feelings and talk about his girlfriend and the disruption in the family since her arrival in the house. I want to join with this man and see if he will work with me:

> I talk with Scott about his difficulty in managing everyone. While supporting him on one hand, I acknowledge the children's needs to grow and strike out on their own. By asking about his own departure from family of origin, I learn he dropped out of high school, worked briefly, got married, and joined the Army. He did a tour of duty in Viet Nam and came home to a son. He went to work for the city and has progressed to supervisor. At 34, he's unhappy with the job routine but can't leave because of his financial obligations; he's responsible for significant credit card debt left from the divorce. "I thought I had it made—a house, two cars, three great kids, and a beautiful wife until I came home early one day to find her with another guy. I went ballistic and nothing has been the same since."
>
> Concerned about boundary issues and the children hearing about their mother's infidelity, I ask their perspective on their parents' break-up. Lisa pipes up, "This was the first guy Dad found out about. There were lots of others he didn't know about." David is quiet and sullen. I gently probe. He reluctantly admits to his mother's indiscretions and it's clear he doesn't want to talk about it. I acknowledge there has been a lot of pain and betrayal in this family so naturally everyone would be concerned about who comes and goes, who is safe and who isn't, which is part of their current distress.

David and Lisa are able to join with me. I acknowledge their need for autonomy, their uncertainty about having an interloper, their concern for their youngest sister, and their allegiances split between mom and dad. I translate for Scott how their feelings are healthy and they need him to tolerate differences lest he end up like his authoritarian father whom he despises.

I outline how family therapy works and identify the goals for our task together: to help this family deal with the changes it is undergoing, for Dad to get on with his life the same as David and Lisa are moving on with theirs, and for everyone to feel connected and safe without intrusions. I inform them I may want to work with the children alone or just with Scott, I will want to see the rest of the family including the newcomers and the rule is to express personal reactions but not to talk about someone who is not there. They agree.

Scott is willing to work with me and the family to address the issues we outlined. He knows it's not going to be easy, a fact I underscore. I tell him therapy is not going to fix everything, as a matter of fact, I predict it is going to make things worse before it gets better. I expect the children to act out in some form. Although I know he doesn't want to hear this, I want him to be prepared for when it happens. And when it does occur, I can tell him, "See, this is beginning to work. Remember when I told you things were going to get worse. Well, we reached that point in treatment. And we may be here for some time. I don't know what's going to happen, but we can work through this."

Scott feels responsible. He wants to take care of his children. He believes it's his responsibility to care for the emotional and physical comforts of his ex-wife; he has yet to grieve the loss of that relationship. He feels indebted to her for helping him move out of his family of origin. She was there when he needed reassurance, safety, and security and he believes he owes her. He is unable to let go of his attachment to her despite the pain and conflict she creates for him and the children. He believes it's his role to provide for and, to take care of women no matter what they do.

Scott has taken on the financial responsibility for Beth and her daughter. He worries about money. He worries about how his children see him; he fears being too authoritarian like his father. He is confused about his relationship with Beth. And he hasn't even thought about his relationship with her daughter.

While some of these issues can be dealt with in front of the children, they do not need to know everything like financial arrangements or his sexual behaviors. Acknowledged as belonging to the realm of adult concerns, some issues are "shelved" until the end of the session when the children are released from the session so the adults can deal with adult concerns. This provides concrete awareness of boundaries and makes clear that the children do not need to know everything in their father's life.

By having the children talk about their fear of Scott's explosiveness and their anger toward him, their sibling subgroup is reinforced. They are given permission to assert their autonomy without defiance. The family learns it is possible to communicate differing opinions without the loss of respect for each other:

> In an emotionally laden third session David and Lisa confront Scott on their feeling replaced by Beth's daughter and their distaste for not only her behaviors but how Scott "let[s] her get away with things. If any of us did that

you'd be down our throats." With tears streaming down his cheeks, David declares, "You don't care about us. All you ever do is yell when I don't do something you want. You just start screaming when you come home. I don't want to even be there." By my helping Scott contain his defensiveness and listen to the children's concerns, he was able to see that his children's reactions to him are just like his reactions to his father. He doesn't want them to hate him the way he hated his father. He knows that by keeping them under his thumb they will harbor resentments and he will push them out of the house faster than he wants. He knows he doesn't want to be angry but he doesn't know how to contain it.

I explain that anger is like a rheostat with multiple variations of intensity instead of a switch which is either off or on: a person can regulate his responses from mild annoyance to full-fledged rage. Full-force is not always necessary to make a point. Scott is able to grasp the concept but is unsure how to apply it in day-to-day events. In the "adults only" time at the end of the session, we look at different things the children do from his youngest leaving her bicycle in the driveway to David not coming home at curfew; Scott rates them in terms of severity of offense and intensity of his response. I clarify age-appropriate behaviors and help him put them in context of the child's needs, not just his own reactions. He asks, "So you mean I don't have to blow my top for every little thing that happens?" It was as if he had never considered that before.

In helping the family negotiate their behaviors and outcomes, both the children and Scott are able to set up a contract where he can enforce consequences for behaviors without destroying a bond by his out-of-control anger.

Traditional male gender roles restrict men's expression of emotion (O'Neil, 1981; Scher, 1979, 1980). By increasing a man's awareness of the array of responses to various situations, he is empowered to gain access to a variety of feelings without fear that any one of them will overpower him in its expression. If all a man knows of feeling is an on-off switch, he is likely to keep the switch off especially for unpleasant feelings or those he considers unmasculine. But if he realizes that emotions come in various shades and that he can control their intensity, he is more likely to try their expression and experience.

By telling Scott that he doesn't have to shoot a cannon to swat a fly, he grasps the concept of expressive variation. This is new information for him, however; he never considered options other than screaming which was what his father did when angry. The analogy of a rheostat helps Scott adjust his reactions to the children's actions, and deal with his out of proportion responses to their age appropriate behaviors.

Borrowing from other theoretical orientations is useful to the client in their making change. Meichenbaum's (1977) stop and think method of cognitive-behavior modification is particularly useful for men to break the task into manageable units, identify strategies, and talk themselves through the event:

> With Scott, I underscore his being under stress and not able to think clearly. I tell him how to build in brakes to delay his response until he can gain presence of mind: to stop and think, to talk to himself during the commute home, to talk himself through an exchange with the children. He likes the concept of varying responses and is willing to try it during the week with my caveat that like any skill, he will need to practice and he will make mistakes before he is able to master it. By using anger as a springboard, we are able to talk about other emotions, like sadness, and how he can also express them in degrees.
>
> In the next family session I learn of Scott's attempts at managing his anger; the children didn't notice any differences. They both are more withdrawn and less talkative. In our private conversation Scott and I review what he was thinking, feeling, and doing during some difficult points and how he could continue to practice in the upcoming week.

Scott is on medication for high blood pressure, smokes a pack of cigarettes a day, and drinks about three or four beers a week, mostly on weekends. These last are behaviors men often use to insulate themselves from feelings, a palliative to ease the discomfort of life:

> I raise health concerns and substance use issues in context of how he copes with stress noting that high blood pressure is the body's signal that he is not dealing with things well. We look at new ways he can cope with life's everyday annoyances. Although this may not be the optimum time to quit his addictions, he realizes his smoking and drinking only exacerbate his situation. He comes up with a plan to decrease the amount of toxins and increase the amount of oxygen he puts in his body. He sets unrealistic goals which need to be made do-able, but if the plan comes from him, it is more likely to happen than if it comes from me.

Men tend not to take care of their health (Eisler, 1995; Meinecke, 1981; Sutkin & Good, 1987). I routinely inquire about the date of their last physical, their ability to relax, interests outside work, aerobic and physical exercise plan, and social relationships. Avoid asking global questions like "How is your health?" which results in global responses like "Good" when in fact, they haven't had a check-up. I frame the questions in context of self-care using an analogy of car maintenance; although I dislike its reductionism, most men easily relate to it.

The initial sessions are spent drawing boundaries, keeping conflicts between Scott and his ex-wife out of discussions with the children, reinforcing the sibling subgroup and their need for guided independence, moving Lisa out of the caregiver role, and moving toward how the family is going to reconfigure when Scott remarries. Despite her complaints about the housework, Lisa is not willing to let Beth move into the adult female role in the family. There are conflicts between them and Scott feels caught in the middle:

> For the first five sessions, Scott would bring only the two eldest children. I want to learn how 6-year-old Laura is coping. Scott asks for a referral for her for individual therapy; he doesn't believe she would find the family sessions useful. I comply with his request noting that at some point I would like to include her because she is very much a part of what is going on in the home.
>
> Scott also isn't ready to bring Beth and definitely doesn't want to include her daughter; we have yet to address his role as stepfather. He appears to be using therapy well: he is able to differentiate between annoyances and legitimate cause for anger, grants more freedom for the adolescents to spend time with their friends as long as he knows where they are and they obey curfew; he starts a work-out regime after negotiating a barter agreement with a health club, and he limits contact with his ex-wife.
>
> The family system appears to stabilize somewhat. I tell Scott our work is not complete but we have reached a plateau unless other family members became part of the therapy. He brings Beth and Laura to the next session.
>
> Excited about starting school the next week, Laura unabashedly offers her analysis of the family: Lisa is "bossy and tries to tell everyone what to do," David "isn't around much," Jennifer "listens to music in her room and doesn't do much," Beth is "nice and takes care of me and daddy," and Scott "worries a lot. He used to come home tired and grouchy, now he just comes home tired." Laura likes visiting her mother but "I like to come back to Daddy" because "Mom sometimes has strange guys there [and] she yells for no good reason." Both Beth and Laura observe improved relationships between Scott and the two oldest which encourages Beth about the usefulness of therapy.
>
> I ask Scott about Laura's observation that he worries. David, Lisa, and Beth all agree that Scott worries. They claim he worries about their mother, money, their health, their friends, drugs, and Beth adds "about the upcoming wedding." Scott is only able to acknowledge his worry by saying, "I just think all the time."
>
> Framing his worry as Scott's way of expressing his concern and care for them, I ask the family to elaborate the ways he worries. Noting it's easier to assign the same feeling word to different intensities and kinds of feelings, I engage the family in a game of "Identify the feeling." Their task is to observe family behaviors and identify what they are feeling and see if it matches with what the other party in the interaction experiences.

Men have difficulty linking actions and thoughts with feelings. The family can help him (and themselves) by identifying what the inner experience is and its effects upon the sequence and pattern of family interactions. To help men distinguish the nuances of different kinds of feelings, I compare the distinctions to being able to identify a '98 BMW 528i from a 328I, a Saab from a Saturn, or saying it's just a blue car. Distinguishing models of cars is more differentiated than distinguishing different brands which is differentiated from discerning a car's color: there are many varieties of the same kind but all are not the same. Most men get the point:

> In the next session, Lisa and Beth identify feelings of jealousy and competition in their interactions. Laura identifies how she feels babied by everyone but Beth who encourages her to work on her own. Scott is able to distinguish between worrying when he's anxious and legitimate concerns, his fear about the shifts in the family, and the changes with his impending marriage. The family looks at ways to incorporate Beth and Jennifer into the family but reaches a stalemate when the adults differ. This leads to a couple's session.
>
> The couple is willing to honestly examine their relationship and determine how they are going to merge families, parenting styles, finances, and deal with external intrusions like Scott's ex-wife. They decide to postpone the wedding; both feel the date is artificial and approaching faster than they and the children are ready to accommodate. Beth points out how Scott is wrapped up with work, the children, and his softball, that she feels overlooked and taken for granted. She accuses him of noticing her only when he wants sex. He argues back that the only time they have to talk without interruption is in bed.

Rosenberg, Rand, and Asay (1985) observe that some people need sex to be intimate while others need to be intimate to have sex. The difference is in individual temperament and the couple needs to negotiate a common meeting ground wherein personal needs can be gratified before the enjoyment of sexual expression can take place. Intimacy involves "sharing your innermost personal thoughts . . . [and] feelings" (Magnavita, 1997, p. 86). It is found in a place where "Both partners value the safe harbor of their relationship, the place where they can put aside their societal masks and truly be themselves. Mature relationships nurture this process of becoming fully known" (Bugen, 1990, p. 50).

In realigning the generational subsets of a family, some time may need to be spent with the couple addressing issues of intimacy, sexual expression as well as parenting and finances. As a facilitator, I help both parties examine their own and the other's positions and reach an understanding. As therapist, I model ways of interacting as demonstrated by my interactions with the family to this point. As a male, I can help them both understand how male gender roles determine expectations of self and other which confuse, limit, and interfere with natural, free-flowing expression of sexuality.

As Levant (1995) observes, men confuse sex with intimacy. This has been my clinical experience as well. In working with the couple subset of the family, sexual expression as an indicator of harmony in the relationship is discussed as well as each person's capacity to be vulnerable, and their ability to work through sensitive, emotionally laden issues. When the issues go beyond the reason for the initial therapy appointment, therapeutic contract with the family is renegotiated. If a referral for couple's therapy is appropriate, I make it. If the family issues appear to be stalemated until the couple works through their issues, I am willing to continue work with the couple, thereby suspending family treatment and redefining boundaries, until a resolve is reached and determination of the family's needs at that time is made:

> As the couple grew more stable and consistent in their parenting style, the system reacted: David was arrested for shoplifting, Lisa ran away and returned to her mother. Scott's ex-wife tried to abduct Laura again but was unsuccessful, in part due to Laura's ingenuity in escaping. Scott proceeded with legal action. Although anxious, he found purpose in his mission to save his children. He helped the attorney strategize by predicting his ex-wife's reactions to the motions made in court. He and the whole family missed Lisa and several sessions were spent talking about her departure. As the court date approached, Scott came to a resolution to acknowledge Lisa's decision even though he disagreed with it.
>
> The court awarded Scott sole custody of David and Laura and joint custody of Lisa. The crisis was over. Life returned to normal with the everyday annoyances and irritations that Scott was able to manage. Although he wasn't Mr. Rogers walking through the front door, he was considerably more calm and contained in his interactions with Beth and the children.
>
> On one month follow-up, boundary issues with Scott's family of origin re-surface and Beth re-asserts her limits. Lisa comes for visits, and the relationship remains strained between Lisa and Beth. Lisa has a hard time dealing with her father's re-marriage and "being replaced." David is busy with high school activities and appears to adjust with no further acting-out. Laura has supervised visitation with her mother who frequently fails to show for their scheduled meeting; Laura continues in individual therapy.
>
> At the end of the session, Scott acknowledges, "Things are not going to change. I have no control over what happens but I have control over how I look at it. If I let it get to me, I'll explode. I watch what's happening inside and Beth is good about letting me know what she sees. You know, I used to think my role as husband and provider meant I had to do everything for everyone. There's no way I can do that! Now, I decide what I can and am willing to do. And I can feel good about myself."

SUMMARY

The family is the incubator of gender roles. In the family, a child learns firsthand about expectations of his own and his parents' gender roles, "what the sexes should be like" (Pleck, 1981, p. 135), and how to deal with variance. Both men and women experience strain in their family roles. Gender role strain is an unspoken ingrained expectation of family members and is colored by cultural variances.

When families exhaust their means to problem solve and disruptions occur, they may enter therapy. Identification of gender role strain and its impact on the family system is an important part of work done in family therapy. A restricted range and/or lack of openness in the expression of feelings, power differentials, value ascribed to money, confusion of sex with intimacy, time available for family interaction including management of the household are all signs of activated gender role strain. Through identification of these symptoms in the assessment, the family therapist can tailor interventions in the structure and sequence of the system to best meet the clients' needs. Gender roles strain is an inherent part of the family system and needs to be incorporated in the diagnosis and treatment of the system. Not to do so is shortchanging the family, and by extension, society, of the power of change.

In addressing gender role strain issues, the family therapist helps the client identify basic beliefs that support the underlying patterns in the family's homeostasis. Through the identification of boundaries, sequence analysis, developmental themes, significant triangles, loyalties, and communication patterns, the therapist can determine gender role strain in how members think and act. The synergistic impact affects the whole. Intervention needs to be made in the structure (how the family is organized), function (roles of members), and processes (the rule and policies that govern) (Ginsberg, 1997).

Like the entire therapeutic process, the goal is not to solve the problem but to help the family alter their functioning so they can solve the problem themselves. By identifying the family's expectation of the members and their gender roles, strain can be identified and altered, thereby freeing up members to deal with other constraints. As demonstrated by the two case examples, when gender role strain is addressed as part of the therapy, it can have a profound effect on the outcome for the client. As in any therapy, the goal is to provide as wide an opportunity as possible for the client to choose a course that includes a variety of options and adds breadth, depth, and richness to life.

REFERENCES

Ajzen, I., & Fishbein, M. (1972). Attitudes and normative beliefs as factors influencing behavioral intentions. *Journal of Personality and Social Psychology, 21,* 1–9.

Bernard, J. (1981). The good provider role: Its rise and fall. *American Psychologist, 36,* 1–12.

Bowen, M. (1978). *Family therapy in clinical practice.* New York: Jason Aronson.

Brooks, G. R., & Silverstein, L. B. (1995). Understanding the dark side of masculinity: An interactive systems model. In R. F. Levant & W. S. Pollock (Eds.), *A new psychology of men* (pp. 280–333). New York: Basic Books.

Brown, L. S. (1986). Gender-role analysis: A neglected component of psychological assessment. *Psychotherapy, 23*(2), 243–248.

Bugen, L. A. (1990). *Love and renewal: A couple's guide to commitment.* Oakland, CA: New Harbinger.

Eisler, R. M. (1995). The relationship between masculine gender role stress and men's health risk: The validation of a construct. In R. F. Levant & W. S. Pollock (Eds.), *A new psychology of men* (pp. 207–225). New York: Basic Books.

Gilmore, D. (1990). *Manhood in the making: Cultural concepts of masculinity.* New Haven, CT: Yale University Press.

Ginsberg, M. R. (1997, June). *Systemic interventions: New models for interventions with individuals, families, and communities.* Paper presented at the 1997 Alaska Summer Solstice Institute, Anchorage.

Good, G. E., Gilbert, L. A., & Scher, M. (1990). Gender aware therapy: A synthesis of feminist therapy and knowledge about gender. *Journal of Counseling & Development, 68*(4), 376–380.

Haley, J. (1973). *Uncommon therapy.* New York: Norton.

Hoffman, L. (1981). *Foundations of family therapy.* New York: Basic Books.

Jackson, D. D. (1957). The question of family homeostasis. *Psychiatric Quarterly Supplement, 31,* 79–90.

Levant, R. F. (1995). Toward the reconstruction of masculinity. In R. F. Levant & W. S. Pollock (Eds.), *A new psychology of men* (pp. 229–251). New York: Basic Books.

Levant, R. F., & Pollock, W. S. (Eds.). (1995). *A new psychology of men.* New York: Basic Books.

Magnavita, J. J. (1997). *Restructuring personality disorders.* New York: Guilford Press.

Meichenbaum, D. (1977). *Cognitive-behavior modification: An integrative approach.* New York: Plenum Press.

Meinecke, C. E. (1981). Socialized to die younger? Hyermasculinity and men's health. *Personnel and Guidance Journal, 60*(4), 241–245.

Minuchin, S., & Fishman, H. C. (1981). *Family therapy techniques.* Cambridge, MA: Harvard University Press.

O'Neil, J. M. (1981). Patterns of gender role conflict and strain: Sexism and fear of femininity in men's lives. *Personnel and Guidance Journal, 60*(4), 203–209.

O'Neil, J. M., Good, G. E., & Holmes, S. (1995). Fifteen years of theory and research on men's gender role conflict. In R. F. Levant & W. S. Pollock (Eds.), *A new psychology of men* (pp. 164–206). New York: Basic Books.

Pleck, J. (1981). *The myth of masculinity.* Cambridge, MA: MIT Press.

Robinson, J. (1977). *How Americans use time: A social-psychological analysis.* New York: Praeger.

Rosenberg, J. L., Rand, M. L., & Asay, D. (1985). *Body, self and soul: Sustaining integration.* Atlanta, GA: Humanics.

Scher, M. (1979). The little boy in the adult male client. *Personnel and Guidance Journal, 57,* 537–539.

Scher, M. (1980). Men and intimacy. *Counseling and Value, 25,* 62–68.

Stanton, M. D. (1988). The lobster quadrille: Issues and dilemmas for family therapy research. In L. C. Wynne (Ed.), *The state of the art in family therapy research: Controversies and recommendations* (pp. 5–31). New York: Family Process Press.

Sutkin, L. C., & Good, G. (1987). Therapy with men in health-care settings. In M. Scher, M. Stevens, G. Good, & G. A. Eichenfield (Eds.), *Handbook of counseling and psychotherapy with men* (pp. 372–387). Newbury Park, CA: Sage.

U.S. Bureau of the Census. (1996). *Statistical abstract of the United States: 1996* (p. 399, Table 625). Washington, DC: U.S. Government Printing Office.

Vogel, E. F., & Bell, N. W. (1960). The emotionally disturbed child as the family scapegoat. In N. W. Bell & E. F. Vogel (Eds.), *The family* (pp. 382–397). Glencoe, IL: Free Press.

Von Bertalanffy, L. (1968). *General systems theory: Foundation, development, application.* New York: Braziller.

PART TWO

ENDURING PROBLEMS, NEW SOLUTIONS

Mourning, Melancholia, and Masculinity: Recognizing and Treating Depression in Men

William S. Pollack

LIKE THE men T. S. Eliot refers to in his poem *The Hollow Men,* many of the men we see in our consulting rooms (and on the streets, on television, in their places of work, or as part of a family system) have been hollowed out by their developmental journey from boyhood to adult masculine self. Men are hollowed by increasingly stressful life events at home or at work, hollowed by substances—genetic and endogenous as well as those self-administered to produce self-soothing. They are then stuffed with gender-straining obsessional duty, plagued by dangerously harsh perfectionistic self-criticism, wracked with conflictual guilt, or deadened by empty despair. Men are increasingly manifesting states of psychic depletion and fragmentation, which would become plain to our view, if only we had the empathic lens through which to see! This epidemic of men's painfully numbed inner experience is best understood as a masculine-specific form of affective dysregulation or (abandonment) depression.

Although melancholia has traditionally been linked with female patients—with some arguing for a lifetime prevalence rate of major depressive episode with a greater than 2:1 female/male ratio—there may be good reason to suggest that affective disorders are a salient, albeit hidden, problem for many men. This chapter will pose and attempt to answer several pressing questions:

1. Are many men today clinically depressed?
2. If so, why do we continue to underdiagnose, and undertreat men's depressions?
3. Are there any stereotypical differences in the presentation/expression of depression in women and men?
4. How may the clinician actively shape the diagnostic and treatment milieu in a way that is more empathic to men's depressive pain?
5. What are the value-added contributions that a developmentally based, depth psychology may bring to a new model for the diagnosis and treatment of depression in men?

This chapter highlights research-based diagnostic, epidemiological and treatment data for affective spectrum disease, new psychoanalytic theories of boy's normative development into manhood (specifically, gender specific vulnerability to trauma/impingement), modern self-psychological findings differentiating guilty and empty depressive states in men (i.e., "stuffed" men vs. "hollow" men), a new diagnostic structure for male-specific depressions (Major Depressive Disorder, Male Type), insights gleaned from experience-near empathic immersion into individual men's depressive psychological disorders, and a rethinking of Freud's psychoanalytic model, in an attempt to address the hidden epidemic of modern men's affective derailment and the need for new treatment models designed for men.

The reader will be challenged to suspend disbelief about our often, too-well rooted, gender stereotypes—those unconscious templates that silently govern so much of our clinical judgment—in return for the opportunity to potentially enhance our recognition of male-based depressive syndromes, and expand our armamentarium for the clinical treatment of depression in men. If successful, we may achieve an empathic improvement in the clinical endeavor with men, as we begin to listen—with a newfound resonance—to men's unique voice of pain. Such an echo of recognition, has manifold therapeutic effects in both the psychological and biological realms.

DEPRESSION AND GENDER

Depression is one of the most serious, pervasive, and costly psychiatric disorders. It has been estimated that when costs for treatment and lost productivity are factored in, depression may cost more than $43 billion per year in the United States alone ("Too Often People," 1997). It is estimated that at least 15 million people suffer from the disorder yearly. Robert Hirschfield has argued that 24% of all American women and 15% of American men will suffer from an affective disorder over the course of their lifetime. Such estimates may be conservative, given the argument of this chapter that many more men suffer from depression than are traditionally diagnosed and treated.

A well-studied disorder epidemiologically, the majority of our data on incidence and prevalence, including differential rates for Major Depressive Disorder between males and females come from the two major completed studies of psychological/psychiatric disorders in the community: The National Institute of Mental Health (NIMH) Epidemiological Catchment Area Study (ECA) (Robins & Regier, 1991) and the National Co-Morbidity Study(NCS) (Kessler, McGonagle, Zhao, et al., 1994). The ECA was completed by the mid-1980s and was a multisite collaborative effort utilizing structured interview, the Diagnostic Interview Schedules, with over 18,000 subjects culled from probability subjects in five key U.S. urban areas. The gender ratio for one year prevalence of Major Depression female/male varied from 1.9: 1 in Los Angeles to 5.0: 1 in St. Louis. Cumulative lifetime risk for depression ratios, again female to male, were calculated by Weissman and her colleagues to be 2.4: 1 (Weissman, Bruce, Leaf, et al., 1991).

The National Co-Morbidity Study (NCS, 1993), was the first to utilize *DSM-III-R-R* criteria with a nationally representative sample. The lifetime prevalence ratio difference between women and men—though still dominated by women—had been reduced to female/male, 1.7: 1 (Kessler et al., 1994). Indeed when chronic or recurrent depression was measured, there were no differences between the genders, with the higher rates of depression for women reflecting reports for greater risk of first-onset illness. Men and women who were depressed did not differ in their recurrence rates, either.

There are clear secular cohort trends for the reporting of major depression, as well. For those groups born after 1945, there appears to be a higher lifetime risk than for those born earlier. Again, here, however, the rise is not distributed evenly by gender, with the rates between the sexes narrowing. As Wolk and Weissman summarize, "for individuals born since World War II, the rates of major depression seem to be rising in men and stabilizing for women" (1994, p. 235). Other subtle gender differences also emerge in this more traditional literature. Women's symptom profiles are more likely to show evidence of anxiety and somatization, than men's (Perugi, Musetti, Simonini, et al., 1990); and men appear to have slightly better response rates to tricyclic antidepressants (Glassman, Perel, Shostak, et al., 1977).

So, although traditional measures of depression do show some increase in the disease for males, with some intriguing differences in presentation by gender, the overwhelming majority of patients at risk for the disorder continue to *appear to be* women. So where do we derive the suspicion that depression is a more significant illness in men than presently reported; that indeed it may represent a hidden epidemic? Our first answers emerge from the shocking data on suicide.

MEN AND SUICIDE: RETHINKING GENDER AND DEPRESSION

Although there is always some debate about the statistics, the most accurate and recent estimates, culled from the National Center for Health Statistics (NCHS) (1996–1997) is that there are 4.2 male completions of suicide for each female completion. In other words, men are more likely to take their own lives four times more often than women. We can also estimate in subgroups that young white males (ages 15–24) are 5 to 8 times more likely to complete suicide than females; and very old males (ages 85+) are 10 times more likely than elderly females. Parasuicides, that is, attempts not completed, are heavily weighted toward females with ratios of 3 to 1, female to male. Men are killing themselves in record numbers, while more women are attempting suicide but are either being rescued or self-aborting the destructive acts. Women's self-destructive, morbid activity is explained by numerous factors, most notably their rates of serious depression. But how can men be committing suicide in these growing numbers, without being depressed—with their rates of depression remaining relatively low in all our classic diagnostic mechanisms?

Perhaps men are more significantly depressed than we have traditionally imagined. In that case, we would be forced to pose the question, Why do we remain blind to this serious affliction in males?

UNDERDIAGNOSIS AND UNDERTREATMENT OF DEPRESSION IN MEN

The definition of depression in men may be too narrowly proscribed for the typical symptom pictures with which male patients either present for help or manifest dysfunction in the community. Biologically oriented psychiatrists have argued long and hard for the linkage between substance abuse disorders (especially alcoholism) and depressive symptomotology, more recently observing common response to newer serotonergic antidepressants to include anxiety-based disorders such as panic and OCD; and even impulse control disorders. Consequently, they conceptualize these illnesses as existing along one axis of psychological dysregulation with myriad symptom constellations but a common core pathology. This concept of a depressive or affective spectrum disorder or set of disorders (Hudson & Pope, 1990; McElroy, Hudson, Pope, Keck, & Aizley, 1992; Winokur, 1979) would fit well within the growing psychological understanding of the unifying features that form a distinctly male stereotyped presentation for depression. For our purposes, it would suffice to attempt a rough empirical test of the spectrum disorder model by observing the recent data of these component disorders in the statistics culled from the NCS Lifetime Prevalence survey, as outlined in Table 7.1.

A rough calculation would find that the combination of anxiety, substance abuse, and "classic" depression yields equivalent prevalence of "depressive spectrum disorder" in men and women. Men, however, are more likely than women to manifest their depression through substance abuse, while women are likely to exhibit a co-morbid pattern with anxiety. This fits the typical clinical pictures in our consulting rooms. In fact, in studies of men already diagnosed with alcohol abuse, we often find equal prevalence of depression as with women (Brady et al., 1993).

Men are clearly manifesting depression through moods and behaviors and self-reports that are different from women, and our diagnostic tools are too often blind to this gender disparity. A Swiss group found that at the same documented level of occupational impairment, men continue to report fewer symptoms than equally impaired women subjects do (Angst & Dobler-Mikola, 1984). Indeed when the operational definition of depression is changed to two weeks duration depressed mood, plus occupational impairment with no minimum number of additional symptoms, no difference in depression rates for men and women is found (Ernst & Angst, 1992). When the NCS data is recalculated with only a one symptom requirement the female: male ratio lowers to 1.4: 1.

There is also the factor referred to by researchers as *differential memory* between the genders, a phenomenon we might better understand as

Table 7.1
Lifetime Prevalence *DSM-III* Disorders*

	Males (%)	Females (%)
Affective disorders	14.7	23.9
Substance abuse	35.4	17.9
Anxiety disorders	19.2	30.5

*From Kessler et al., 1994.

repression based upon social expectation and the differences between masculine and feminine internalized ideal selves. Men tend to "forget" their depressions, while women remember all their symptoms. Angst and Dobler-Mikola (1984) found that for the few months surrounding the episode, men and women will report the same number of symptoms, but at one year and beyond, men's memory diminishes and fewer symptoms are recalled. The argument for cultural and psychological suppression of vulnerable experience in men leading to under-reporting is supported by a study of college populations. This is a population where you would expect less traditional male suppression and, indeed, Nolen-Hoeksema (1990) did find the smallest disparity between the genders in reported rates of depression in college students. If men remember, or report, fewer distinct symptoms of classic depression, then a diagnostic model like the *DSM-IV* (with requisite numbers of symptoms per diagnosis) is likely to yield fewer diagnoses of depressed men.

A FEMINIZED VIEW OF DEPRESSION

Is it possible that the same medically based gender bias that tends to over pathologize women, underestimates men's pain? After all the traditional psychiatric model of male doctor/female patient, with doctor = active and well, while patient = sick and passive, works no better when the male is placed in the one-down patient role, pushed to comply with medical advice. Indeed a subsection of the Rand National Outcomes Study of medical care, involving 23,000 patients and over 500 practitioners, analyzed for accuracy in depression diagnosis appears to lend credence to this hypotheses. Potts, Burnam, and Wells (1991) compared the treating physicians' diagnosis with random administrations of an objective diagnostic instrument, the Diagnostic Interview Schedule (DIS). They found that 65% of men's verified depressions went undetected and undiagnosed. In other words, 3 out of 5 men who were actively suffering from a depression (even when detected by an instrument we have already shown to be biased against recognition of male symptoms) had their illness undetected and untreated. The incidence of completed male suicide begins to come into sharper focus.

This under diagnosis of men's depression may hinge on three factors:

1. Men are more likely to deny depression because it is unacceptable to their self image (due to the shame-hardening socialization mechanisms, described next).

2. Men are less likely to express overt affects or mood shifts than are women.

3. Clinicians being affected unconsciously by the same societally imbedded gender stereotypes are reticent to ask men about depressive symptoms or to inquire in depth against any resistance.

Gjerde, Block, and Block (1988) noted a channeling of sadness, distress, or depression by gender. They delineated four styles of male-based depression, only one of which would be overlapping enough with our feminized classical models to be read by external observers as depressed. This style they called "discontent with self." The other three included "interpersonal antagonism" (blaming), "unrestraint" (impulsivity), and "unconventionality" (rebelliousness). If we were to reconfigure these styles slightly to anger, rage, and risky behavior, we might begin to see where such male depressions tend to surface: as disorders of conduct, dangerous behaviors to self and others, and the types of lifestyles that create stress-induced, hostility-based physiological disorders. While outside the general scope of this chapter, it is important to note that depression has been linked to two disorders of great significance to men: hypertension and heart disease. Jonas (1997) found a 60% greater chance of developing hypertension if patients were depressed. Barefoot and Schroll (1996) demonstrated a four time greater risk for myocardial infraction for patients with Major Depressive disorder over a 14-year prospective study—a risk factor greater than cholesterol levels. One can only wonder how much this cardiac distress and morbidity in men is due to undiagnosed or undertreated depression or some of its male equivalents like anger or chronic rage. Indeed Goodman et al.'s lab (1996) reported a strong correlation between restenosis post-angioplasty and hostile Type A personality, a character structure we might better understand as depressed Type M-for male.

HOW DO MEN GET THIS WAY?

This chapter will attempt to create an empathic foundation for a *new diagnostic and therapeutic treatment model for men's depression*, integrating phenomenological data, psychopharmacological intervention, and a modern psychoanalytic (developmental/self-psychology) perspective. Experience-near listening will reveal a fissure in many men's self-systems, one beginning well before the Oedipal period. Specifically addressed will be the author's theory that historical, cultural, and economic forces have effected parenting styles so that as boys, men will suffer a traumatic disruption of their early holding environment, a premature psychic separation from both maternal and paternal caregivers. This is a normative male, gender-linked loss, a trauma of abandonment, for boys, which may show itself, later, as an adult through symptomatic behavior, characterological defense and vulnerability to depression.

As a result of the unconscious sense of *shame* accompanying this frightening sense of loss and deficit, many men seek treatment only reluctantly and under pressure from significant others. Often they present empathic disruptions in their relationships (love/desire splits in romance or an inability to commit) as an attempt to unconsciously protect against further loss, restricted emotionality with an inability to tolerate feelings of vulnerability or to express and bear sadness; and, consequently, an impingement in the capacity to grieve, *to mourn,* and to change. Such a combination of defense is often incorporated into a syntonic character armor that blocks the overt expression of all strong feelings, except anger, and is consciously maintained, indeed valued, as a (false) self-sufficiency—a process I have described elsewhere as defensive autonomy (Pollack, 1990, 1995). In many cases, such men's pain may be better understood as the emergence of a neurotic, relationally embedded, abandonment depression.

Many men's normative traumatic experience of premature separation, abandonment, though often not consciously remembered, forever casts a shadow on their relationships. Men are constantly seeking, yearning to be connected. However, they are terribly frightened of the shameful depressive dependency such connection may bring forth. Too often the psychology of men has been to suppress the anxieties and the depressive defenses such connections elicit and to replace experience of fear with a model of sexually based conflict. Men are not merely independent aggressive competitors, autonomously disconnected from others. They are frightened searchers, looking to connect, but are wary should the bond once more be tragically broken, and are catapulted helplessly into a state of disconnected despair. To help men to become more empathic to their own selves, as well as to others, we must provide a psychotherapy that is more empathic to men.

THEORY AND TREATMENT

We continue to view healthy masculine development as either Oedipally based unrequited desire and problematic aggression, or as pre-Oedipal struggles to master separation and to achieve independence. Indeed, the achievement of autonomy has become so central a construct in our conceptualization of the normal tasks of early male development that we have actually created an extra hoop of separation for boys to jump through—the so-called *disidentification* stage (Greenson, 1968). Within this model the pre-Oedipal boy is required to dis-identify with his maternal caretaker in order to move psychically closer to the father, thereby achieving a more secure male gender identity. Modern feminist theorists (like Chodorow, 1978, 1989) have also embraced this extra-separation stage for young boys, reframing it as the fault line upon which adult male identity precariously rests. From this perspective, boys and men are constantly fending off the psychic sense of feminine identification for fear of being pulled back into a symbiotic union with the mother and thereby losing their masculine sense of self.

My own clinical work with men and research on fathering and its effects on child development suggest a significantly different view (Pollack, 1990, 1995). We see many men in treatment who have felt forced to distance themselves at an early age from their mothers in order to create proto-masculine, nascent autonomous selves. But such events are rarely remembered as part of a sequence of healthy development. Rather, if one listens empathically (free from the bias of a dis-identification/separation model), a different affective experience emerges. Unearthed from layers of repression and anger, a deep sadness often comes forward, a delayed mourning for a tragic loss. This premature push for separation in boys is not a healthy form of self-differentiation but rather a traumatic disruption of their early holding environment. We may be seeing a developmental basis for a normative male-gender linked trauma (or impingement)—a life-cycle loss in boys that may show itself later in adulthood in symptomatic behavior and characterological disturbance. Many men who seek treatment often present with empathic disruptions in relationships; restricted emotionality and an inability to commit (often as an attempt to protect against loss); an inability to tolerate feelings of vulnerability, especially to express sadness or to grieve and mourn; and a type of syntonic character armor blocking the expression of strong emotional feeling, a false self-sufficiency which I have described previously as defensive autonomy.

We never stop to wonder what it must feel like for a young boy to lose his connection to mother. Such an enforced separation from the most cherished, admired, and loved person in his life must come as a terrible loss—all the more so in a family structure in which girls of the same age are encouraged to remain bonded and where fathers are often unable or unwilling to assuage their son's fall from the maternal safety net with an equally nurturant form of caregiving. Men's traumatic experience of abandonment in boyhood, though not consciously remembered, forever casts a shadow on their relationships. It is a sadness without a name, a yearning without clear object. It cannot be remembered, not only because it occurs so early in life and is repressed, nor merely because of the traumatic nature of the loss, but also because of the shame and humiliation which unrequited love elicits. Without the capacity for conscious awareness, men are unable to grieve, to mourn this psychic disruption, and are often never able to face or bear it directly.

Later, adult heterosexual relationships are likely to revive in men deeply repressed yearnings for the earliest mother. The result may be the creation by many men to transitional object or self-object relationships with women who function unconsciously as mother substitutes in a manner meant both to repair and assuage the unspeakable hurt of premature traumatic separation, while allowing men to consciously deny the loss of, or need for, a relational bond. In their unconscious yearning for closeness, men may seek out women who meet these repressed needs, only to deny such women any mutually empathic response. This occurs not because these men are immature, bad or fear symbiotic reunion. Rather, they need to protect themselves from the danger of re-experiencing the repressed pain, sadness, or depression that the new affiliation threatens to evoke and which they feel unable to mourn or to tolerate. Such men, maintain that they are self-sufficient while they are in the midst of a deeply dependent or interdependent connection.

This paradoxical situation may lead to the misunderstanding that we see in traditional, intimate relationships between men and women, and may account for much of the pain experienced by the two genders as they attempt to listen to and interpret each other's "voice." It may also begin to explain the apparent resistance that men show in unmodified forms of dynamic psychotherapy, and the preponderance of the diagnosis of narcissistic personality disorder among males. Following Modell (1976), dynamic treatment must pay close attention to the requirement for creating a symbolic recreation of the early holding environment in the treatment of narcissistic issues. Kohut's (1971, 1977) understanding of the need for facilitating and maintaining (for long periods of time) an experience-near, nonjudgmental, stabilizing self-object transference arrangement— either of a mirroring or idealizing type—may broaden our capacity for empathic connection with patients, who most frequently are men, so conflicted about relationship itself.

Added to the intrapsychic and interpersonal separation-based traumas in boys' childhood's are the ravages of our shame-hardening gender-bifurcated socialization systems and the biological vulnerability of male infants. Beyond the specific scope of this review on men and depression, it is important to note that our society continues to shame boys into the suppression of all vulnerable emotions, redefining them as feminine and like all things so delineated as an anathema to normal masculinity, thereby decrying the natural yearnings for dependency and succor in males beyond the latency period. The result is the creation of a highly shame phobic stereotypic male character with a propensity to funnel most hurt and pain into the one undifferentiated affect of anger/rage. This, in turn, stifles the inborn, genetic mechanisms for empathy in males leading to impulsive activity as the "favorite son" of men's expression of caring. In addition, the biologically more emotionally expressive male infant, with increased vulnerability to maternal rejection is quickly shaped into a more compliant baby, soon showing less vocal expression of feeling and later, as a young child, beginning to suppress the expression of affects with both peers and adults (see Pollack, 1995).

So-called "healthy" traditional masculine gender identity (replete with rigid differentiation from femininity [dis-identification]) is at least, in part, a false self construction with an ungrieved abandonment depression at its core (see Table 7.2). The self is structured and rests upon two faulty psychic foundations:

1. An identification with the absent aggressor father (Mitscherlich, 1963) creating a harsh self-critical and perfectionistic superego that demands neverending production oriented successes to fend off rageful states of depressed self esteem—the stuffed sense of men, and

Table 7.2
Disorder of the Self: Male Type

- Partial affective/intellectual split
- Anger prominence or "repression" personality
- Walling off of vulnerable core self
- Phobic avoidance/denial of interdependent object relations: sexualized self-object yearnings
- Shame sensitive/shame phobic
- Action blunting of empathic recognition
- Incapacity to translate feelings into language: alexithymia
- Harsh unconscious self-criticism: sometimes projected onto others
- Perfectionistic need to master: workaholism
- Inability to grieve/mourn
- Vulnerability to substance abuse and depression (male type)

---

2. An impinged upon, enfeebled, narcissistically depleted core shamed into hiding its prematurely disrupted sense of needing to be held, hiding behind a false self of angry defiance and pseudoindependence—the hollow sense of men. One of the psychological consequences of such a faulty foundation is the vulnerability of men to a type of abandonment depression.

MOURNING, MELANCHOLIA, AND MEN

Over 80 years ago, Freud, called our attention to the striking resemblance between the normal processes of grieving—mourning—and the pathological phenomena in depression—melancholia. One striking difference was evident, however: The presence of severe self-reproaches in melancholic depression. Freud believed that these inner attacks upon the self were actually unconscious criticisms aimed against another loved one, who either disappointed or left that person. The response toward this unavailable object was to deal with the loss and the resultant ambivalent attachment to them, by taking 'the disappointing other' into the self, that is, identifying with them:

> Thus the shadow of the object fell upon the ego, and the later could henceforward be judged by a special agency, as though it were . . . the forsaken object (Freud, 1912/1957)

Here we have the beginning of a theory of superego. But for our purposes, from a clinical, experience-near perspective, Freud is describing how a traumatic loss of a sustaining person, may lead psychologically to a conflictual ambivalent unconscious identification with them, and thereby leads to a barrage of inner, hostile criticism (once meant for a disappointing love object), now, aimed against the self. The root loss would likely remain out of conscious awareness and our patient would feel depleted, guilty, and self-critical without becoming aware of the inner sense of loss. Consequently, he would be stuck in this conflicted, depressed state without the capacity to grieve or mourn.

Such a conflict-based depressive position, in which the patient is wracked by guilty and perfectionistic self-reproaches of conscience, leading to varying degrees of self-limiting depression, so well described by Freud, is categorized by Heinz Kohut, the founder of self-psychology as the quintessential fate of *guilty man*. Counterpoised with such a conflict-based depressive dynamic for men is Kohut's alternate model of a despairing, empty depression in which guilty feelings play little or no role.

Here, in *tragic man* we find, instead, a guiltless despair of a depleted core self that has not received adequate opportunity to strive—with healthy exuberant support—to reach its own ideals, based upon a realistic assessment of real skill and talent. In other words, men who have been denied the chance for genuine responsiveness to their legitimate needs for dependent support in childhood (a psychic trauma which is common due to gender-bifurcated developmental models and cultural mores) or whose role models did not allow for optimal idealization, (e.g., Herzog's "father hunger"), would be susceptible to varying degrees of depletion and fragmentation—best understood as stereotypically male-based depressions.

Often, however, such depleted states would be defended against, or partially repaired by behavioral actions that are meant to assuage the depressive anxiety and to diminish the intense feelings of shame that depressed men feel. Such behavior might include serial sexual affairs, intermittent substance abuse, phobic avoidance of object relationships that demand commitment, apparently impulsive work, and love-based decisions/activities (action disorders in men), and, either in chronic form or during acute crises—which threaten an already compromised self stability—a range of anger/rage reactions instituted as last ditch efforts at narcissistic repair of core depressed self. Indeed, we might argue that one reason that men don't attempt suicide, but, rather, complete it, is that, with unrecognized depression in men, suicidal enactment is the final face-saving defense against the shame of failing to live up to one's perfectionistic ideals.

Some have suggested that such shame-based narcissistic depressions are particularly prominent in mid-life crises (e.g., Bibring, Morrison). But it seems likely that such tragic shame-based failures to meet one's ideals can occur throughout the life cycle, as men remain particularly susceptible due to unconscious, normative psychic disruptions or impingements within their early holding environments, and the continued shame which adheres to dependency or passivity in adulthood.

So, in their own language, we may find in Freud and Kohut, the seeds of understanding the dilemmas of stuffed (guilt-ridden, self-critical) men and hollow (empty, depleted, angry) men, both of whom, in ways characteristic to their particular developmental derailments and conflicts, are manifesting a myriad of symptoms best understood, I've argued, as variants of abandonment depression in men. However, while such clear distinctions between *guilty man* and *tragic man* may be useful for heuristic purposes, in clinical practice, it is most likely to find men with mixed presentations of depression and to discover underlying fault lines of both developmental failure and psychic conflict. To become and remain empathic in our treatment models for depression in men, we must learn to listen in a new way to a wide range of often hidden depletions and self-criticisms. Therefore, I suggest we adopt the new construct, outlilned in Table 7.3, with which to better sensitize ourselves to stereotypical depressions in men.

To provide experience near empathic treatment of depression in men requires the following elements:

1. Recognition of the gender specific syndrome as a bona fide defensive structure with biological proclivities without recourse to moralistic judgment or critical misunderstanding by the therapist
2. A sensitivity to men's shame increased by the man's seeking of help, attempting to actively interpret and diminish the parent's harsh self-criticism and being vigilant to avoiding further shame by either hiding behind a mask of "neutrality" or using "therapeutic confrontation"
3. The creation of a therapeutic holding environment or cocoon (Modell, 1976) that simultaneously sustains the enfeebled male patient while allowing him to save face and deny his dependence upon the

Table 7.3
Major Depressive Disorder-Male Type

1. Increased withdrawal from relationships: May be denied by patient
2. Overinvolvement with work activities: May reach a level of obsessional concern, masked by comments about "stress" (burnout)
3. Denial of pain
4. Increasingly rigid demands for autonomy
5. Avoiding the help of others: The "I can do it myself" syndrome
6. Shift in the interest level of sexual encounters: May be either a decrease or an increase (differentiate from mania)
7. Increase in intensity or frequency of angry outbursts
8. New or renewed interest in psychoactive substance self-administration: To create self-numbing tension relief states without classic dissociative mechanisms
9. A denial of any sadness and an inability to cry
10. Harsh self-criticism: Often focusing on failures in the arenas of provider and/or protector
11. Impulsive plans to have loved ones cared for in case of patient's death or disability: "The wife and/or kids only need me for the money."
12. Depleted or impulsive mood
13. Concentration, sleep, weight disorders

therapist, if necessary, allowing the formation of a stabilizing selfob-ject transference (Kohut), which understands narcissistic defense as a thwarted need to grow (Ornstein) and re-institutes the human growth enhancing developmental environment (Pollack, 1990, 1995)

4. An integration of biological interventions with psychological treatment

The case of an "angry" older man, Hal, illustrates this new empathic therapy for gender-specific depressions in men.

CASE STUDY: HAL

Hal, a married middle-class Jewish professional man in his late sixties first contacted the therapist via a telephone call to his staff: "I'm trying to reach Dr. P. I'm angry and don't want to speak with anyone else. I want to talk with him! I got his name as an expert on men and anger. Please have him call me today!" Not taking "maybe" as an answer, he followed up, several hours later, with a call to the voice mail: "When can I expect to hear from you? I need an appointment immediately!"

Needless to say, such a "pre"-contact did not generate a wholly positive countertransference expectation in the therapist. And when at the begin-ning of the first evaluation session, Hal began by berating the "idiot" who had answered the phone during his final demanding call, the therapist had to work hard in retaining an empathic stance, as that particular idiot was the therapist's wife!

Indeed, Hal was an angry man. He had come at the insistence of his wife (and upon the recommendation of his wife's therapist), when his chronic verbal attacks on his spouse had intensified in vehemence, in-creased in frequency, and led on two occasions to overt aggressive out-bursts. His immediate attitude toward the therapist betrayed a mixture of suspiciousness, hostility, and demeaning sarcasm, so much so that a clinician might not have been technically incorrect in hypothesizing a diagnosis of character disorder: with mixed features of a narcissistic, paranoid, and explosive type.

Yet there was something about this man's almost heroic struggle to maintain contact, with the very souls whom he berated and that betrayed—to the therapist—mind, a fragile core, a core self hidden behind a false fa-cade of angry distance demanding understanding and, perhaps requiring nurturance. Hal appeared to be both hollowed out and stuffed—hollowed with the sense of an empty, depleted inner self still searching for recognition and stuffed with a guilt-inducing rage that stalked his every outburst, generating endless self-criticism, and keeping him apart from the people he genuinely loved. Hal was depressed.

Indeed, Hal complained that no matter how much he attempted to reach out to his son or to reconcile with his wife, he was rebuffed. He was constantly "attacked" by his librarian colleagues, was unable to sleep at night, and felt a growing loss of concentration capacity. When asked about his feelings, he could come up with only one—an overwhelming, and at times almost paralyzing, rage.

The therapist suggested to Hal that it was unfair that he was burdened so frequently with others' insensitivity and rebuff, and that a trial attempt at psychotherapy might help to clarify his concerns and might even—although there could be no promises—uncover some unique approach to alleviate his distress. The therapist also suggested if Hal recognized even the faintest glimmer of dissatisfaction or anger toward therapy or toward himself, he would suspend his normal operations of civility and patience, and mention his irritation immediately. Needless to say, Hal had little trouble complying, immediately, with this request.

Before the end of the first evaluation session, the therapist suggested to Hal that although our meetings might well—in and of themselves—prove beneficial, his symptoms could also respond to new medications now available. Although often labeled anti-depressants, it was not necessary for him to feel depressed in order to experience their efficacy and that some of these drugs might target his symptoms of depletion, sleeplessness, irritability, and poor concentration. The level of his distress was not severe, but still distressing to him, and there was no reason for him to deny himself the choice of medical intervention. Hal was surprised by, and grateful for the concern, but worried about becoming dependent (like his wife) on drugs.

The therapist helped Hal to understand that the psychological treatment could progress, at this point, with or without medication, and that the therapist felt comfortable with either approach. Reassured by this level of openness, Hal requested a psychopharmacological consultation and a return appointment with the therapist, simultaneously. Indeed, by the time Hal returned to his second hour he had already been seen by the consulting psychopharmacologist, who recommended an SSRI as adjunctive treatment, but only if Hal were interested or willing.

During his second session, Hal discussed how his son, earlier that day, during an argument, had infuriated him. Asked to share his associations,

Hal paused when he came to the phrase, "He really put me down." When the therapist inquired whether that was a common feeling, he replied, "I didn't know that 'put-down' was a feeling. Then, yes, I feel that way all the time." Soon after, Hal began to recollect his earliest memories of continual criticism and put down by his father.

A depression baby, Hal was only five years old when his shy and non-communicative father lost his job. Fearing for his family's security and narcissistically wounded by his inability to put food on the table, Hal's father became increasingly sullen and depressed, as well as enraged—taking out much of his anger on his son Hal. Hal was made to feel puny, stupid, and weak, trying endlessly to assuage his father's demands, but frequently failing, never able to measure up in father's eyes. Much to his own surprise and with some initial shame, Hal began to tear up, and cry, sobbing profoundly.

What followed in relatively rapid succession, during the now regular bi-weekly therapy, was the piecing together of many of Hal's previously confusing failures in his work and love life. He identified, with support from the therapist, the *critical voice* inside him, an inner self-directed rage that tore apart every success he had achieved, depressing his affect and making him irritable, and therefore, difficult for others to deal with. As he became more empathic to himself, his perfectionistic demands upon both self and others diminished. He became painfully aware of how he had recreated these put-downs with his own son, apologizing now with no expectation of immediate improvement in the relationship—other than his own enhanced self-esteem. He gained an increasing interest in his own emotional inner life with the excellent side-effect of becoming more empathic to and respectful of his wife's depressive affect.

With the diminished shame about the possibility of taking medication and by beginning to work through his depressive sadness in psychotherapy, Hal was able to conquer his symptoms without medication. His wife's medication could be discontinued sooner due to the enhanced support she felt from the marriage, now that Hal's depleted, self-critical, perfectionistic, rageful self-fragments were healing. "I've been hurt and angry so much of my life," Hal remarked, "it's sad to reflect on it. I still cry from time to time . . . But oddly enough I don't feel tired or down any more. Therapy must really be helping me!"

Recently, Hal felt that he had hit a wall in treatment and wondered if medication would be a useful therapeutic adjunct. An SSRI (sertraline) was added and with this additional safety net in place, Hal began to notice something strange happening in the therapy sessions. His need to control matters was diminishing and, "my mind seems to go or wander wherever it pleases." Free association and its benefits was reintroduced into the therapy and Hal began to share a series of obsessional ideas that had plagued him—some for over 40 years! Some were thoughts, fantasies really, of injuring his children and the other memories of sex play and experimentation with his own siblings as a child. Verbalizing these lonely and burdensome ruminations elicited harsh self-criticism, guilt, and shame. When these self-reproaches—"I'm a murderer, I'm a pervert"—were actively confronted and dispelled, Hal showed an almost visceral sense of relief. "I don't know if talking about this will help, but it sure feels better to finally talk to someone about all of this!"

SUMMARY

Embedded within a cool facade of stoic tolerance, alcoholic alexithymia, stress-based cardiac toxicity, and repression-generated gastrointestinal distress, men are in pain—men are sad, men are *depressed*. Men's psychic suffering is palpable to those who are willing to plumb the depths hidden behind the often smooth surfaces of compliance and dutiful productivity. Stuffed with burdensome duty and responsibility chaining them to the grindstone; and hollowed out by the demands of pseodoautonomy and separation based paradigms of self-esteem, many men are yearning to come in out of the cold. Such yearning is often itself an anathema to men, for to be in need, to betray vulnerability or dependence, is to court shame and with it the threatened depletion of an already strained reservoir of ideal self-image, the dangerous emergence of anxiety about dissociative affective connections and the depressive panic of long-repressed abandonment. It is only too easy for clinicians—male and female—to collude in this cultural process of self-deception, eschewing our own demons of loss and uncertainty by seeing men as either too healthy to need depth-oriented dynamic psychotherapy, or too sick, disconnected, or defensive to benefit from it.

Men may greatly benefit from treatments, if and when, we are able to reframe our therapy paradigms to models that are genuinely empathic to men's needs—both conscious and unconscious. Such a task, and with it the enhanced diagnosis and remediation of men's abandonment depressions, promises to be transformative to the men in our consulting rooms, the men in our society, and the other men, women, and children who love them. For if we succeed in our endeavor, as clinicians, we may help men to acknowledge, bear, and put into perspective their deepest pain—helping them, then, to grieve and to mourn—transforming destructive rage into sadness, and melting their protective armoring with the tears of liberation, tears we may now expect to share together.

REFERENCES

Angst, I., & Dobler-Mikola, A. (1984). Do the diagnostic criteria determine the sex ratio in depression? *Journal of Affective Disorders, 7,* 189–198.

Barefoot, J. C., & Schroll, M. (1996). Symptoms of depression, acute myocardial infarction, and total mortality in a community sample. *Circulation, 93,* 1976–1980.

Ernst, C., & Angst, J. (1992). The Zurich study XII: Sex difference in depression: Evidence from longitudinal epidemiological data. *European Archives of Psychiatry and Clinical Neuroscience, 241,* 222–230.

Freud, S. (1957). Mourning and melancholia. In J. Strachey (Ed. & Trans.), *The standard edition of the complete psychological works of Sigmund Freud* (Vol. 14, pp. 237–260). London: Hogarth Press. (Original work published 1912)

Gjerde, P., Block, J., & Block, J. (1988). Depressive symptoms of personality during late adolescence: Gender differences in the externalization-internalization on symptom expression. *Journal of Abnormal Psychology 97,* 475–486.

Glassman, A. H., Perel, J. M., Shostak, M., et al. (1977). Clinical implications of imipramine plasma levels for depressive illness. *Archives of General Psychiatry, 34,* 197–204.

Goodman, M., et al. (1996). Hostility predicts restenosis after percutaneous transluminal coronary angioplasty. *Mayo Clinic Proceedings, 71,* 729–734.

Greenson, R. (1968). Disidentifying from mother. *International Journal of Psychoanalysis, 49,* 370–374.

Hudson, J. I., & Pope, H. G. (1990). Affective spectrum disorder: Does antidepressant response identify a family of disorders with a common pathophysiology? *American Journal of Psychiatry, 147,* 552–564.

Kessler, R. C., McGonagle, K. A., Zhao, S., et al. (1994). Lifetime and 12-month prevalence of *DSM-III-R* psychiatric disorders in the United States: Results from the national comorbidity study. *Archives of General Psychiatry, 51,* 8–19.

Kohut, H. (1977). *The restoration of the self.* New York: International Universities Press.

McElroy, S. C., Hudson, J. I., Pope, H. G., Keck, P. E., & Aizley, H. G. (1992). The *DSM-III-R* impulse control disorders not elsewhere classified. *American Journal of Psychiatry, 149*(3), 318–327.

Mitscherlich, A. (1963). *Society without the father.* New York: Harcourt.

Modell, A. H. (1976). The "holding environment" and the therapeutic action of psychoanalysis. *Journal of the American Psychoanalytic Association, 24,* 285–308.

Nolen-Hoeksema, S. (1990). *Sex differences in depression.* Stanford, CA: Stanford University Press.

Perugi, G., Musetti, L., Simonini, E., et al. (1990). Gender-mediated clinical features of depressive illness: The importance of temperamental differences. *British Journal of Psychiatry, 157,* 835–841.

Pollack, W. S. (1990). Men's development and psychotherapy: A psychoanalytic perspective. *Psychotherapy, 27*(3), 316–321.

Pollack, W. S. (1995). No man is an island: Toward a new psychoanalytic psychology of men. In R. Levant & W. Pollack (Eds.), *A new psychology of men.* New York: Basic Books.

Potts, M. K., Burnam, M. A., & Wells, K. B. (1991). Gender differences in depressive detection: A comparison of clinician diagnosis and standardized assessment. *Psychological Assessment, 3*(4), 609–65.

Robins, L. N., & Regier, D. A. (1991). *Psychiatric disorders in America: The epidemiological catchment area study.* New York: Free Press.

Too often people suffering from depression are left undiagnosed. (1997, January 21). Reuters News Letter.

Weissman, M. M., Bruce, M. L., Leaf, P. J., et al. (1991). Affective disorders. In L. N. Robins & D. A. Regier (Eds.), *Psychiatric disorders in America* (pp. 53–80). New York: Free Press.

Winnicott, D. W. (1974). *The maturational processes and the facilitating environment.* New York: International Universities Press.

Winokur, G. (1979). Unipolar depression: Is it divisible into autonomous subtypes? *Archives of General Psychiatry, 36,* 47–52.

Wolk, S. I., & Weismann, M. M. (1994). Women and depression: An update. In J. M. Oldham & M. B. Ruba (Eds.), *Review of psychiatry* (Vol. 14). Washington, DC: American Psychiatric Press.

CHAPTER 8

Men's Shame and Trauma in Therapy

Steven Krugman

S HAME IS a central emotional issue in the lives of many men (Krugman, 1995). It is a by-product of male socialization and gender role strain (Pleck, 1981). As a primary self-regulating emotion, shame, in its various manifestations, shapes male development throughout the lifecycle. It is a regulator of attachment and connection and serves as a signal of vulnerability and exposure. Boys learn many early and often painful lessons as to how to manage feelings of shame, and shame-producing situations. In fact, shame affects are among the most potent motivators of male character armor—"machismo," "cool," "strong and silent," "poker faced," and other familiar poses. Shame, as a powerful affective state, also motivates defensive reactions like withdrawal and rage responses and plays an important part in maladaptive coping mechanisms, like substance abuse. Treating shame and shame-related conditions is one of the central technical challenges facing therapists working with male populations (Krugman, 1995; Lansky, 1992; Wright, 1987).

The psychotherapy of shame is the focus of this chapter. I present the case of Paul, a 42-year-old man. Much of the shame in his life has its origins in the abusive maltreatment he received in his family of origin. Normative male development generates considerable shame in its own right. Maltreatment, along with familial alcoholism, among other conditions, are significant non-normative sources of shame in male development. These sources of shame interact with normative shame experiences, motivating the creation of character defense. I will present Paul's story from the point of his entrance into psychotherapy, and will discuss his symptomatic, behavioral, and characterological issues as they unfold in the context of his treatment. This case gives us an opportunity to look at some of the major sources of shame in men's lives. Paul's experience captures both the problem of shame in men's lives, as well as the particular role of shame dynamics in the life of an abused man. The problem of shame has been addressed by a variety of clinical theorists and practitioners (Lewis, 1971; Morrison, 1989; Nathanson, 1987; Wurmser, 1981). I will discuss some of these issues by setting the stage for my own approach to the shame-based issues in Paul's life.

THE DYNAMICS OF SHAME

"Shame plays a prominent, but unspoken, role in men's lives" (Krugman, 1995). Shame states are known to all of us, ranging from the passing embarrassment of forgetting to zip one's fly, to the burning feeling that erupts upon learning one has been "made a fool of," to the unspeakable feelings of humiliation that often accompanies being beaten and/or raped.

The shame response is part of an innate system that includes blushing, along with a sequence of movements like lowered eye gaze, head down, and turning away. Global, undifferentiated shame responses often trigger rage or flight (Tomkins, 1987). Shame is a basic emotional response to the loss of interest and attention by a significant other (Tomkins). It is an innate response to exposure that is linked to the autonomic nervous system, generating blushing and hot feelings, intense arousal, and the disruption of smooth cognitive and motor functioning. Shame states include a wide range of responses and associated reactions. In this culture, we recognize embarrassment, humiliation, and mortification. Contemporary theorists and researchers have also pointed to the powerful connection between humiliation and rage, the likelihood that guilt is a later derivative of shame, and the wide range of defensive behaviors triggered by and associated with shame states (Scheff, 1988). The most important of these include silence, withdrawal, flight, and intensification of self-conscious cognitive activity (by-passed shame). Shame, because of its primary association with contact and acceptance by the other, quickly becomes a critical affect in the regulation of self-other relationships. Though we generally think of shame as a predominantly negative experience, contemporary theory and research leaves little doubt that shame also serves critically important prosocial and adaptive functions (Lewis, 1987; Nathanson, 1987).

Shame is the affect of the exposed self. It is an emotion signaling that we are vulnerable, exposed, different, and not in control. These powerful response tendencies are quickly recruited by the process of socialization. The child who learns to acknowledge shame and to integrate it into his or her sense of self, into social life, develops a finely attuned set of internal and interpersonal signals as to when to come forward and when to hold back, when to show off and when to be modest, and when to challenge an adversary and when to back-off in the face of danger (Malatesta-Magai, 1991). Male and female gender socialization offers boys and girls rather different messages and means for dealing with shame (Gross, 1996). Girls seem more alert and sensitive to shame signals; they learn to recognize them early in life, learn to read them in their relationships; and then allow these signals to direct their social interactions. By contrast, boys are relatively more phobic and avoidant with respect to shame, and remain more vulnerable to shame affects as they arise in the course of social life. Girls are more likely to reveal their hurt, while boys are more likely to mask their feelings by cognitive constriction or increased belligerence. For males, shame states carry a greater risk of emotional fragmentation.

Shame is a basic emotional response to the loss of interest and attention by a significant other (Tomkins, 1987). It is an innate response to exposure that is linked to the autonomic nervous system, generating blushing and "hot" feelings, intense arousal, and the disruption of smooth cognitive and motoric functioning. Shame states include a wide range of responses and associated reactions. In this culture we recognize embarrassment, humiliation, and mortification. Contemporary theorists and researchers have also pointed to the powerful connection between humiliation and rage, the likelihood that guilt is a later derivative of shame, and the wide range of defensive behaviors triggered by and associated with shame states (Scheff, 1988). The most important of these include silence, withdrawal, flight, and intensification of self conscious cognitive activity. Shame, because of its primary association with contact and acceptance by the other, quickly becomes a critical affect in the regulation of self-other relationships.

In my inquiry into the role of shame in male development (Krugman, 1995), I concluded that four psychosocial factors associated with male development impede the socialization and integration of shame. First, boys typically undergo a complex process of consolidating their sense of autonomy, often at the cost of their previously comfortable connections with their mothers. Much shame is stimulated by an inadequate sense of autonomy, by unresolved dependent needs, and by fears/wishes to be engulfed by women. Second, boys frequently must rely on problematic male identifications in the crafting of their own male identities; thus, having a dysfunctional or absent father is usually a source of complex shame experience. If one's primary male role model is a repetitive source of humiliation and fear, shame becomes a highly sensitized state, which requires considerable defensive adaptation. When one is both shamed by, and ashamed of, one or both parents, there is little or no help in working through normally occurring narcissistic and grandiose states. Ego weakness and emotional instability are common consequences. The third factor is also rooted in male identification, this time with the peer group. Typically, the male peer group encourages boys to extinguish and hide vulnerable states that produce shame reactions. This is done through teasing and/or mocking the appearance of vulnerability. In this process, boys learn to hide, to counter shame, and to be aggressive in defense of themselves and their friends. For many males, poorly integrated shame is quickly transformed into flight-fight reactions. Humiliated fury, a rage reaction associated with shame, is believed to stave off impending ego collapse (Lansky, 1992). Finally, this same traditional male subculture disinclines males from normalizing and detoxifying shameful experiences through talking and connecting with others. Instead, it rewards and promotes action, compulsive behavior, drinking, fighting, and the like. The net effect is that these significant psychosocial factors mitigate against successful shame socialization among males.

POST-TRAUMATIC SHAME

Like fear, anxiety, and rage, shame is one of the core affective responses to traumatic exposure. The loss of control and helplessness that is inherent in traumatization typically evokes powerful feelings of humiliation. (In severe instances of traumatic threat, victims may lose bladder or bowel control, with additionally strong feelings of shame.) The failure of the self to respond adequately to a traumatic situation may remain a long-standing source of shame; one that can interact with gender role expectations of heroism or fearlessness. Often, the traumatized person has undergone a demeaning or debasing experience that is central to the memory of the event. In some instances, it is the intent of the perpetrator (where one is involved) to inflict humiliation on his victim. The internal experiences of loss of control and helplessness are, in themselves, humiliating.

Maladaptive coping with subsequent vulnerability—through substance abuse, sexual acting out, or other means—leaves one actively re-experiencing the humiliation.

MALE GENDER EFFECTS

Maltreatment and the shame associated with it interacts with male gender socialization in significant ways. One of the major developmental tasks of boyhood for males is the construction of a coherent sense of self that includes a secure and sturdy sense of their own identification as male. Maltreated boys turn to the process of male socialization for a framework within which to organize their experiences and assign meaning. The physically or sexually abused boy measures his response to being beaten, molested, or raped, against what he has learned about being a man. As David Lisak (this volume, Chapter 10) points out so well, the vulnerabilities that accompany traumatization pose a profound challenge for traditional male roles. Male codes of toughness and invulnerability are profoundly disrupted by surging anxiety, shame states, and with fears of reinjury.

Traumatized men live with a sense of shame over their fears and sense of frailty. As boys and men struggle to cope with post-traumatic affects, their response to shame shapes their mode of adaptation. Those who internalize blame for what has happened to them, find that shame permeates their body images, their self-representations, and their expectations of others. Self-hatred, substance abuse, and re-victimization often follows. For those whose externalize, projected shame takes its toll on significant others in the form of contempt, disdain, and devaluation; these are often preludes to violence and perpetration. Unbearable shame feelings are associated with high risk behaviors, including suicide (Lansky, 1992).

For the maltreated man, shame is omnipresent and surrounds the wounded self. It covers and protects vulnerable post-traumatic self-states. If these are to be accessed and reworked or integrated, shame, like some mythic guardian, must be tamed and laid to rest.

CONTEMPORARY THEORY AND RESEARCH

The phenomena of shame has received considerable attention over the last 10 years. This renewed interest can be traced initially to the work of Helen Block Lewis (1971) whose careful scrutiny of tape recordings of psychotherapy sessions alerted her to the impact of unacknowledged shame in the psychotherapy process. In case after case, she found that these moments frequently preceded treatment impasses or, at times, the complete breakdown of treatment. A generation of clinicians and researchers have followed her lead in their inquiry into the critical importance of this not so well understood affect (see Krugman, 1995).

Much of the contemporary research work on shame has been aimed at validating shame as an empirical construct, and either differentiating it from guilt (Hobliztzelle, 1982; Lewis, 1987), or investigating its relationship to other variables such as depression, self-esteem, or gender (Severino, McNutt, & Feder, 1987). While the empirical study of shame has yet to contribute significantly to the treatment of shame-based conditions, the growth of clinical theory has generated important advances both in overall approaches to the problem, as well as in specific techniques. Clinicians have become sensitized to the disruptive impact of shame on interpersonal relationships, and shame's promotion of acting out. Clinicians working with shame-sensitive subgroups (e.g., incest survivors, eating disorders, ethnic minorities) have themselves grown more sensitive to their patient's vulnerability to shame. The heightened awareness of shame's impact on interpersonal behavior has also led to an increased appreciation of the role of shame in familial alcoholism and domestic violence, and other sources of interpersonal conflict. Self-psychological and object-relational approaches to shame (Alonso & Rutan, 1988; Morrison, 1989) have also highlighted the role of shame in narcissistic and depressive disorders.

Shame's role in male development suggests several prominent sources of shame formation in the male lifecycle. Approaches to the treatment of male shame should consider these sources during the course of assessment. The first significant occasion for shame formation occurs early in the boy's life, where conflicts around attachment and identification give rise to anxieties related to separation and individuation from parental figures. Shame arises, and becomes an associated feature of, the insecure points of contact between the child and his parents. Shame is generated as the boy discovers his parents' negative reactions to parts of himself. Shame may accompany the boy's efforts to become psychologically separate from maternal and paternal figures.

The clinical issues related to the development of shame during the first years of life are often best addressed by psychodynamic object relations theories. Clinical theorists like Blatt (1990), along with self psychologists like Morrison (1989) and Lansky (1992) provide important perspectives on the role and manifestations of shame in the presentation of self. Blatt theorizes that each individual works to integrate attachment/dependency needs with complementary needs for autonomy. Needs for connection (anaclitic) exist in a tension state with needs for autonomy and identity consolidation (introjective). These two fundamental styles are associated with differing cognitive styles (e.g., field dependence and independence), predisposition to depression, success in psychotherapy, and different types of shame. Hibbard (1994) distinguishes between libidinal shame and aggressive shame. The former is more characteristic of anaclitic types and concerns over loss of self, while the latter is related to strivings for independence, and is characteristic of introjective types. The clinical implications of this line of investigation center around how the individual in treatment is able to balance needs for connection with needs for psychological autonomy. The therapist seeking to support the development of such balance needs to address both elements of the patient's shame. Many men are deeply conflicted over their anaclitic/dependent needs. Their aggressive behavior—whether it be overt and direct or covert and passive—is itself often a source of shame. As a result, differentiation may be inhibited, and counterdependent behavior may be stimulated.

A second prominent source of shame arises out of "normative" male socialization pressures and concerns over measuring up to these norms. Male gender role strain (Pleck, 1981) is another significant source of shame formation. Levant (1995), O'Neil et al. (1986), along with Pleck and others, have established that many men experience themselves as failing to live up to male gender stereotypes. Whether it be internalized demands for toughness, competitiveness, or sexual performance, the gap between the ideal male self and the real male self is a potent shame generator. This particular source of shame affects and cognitions is toxic to male self-esteem, and gives rise to characterological defenses against being revealed, such as hypermasculine machismo-like posturing and the cool pose (Lazur & Majors, 1995). Therapists associated with a feminist or social constructivist perspective (e.g., Levant, Chapter 2; Lisak, Chapter 10, this volume) often use a cognitive approach in an effort to "deconstruct" the internalized male gender schema. This is, in effect, a strategy for diminishing super-ego pressure and criticality. To the extent that this can be accomplished, there is often a reduction in felt shame and an enhancement of self-esteem.

The last major source of shame in men's lives centers in their experiences with familial dysfunction and psychopathology; most specifically with familial alcoholism and domestic violence. A significant number of boys grow up in families troubled by one or both of these disorders. The impact on emotional, cognitive, and social development is widespread (Pynoos, Steinberg, & Goenjian, 1996). Where fathers are actively alcoholic and/or violent or sexually abusive, boys experience, among many other feelings, powerful shame states. On the strength of their own feelings, they are likely to be frightened, critical, and even disgusted with their

father's behaviors. By virtue of their connection with mother and other siblings, their fears and criticisms are amplified. They are ashamed of their
identifications with him, their weakness in the face of him, and their fear
that they will become like him. To the extent that adult men either re-enact
paternal patterns or develop these tendencies in response to other factors,
these men also struggle with much shame and self-hatred (Lansky, 1992).

The shame of alcoholism has given rise to therapeutic movements such
as Alcoholics Anonymous, Ala-Non, adult children of alcoholics groups,
and other approaches to recovery. Similar models have arisen in the area of
domestic violence. Cognitive interventions, well as holistic and spiritual
approaches to treatment are widely used by the individuals themselves
utilizing self-help literature and groups. Therapists working within the
framework of the recovery movement also make extensive use of transactional analysis notions of the inner child as a way of accessing the hurt,
shamed, self (Fossum & Mason, 1986). Where shame states are embedded
in complex interpersonal processes like domestic violence or familial alcoholism, their resolution often requires intervention at the familial level.
Where shame is secondary to loss of self-control (as with addictive behavior
or impulsive behaviors), amelioration may come with increased control
over the behaviors in question, often accomplished with the aid of group
based programs.

A SHAME-GUIDED PSYCHOTHERAPY

My work with men maltreated as boys is guided in large measure by my
perspective on shame. These men are like most men, but more so. Their experience of maltreatment intensifies their sense of vulnerability and need
and poses challenges to their rigid sense of maleness. They often present,
as did Paul, with a heightened awareness of traditional male conflicts. Asking for help violates traditional male gender role expectations of being self-
sufficient, on the one hand, and revealing personal vulnerability, on the
other. In treating men with histories of maltreatment, Lewis' (1987) observation regarding the impact of unacknowledged shame on the treatment
process is an important beacon for keeping the treatment on track. As I become aware that shameful material is emerging, or as a transaction between myself and my patient has the potential to be embarrassing or
worse, I use this awareness as a signal to proceed with caution. Early alliance building with shame sensitive men takes on particular importance.
For example, in one very dramatic instance, I was attempting to clarify an
outstanding bill early in the treatment of one such man. As he understood

that I was questioning him about his unpaid balance, he became infuriated, rose from his chair saying, "I don't have to take this shit from you," and made his way to the door. Surprised, if not stunned by his reaction, I asked him to stay at least long enough to tell me what had just happened. It seemed that my transparent look of bewilderment diminished his sense of threat. He sat down again and explained that he felt, and thought, that I was bringing up the billing issue to test him, to see if I could humiliate him about owing me money. As he articulated his concern, it seemed improbable to him that I would want to do that and the situation was defused.

PSYCHODYNAMIC PERSPECTIVE

The psychodynamic treatment described herein took an integrative approach to Paul's multilevel difficulties. My primary stance, however, was that of an interpersonally oriented, psychodynamic psychotherapist. Such an orientation is the most effective approach to working through the deeper personality patterns and self-experiences engendered by growing up in an environment of familial maltreatment. At the same time, I draw upon other approaches in response to particular challenges within the treatment. As a psychodynamic psychotherapist, two fundamental principles organize my attention. One is the assumption that adult behavior is the adaptive and cumulative outcome of the developing person's efforts to integrate his changing needs within the context of his familial and social environment. From this point of view, taking a personal and familial history is particularly important; as is the analysis of the patient's contemporary experience and behavior in light of his responses to abandonment, physical abuse, and problematic paternal love. While the present is far more than the re-enactment of the past, problematic behaviors are seen as heavily influenced by earlier developmental deficits and conflicts.

Another core belief highlights the importance of the therapeutic relationship as the curative medium within which change occurs. The patient's experience of acceptance in therapy provides the emotional safety to acknowledge and work through his competing needs for a secure interpersonal connection, on the one hand, and emotional autonomy, on the other. In the case of Paul, we were able to access powerful, destabilizing constellations of shame, and associated cognitions, through our close attention to his internal object ties to his parents, his re-enactments in the interpersonal world, and the transference-countertransference process. It is often through this medium that shame becomes accessible to therapeutic dialogue and amelioration.

TECHNICAL ISSUES IN TREATING MEN

From the beginning of my work as a psychotherapist it seemed apparent that there were any number of significant obstacles to men utilizing psychotherapy (Osherson & Krugman, 1994). Some of these are the aforementioned male subcultural biases against help-seeking and talking about vulnerability. Others involve the process of psychotherapy itself. For one thing, the doctor-patient model amplifies male anxieties related to power, control, being diminished, and being exposed to possible humiliation. For another, certain elements of traditional psychodynamic psychotherapy are likely to heighten a man's sense of vulnerability, intensifying concerns over "failing" to live up to the traditional male role. Thus, the emotionally "neutral" therapist who assumes a personally distant stance may intensify a man's anxiety over being judged, and fears of being critically evaluated by someone experienced as occupying a superior position. Other technical aspects of the psychodynamic tradition, such as the practice of responding to the patient's questions with the question "Why do you ask?" is likely to increase resistance, and promote control struggles at the outset of the treatment.

These and other perspectives from my work with men began to shape my approach to treatment. I assumed that embedded in the man's early questions were concerns about loss of control, safety, and mutual respect. Rather than expose these concerns prematurely, I found that a rather direct response to all reasonable inquiry fostered the building of a working alliance and increased the likelihood that my male patients would stay in treatment. My awareness of shame as a covert male concern also led me to "name the issue" as it became apparent within a man's narrative material, or in our relationship. By naming this powerful source of resistance and destabilization, I find that men are more likely to begin talking about their shameful experiences rather than reacting to them by hiding, acting out, or fleeing treatment. Finally, these issues seem best contained, particularly during the early phases of treatment, by adopting an intersubjective approach that acknowledges our effort to build a relationship, that is, long on empathy and short on penetrating interpretation.

CASE STUDY: PAUL

THE PRESENTING PROBLEM

Paul is a 41-year-old, single, white businessman who came into psychotherapy because he often felt quite depressed and worthless and experienced considerable despair over the prospect of living life without an intimate partner. He talked about feeling raw and vulnerable in everyday business dealings, and of the similarities between these experiences and the way he had felt in his family of origin. He said that he was troubled by great swings of mood and behavior that ranged from explosive confrontations with other men following a perceived or real slight, to fears of losing all his important relationships. While Paul no longer used drugs, he still drank, and actively pursued sex with male prostitutes on an episodic basis, which left him feeling deeply shamed and paranoid.

Paul is an athletic man whose emotional vulnerability reveals itself in his demeanor: he often looks away rather than make direct contact and carries himself in a slouch, minimizing his stature. He is of above average intelligence and has some hesitancy in his speech, reflecting underlying anxiety or conflict. He owns a small but successful business and has several important male friendships, some of which are quite volatile. His relationships with women are more problematic, all full of yearning, mistrust, and anger. He has a history of impulsive aggression with men and can become quite depressed.

Paul was born in a small midwestern city, the youngest of two sons of a prominent, powerful, yet brittle, man. He has only dim and distant memories of his mother who was unavailable to him as a small child, and remained cool and distant throughout his life. Soon after he was born, his mother suffered a mild stroke which required her hospitalization and several months of convalescence. He was cared for by an aunt and a nanny, and while the care seems to have been adequate, this event has had defining significance in his life. When his mother recovered, she was portrayed as a precious and fragile object that needed to be protected against the demands of her children. His father and brother "blamed" him for his mother's illness, and scapegoated him throughout his childhood. Paul's interest in his mother and demands upon her were experienced in the family as threats to her stability. He was physically beaten by his father with some frequency and, on several occasions, seriously abused, suffering visible bruises and broken bones. At the same time, he felt deeply attached and dependent upon his father, both admiring and fearing him.

Paul's childhood and adolescence were marked by his response to his home environment. Like many abused boys, he struggled with depression, self-destructive behaviors, and substance abuse. At the same time, his intelligence, friendliness, and athletic ability provided him with opportunities for success and social contact. By the time he had graduated from college, however, the cumulative drag of feeling unloved and feeling vulnerable to being hurt, the low self-esteem and rage that fueled his maladaptive behaviors, and his unstable mood states, had begun to isolate him and plunge him deeper into depression and substance abuse. He was able to build an independent adult life, though one that was rather isolated with the exception of his enmeshed relationship with his aging father. He yearned for intimacy with an accepting woman.

Paul's Psychotherapy

I began to see Paul twice a week in individual therapy. The therapy continued over a period of six years. There were several major issues that Paul brought to treatment. His poor self-esteem and difficulty regulating his own needs and behaviors contributed to a chronic, low level, depression that left him feeling empty and alone, overly dependent upon problematic relationships. He spoke of being "all entangled" with his aging father and mother. While having stopped using cocaine, Paul continued to use alcohol to manage his despair and, from time to time, while drinking, would engage in anonymous homosexual sex. He also reported that his professional life was troubled by his volatile temper, and he was prone to episodes of "road rage."

The account of the treatment that follows focuses closely upon Paul's experience of shame, as an underlying affect and motive for many of his problematic behaviors. During the six-year treatment, Paul made considerable progress. By the third year, much of his problematic behavior was under better control and his life was more stable. During the fourth year of treatment, Paul met and married a woman from his hometown. After much ambivalence, he terminated treatment after the sixth year.

The Struggle for Safety

Paul's intense vulnerability and need for acceptance was apparent from the first meeting. He was quite depressed. Things were not going well. His latest effort at romance had failed suddenly when his girlfriend had broken off their relationship and left town. He was drinking again, feeling quite hopeless about ever having a successful relationship with a woman. Along with his depression, shame was the most prominent of his feelings. He struggled with feelings of shame related to his sense of inadequacy and failure: to separate from his parents, to achieve a marriage, to keep himself under emotional control. He felt humiliated when he thought of his liaisons with male prostitutes. He hated his ruminations over the breakup of an unsatisfactory relationship.

Paul made little effort to conceal his ambivalence toward women. It was thinly disguised and readily talked about. At the same time, he was extremely suspicious of me. Men in his life were every bit as problematic as women. His father, whom he loved and idealized, had beaten him and favored his other brother. His brother had either bullied or ignored him. His professional relationships with other businessmen were volatile and combative. His previous experiences in therapy had not been successful ones. Despite this history, I wasn't prepared for his challenge to me in our second session.

Toward the end of our second hour, as we were contracting to begin psychotherapy he asked if I were gay. Surprised and taken off guard, I asked him to say more about his question. "I had a close friend in high school. I looked up to him, but he always busted my balls, teased me. I always wanted to be friends. Then it turned out that he was gay. I still wanted to be friends. When I didn't want to have sex with him, he dumped me. It felt like I wasn't important enough to him."

I asked, "I wonder if you're worried about some of the same kinds of issues between you and me?"

"I don't know what you want from me," he said. "You want my money. You say you want to help me but maybe you just want to humiliate me. I feel terrible about some of what I feel and do. I feel like a baby. You can just make a fool of me."

Feeling like I had a handle on the question I suggested that "it's probably not so easy to trust someone like me after experiences like these." I was again surprised when he said, "But I need to trust you; I need you, your help. I'm really screwed up about women. Its not much better with men. My relationship with both my mother and father are ones for the books. I need to deal with this. I don't really trust you, but I feel like I have no choice."

In an early session Paul said, "I feel very confused about women. This woman who I broke up with—we didn't like each other. But we dated for months; we slept with each other, and treated each other badly. Finally she broke some plans we had and I told her I didn't want to see her. She said "fine." I was home over the holiday weekend. I was so depressed I called a prostitute."

[T]: Is that why you called me?
[P]: Well, my primary care doc gave me your number months ago but I was afraid to see a man even though I knew I needed to.
[T]: A man who would listen?
[P]: I'm really angry at women. It embarrasses me to talk about it.

[T]: You think you can tell me about it?

[P]: I would have to trust you.

We struggled for months around these themes of need, trust, men, and women. Shame pervaded his every need. The intensity and overwhelming character of these feelings left him feeling internally raw and completely exposed. Needs for others would evoke feelings of shameful inadequacy along with defensive anger, on the one hand, and resentment over being so needy, on the other. Relationships with both men and women fell prey to this intense constellation of feelings. If Paul allowed himself to be drawn close toward another person, he would begin to experience powerful longings, increased vulnerability, and later, a sense of paranoia. These longings would press through his personal resolve not to get too close to anyone. He would begin to see the object of his need as a potentially threatening person. He had an exquisite sensitivity to slights, real and imagined. Since he felt so badly about himself, he could only imagine that other people, including me, wanted to be with him either to use him or humiliate him.

BUILDING AN ALLIANCE TO WORK ON SHAME

Initial Resistance

In Paul's case, much of the early work in therapy revolved around building a trustworthy treatment alliance in which he felt safe enough to disclose his fears of dependency and speak about the behaviors about which he felt ashamed. Initially, we engaged in a kind of emotional wrestling in which the frame of our treatment relationship was forged. First there were struggles over some of the concrete frame issues: when would we meet, how much would I charge him, what about missed sessions, telephone calls, etc. As these were settled, his anxiety focused on the limits of our relationship: how angry could he be with me; would I retaliate; how special was he to me? It was quite clear, early on, that our real, here-and-now relationship was subject to significant transferential distortions based in his early experiences with important male figures. To his credit, Paul was able to recognize this as well. Even when an exchange would get heated, he would usually be able to step back and say, "You know, I'm not really so angry at you about this. It's just that it feels like so many other times with other people who I trusted and who hurt me."

Around the frame issues I found it important to be direct. When we discussed my fee, Paul needed to know whether I was charging him full fee. I was inclined to explore the meaning of this with him before actually setting the fee. He found the ambiguity of this process intolerable. Later, the phrase "full fee" turned out to have many meanings, including "did I feel sorry for him" (he wanted me to but was humiliated by the thought that I might pity him); "was he man enough to pay the whole fee or did he need a break," and would I see him as "special." During one particular phase of treating in the second year, Paul began to compare my taking of money with his paying the male prostitute he saw from time to time. He was full of contempt. After listening to his insinuations and containing his anger/shame over having to pay to be cared for, I suggested that his needing me emotionally filled him with shame. He paused and was able to take in the interpretation. He went on to talk about his fury and disappointment that his parents should have left him so full of need.

Shame as a Defense

Where shame is as prominent as affect and defense, it is important to make room for it in the therapeutic dialogue early in the relationship. With Paul I was able to address it directly:

[T]: It seems hard for you to let me know about being out of control.
[P]: Well, I feel foolish. I think you'll think I'm a jerk.
[T]: The shame you feel about this stuff is the key to getting to the bottom of this. I know its hard to talk about embarrassing things but if we can get comfortable with the discomfort of it, tolerate it, we can probably make sense out of these experiences.
[P]: I'd have to trust you not to make a fool of me.
[T]: Yes, you would.

Making a place in the therapy for shameful feelings and behaviors provided Paul with considerable relief. Even naming the dreadful feeling as shame provided us with a point of reference. Trust became less of an abstract question; it now boiled down to whether I'd laugh at him or humiliate him like others had. Even as we established a way of talking about the shameful feelings and events of his life, moments would arise in which he would pull back warily and say, "What did you mean by that?" or "Are you laughing at me?"

These early phases in Paul's treatment are familiar to me from my work with many different types of men. A male patient's initial anxiety over needing another's help, of being vulnerable, and potentially humiliated, are common defensive concerns which are heightened by traditional male gender norms. Men are often more accustomed to revealing their vulnerable sides to women intimates. In that scenario, the man may maintain his sense of control by overt or covert feelings of detachment, superiority, or dominance. In any event, there may be enough emotional safety for a man to let down his guard, to cry, to be seen as not having it together. Being taken care of by a woman is traditionally more congruent for many men, particularly if it occurs in a sexualized context. To let down one's guard, to be in need, in the presence of another man is fraught with fantasies of psychological and even physical danger. Male socialization codes carry the implicit warnings that to let another man see one's weaknesses is to risk being put down and taken advantage of. At a deeper, often unexpressed level, males become anxious over homosexual concerns. Anxiety over being vulnerable with or being cared for by another man may also give rise to sexualized feelings or fears. In Paul's case, there were certain instances in which his dependent needs gave way to homosexual impulses that were acted out. At the same time, he was extremely conflicted about these feelings and became quite anxious when they arose in relation to me.

Paul's real experience in his family reflected these traditional male fears. His needs for parental care were often dismissed or violently rebuffed. In his fantasy life, his need for his father, his experiences of being humiliated by this man, became sexualized. His homoerotic fears were admixed with desire. In the course of treatment, he eventually was able to acknowledge wishes of being feminized, of being penetrated; if he were a woman, things wouldn't have been so hard. These feelings emerged slowly over time. More prominent and, in a sense, problematic was his eroticization of his dependency. Paul struggled to gain access to his disconnected homosexual longings. Along the way he acted them out under dangerous circumstances.

Paul's predicament reflects the two sets of forces that shaped his early life. First, the physical and emotional loss of his mother to the cerebral incident that followed his birth, engendered in him a deep and permanent sensitivity to loss and abandonment concerns. Fears associated with this early disruption of the mother-son connection resulted in an anxious and vigilant guard against being left, being blamed, or, for that matter, being in need. Second, Paul's disconnection from his mother and his sense that his need for her was harmful to her, left him narcissistically vulnerable, and easily wounded. As Paul talked of his early history, some of the painful yet soothing behaviors he'd engaged in as a child—chiefly, head banging and biting himself—took on new meaning for him. Connecting his current feelings with his near forgotten, but still embarrassing, childhood behaviors, produced an enhanced sense of cohesion and integrity, as if "connecting the dots" helped him feel more whole. It also gave us increased leverage in seeking out the contemporary versions of the self-soothing behaviors of his childhood. Not surprisingly, his predilection for cocaine and alcohol, his homosexual fantasies and liaisons, seem to have their origins in these early deficits.

Paul's earliest sense of shame probably had its origins in his early childhood. While the infant boy may not have had the cognitive capacity for true shame, his experience of not being emotionally received by his mother, of discovering that his basic needs were labeled as being "too much" for her (and probably were), laid the groundwork for a shame-sensitized sense of self. Feeling and believing this, my initial approach to his treatment was very sensitive to any narcissistic rebuff. My early stance toward him was largely empathic. I consistently recognized his behavior as reflecting his best efforts at coping with the cards he'd been given. I spoke openly and often about how painful, uncomfortable, and disappointing many of his experiences felt. I recognized his desire to be noticed by me and worried over. At times, however, he commented that my expressed dismay over how he had been raised left him feeling very confused. Sometimes he felt that I understood what his life had been like; at other times, he felt like he needed to defend his family and his self-esteem—against my empathic response to his deprivation.

This situation calls attention to one of the paradoxical aspects of treating shame-sensitive men. Relief from shame requires that a trusting context and the presence of an empathic other. The shame—often about threatening feelings—can be ameliorated to the extent that the man in question gains recognition and acceptance for his vulnerable states of feeling. As the therapist offers to name the unspoken pain or is empathic to an underlying fear or anxiety, the patient may feel flooded by the affect itself, shame over being seen, and anxious about being too close to the therapist. A slow, negotiated, process is required to tease apart these reactions to too much feeling. Successful titration of the intensity can result in a resolution of these tensions with considerable gain.

WORKING THROUGH THE SHAME

Paul and I wrestled over one thing or another for many months. In the course of these struggles, or by means of them, we established a trustworthy alliance. Paul came to feel that I was predictable, on his side, and not retaliatory—that I wasn't going to humiliate him or kick him out. As the therapy progressed, I learned more about the sources of his shame, and its disorganizing impact upon him. One major constellation of experience revolved around his relationships with other men. A second concerned his sexual behaviors. These, in turn, were rooted in his unresolved issues with his parents. Running through these and related issues was the question of self control, and control over his emotional states.

A Critical Constellation

One of the troubling aspects of Paul's public life centered on his reactivity to conflicts with other men. He reported becoming easily enraged when, at a business club meeting, someone would show signs of disrespect. Though he knew that he was overly sensitive, he found himself exploding on a regular basis. (These experiences of loss of control were, in themselves, quite embarrassing, and threatened his social standing and membership in important business settings.) He also spoke of other situations, such as one in which another driver would cut him off or beat him to a parking space. These encounters might also trigger a rage reaction and, occasionally, lead to violence.

As the therapy proceeded, we gradually uncovered the deeper structure of these humiliating incidents by revisiting them again and again. In retelling them, Paul desensitized himself while developing an enhanced perspective on these experiences. He became increasingly able to focus on the associations evoked by the memories. Not surprisingly, his associations led to a core of memories that included being beaten and being humiliated by his father. He believed that when he sought out his parents' attention, or would try to claim a special place, he'd be slapped down and "put in his place." Many of the angry encounters with men that he'd spoken about contained similar elements. A common scenario might involve him claiming his place (at a meeting, in a line, in a parking lot); someone, almost always a man, would challenge him (or so he thought). Many of these were competitive confrontations of a professional sort; others, however, were random occurrences on the road or in a store. Depending on how thin-skinned he felt, he would feel slighted, would imagine that the other was trying to put him down, or would feel the need to defend himself. He would then rise to the occasion fortified by an old resolution that he would never again let any man humiliate him.

Paul was deeply embarrassed by these events. Not only had he felt the fool on many occasions, he had been in several fistfights and arrested once. He felt immature and weak. Initially he was quite hesitant to talk about these incidents, expecting that I would mock him. Slipping into a paranoid mode, he worried that I would use his "rawness" to "get him."

In the repetitive nature of these encounters, Paul would experience himself at risk of being overwhelmed by feelings of not being as important as his adversary. He feared "losing his place," and perhaps his identity as a man. At times, in the treatment, this material would appear as competitive, male-male, Oedipal re-enactment. At other times, and perhaps more profoundly, the competitive element seemed less central than the dread of being overwhelmed by shame and losing self-cohesion. The prominence of his shame as a defense against deeper vulnerability points to the central role of shame in the larger transactional dynamic.

The defensive function of shame motivates hiding the wounded, or inadequate, self. Neutralizing shame requires increased awareness of situational cues, rising affective states, and increased affect tolerance. Feelings of embarrassment warn against impending exposure and become signals to avoid potentially shaming encounters. Paul learned to be increasingly aware of early signs of these feelings. With his growing awareness and increased sense of containment in treatment, he was able to forestall the preconscious rush from embarrassment to humiliation to rage. The threat of losing control of himself in public began to diminish.

Paul and I worked on this constellation of shame-laden schemas in relation to both contemporary encounters and historical associations. When he would bring in a fresh experience of losing his temper, or feeling provoked by a male rival, we utilized a cognitive restructuring approach to these encounters. Each was de-constructed and analyzed. What were the meanings embedded in the situation? What was in his best interest? What was the motivation of his rival? How could he have handled it differently? At what point did he begin to feel shamed? We anticipated social situations where he was likely to be tested; we rehearsed random encounters (e.g., conflict over parking space) with guided imagery. The antidote to shame is safe exposure. Each time we identified the shaming moment and talked about it, we de-toxified it. Each bit of understanding, each contextualization of his experience helped to diminish his triggerlike reactivity.

As Paul gained mastery over the threat of humiliation in the present (and in the transferential relationship) he gained more access to childhood memories of abuse. He recalled memories of times in the past when his father or brother had humiliated him, with mockery and physical punishment. In the aftermath of these instances, he would silently comfort himself with the belief that when he was bigger no one would do this to him. Beneath this, however, was the painful belief that only a bad son would be treated so badly by his powerful, idealized father. We accessed this configuration of memory by recounting several incidents in which he had been beaten and humiliated. In doing this, I adopted a technique used in treating other types of traumatic events (Rothbaum & Foa, 1996). In essence, a narrative script of the incident is developed by the patient with help from the therapist. This can be as simple as a tape of the patient's account, a transcript of same, or the patient's own written or dictated account. Once an account has been created, it is reviewed on multiple occasions. In Paul's case, much resolution was achieved by means of his organizing his memories of abuse and recounting his experiences to me. These were tales that had never been told; tales in which he believed himself to be unjustly punished, on the one hand, and guilty on the other. As in the above cognitive restructuring, the abuse memories began to take on somewhat different meanings. The shame embedded within these memories made it initially quite hard to focus on them. Paul was deeply embarrassed to have me see him as a helpless boy being whipped with his pants down. He was ashamed that his father would have treated him this way. As to whether he deserved the whippings, the gradual retellings allowed our conjoined adult egos to answer "No." My interest in him, my empathy for his historical situation, and my focus on shame as a trigger in the present, began to transform the shame from a major defense to an affect associated with painful memories, as well as a signal affect in social encounters.

Paul was able to use therapy to revise his view of the abusive treatment he received at the hands of his father and brother. His ability to do this involved the de-idealization of his paternal introject. He became able to use his identification with me to support his growing psychological differentiation from his father.

EMERGING PRIDE

In the wake of this work and the resolution that seemed to accompany it, Paul began to experience a sense of pride. Pride, the counter to shame, emerged as he gained trust in the strength of his connection and identification with me. Using our relationship as a foundation, he was able to feel and believe that he did not deserve the maltreatment he'd received; that there was "nothing about him" that would merit such treatment. Pride can reflect a sense of accomplishment and pleasure in attaining an idealized experience of self. For Paul, it was the pleasure of feeling and trusting his own experience, without being governed by fears that his independence would destroy his relationship with his father (and perhaps, actually destroy his father).

In male development pride can also reflect an inflated sense of self-sustained by compensatory behaviors and attitudes. This false pride is supported by posturing and braggadocio rather than competence pleasure (Broucek, 1979). In the past, Paul had been quite vulnerable to prideful showdowns with other men. As he felt less shame-ridden and guilty over his aggression toward his father, these showdowns diminished dramatically. He would report feelings of pride when his sense of self-control enabled him to negotiate a charged emotional situation, or resist the temptation to engage in behaviors he knew would leave him feeling humiliated. Increasingly, he was able to notice my pleasure in his success.

SHAME IN THE TRANSFERENCE-COUNTERTRANSFERENCE

Our therapeutic relationship evolved through a series of tests, errors, rescues, and confrontations. Weeks of solid therapeutic work would intensify our relationship. Paul's ordinary sensitivity to slights would take on an exquisite edge. Inevitably he and I would misunderstand something, try to untangle it, only to become ensnared in a deeper sense of misunderstanding. These *disconnections*, as we came to call them, would frighten Paul, regenerating a pervasive sense of mistrust and hopelessness. As we came to understand them, these disconnects seemed generated by Paul's deepening sense of dependence upon me.

In the course of four years, I had become the idealized good father upon whom Paul could rely on without fear of humiliation and punishment. He spoke of needing to depend on me to see him through to a sense of secure manhood, to help with his career, to coach in his marriage. Yet as his conscious need grew, he came to re-experience how dangerous and humiliating dependency upon a man could be. To the degree I was subject to distorting paternal transferences, Paul would become increasingly anxious and even paranoid about my intentions and behaviors. An ordinary billing error might again be taken as a sign that I was "messing with him." He spoke of "having to eat it," paying me even when the amount due didn't seem right to him. It was too risky to take me on; his anger toward me frightened him and needed to be warded off.

As we continued to sort out Paul's expectations of treachery and aggression and work them through, he became more aware of his ambivalent feelings about becoming more autonomous. Paul did, indeed, love me, and did not want to leave me. There were even moments when he could acknowledge his homosexual impulses toward me. At the same time, he felt he needed to leave me, stand on his own, and become independent. Not so much because it was "unmanly" to be dependent, but because he needed to know that he could handle the vicissitudes of emotional life on his own. During this phase of the treatment that lasted more than a year, we became aware that the paternal transference toward me had been replaced by an increasingly maternal one.

I was also aware of the depth of my own feelings toward Paul's deep and honest struggle to emerge. I was often moved by his hard work and grudging persistence. His growth and struggle to separate himself from the humiliating attachment to his parents won my admiration. I could feel my own pull to step into that damaged psychological space. I worked to keep my own ambitions to be "too helpful" in check. He had allowed me inside his defenses, into the heart of his problematic parental identifications. I knew how costly it was for him to need me as he did. At times the alternative to remaining connected with me seemed to be a slow slide into degradation and despair. I had to pay careful attention to my impulses to push him out of the nest because it did seem like he *should* be able to stand on his own by now. I wondered about my own countertransference in this regard. There was the risk that I might humiliate him by focusing too much on the anaclitic relationship between us. I became aware of my own attachment needs were a factor in the relationship: I didn't want him to leave; he would always need me; he could always come back.

In the course of time, however, Paul and I developed a plan to help him wean himself. We went from weekly meetings to biweekly meetings and then to monthly meetings. These continued for more than 10 months; he would call in between as often as he needed. His life was now quite on track. After this period, he terminated treatment.

SUMMARY

I have presented my treatment of Paul in order to discuss the treatment of shame in psychotherapy with men. My experience with Paul and other men from similar backgrounds, affirms and extends the wisdom of Helen Block Lewis' observation that unacknowledged shame is an obstacle to psychotherapeutic treatment. It is also often true that acknowledged shame protects the therapeutic alliance and deepens the treatment. Men often have a difficult time learning to integrate their shame experiences so that they are less vulnerable and less volatile when challenged or revealed. Conducting the business of psychotherapy with an eye toward male shame vulnerability diminishes the likelihood of giving offense before the treatment has even begun. Learning to de-code the language of shame reveals much about men in treatment.

This chapter details the treatment of shame in the life of a man who experienced considerable childhood maltreatment. His problems with shame are built upon the normative male socialization experience. He shares with many men a deep shame sensitivity that reflects how difficult it is for men to find safety in their relationships. Focusing on the treatment of shame in the psychotherapy of men provides a rich inroad into the hidden self of all men.

REFERENCES

Alonso, A., & Rutan, S. (1988). The experience of shame and the restoration of self respect in group therapy. *International Journal of Group Psychotherapy, 39,* 1.

Bergman, S. J. (1991). *Men's psychological development: A relational perspective* (Work in progress no. 48). Wellesley, MA: Stone Center.

Blatt, S. J. (1990). Interpersonal relatedness and self-definition: Two personality configurations and their implication for psychopathology and psychotherapy. In J. Singer (Ed.), *Repression and dissociation: Implications for personality theory psychopathology and health* (pp. 299–335). Chicago: University of Chicago Press.

Brody, L. (1985). Gender differences in emotional development: A review of themes and research. *Journal of Personality, 53*(2), 102–149.

Broucek, F. J. (1979). Efficacy in infancy. *International Journal of Psychoanalysis, 60,* 311–316.

Broucek, F. J. (1982). Shame and its relationship to early narcissistic developments. *International Journal of Psychoanalysis, 63,* 369–378.

Cicchetti, D., & Toth, S. L. (1991). *Internalizing and externalizing expressions of dysfunction: Rochester Symposium on Developmental Psychopathology.* Hillsdale, NJ: Erlbaum.

Fossum, M. A., & Mason, M. J. (1986). *Facing shame: Families in recovery.* New York: Norton.

Gross, C. A. (1996). *Shame—the self and relatedness.* Unpublished dissertation, Fielding Institute, Santa Barbara, CA.

Hibbard. S. (1994). An empirical study of the differential roles of libidinous and aggressive shame components in normality and pathology. *Psychoanalytic Psychology, 11*(4), 449–474.

Hoblitzelle, W. (1987). Differentiating and measuring shame and guilt: therelation between shame and depression. In H. B. Lewis, (Ed.), *The role of shame in symptom formation.* Hillsdale, NJ: Earlbaum.

Horowitz, M. (1981). Self-righteous rage and the attribution of blame. *Archives of General Psychiatry, 38,* 1233–1237.

Izard, C. (1977). *Human emotions.* New York: Plenum Press.

Kinston, W. (1983). A theoretical context for shame. *International Journal of Psychoanalysis, 64,* 213–226.

Krugman, S. (1995). The role of shame in male development. In R. Levant & W. Pollack (Eds.), *A new psychology of men*. New York: Basic Books.

Lansky, M. R. (1992). *Fathers who fail: Shame and psychopathology in the family system*. Hillsdale, NJ: Analytic Press.

Lazur, R. F., & Majors, R. (1995). Men of color: Ethnocultural variations of male gender role strain. In R. Levant & W. Pollack (Eds.), *A new psychology of men*. New York: Basic Books.

Lewis, H. B. (1971). *Shame and guilt in neurosis*. Hillsdale, NJ: Erlbaum.

Lewis, H. B. (Ed.). (1987). *The role of shame in symptom formation*. Hillsdale, NJ: Erlbaum.

Malatesta-Magai, C. (1991). Emotional socialization: Its role in personality and developmental psychopathology. *Internalizing and externalizing expressions of dysfunction: Rochester Symposium on Developmental Psychopathology*. Hillsdale, NJ: Erlbaum.

Morrison, A. P. (1989). *Shame: The under side of narcissism*. Hillsdale, NJ: Analytic Press.

Nathanson, D. L. (1987). A timetable for shame. In D. L. Nathanson (Ed.), *The many faces of shame* (pp. 1–63). New York: Guilford Press.

O'Neil, J. M. Helms, B., Gable, R. K., David, L., & Wrightsman, L. S. (1986). Gender-role conflict scale: College men's fear of femininity. *Sex Roles, 14*, 335-350.

Osherson, S. (1992). *Wrestling with love: How men struggle with intimacy, women, children, parents and each other*. New York: Ballantine Books.

Osherson, S. & Krugman, S. (1990). Men, shame, and psychotherapy. *Psychotherapy, 27*(3), 327–339.

Pleck, J. H. (1981). *The myth of masculinity*. Cambridge, MA: MIT Press.

Pynoos, R. S., Steinberg, A. M., & Goenjian, A. (1996). Traumatic stress in childhood and adolescence: Recent developments and current controversies. In B. Van der Kolk, A. McFarlane, & L. Weisath (Eds.), *Traumatic stress: The effects of overwhelming experience on mind, body, and society*. New York: Guilford Press.

Rothbaum, B. A., & Foa, E. (1996). Cognitive-behavioral therapy for post traumatic stress disorder. In B. Van der Kolk, A. McFarlane, & L. Weisath (Eds.), *Traumatic stress: The effects of overwhelming experience on mind, body, and society*. New York: Guilford Press.

Scheff, T. J. (1988). Shame and conformity: The deference-emotion system. *American Sociological Review, 53*, 395–406.

Severino, S. K., McNutt, E. R., & Feder, S. L. (1987). Shame and the development of autonomy. *Journal of the American Academy of Psychoanalysis, 15*(1), 93–106.

Tomkins, S. S. (1987). Shame. In D. L. Nathanson (Ed.), *The many faces of shame* (pp. 133–161). New York: Norton.

Wright, F. (1987). Men, shame and antisocial behavior: A psychodynamic perspective. *Group, 11*(4), 238–246.

Wright, F., O'Leary, J., & Balkin, J. (1989). Shame, guilt, narcissism and depression: Correlates and sex differences. *Psychoanalytic Psychology, 6*(2), 217–230.

Wurmser, L. (1981). *The mask of shame*. Baltimore: John Hopkins University Press.

CHAPTER 9

Gender Role Stress and Male Erectile Disorder

Larry A. Morris

A T LEAST once during his lifespan nearly every male will find himself unable to get an erection. Most males who experience difficulties with achieving or maintaining an erection feel emasculated and ashamed. Even males who have no history of an erectile dysfunction often become panicky and desperate when they experience a "failure" for the first time. Males who seek professional help regarding erection problems often present as anxious, depressed, and unable to understand how "it" could have happened to them.

In spite of most men's fears that one experience of so-called impotency is the death-knell for their sexual life, isolated episodes of not being able to achieve an erection or losing an erection during sexual activities are common. Solitary or infrequently occurring erection problems do not necessarily mean that a man has a sexual dysfunction. In fact, a total absence of erection is rare except for specific medical conditions. More common is an occasional loss of erection as a function of a variety of situational factors.

Historically, males who experience problems in achieving an erection have been labeled impotent. A man who has never succeeded in completing an attempted coitus has been referred to as experiencing *primary impotency*. While this condition exists, it is rare. Mostly, erectile problems occur following a history of successful attempts at intercourse. The historical term for this condition is *secondary impotency*. For most males, any loss of sexual power can be virtually overwhelming and the term impotency seems foreboding. Fortunately, these terms are increasingly being replaced by diagnostic descriptors absent an association of sex with power. For example, the *Diagnostic and Statistical Manual of Mental Disorders-Fourth Edition (DSM-IV)* (American Psychiatric Association, 1994), describes male erectile dysfunction, generally, as a sexual arousal disorder involving a persistent or recurrent inability to achieve or maintain an erection sufficiently firm enough to allow for the initiation and/or completion of sexual activities.

Since males are culturally trained to view sex as related to power, manhood, and some form of performance, many men also learn to be anxious about not living up to cultural expectations. For example, in a recent survey of sexual behavior in America, Michael, Gagnon, Laumann, and Kolata (1994) found that while women, in general, appear more affected by sexual problems than men, males report more anxiety about performance and climaxing too early. And anxiety is thought to be the most frequently occurring factor related to temporary, situational erectile difficulties and the tendency for these episodes to eventually develop into a more persistent problem.

This chapter provides the clinician with gender-appropriate information and skills to evaluate and effectively treat men who present with some form of erectile problem. The proposed treatment approach is based on men's studies and clinical experience suggesting that a major component in the development of sexual problems by males emanates primarily from the male socialization process. Central to this perspective is that anxiety springs from some form of gender role strain or conflict related to the development of masculinity and male sexuality.

GENDER ROLE STRAIN, ANXIETY, AND MALE ERECTILE DISORDERS

Most clinicians find that anxiety related to sexual performance is a major factor in erectile dysfunctions, but analogue studies conducted in laboratory settings suggest that anxiety may only be a coconspirator. For example, Barlow, Sakheim, and Beck (1983) found that subjects who were told they would most likely receive an electrical shock if they did not achieve an adequate level of sexual arousal while watching a film with explicit sexual scenes (anxiety-inducing condition), produced a higher level of sexual arousal, as measured by a penile strain gauge, than a group in a noncontingent shock situation and a no-shock control group. Anxiety did not seem to produce a negative effect on sexual arousal for men in this study. In a follow-up study, men with a history of sexual dysfunctions responded to contingent and noncontingent shock threat conditions with less sexual arousal than men without a reported history of sexual dysfunctions (Beck & Barlow, 1984). These findings suggest that performance anxiety may have more of a negative impact on already sexually dysfunctional men than on men who appear to be sexually functional. Other studies also suggest that anxiety-inducing erotic films increase sexual arousal in sexually functional men, while producing lower levels of sexual arousal in sexually dysfunctional men (see Beck, 1988).

While anxiety appears to be present in most sexual dysfunctions, cognitive variables also play an important role and may actually set the stage for so-called performance anxiety. Barlow (1986) proposes that sexually functional men establish a cognitive feedback loop consisting of an accurate representation of the cues. This includes erectile responses, positive affect, a perception of control, and an increasingly efficient focus on the erotic stimuli, in spite of autonomic arousal related to anxiety. On the other hand, sexually dysfunctional men tend to establish a negative feedback loop consisting of an inaccurate representation of cues, expectations, and erections. Negative affect, a perceived lack of control, and an increasingly efficient focus on non-erotic issues, such as the perceived negative consequences of not being able to perform sexually, follow. In my experience in working with men with sexual dysfunctions, nearly all report worry about performance, concern over the consequences of not performing adequately, and negative affect associated with a perceived lack of performance.

Barlow's model differentiates between the cognitive processes of sexually functional and dysfunctional men, but his model does not address the issue of why some men, with no history of sexual problems, suddenly succumb to irrational fears and anxiety following an isolated episode with an erectile problem, while other so-called sexually functional men take this transitory problem in stride and do not engage a destructive cycle of anticipatory anxiety leading to a more persistent sexual problem. The answer lies deep within the male socialization experience.

Herb Goldberg, in *The Hazards of Being Male* (1976) and *The New Male* (1979), warned that the myth of masculine privilege and power was misleading men into believing that traditional masculinity was healthy masculinity. He encouraged men to free themselves from a pattern of self-destructive stereotypic ideas and behavior associated with predefined masculine roles. In *The Myth of Masculinity*, Joseph Pleck (1981) criticized the theoretical perspective that men have an inherent need to develop a gender role identity based upon traditional ideas about the masculine role. This concept, known as the *Gender Role Identity Paradigm*, is based on the notion that a relatively stable masculine essence exists and that a male's need to achieve a masculine identity is met only to the extent he assimilates the traditional ideas about and norms regulating the male gender role. Historically, avoiding femininity, restrictive emotionality, seeking achievement and status, self-reliance, aggression, homophobia, and nonrelational attitudes toward sexuality are commonly considered the essence of traditional male role norms (see Levant et al., 1992).

Since Pleck (1981) found little support from research studies for the Gender Role Identity Paradigm, he proposed, instead, the *Gender Role Strain Paradigm*. This concept is based on the notion that gender identity is not inherent and stable but socially constructed and subject to change. As such, gender roles are defined by prevailing stereotypes and norms that are communicated to children by the various socialization agents in the child's social milieu. Being socially constructed, gender roles often are contradictory and inconsistent. Pleck's paradigm proposes that most people violate gender roles, even in the face of strong condemnation and other negative consequences, but males are more severely punished for violating gender roles than are females. And some males tend to overconform to gender roles, fearing any type of infraction (see Garnets & Pleck, 1979; Pleck, 1981).

Using Pleck's Gender Role Strain Paradigm as a foundation, James O'Neil and his associates propose that many men actually experience a conflict with traditional gender roles (O'Neil, 1981a, 1981b, 1982, 1990; O'Neil & Egan, 1992a, 1992b, 1992c; O'Neil, Egan, Owen, & Murry, 1993; O'Neil & Fishman, 1992; O'Neil, Fishman, & Kinsella-Shaw, 1987; O'Neil, Helms, Gable, David, & Wrightsman, 1986). They define gender role conflict as a psychological state in which socialized gender roles have negative consequences on the person or others. They propose that gender role conflict is a multidimensional and complex concept that is experienced at four overlapping levels: cognitive (restrictive views of gender roles), affective (emotional turmoil about masculinity and femininity), behavioral (actual conflict experienced with masculinity-femininity as we interact with ourselves and others), and unconscious (intrapsychic and repressed conflicts with masculinity-femininity). According to this perspective, gender role conflict occurs when men deviate from traditional gender role norms; attempt to meet or fail to meet masculine gender role norms; observe discrepancies between their real self-concept and concepts based on idealized gender role stereotypes; devalue, restrict, or violate themselves; experience devaluations, restrictions, or violations from others; and devalue restrict, or violate others as a function of adhering to gender role stereotypes.

In a recent review of the research literature associated with the development of masculinity, Pleck (1995) found both critics of and data supporting his perspective that traditional masculinity ideology is a major factor in male role strain and the concomitant problems many males experience. He writes, " . . . by shaping the gender expectations that men apply to themselves (and others apply to men) and by influencing how discrepancies from these expectations are experienced, masculinity ideology is an essential cofactor in male role strain. It also promotes trauma, inhibits the working-through of trauma, and leads men to persist in dysfunctional behavior" (p. 21). A comprehensive review of the research on men's gender role conflict by O'Neil, Good, and Holmes (1995) also revealed evidence that there are relationships between men's conflict with their gender roles and many psychologically negative outcomes such as anxiety, depression, lower self-esteem, marital dissatisfaction, stress, negative attitudes toward help-seeking, and sexual coercion. Clearly, the gender role strain or the gender role conflict position is that men need to prove their manhood because men are socialized to believe that their masculinity is something they have to prove. Proving manhood in the traditional sense can bring lots of grief to many men. Nowhere is this more true than in the development and validation of traditional ideas about masculine sexuality.

American culture embraces the Judeo-Christian dogma that all sexual behavior is sinful and prohibited, except procreational sexual activities by married heterosexuals, but conflicting messages encouraging various types of nonrelational sexual behavior, especially for heterosexual males, also abound. This confusion and misinformation about sexuality are transmitted through various agents of Western society in a process Morris (1997) describes as the "sociocultural abuse of sexuality" (see also: Bolton, Morris, & MacEachron, 1989). This model proposes that sexuality is a naturally occurring developmental factor existing from conception forward throughout the lifecycle. The sociocultural abuse of sexuality model also proposes a continuum of developmental environments that range from the promotion of normalized sexual development in both genders to approaches that are detrimental and significantly increase the probability of future dysfunctional sexual responses. This formulation rejects the notion that there is an essential masculine sexuality attached to naturally occurring sexual responses that is inherent in each man and must at some point be actualized. The sociocultural abuse of sexuality perspective is that sexuality is a developmental variable molded by many forces, especially culturally sanctioned notions about and expectations based upon gender role stereotypes.

Accepting the proposition that sexuality is nothing more than just another developmental variable waiting to be nurtured or abused provides the opportunity to design a social environment to foster, rather than hinder, the development of healthy sexual attitudes and behavior. Instead, social, political, and religious agendas provide the foundation for attitudes toward sexuality in Western society. Sadly, most of this "information" about sex is based on fears, myths, and gender-role stereotypes. Bernie Zilbergeld (1992) identifies many of the culturally driven myths many males believe about their sexuality. For example, males are taught that their essence is linked to their penis; it is not enough to just have a penis but you must have a big one that stands ready at all times to perform spectacular sexual feats. Morris (1997) refers to these exaggerated gender role expectations as the "Birth of Superpenis." Gary Brooks (1995) also points out that men are culturally conditioned to seek out "trophy" women (exceptionally beautiful young women who, once won, become symbols of a man's sexual prowess) and use sexual performance as a measuring stick for their masculinity. Similarly, Krugman (1995) connects normative male socialization experiences with anxiety and strong shame responses about sexual matters, especially premature ejaculation, size of penis, and erectile problems.

The existence of this pattern of myths, misinformation, and unrealistic expectations related to masculinity and sexuality in so many men who seek therapy for sexual problems supports the abuse of sexuality perspective and Pleck's (1981) argument that role strain results from the cultural expectation that males conform to an impossibly narrow definition of masculinity. David Lisak (1991) suggests the term *self-mutilation* to describe this tragic endpoint of the male child's masculine identification. He writes, "Masculine identification emerges as the expression of a relatively narrow range of experience and behavior. This narrowness tends to entrench distortions in personality by arbitrarily limiting what can be expressed and by precluding the possibility of embracing the full range of human experience and behavior" (p. 246).

Thus, the foundation for future problems with sexuality, especially erectile problems, is laid early on in the male socialization process. As Masters and Johnson (1970) noted, "From his initial heterosexual performance through the continuum of his sexual expression, every man constantly assumes a cultural challenge to his potency" (p. 168). William Betcher and William Pollack (1995) also warn, "By turning sex into a competitive Olympic event, men are more likely to fall prey to impotence and, even more commonly, to become sexually dissatisfied" (p. 197). Male sexual disorders appear to be the hernia of masculine gender role strain.

TOWARD RELIEVING THE STRESS AND RESTORING ERECTIONS

The primary focus of the proposed evaluation and treatment plan is on the male socialization experience and its negative consequences on male sexuality. Of special concern is the sexual conditioning that leads men to believe that much of their status as a "real man" is contingent on their ability to produce a throbbing hard penis regardless of the conditions. The proposed model incorporates gender role sensitive or gender role psychotherapy concepts in which major goals are increasing flexibility in male role attitudes and behavior (see Brooks, 1990; Brooks & Silverstein, 1995; Solomon, 1982), reconstructing masculinity (Levant, 1995; Levant & Kopecky, 1995; Levant & Pollack, 1995), and reconstructing male heterosexuality (Morris, 1997). Also molded into the treatment plan are well-established therapeutic techniques proposed by William Masters and Virginia Johnson (Masters & Johnson, 1966, 1970, 1976; Masters, Johnson, & Kolodny, 1985, 1988) and elaborated upon by noted sex therapists such as Helen Singer Kaplan (1974, 1975, 1979) and Bernie Zilbergeld (1992). As a composite they produce a comprehensive and gender-appropriate approach to treating male erectile problems.

THE EVALUATION PROCESS

RULE OUT MEDICAL FACTORS

Most males who experience erectile problems seek medical advice initially from their family physician or a medical specialist, such as a urologist. If no medical problem is detected, referrals are then made by the physician to appropriate practitioners. Other males recognize that their erectile problems are probably related to a nonmedical issue and seek help directly from mental health practitioners, especially therapists known to specialize in sexual disorders. It is recommended that males who report erectile problems to a nonmedical practitioner be referred to their family physician or a medical specialist, such as a urologist or endocrinologist, for a physical examination before embarking on a nonmedical treatment program. Common medical conditions known to have a negative effect on the erectile response in some males are heart disease, diabetes, and various hormonal imbalances.

Rule Out Alcohol and Other Drugs

While some males find that the moderate use of alcohol or other drugs may be relaxing and actually enhance their sexual experiences, alcohol and most other drugs have a negative effect on judgment about sexual partners and behavior, sexual desire, and the physiology related to the human sexual response. This is especially the case with the heavy or regular use of any intoxicating or mind-altering substance. It is not uncommon for the first sexual miscue to occur following a bout with heavy use of alcohol and/or other drugs. Once this miscue occurs, gender role strain or conflict factors soon come into play. A number of prescription drugs are also known to affect sexual functioning adversely in some men. Some of the most common are medications for high blood pressure, depressive disorders, and anxiety.

Assess Development of Sexuality and Gender Role Strain/Conflict

Structured Clinical Interview

In order to determine the level of gender role strain or conflict associated with sexual responses, a detailed sexual history must be obtained. While this may seem like an easy task because most males appear eager to talk about sex, obtaining accurate and complete information from males about the development of their sexuality can be difficult. For example, many males appear reluctant to reveal sexual experiences that they consider inconsistent with the traditional male role. And most males think of their sexual history as beginning with the first time they "got laid," and ending with their current sexual problem. A structured clinical interview format can assist in this regard. It is helpful to request sexual information within a developmental framework, starting with early childhood curiosity and experimentation experiences and proceeding sequentially into the person's present age category. Within this structured format, clients can be guided into providing sensitive personal information they might otherwise be reluctant to disclose. Examples of the variety of information to be explored are presented in Table 9.1.

Evaluation Instruments

In addition to obtaining information through a clinical interview, questionnaires and inventories can be used. Although most questionnaires used to assess male gender roles or norms have been developed as research

Table 9.1
Guidelines for the Assessment of Sexuality and
Gender Role Strain/Conflict

Sociocultural Messages

1. Sexual attitudes and behavior exhibited by family members and other persons important to the person's socialization experiences
2. Sources for and type of information about sexual matters such as parents, other adults, peers, magazines, books, movies, television
3. Religious teachings about sexual behavior
4. Uncomfortable or inappropriate sexual experiences initiated by others

Ideas and Feelings about Sexual Matters

1. First awareness of and feelings about anything he considers related to "sex"
2. Sexual fantasies
3. Sexual satisfaction and preferences
4. Sex and marriage
5. Sex and infidelity
6. Attitudes toward women and sex
7. Attitudes toward men and sex
8. Self-concept as it relates to his sexual feelings and activities

Sexual Experiences

1. Childhood curiosity and exploration activities
2. Masturbation, including age of first autoerotic experience, fantasies, and frequency of subsequent masturbatory activities
3. Dating experiences
4. First consensual heterosexual experiences including age of first experience, partner, and frequency of subsequent heterosexual experiences
5. Number of sexual partners
6. Homosexual experiences

Problem Areas

1. Sexually transmitted diseases
2. History of problems with sexual functioning
3. Previous counseling for sex related matters

instruments and continue to evolve as data are collected, the Gender Role Conflict Scale (GRCS) and the Male Role Norms Inventory (MRNI) show promise in assisting the clinician in assessing men's attitudes toward gender roles. These and the other instruments described in Table 9.2 are especially helpful in assessing sexuality and/or attitudes toward gender roles. An excellent source for additional tests associated with the assessment of gender roles is Beere (1990).

Table 9.2
Instruments for Assessing Sexuality and Gender Roles

Overall Sexual Information

1. *Sexual Adjustment Inventory.* Designed to obtain sexual information from couples in preparation for a marital and/or sexual treatment plan (Stuart, Stuart, Maurice, & Szasz, 1975)
2. *Wilson Sexual Fantasy Questionnaire.* Designed to assess an individual's fantasies associated with a wide range of sexual activity within four themes: Exploratory, Intimate, Impersonal, and Sado-Masochistic (Gosselin & Wilson, 1980)

Attitudes toward Women

1. *Attitudes toward Women Scale.* Designed to measure an individual's attitudes toward women and their roles associated with several areas, including vocational, educational, intellectual, freedom and independence, dating, sexual behavior, and marital relationships (Spence & Helmreich, 1972, 1978a, 1978b)

Gender Roles

1. *Gender Role Conflict Scale (GRCS).* Designed to assess men's degree of comfort or conflict in specific gender role conflict situations (O'Neil, Helms, Gable, David, & Wrightsman, 1986; see also O'Neil, Good, & Holmes, 1995)
2. *Male Role Norms Inventory (MRNI).* Designed to assess absolute role norms associated with seven areas: Avoidance of Femininity, Homophobia, Self-Reliance, Aggression, Achievement/Status, Attitudes Toward Sex, and Restrictive Emotionality (Levant et al., 1992)

Note: Copies of the current version of the GRCS can be obtained from: James O'Neil, School of Family Studies, UBox 58, University of Connecticut, Storrs, CT 06269. The MRNI with scoring instructions is available at a nominal cost from: Ronald F. Levant, Dean, Center for Psychological Studies, Nova Southeastern University, 3301 College Avenue, Fort Lauderdale, FL 33314.

Men's responses to this type of structured clinical interview with a few specialized questionnaires will provide valuable information regarding their level of acceptance of socialized gender roles and the degree and type of strain or conflict they experience regarding sexual matters. This information can then be used to develop an individualized treatment plan to assist in resolving gender role conflict, reducing stress, and resolving erectile problems.

THE TREATMENT PLAN

LEARNING A DIFFERENT LANGUAGE

Many men display an inability to correctly identify, name, and verbally describe their feelings. This condition, commonly referred to as *alexithymia,* often leaves men emotionally isolated from loved ones and themselves (Krystal, 1979; Levant, 1992, 1995; Levant & Kelly, 1989; Sifneos, 1967). Men who overcome alexithymia by learning to identify and express their emotions, especially feelings of vulnerability, frequently show improvement in a number of physical and psychological health areas (Levant & Kopecky, 1995). A similar language problem exists associated with men's ability to correctly identify and describe certain aspects of their sexuality, especially as they relate to erections and sexual intercourse. Most terms used by men when they refer to males with an erectile problem have strong negative connotations and do not accurately reflect the nature of the problem. For example, besides being called impotent, men with erectile problems are often called wimps, pussies, little boys, no-dicks, inadequate, failures, and other equally derogatory terms.

Men also use terms reflecting a belief that males can control their penis to perform sex. *Performance anxiety* is a common term used by professionals to explain why men fail to perform. Through the gender role socialization process, men have learned to believe that their penis is the center of the universe and it should be paraded around in all of its throbbing hard glory. If sex were a circus, the penis would be the star attraction, always thrilling spectators with death-defying acts of remarkable skill and endurance.

Like alexithymia, this language problem related to sexuality is a result of gender-role socialization experiences. It can also be overcome by learning a new language. The first step is for professionals to correct their own descriptions of erectile problems. For example, *impotency* should be banished forever from the therapeutic lexicon. Replace it with less harmful and more accurate descriptors such as *sexual problem, partial erection,* or *no erection.* Remember, the term *impotence* is from the Latin *posse,* meaning *to be able.* To be *potent* means to have authority and power. For males, impotent means having no sexual power. Note that the use of loss-of-power terminology is associated only with male sexual behavior. We do not refer to women who are unable to produce clitoral erections as impotent. Since gender role socialization emphasizes that real men have power, especially sexual power, the loss of that power seems to have warranted the term *impotent.* This harmful gender role distortion about power and sexuality must be corrected. Although many references to impotency in the professional literature are being replaced with less prejudicial nomenclature, many researchers and health care providers continue to refer to erectile problems as impotency. And most men still use the term as though it accurately reflects their sexual problem. It does not.

The next step is to help men understand that the terms that most males use to describe sexual problems are part of the problem and then teach them a language to more accurately talk about their sexual problems. Guide men away from harmful and inaccurate language to more accurate descriptions of the problem. Three examples follow:

Impotency

"Doc, I think I am impotent."

"What happened to make you think that you're impotent?"

"I want to have sex but I keep losing my erection."

"I see, you want to have sex but you are having problems with your erection. We used to call this impotency but we don't anymore because impotency means not having power and having problems with an erection has nothing to do with power. So, it might be more helpful if we talk about your loss of erections without using the term impotence. Let's just call it what it is, a problem with maintaining an erection. That way we can figure out what is causing the problem without having to worry about power or the loss of it."

Performance

"No matter what I did I just couldn't get it up. She was ready and willing and I just couldn't perform."

"Lots of men think that they have to perform in bed and with that kind of pressure they sometimes have trouble with their erections. Let's start by not calling sex a performance and take the pressure off. After all, sex really doesn't have anything to do with staging a performance. Let's call it something else like having intercourse or making love."

Failure and Inadequacy

"I felt like such a failure. I didn't know what to do because I never had trouble with erections before. I guess I am really inadequate after all."

"You are right about having trouble with your erection, but this does not mean that you are a failure or inadequate. All it means is that, for some reason or another, you were not aroused enough to become erect. Let's steer away from calling your situation a failure because it is not. Rather, let's just look at the situation so we can find out why you were not aroused enough to get an erection."

REFRAMING GENDER-RIGID IMAGES

A reversal of traditional gender roles often creates anxiety, anger, fear, and confusion in males who embrace conservative rather than egalitarian notions about women and sexuality. For example, new rules proposed by feminists state that males must accept females as equal partners in sexual matters instead of traditional ideas related to males as dominant and females as subordinate. Men who have severely restrictive views of gender roles often experience gender role conflict when they perceive a devaluation or restriction of their revered masculine role. This conflict often leads to sexual problems, especially erectile disorders. I found an increase in this type of case during the onset of the women's movement and the so-called sexual revolution during the late 1960s and early 1970s. Some males welcomed the more assertive sexual approaches by newly liberated females; many responded with erectile problems. This anxiety and fear often generalized to other women and the mechanics of more persistent erectile problems were put into motion. While some progress has been made over the past several years in equalizing the sexual playing field, rigid ideas about gender roles remain strong in some men as the following case illustrates:

Chad reluctantly referred himself to therapy after several unsuccessful attempts to engage in sexual intercourse with a new girlfriend. He presented a history of no sexual miscues other than a transitory problem with premature ejaculation as a sexual neophyte. His social history revealed a traditional household consisting of a politically and socially conservative father who was the primary breadwinner and head of the household. His mother was a homemaker who took pride in her child-rearing abilities and well-managed home. He received little information about sexuality from his parents as a child. When Chad began to date, his father told him to "be careful and don't get anybody pregnant." As a young adult he had been successful in courting and bedding several "trophy" women. He thought he would eventually marry the "ideal woman," most likely a beautiful virgin, once he decided to settle down. Recently, he met a young woman who was bright, physically attractive, independent, and assertive. Chad made the initial approach to her in his usual manner, but she didn't seem very interested. A few days afterwards, she called and invited him to dinner. Chad was surprised, but accepted her invitation. They met at a restaurant and had an enjoyable conversation, even though he did not agree with most of her rather liberal and feminist ideas. When she insisted on paying the check, he began to feel uncomfortable. She then invited him to her place for after dinner conversation and drinks. He said, "At her place she told me that she enjoyed sex with men who have learned to understand what women really want in a relationship and in bed. Of course, I thought I understood women and knew that all any woman really needed and wanted was a good fuck from a real man. And, of course, I was just the man to give it to her. But she redirected most of my best stuff and soon she seemed to be in control of the situation. The more she took control, the more anxiety I felt. I couldn't understand it. I had been seduced by females before and found it exciting. But this did not seem like seduction. It seemed different somehow, but it should not have mattered because I knew I was going to get laid. When we finally got in bed, I couldn't get an erection. I started to make excuses about being tired and having too much to drink but neither was true. I gave up and went home. I was very embarrassed and I knew that I would never hear from her again, but she called the next day. We went out a few more times but I still could not perform. I have not dated anyone for the past month because I am afraid I will not be able to get it up again with anyone."

Therapeutic work with the type of gender-rigid case illustrated by Chad must include a focus on liberating men from the grasp of a belief system that allows only a very narrow definition of masculinity, femininity, and sexuality. Getting these men to see the world through a different lens is not an easy task. An approach that seems to work is to use the positive attributes of masculinity such as problem-solving skills, logical thinking, and risk taking as a springboard to examining the negative aspects of traditional gender roles. That is, therapists can point out that the man has identified a problem (no erection) and that the problem is most likely related to various socialization messages that males receive in this culture about men, women, and sex. The therapist can then advise him that the best way to begin solving the problem is to explore those messages as they relate to his relationships with various kind of women. Then throw down the gauntlet. Tell him that the task may be difficult and not without some risk, but the interpersonal and sexual payoff could very well be worth the personal investment. These are concepts that most men understand. Once he responds to the challenge, as most men do, his skills related to logical thinking and problem solving can be employed to explore and resolve issues associated with constricted ideas about gender roles.

In other gender-rigid cases, males strain to live up to a narrowly defined and exaggerated portrayal of a "real man." The result is often a distorted and fragile imitation of masculinity subject to disintegration under fire. Consider the case of Mike:

Mike is so conditioned by the traditional male socialization model that he insists on driving only a pick-up truck and wearing macho clothing such as denim pants, work boots or cowboy boots, flannel shirts, and white underwear. He believes that anything less than a "Marlboro Man" image is unmanly and subject to suspicion. Mike was so rigid in his approach to sexuality that his wife was consistently unsatisfied and eventually began to lose interest. Her waning interest in sexual contact confused and angered Mike because he knew that he was "performing" as a real man should and his wife should be more appreciative of his sexual prowess. His ability to "perform like a real man" quickly diminished when his wife suggested that a slower and more romantic approach might help her become more aroused and interested. He responded by seeking refuge in alcohol and extramarital sexual activities, neither of which alleviated his erectile problem. Mike resisted his wife's efforts to seek counseling because he believed that all male counselors were "sissies sitting around an office wearing ties." He absolutely refused to talk about sexual problems with a female counselor. When Mike's wife threatened him with divorce, he reluctantly agreed to try therapy.

A major focus in this second type of gender-rigid case is on helping men expand their definition of "real man" masculinity. But most of these men hold such a rigid view of masculinity that they believe that showing any sign of nontraditional masculinity suggests weakness, femininity, or even homosexuality. Suggesting that macho men let their feminine side show will initiate a barroom brawl. While these extremely narrow ideas about masculinity are deeply entrenched and difficult to dislodge, most men will eventually admit that trying to be so macho all the time is tiring and not very satisfying. This is especially so if they are no longer able to "get some pussy." The approach consists of gradually introducing an expanded view of masculinity while reducing the importance of the distorted concepts. Most men are interested in learning how to be a better lover and will listen to suggestions if they are not too radical at first. For example, the therapist can say something like, "Your wife loves you and she really likes it when you kiss her and touch her. It turns her on and she really wants to have sex with you. Maybe it could be fun for both of you if you kissed and touched her for a little longer before you attempt penetration."

I have also suggested to extreme macho men that they attempt to wear just one item of nontraditional masculine clothing to see what happens. When they discover that they do not have to defend their manhood on the street, some flexibility is born. As macho men become less rigid about their notions of masculinity and real man sexuality, they become more receptive to additional treatment strategies.

Undoing Unrealistic Expectations

Most males are conditioned to believe that they have an unlimited supply of sexual desire and that nothing will interfere with this desire and their ability to engage in sexual intercourse at every opportunity. Some males even believe that they can override an occasional bout with an erectile problem by commanding their reluctant penis to "stand up straight and act like a man." Gender role expectations and reality soon clash. Males, in their quest to become Superpenis, often deny the existence of fatigue, disinterest, preoccupation with other matters, and other similar elements which typically reduce the sexual responses in most regular humans. Most men need guidance in learning how to assess and respond to their overall feelings about a potential sexual situation instead of succumbing to the cultural messages insisting on sexual performance regardless of conditions. Neutralizing the ideas that men must engage in sexual activities even when they secretly know that they are not really interested is an important step in reducing gender role strain associated with sexuality. Not all sexual opportunities should or can be seized. Consider the following case:

> Jim, a 53-year-old, self-employed professional with no history of sexual problems throughout his 29 years of marriage, reported that he feared becoming "impotent." He described two recent episodes of being unable to respond to his wife's initiation of sexual contact. He reported that he and his wife maintained a rather active and compatible sexual relationship. Normally he would become aroused when she initiated sexual contact, which she did on a fairly regular basis. He was surprised that he was so unresponsive and began to experience anxiety about his lack of erection. Since this was so uncharacteristic of Jim, his wife also became concerned. When asked to describe his activities on the days preceding the "sexual failures," Jim reported several physically demanding activities associated with his participation in organized sports events. He also had experienced some problems at work with an employee and the conflict was not yet resolved. Jim entered the marital bed on those nights physically fatigued and mentally distracted. While he thought at the time that he was interested in responding to his wife's sexual overtures, in retrospect he admitted that he felt only that he *should have* been interested. In reality, he was very tired and just wanted to get some rest.

Jim's case was easily resolved by reducing his unrealistic expectations that he should be able to engage in sexual behavior regardless of his temporary lack of interest and diminished physical condition. He was advised to wait a week or so before engaging in sexual intercourse with his wife. During that time, he was instructed to avoid becoming overtired. He was also advised to resolve the conflict at the office, if possible. If the conflict could not be resolved in the time period, he was instructed to make an attempt not to carry the problem to bed with him. At home he was to focus on creating a positive atmosphere for sexual activities as he and his wife had been doing for years, instead of worrying about not living up to myths of masculinity. Within a few weeks, Jim and his wife resumed sexual contact as usual.

While Jim's case was resolved fairly easily, other cases of unrealistic expectations may require more extensive work beyond simply neutralizing the gender-driven urgency to get an erection regardless of conditions.

RESPONSIVE RELAXATION

One of the most effective antidotes to anxiety is relaxation. Although many males report seeking relaxation through some form of physical activity, watching sports, or drinking with their buddies, this action-oriented form of relaxation typically does not transfer well to an anxiety-inducing sexual situation. Rather, a more directed and personal form of relaxation is needed to counter anxiety associated with sexual problems. A typical form of relaxation training is a much abbreviated version of progressive relaxation techniques pioneered by Jacobson (1938, 1964). Over the past several decades, many variations of Jacobson's original procedures have been developed and used successfully (see Wolpe & Lazarus, 1966). In some cases, therapists may prefer to employ other procedures such as hypnosis; biofeedback; autogenic training; or a combination of imaging, meditation, and breathing exercises. The choice of relaxation training is dependent upon the therapist's own treatment philosophy and experience with relaxation procedures, as well as the patient's response to the procedure selected. The net result must allow the patient to apply relaxation to reduce anticipatory anxiety associated with sexual matters, as well as to neutralize anxiety during actual sexual activities. For males in the throes of a gender-role conflict, the benefits of achieving a self-controlled deep relaxation response are many. For example, the individual learns a pleasant and effective stress management technique that can be used in place of inappropriate coping strategies such as substance abuse or extramarital affairs. It can provide the sexually anxious man with a rare sense of control and self-worth as he addresses his sexual problems. And relaxation is a positive emotional experience by itself.

Playful Pleasuring

Masters and Johnson (1970) developed "sensate focus exercises" to gradually eliminate the barriers to the natural process of sexual excitement and sexual responsivity. The technique involved a series of tactile activities designed to reduce tension and increase pleasurable sensations. Both partners are given the opportunity to give and receive pleasure from each other. This type of pleasuring is conducted without the pressures of having to engage in sexual intercourse. In fact, sexual intercourse is specifically excluded from the exercises during most of the treatment plan. After the couple has experienced successful mutual nonsexual pleasuring, extracoital genital pleasuring is introduced. Eventually, and without demand, sensate focus exercises include the gradual reintroduction of penile-vaginal contact and, ultimately, coitus. In this way, males learn that sexual behavior is more than a need to "get a hard on and stick it in before it goes down." Both partners learn that touch, smell, sound, and sight, as well as thought processes, are important to restoring the natural process of sexual responsivity.

SUMMARY

After several years of observing and studying sexual behavior more closely than any other sex researchers, William Masters and Virginia Johnson (1970) proclaimed sex a natural physiological function. These intrepid explorers of the human sexual response also indicated that sexual responsivity was interpreted through an individual's psychosocial sexual history, but specific socialization experiences were not identified. Now, nearly three decades later, findings from gender studies and clinical experience point to abuse of sexuality socialization experiences and gender role strain or conflict as major players in male sexual problems.

Western culture routinely relies upon traditional Judeo-Christian doctrine about gender roles and sexuality to assure gender role conformity among its constituency. Included are prohibitions against most sexual behavior, except activities used to propagate the species and beliefs that men are inherently superior to and have a higher sexual drive than women. The gender role differential resulting from these notions is a double standard script stating that men are full of lust and women are full of resistance. For males, one of the most important rites of passage into manhood is to overcome women's resistance to sex. And to be initiated into the "Royal Order of the Real Man," males must display a huge penis that stands ready to penetrate at every opportunity, regardless of countermanding forces.

As long as males are raised to be sexual warriors there will be casualties. Sexual warriors learn to become isolated from their feelings and are discouraged by gender role expectations from standing down from any sexual challenge. They continue to pursue the enemy as trained, seemingly unaware that the training is flawed and directs many of them toward harms way.

To reduce the stress of gender role conflict found on the sexual battlefield, a gender appropriate therapeutic approach is proposed with a focus on male socialization experiences and their negative effects on male sexuality. The treatment model is an amalgamation of three major components:

1. The gender role strain or conflict perspective
2. The reconstruction of masculinity and male heterosexuality
3. Well-established therapeutic techniques designed to treat glitches in the human sexual response

After ruling out medical conditions and factors associated with alcohol and other drugs, several gender appropriate evaluation and treatment strategies are proposed. First, the therapist assesses gender role strain or conflict associated with sexual responses. To gather this information, a structured interview based upon a developmental perspective, as well as several questionnaires, are recommended. Proposed next is an individualized treatment plan with several components, including learning a different language to replace incorrect and prejudicial terminology with more accurate and therapeutic nomenclature for men's sexual problems, procedures for reducing anxiety associated with men's "failures" to live up to gender-role-driven expectations of masculinity and sexual "performance," and a description of playful pleasuring based on basic concepts contained within the sensate focus paradigm. Table 9.3 summarizes the proposed gender role sensitive evaluation and treatment process.

This therapeutic treatment plan derives from the position that most men's sexual problems, especially erectile disorders, are a function of the stress or conflict men experience when they are unable to meet the socialized, gender role-driven expectations and myths of masculinity and sexuality. Men with strong convictions that an essential nature of man and

Table 9.3

Gender Role Sensitive Evaluation and Treatment Process

Rule Out Nongender Role Factors

1. Medical conditions
2. Alcohol use or abuse
3. Prescription or other drug use or abuse

Assess Development of Sexuality and Gender Role Strain/Conflict

1. Sociocultural messages
2. Ideas and feelings about sexual matters
3. Sexual experiences
4. Problem areas
5. Overall sexual information
6. Attitudes toward women
7. Gender roles

Treatment Components

1. Learning a different language
2. Reframing gender-rigid images
3. Undoing unrealistic expectations
4. Responsive relaxation
5. Playful pleasuring

---

masculinity exists and this essence includes the myths of male sexuality, will have more difficulty with the proposed therapeutic program than men who do not embrace myths of masculinity so tightly. Typically, men with a strong faith in the traditional male role will require a full range of the proposed therapeutic strategies in order to make the language, cognitive, and behavioral changes necessary for recovery. Men who already show some flexibility in their belief system about gender roles often require only an abbreviated form of the overall therapeutic program to restore erectile functioning. Therapists who accept the gender role strain or conflict paradigms and have developed a good understanding of the concepts proposed within the reconstruction of masculinity perspective will find the proposed treatment approach familiar and should be able to apply these techniques with skill. Therapists who are not yet familiar with the differences between the gender role stress or conflict perspective and the gender role identity paradigm may experience some difficulty in managing the proposed gender-appropriate program effectively. And any therapist applying the proposed strategies to reduce gender role strain or conflict should also be knowledgeable and experienced in the overall Masters and Johnson approach to treating male sexual dysfunctions.

REFERENCES

American Psychiatric Association. (1994). *Diagnostic and statistical manual of mental disorders* (4th ed.). Washington, DC: Author.

Barlow, D. H. (1986). Causes of sexual dysfunction: The role of anxiety and cognitive interference. *Journal of Consulting and Clinical Psychology, 54,* 140–148.

Barlow, D. H., Sakheim, D. K., & Beck, J. G. (1983). Anxiety increased sexual arousal. *Journal of Abnormal Psychology, 92,* 49–54.

Beck, J. G. (1988). *Love is never enough.* New York: Harper & Row.

Beck, J. G., & Barlow, D. H. (1984). Current conceptualizations of sexual dysfunction: A review and an alternative perspective. *Clinical Psychology Review, 4,* 363–378.

Beere, C. A. (1990). *Gender roles: A handbook of tests and measures.* Westport, CT: Greenwood Press.

Betcher, R. W., & Pollack, W. S. (1995). *In a time of fallen heroes: The recreation of masculinity.* New York: Guilford Press.

Bolton, F. G., Morris, L. A., & MacEachron, A. E. (1989). *Males at risk: The other side of child sexual abuse.* Newbury Park, CA: Sage.

Brooks, G. R. (1990). The inexpressive male and vulnerability to therapist-patient sexual exploitation. *Psychotherapy: Theory, Research, Training, 27,* 344–349.

Brooks, G. R. (1995). *The centerfold syndrome: How men can overcome objectification and achieve intimacy with women.* San Francisco: Jossey-Bass.

Brooks, G. R., & Silverstein, L. B. (1995). Understanding the dark side of masculinity: An interactive systems model. In R. F. Levant & W. S. Pollack (Eds.), *A new psychology of men* (pp. 280–333). New York: Basic Books.

Garnets, L., & Pleck, J. (1979). Sex role identity, androgyny and sex role transcendence: A sex role strain analysis. *Psychology of Women Quarterly, 3,* 270–283.

Goldberg, H. (1976). *The hazards of being male: Surviving the myth of masculine privilege.* New York: Signet.

Goldberg, H. (1979). *The new male: From self-destruction to self-care.* New York: Morrow.

Gosselin, C., & Wilson, G. (1980). *Sexual variations: Fetishism, sado-masochism, and transvestism.* New York: Simon & Schuster.

Jacobson, E. (1938). *Progressive relaxation.* Chicago: University of Chicago Press.

Jacobson, E. (1964). *Anxiety and tension control.* Philadelphia: Lippincott.

Kaplan, H. S. (1974). *The new sex therapy.* New York: Brunner/Mazel.

Kaplan, H. S. (1975). *The illustrated manual of sex therapy.* New York: Quadrangle/New York Times Book.

Kaplan, H. S. (1979). *Disorders of sexual desire.* New York: Bruner/Mazel.

Krugman, S. (1995). Male development and the transformation of shame. In R. F. Levant & W. S. Pollack (Eds.), *A new psychology of men* (pp. 91–128). New York: Basic Books.

Krystal, H. (1979). Alexithymia and psychotherapy. *American Journal of Psychotherapy, 33*, 17–30.

Levant, R. F. (1992). Toward the reconstruction of masculinity. *Journal of Family Psychology, 5*, 379–402.

Levant, R. F. (1995). Toward the reconstruction of masculinity. In R. F. Levant & W. S. Pollack (Eds.), *A new psychology of men* (pp. 229–251). New York: Basic Books.

Levant, R. F., Hirsch, L. S., Celentano, E., Cozza, T. M., Hill, S., MacEachern, M., Marty, N., & Schnedeker, J. (1992). The male role: An investigation of contemporary norms. *Journal of Mental Health Counseling, 14*, 325–337.

Levant, R. F., & Kelly, J. (1989). *Between father and child.* New York: Viking.

Levant, R. F., & Kopecky, G. (1995). *Masculinity reconstructed: Changing the rules of manhood-at work, in relationships, and in family life.* New York: Dutton.

Levant, R. F., & Pollack, W. S. (Eds.). (1995). *A new psychology of men.* New York: Basic Books.

Lisak, D. (1991). Sexual aggression, masculinity, and fathers. *Signs: Journal of Women in Culture and Society, 16*(2), 238–262.

Masters, W. H., & Johnson, V. E. (1966). *Human sexual response.* Boston: Little, Brown.

Masters, W. H., & Johnson, V. E. (1970). *Human sexual inadequacy.* Boston: Little, Brown.

Masters, W. H., & Johnson, V. E. (1976). *The pleasure bond.* New York: Bantam.

Masters, W. H., Johnson, V. E., & Kolodny, R. C. (1985). *Human sexuality* (2nd ed.). Boston: Little, Brown.

Masters, W. H., Johnson, V. E., & Kolodny, R. C. (1988). *Masters and Johnson on sex and human loving.* Boston: Little, Brown.

Michael, R. T., Gagnon, J. H., Laumann, E. O., & Kolata, G. (1994). *Sex in America: A definitive survey.* Boston: Little, Brown.

Morris, L. A. (1997). *The male heterosexual: Lust in his loins, sin in his soul?* Thousand Oaks, CA: Sage.

O'Neil, J. M. (1981a). Male sex-role conflict, sexism, and masculinity: Implications for men, women, and the counseling psychologist. *Counseling Psychologist, 9*, 61–80.

O'Neil, J. M. (1981b). Patterns of gender role conflict and strain: Sexism and fear of femininity in men's lives. *Personnel and Guidance Journal, 60*, 203–210.

O'Neil, J. M. (1982). Gender role conflict and strain in men's lives: Implications for psychiatrists, psychologists, and other human service providers. In K. Solomon & N. B. Levy (Eds.), *Men in transition: Changing male roles, theory, and therapy.* New York: Plenum Press.

O'Neil, J. M. (1990). Assessing men's gender role conflict. In D. Moore & F. Leafgren (Eds.), *Men in conflict: Problem solving strategies and interventions.* Alexandria, VA: American Association for Counseling and Development.

O'Neil, J. M., & Egan, J. (1992a). Abuses of power against women: Sexism, gender role conflict, and psychological violence. In E. Cook (Ed.), *Women, relationships, and power: Implications for counseling.* Alexandria, VA: American Counseling Association Press.

O'Neil, J. M., & Egan, J. (1992b). Men's and women's gender role journey: Metaphor for healing, transition, and transformation. In B. Wainrib (Ed.), *Gender issues across the life cycle*. New York: Springer.

O'Neil, J. M., & Egan, J. (1992c). Men's gender role transitions over the life span: Transformations and fears of femininity. *Journal of Mental Health Counseling, 14*, 305–324.

O'Neil, J. M., Egan, J., Owen, S. V., & Murry, V. M. (1993). The gender role journey measure: Scale development and psychometric evaluation. *Sex Roles, 28*(3/4), 167–185.

O'Neil, J. M., & Fishman, D. (1992). Adult men's career transitions and gender role themes. In H. D. Leas & Z. B. Leibowitz (Eds.), *Adult career development: Concepts, issues, and practices* (2nd ed.). Alexandria, VA: American Counseling Association Press.

O'Neil, J. M., Fishman, D. M., & Kinsella-Shaw, M. (1987). Dual-career couples' career transitions and normative dilemmas: A preliminary assessment model. *Counseling Psychologist, 15*(1), 50–96.

O'Neil, J. M., Good, G. E., & Homes, S. (1995). Fifteen years of theory and research on men's gender role conflict: New paradigms for empirical research. In R. F. Levant & W. S. Pollack (Eds.), *A new psychology of men* (pp. 164–206). New York: Basic Books.

O'Neil, J. M., Helms, B., Gable, R., David, L., & Wrightsman, L. (1986). Gender role conflict scale: College men's fear of femininity. *Sex Roles, 14*(5/6), 335–350.

Pleck, J. H. (1981). *The myth of masculinity*. Cambridge, MA: MIT Press.

Pleck, J. H. (1995). The gender role strain paradigm: An update. In R. F. Levant & W. S. Pollack (Eds.), *A new psychology of men* (pp. 11–32). New York: Basic Books.

Sifneos, P. E. (1967). *Clinical observations on some patients suffering from a variety of psychosomatic diseases*. Proceedings of the seventh European Conference on Psychosomatic Research, Basel, Switzerland.

Solomon, K. (1982). The masculine gender role: Description. In K. Solomon & N. Levy (Eds.), *Men in transition: Theory and therapy* (pp. 45–76). New York: Plenum Press.

Spence, J. T., & Helmreich, R. L. (1972). The attitudes toward women scale: An objective instrument to measure attitudes toward the rights and roles of women in contemporary society. *Psychological Documents, 2*, 153.

Spence, J. T., & Helmreich, R. L. (1978a). *Attitudes toward women*. Austin: University of Texas Press.

Spence, J. T., & Helmreich, R. L. (1978b). *Masculinity & femininity: Their psychological dimensions, correlates and antecedents*. Austin: University of Texas Press.

Stuart, F, Stuart, R. B., Maurice, W. L., & Szasz, G. (1975). *Sexual adjustment inventory*. Champaign, IL: Research Press.

Wolpe, J., & Lazarus, A. A. (1966). *Behavior therapy techniques: A guide to the treatment of neuroses*. New York: Pergamon Press.

Zilbergeld, B. (1992). *The new male sexuality*. New York: Bantam Books.

CHAPTER 10

Confronting and Treating Empathic Disconnection in Violent Men

David Lisak

THE UBIQUITY OF MALE VIOLENCE

W HETHER YOU've seen it on your own block, or on the nightly news, or on one of the real-life cop shows, the scene is by now very familiar to most Americans: a tattooed and handcuffed man is being hauled to a patrol car, his tense and agitated body still vibrating from the violence he has just committed. On the steps of the house he leaves behind sits a shaken and battered woman, and behind her, two terrified children.

Violence committed by males has become a normal part of our visual and mental landscape. And even without the nightly news broadcasts and the real-life cop shows, there is ample evidence of its normality. American jails and prisons are overflowing with ever-increasing numbers of prisoners, and while the number of incarcerated females is growing, it is still dwarfed by the numbers of men. Our prisons can be accurately described as warehouses for violent men.

Nor is it simply that men are more likely to be arrested for their violence. Research on various types of hidden male violence—interpersonal violence that is never reported to authorities—tells us repeatedly and indisputably that the vast majority of such violence goes unreported.

Interpersonal crimes, especially those that take place within families or between acquaintances, are rarely reported to authorities, and even more rarely result in arrests and convictions (Martin, Anderson, Romans, Mullen, & O'Shea, 1993). For example, in their national sample of college women, Koss, Gidycz, and Wisniewski (1987) found that only 5% of the rapes reported by their respondents were ever reported to the police. In Russell's (1983) random community survey, only 2% of intrafamilial and 6% of extrafamilial child sexual abuse cases were reported to the police.

There is corresponding evidence from the other side of the violence ledger—from studies of men who perpetrate the violence uncovered by researchers such as Koss and Russell. For example, in two studies conducted at the University of Massachusetts–Boston, in which approximately 1,200 men participated, 24% acknowledged perpetrating sexual or physical violence against adults or children (Lisak, Hopper, & Song, 1996; P. M. Miller, 1996). The violence acknowledged by these men included battery of adult, intimate partners, rape and attempted rape of adults, physical abuse of children, and sexual abuse of children. From interview studies that have been conducted with subsets of these types of samples, we know that almost none of the men were ever reported or prosecuted for these acts of violence (e.g., Lisak & Roth, 1990).

Nor are these kinds of violence—with women and children as the predominant victims—the only kinds of hidden violence. Male-on-male violence—from simple assaults, to robberies, to gang violence, to murder—is an established and deeply embedded part of American culture. Perhaps the most hidden form of male-on-male violence occurs in our juvenile detention centers, our jails, and our prisons. This violence is so well hidden that it has received hardly any attention from researchers. Based on the few systematic studies that have been conducted, it is conservatively estimated that nearly 300,000 men are raped each year in American jails and prisons (Donaldson, 1993). Since a large proportion of these men are raped repeatedly, the actual number of rapes occurring each year probably exceeds a million.

There is little room for doubt either about the reality and ubiquity of interpersonal violence, or about the fact that it mostly goes unnoticed by authorities and that the vast majority of it is being perpetrated by males. Nor can there be much doubt that the task of curbing and preventing this violence falls well outside the range of impact of the discipline of psychology—if it is defined in traditional, individualistic terms. Psychologists, through determination and skill, may succeed in changing the behavior of an individual violent male, but in the time that treatment takes, how many more violent men will be shaped and created?

Very often the same personality and developmental characteristics that shape men's violence also make it unlikely that they would ever seek psychological treatment or cooperate with it if they were forced into it. The history of efforts to treat sex offenders indicates that only highly restrictive, comprehensive, and multimodal treatment programs have much hope of success with some forms of violence. Nevertheless, understanding the multiple roots of male violence is critical to shaping treatment strategies that have some chance of success in what are typically high risk and low-odds treatment scenarios.

Violent men do not comprise one diagnostic category. There is no single or even short list of personality traits that characterize violent men. Violence, after all, is a behavior, and it can have an almost infinite number of causal roots. As with any treatment, successful treatment of a violent male patient requires very careful assessment and targeting of the unique factors that determine his behavior. Despite the heterogeneity in the causes of male violence, there is increasing evidence of a number of developmental factors common to many violent men. In this chapter, I will focus on two of these factors—the male gender socialization process and early trauma—and how these factors can be targeted in treatment.

THE ROOTS OF MALE VIOLENCE

It is often argued that men are biologically predisposed to violence, and that this biological difference between the sexes accounts for the difference in expressed violence. Although this issue will be addressed briefly, it is important to remember that it is neither the critical question nor the critical answer when it comes to preventing violence or treating its perpetrators. Regardless of whether men's violence can be traced to biology, gender socialization, economic and social conditions, or the combination of all of these and other unnamed factors, the majority of men *are not* violent. Therefore, the primary focus of our research efforts must be on analyzing the factors that distinguish violent men, for these are the factors that prevention and treatment efforts must address.

Perhaps the most widely argued of the biologically based theories is the sociobiological explanation: that male aggression stems from biologically ordained male reproductive competitiveness—the chronic, intermale fight for access to females (Daly & Wilson, 1985). In this view, aggressive and dominant behaviors have been genetically rewarded and have therefore become an inherent aspect of the male genetic heritage. While this theory has some appeal as a broad-brush explanation of the presumed sex difference in predisposition for aggressive behavior, as a theory, it leaps over an enormous number of factors that have been empirically associated with male violence. Factors such as economic conditions, gender socialization, and violent role models have been isolated as far more proximate variables that distinguish violent from nonviolent men. And again, it is this process of distinguishing the violent from the nonviolent that is our most urgent task. It may be that the male half of the human species is more predisposed to commit violence than the female half, but such a determination does virtually nothing to guide our efforts toward preventing violence or treating the men who perpetrate it.

Finally, any effort to isolate the causal role of genes in producing male violence runs into an enormous confounding variable—male gender socialization: the deeply, culturally embedded process whereby male children are systematically and often traumatically shaped to conform to culturally determined gender norms. These norms dictate everything from behavior to dress to emotional expression to emotional experience. This socialization process quite literally begins in utero, in the parents' already-formed and internalized gender ideologies and the expectations about the newborn and his behavior that these ideologies dictate. It is a process that accelerates rapidly from early childhood, accumulating growing numbers of participants: siblings, peers, babysitters, teachers, daycare workers, films, books, video games; all of which pound in a largely consistent message about what is and what is not acceptable masculine behavior.

Despite intercultural variations in the content and severity of masculine socialization, there is considerable consistency across most cultures (Gilmore, 1990). It can be argued that converting one of the two sexes into that state of being called "masculine," the end-goal of the masculine socialization process, provides a culture with an adaptive advantage, particularly when the culture is attempting to survive in a competitive or harsh physical environment. According to this argument, masculinity actually consists of a subset of human characteristics, in particular, strength, stoicism, toughness, independence, as well as the abnegation of another subset of human characteristics, namely those the culture associates with femininity (passivity, emotionality, dependence). By socializing a large number of its members into such a masculinity, a culture produces a large number of pre-initiated warriors. Masculine socialization is essentially pre-basic training. Males who have undergone this process have internalized a coherent set of values which dictate that their core value as human beings hinges on the degree to which they can adhere to that restricted set of human characteristics that are defined as masculine. Once he has been so socialized, the masculinized male will feel intense shame at any inward or outward display of nonmasculine behavior; for if masculinity has become the core of your identity, then the loss of it is tantamount to the loss of the self; to psychic death.

How else do you explain the following scene, depicted in untold numbers of memoirs, novels, and films about World War I:

> Ten thousand men stand shoulder to shoulder, in a trench, with mustard gas swirling around them. At the sound of the officers' whistles, ten thousand men climb up out of the trench and directly into the path of the machine guns that only moments before slaughtered the previous ten thousand.

Something extremely powerful must be at work to so reliably counteract the instinct for self-preservation among so many thousands of men, in war after war, century after century. That *something* is the socialization process whereby human vulnerabilities, whether physical or psychological, are denigrated and suppressed. This suppression of vulnerability necessitates a radical constriction in emotional experience and emotional expression. In the textbook of masculinity, the realest men in the trench are those who feel no fear; the next realest are those who feel it but do not show it; the failures are those who show it; those who show it and act on it get shot by their officers.

The trench warfare of World War I may seem like an exaggerated analogy for arguing about the effects of normative masculine socialization. However, history leaves little room for doubt that one of the primary purposes of masculinity is indeed warfare—the preparation of males for acts of violence. To endure it and to commit it. To be hurt and not cry. To hurt others and not be emotionally crippled by it. The military's basic training has often been compared to initiation processes found in other cultures: separating the initiate from his past; de-individuating him; creating a new warrior identity in which the military's values are internalized. Those values are highly masculinized. Socializing masculinity has historically been linked to the socialization of the capacity for violence.

So the normatively masculinized male is somewhat preconditioned to violence, trained to be relatively disconnected from his own vulnerabilities and vulnerable emotional states, and to suppress what he cannot disconnect from, and to denigrate what he suppresses. In so doing, his capacity to resonate and sympathize with the vulnerabilities of others is significantly diminished. It has been consistently documented that males are less empathic than females (Eisenberg & Lennon, 1983).

This diminished capacity for empathy creates a general, increased capacity for interpersonal violence, for empathy is clearly an important inhibitor of violent and aggressive impulses. This relationship—between decreased empathy and aggression—also has been well documented (P. A. Miller & Eisenberg, 1988). But while normative masculinization may create a general, increased capacity for violence, there are clearly other factors that further heighten the risk. First, the masculinization process itself is a variable, in that it varies in both content and severity. Not all males within the same culture are socialized either in the same way or with the same effect. How harshly and rigidly a male is masculinized— by his parents, particularly his father; by his peers; by cultural institutions such as the military—can have an important impact on his capacity for violence.

Another critical factor is early trauma. Recent research on male victims of childhood abuse indicates that such early trauma is far more prevalent than has been generally acknowledged. In seven years of studies at the University of Massachusetts–Boston, in which we have assessed more than 1,600 men, more than 40% meet relatively conservative criteria for childhood physical or sexual abuse (Hopper, 1997; Lisak & Luster, 1994; Lisak et al., 1996; P. M. Miller, 1996). While the majority of men who suffered abuse during childhood *do not* perpetrate interpersonal violence, a strong majority of those who do perpetrate violence were themselves abused as children. For example, in one of these studies (Lisak et al.) 70% of perpetrators reported histories of either physical or sexual abuse. Among perpetrators of child abuse, the figure was 79%. In a more recent study, this figure was 83% (Hopper, 1997).

The relationship between childhood abuse and the perpetration of violence is undoubtedly forged by numerous factors, but among them is a potentially toxic amplification of the normative effects of masculinization. Abused children experience extremely intense emotional states: fear and terror, helplessness, shame, and rage. With the exception of rage, all of these intense emotional states directly conflict with the masculine norms the male child is concurrently in the process of internalizing. If the abused child attempts to resolve this conflict by adhering rigidly to those masculine norms, then he has little choice but to engage in an enormous effort to suppress his vulnerabilities and to disconnect himself from much of his emotional experience. His pain becomes a marker of shame, of femininity, of weakness. Internalizing masculinity, he reacts harshly to any sign of such vulnerability within him, and he may react equally harshly to any such sign in others around him.

Our research at the University of Massachusetts–Boston has documented many of the components of the relationship between childhood abuse, masculinization, and violence. Compared to abused men who *do not* perpetrate, abused perpetrators are more rigidly masculine, more emotionally constricted, and less empathic (Hopper, 1997; Lisak et al., 1996).

Thus, the masculinization process, early trauma, and the intertwined and interacting emotional legacies of both appear to be important and relatively common factors in men who commit violence, whether it be the unincarcerated men we study at the University of Massachusetts–Boston, or the incarcerated men discussed by Gilligan (1996), or the death row prisoners I have evaluated in my forensic practice.

What follows is a case study of a prisoner on death row. It illustrates the unraveling of the trauma-masculinization-violence causal sequence and the therapeutic effects of this unraveling on a particular man's capacity to experience emotions and to empathize. It is included here because of the clarity it offers, a clarity no doubt sharpened by the intense existential pressures of living under sentence of death.

CASE STUDY: SAM—RESURRECTING HUMANITY ON DEATH ROW

In a dusty and over-heated desert trailer park in semi-rural Utah, Sam and his older sister and younger brother were raised by their alcoholic parents. The family was chronically poor. Sam's father could never keep a job because of his drinking, and because he was constantly getting into fights with coworkers or with his supervisors. Often, the family skipped meals when the food money ran out, although there was always money for alcohol. For weeks at a time, the children lived on macaroni-and-cheese dinners.

Sam grew up a skinny kid and a hungry one. When he got to be school age, his meager school records included several notes indicating that some of his teachers suspected he was malnourished. He had trouble with bleeding gums. Thirty years later, he remembered vividly his intense craving for food and the unbearable shame he felt about it. These competing physical and emotional states began to rule his behavior at school. He would steal lunches from other children, he would get caught, and he would fight viciously out of rage at his own humiliation.

Sam fought constantly with other children in large part because violence, along with hunger, had always been the central texture of his home life. His father beat his mother regularly, sometimes slapping her with his open hand, sometimes punching her so that her face was a mass of purplish bruises, sometimes kicking her. One time—that Sam could remember—his father choked his mother, his hands wrapped around her neck, lifting her off the floor against the refrigerator. Another time, his father went berserk, screaming incoherently and slashing the air with a butcher knife while everyone—mother and children—hid in terror under table and chairs and then fled out of the trailer. Many nights, Sam and his brother and sister heard their mother's screams and felt the flimsy trailer shake from the weight of their mother falling against walls or to the floor. Sam would lay in bed in helpless rage, imagining his mother's body and its injuries. In the morning, he would see them for real.

As the oldest boy, Sam received the worst beatings from his father and the worst torments and humiliations. His father put him in charge of the decrepit household and then held him responsible for its shabbiness, its broken parts, and even the lack of food. As a result, there was always a reason for a beating. As a result, Sam was beaten whenever his father felt like it. His father beat him with his fists, with a large and heavy wooden spoon, and with a broken broom handle that he seemed to keep only for this purpose. The beatings were so constant and so unpredictable that they became simply another facet of Sam's childhood. It took numerous questions to uncover the extent of these beatings, because to Sam it was as if I was asking questions about the weather. To the end, he never really understood why I was asking.

Far more salient to him were the unique tortures his father inflicted. When Sam was about 8 years old, he found an abandoned puppy in the trailer park and took it home. He fed it what he could, kept it alive, and nurtured it. For days his father paid no attention to the puppy. Then one night his father came home drunk and burst into the children's bedroom and violently jerked Sam out of his bed and dragged him out of the trailer and into the yard where the puppy was lying in its cardboard box. As Sam watched in mute horror, unable to make out the words his father was screaming, his father grabbed the puppy, held it in front of Sam's face and snapped its neck.

Subject to the relentless violence and oppression of his father, Sam at an early age learned to be stoic. Since his father's rages were always intensified if Sam cried, Sam learned how not to cry. Since his father reacted violently to any sign of fear, Sam learned how not to show fear. This training became adaptive in other ways. In the face of his helplessness to stop the beatings and the torments, not feeling was far more adaptive than feeling. Eventually, there was little need to suppress his feelings, for they rarely ever entered his consciousness.

If the violence he was subjected to provided the adaptive purpose for emotional disconnection, then masculinity provided its ideology. Beaten, neglected, and malnourished, Sam was at a disadvantage at nearly every facet of development—except the task of becoming masculinized. The harsh dictates of the masculine creed—to show no fear or vulnerability—were already a part of his being. Masculinity became something he could be truly good at.

Sam became a leader among a small group of delinquent youths who emerged from his and a neighboring trailer park. It was through the gang that he learned of the anesthetizing effects of alcohol and the mind-numbing effects of other drugs. He climbed in the gang hierarchy and by his mid-teens was organizing the petty thefts and robberies the gang conducted. By the age of 16 he was well-known to the local sheriff's office and before he was 17 he had been arrested for car theft and robbery. He was sentenced to a juvenile detention center. His parents were asked to participate in his treatment but refused. Before his eighteenth birthday he escaped and fled the state.

Sam lived on the run, although no one, neither his parents nor the juvenile authorities back in his home county, seemed the slightest bit interested in his whereabouts. He wandered from city to city and state to state, a homeless, penniless adolescent. He ate garbage, scrounged meals, and stole food. He slept in shelters, under highway overpasses, and in alleys. At desperate points, he prostituted himself in exchange for rare cash and once simply for a warm bed on a very cold night. He lived mainly for drugs, for the small pockets of relief they provided from his misery and his fear.

Sam descended from this depression into a deepening and nihilistic despair. He befriended a man at a shelter who owned a gun and together they pulled off several muggings. One night, a mugging went bad. Their prey, a 40-year-old businessman and father of three children, resisted their attack and either Sam or his friend shot him dead. Within days, both Sam and his friend were arrested. Each fingered the other as the trigger man. Both were convicted of capital murder and sentenced to death.

For eight years Sam waited out the slow unraveling of his appeals through the state and federal courts. Vulnerable and terrified by the other inmates, each night he barricaded himself in his cell, never trusting the lock on his cell door. In this chronically frightened state, alone with himself most of each day, every day, year after year, Sam ruminated about his life. He was a 28-year-old middle-aged man by the time his defense lawyers arranged for a comprehensive psychological evaluation as part of a last-ditch effort to overturn his death sentence.

Sam's appearance mirrored the brief contradictory existence he had sustained during his short life on the outside. His light brown hair hung long and limply down the sides of his lined, pasty, and scarred face. His forearms each bore large tattoos. In his prison denims, his appearance fit everyone's stereotype of a convict. But barely beneath the surface of this tough facade were all of the legacies of the terrified and beaten child. The muscles around his eyes twitched involuntarily, unable to contain the decades of pain they had been marshaled to mask.

Initially, Sam described his childhood with the voice and the hardened demeanor of the convict. He joked about being beaten. He punctuated his sparse descriptions with short, exhaled laughs that betrayed only a hint of bitterness and almost no pain. What Sam was unaware of was that an enormous amount of information about his childhood had already been collected from interviews with his siblings and his mother and even neighbors in the trailer park; from his school and juvenile records. While he had signed releases to permit the collection of these data, he did not understand how discrepant his own heartless recounting would be when compared with the accounts of those who witnessed the violent beatings of a helpless child.

The break in Sam's facade of invulnerability was preceded by a gradual deepening of his trust. It was prompted by a simple question about the snapping of the puppy's neck. Sam's face collapsed on itself. All of the tensed and hardened muscles, all of the fragile toughness simply dissolved. His head dropped suddenly to the wooden table and he began to weep uncontrollably. So began the second phase of the evaluation, a long, slow, torturous reliving of years of terror, humiliations, helpless rage, and despair. What came out in this phase was the Sam who had slowly emerged during the years of long nights alone in a tiny cell with no way out. A prematurely middle-aged man who only by night revealed to himself how truly frightened and alone he was, how much pain he felt. When at last he began to translate this long-germinating experience into words, what emerged was a remarkable analysis of his life; a description of the emotional legacy borne by the abused child, and of the adaptive and yet futile and ultimately destructive solution provided by masculinity.

On one occasion he was escorted into the interview room by the usual two guards who then removed his wrist shackles. As he approached the table it was apparent that he had been crying. Tears had wetted his cheeks and he had been unable to wipe them away because his wrists had been chained to his waist-chain. He sat down and said, "Man, those guards think I've lost it." There was a mixture of irony and shame in his voice. He was in conflict and he suddenly began to give voice to what had long been simmering:

> It's fucking crazy, man. All these guys in here, and I mean the guards, too. They're all in there hurting just like I am. Sometimes I hear the sobs at night from under their blankets. But they all try to act tough. It's fucked up, man. We're all fucked up. We're all scared shitless and we're all pretending it's no big deal. Every one of us is carrying around this pain like I've been talking to you about. Most of these guys have probably had it worse—much worse than I did. But they got to pretend. They think they've got to be big, tough men.

Toward the end of that interview session, after he had been once more crying from the pain of betrayal and abandonment he had suffered as a child, Sam offered a kind of conclusion to his analysis of emotions and masculinity in prison:

> You know I'm not going to apologize to you for crying like this. There shouldn't be anything wrong with this. I'm just a human being. And so are the rest of these guys here. Underneath all of that he-man bullshit we're all the same.

The lengthy evaluation of Sam had been proceeding serendipitously forward through his life. When the focus turned to the brief spree of crime that had preceded his arrest and conviction for murder, his speech became stilted once more. He was clearly conflicted and trying hard not to reveal something. However, it did not take much to break through this conflict. Haltingly, once again fighting desperately to hold back tears, Sam described the look of terror he had seen on the faces of his robbery victims, a terror that resonated within him, but a resonance that he had kept hidden from himself for almost a decade. He began sobbing uncontrollably but soon raised his head and angrily tried to stop, wiping away the tears even as they poured out of his eyes. "I've got no right to cry like this. *I* did it! *I* did it to them! *Me!*" And with that he jabbed himself violently with his accusing index finger. His newly found capacity to empathize with his victims produced what would become almost unbearable guilt. He derided himself and belittled his own pain. He revoked from himself his right to cry about his misery, declaring that he had forfeited that right by inflicting that pain on others.

Eventually, Sam began to find a way to reconcile his conflict, to bear the burden of his guilt and remorse and still feel compassion toward himself for the pain that was a permanent legacy of his childhood. He began to talk about his life as a tragedy, as an almost predestined unfolding of forces that he only now could see clearly. And he found a new villain to carry at least a small portion of the guilt that weighted him. He began to rail against the profoundly damaging effects of his masculine socialization. He derided the facade of machismo as a fraud that actually betrayed the inner weakness and fragility of the men who adopted its credo. Sam began to repeat a mantra that became a kind of personal political slogan: "None of that macho shit for me anymore. I'm a human being."

Eight years on death row and the process of a psychological evaluation had effected an essential transformation in Sam. As his defenses against his own pain eroded, his capacity to experience his emotions gradually was restored. But this restoration could not be completed without the restoration of his capacity to feel empathy for himself—to feel compassion for himself and his suffering. Once *this* capacity was restored, the door opened to feeling empathy and compassion for the pain of others—the pain he was responsible for.

IMPLICATIONS FOR TREATMENT

There are obvious dissimilarities between Sam's case and almost any situation in which a therapist would find themselves treating a violent man. Most men don't live under a death sentence and aren't locked alone in a cell with no mechanisms for escape. Further, the transformative process that Sam completed, by itself, neither assures rehabilitation nor comprises a sufficiently comprehensive treatment plan for a violent man. Nevertheless, it illustrates clearly what is one of the most crucial processes that must occur for a violent man to become truly *un-violent*. For we know that the capacity to experience one's pain and to empathize with the pain of others inhibits aggression, and the lack of these capacities facilitates aggression. So, while the particular mechanisms involved in Sam's transformation may not be generalizable, it is just such a transformation that therapy must create if the engine that drives so much of male violence is to be neutralized.

Creating and sustaining the conditions in which such a transformation can occur is arguably one of the most difficult tasks that any therapist could face. It requires creativity, flexibility (a willingness to suspend rules), a willingness to be very real in the therapy relationship, a willingness to take risks, and a willingness to accept the inevitable failures. What follows are several techniques and approaches that, depending on the individual, may prove effective. It is by no means an exhaustive list, but rather is illustrative of approaches that can be tried in the immensely difficult task of changing men who are uniquely well-armored against such change.

THE WELL-SEALED PRESSURE COOKER

It has been well documented that men are far less likely than women to seek treatment for psychological problems (Levant, 1990). Indeed, they may be far less likely to acknowledge, either to themselves or to others, that they have psychological problems that might require treatment. For similar reasons, men may be far more likely to quit treatment that they have initiated. Most of us are sufficiently aware of these characteristics of the male patient that—consciously or unconsciously—our approach to working with them often is influenced. We may become tentative, fearful of precipitating the sudden departure that we anticipate.

But there is an unfortunate paradox. These same psychological defenses and internalized gender beliefs that create the reluctant male patient also create the impervious male patient. That is, it is often the very clinical judgments that we (quite reasonably) make to ensure his continued commitment to treatment that undermine the potential efficacy of that treatment. Put bluntly, we use kid gloves in an effort not to scare him off, and as a result never meaningfully challenge the defenses that wall him off from the potential for change.

If this paradox applies somewhat to the "male patient" in general, it typically applies much more so to the violent male patient. Violence is often the product of the externalization of psychological pain and distress. Therefore, confronting externalizing defenses tends to evoke the pain that underlies them, which quite automatically triggers more externalizing defenses. Witness the following exchange:

THERAPIST: Your voice is matter-of-fact but in your face I see fear.
PATIENT: (Face tensing, eyes narrowing in anger.) If there's anyone afraid in this room it should be you.

There is a quite natural tendency to try to derail this cycle by diminishing the level of confrontation. Unfortunately, in so doing, we essentially become coconspirators. We collude in the fiction that this man cannot bear to confront his pain or his fears; that they will overwhelm him; that he is too fragile to face them. Further, we also collude in producing the outcome that he either secretly—or most likely openly—predicts will happen: Therapy won't accomplish anything.

How then to evade this dilemma? How do you not collude when confrontation will undeniably threaten the fragile fabric of the therapy itself?

First, we must be willing to take risks. Psychotherapeutic treatment of a violent man is inherently a risky undertaking that is, frankly, not all that likely to succeed. By accepting that as the framework, we can be freed to take the risks necessary to exploit the openings that do present themselves for creating meaningful change.

Sometimes, the answer to externalization is—externalization. Continuing the exchange:

THERAPIST: Your voice is matter-of-fact but in your face I see fear.
PATIENT: (Face tensing, eyes narrowing in anger.) If there's anyone afraid in this room it should be you.
THERAPIST: You know, trying to make me feel your fear for you won't do you any good. How about I feel my fear and you feel yours?

The goal of such a response is to bounce back to the patient his own challenge. It is undeniably risky and must be done carefully. The goal is to be challenging enough to keep him on the therapeutic playing field—interpersonally engaged—while not being so confrontational that the exchange reduces to a very untherapeutic "pissing contest." Often this can be done by turning hypermasculine, externalizing defenses back onto themselves, and in so doing, redefining the terms of the engagement. The therapist's challenging stance must be interwoven with warmth and compassion, qualities that must be communicated concurrently with the confrontation. Therein lies the art. With this blend of warmth and confrontation, the patient can be cajoled toward joining the therapist in challenging the patient's assumptions—in this case, for example, about fear. Courage becomes not the absence of fear, but the willingness to face fear. Toughness becomes not the absence of vulnerability, but the strength to acknowledge it. Strength becomes not the absence of pain, but the capacity to openly bear it.

By openly, confidently, and sometimes dramatically confronting the externalizing, masculine credo, the therapist moves toward accomplishing what is the prerequisite for the kind of transformation achieved by Sam on death row: closing off the escape routes; sealing the pressure cooker that is the precondition to fundamental change. Undermining the gender-based foundation of emotional disconnection is often an effective, sometimes a necessary precondition to sealing the pressure cooker. If the patient's masculine ideology remains unchallenged, any successful evocation of genuine emotion, of vulnerability, is likely to be immediately defused by well-entrenched mechanisms. Either the affect will be disconnected from conscious experience, or it will be transformed into the acceptable masculine affect—anger. Either way, the seal is broken.

Without a sealed therapeutic environment, genuine change in the patient's capacity to experience his emotions is unlikely. For if there is a truism about the psychotherapeutic treatment of violent men, it is probably that such fundamental change cannot and will not happen outside of a highly pressurized and contained environment. Escape must either be impossible or more painful than endurance.

MODELING A MORE INTEGRATED MASCULINITY

If the answer to externalizing defenses is often a challenging and externalizing response, how does one prevent therapy from descending into an ill-fated, verbal sparring match? The answer is that not all externalization is the same. For example, in the brief therapy exchange above, the therapist implies quite directly that he is both capable and willing to feel his own fear; all he asks is that the patient do the same. If this challenge comes from a male therapist, then the challenge is softened by the therapist's disclosure that he does feel fear. It is also softened by a particular contradiction being modeled in this exchange: The therapist demonstrates that he is man enough to openly talk about feeling fear. In so doing, he models something that the patient may never have encountered before; a male human being who is tough enough to stand up to the patient's effort at intimidation, and who simultaneously acknowledges the very human experience of fear.

Modeling such seeming contradictions is essential to the process of breaking down the patient's internalized beliefs about masculinity and their control over his emotional experience. The masculinized experience is one of dichotomies and splits. It is a world of hard and soft in which masculinity embodies hardness. Every time the therapist models behavior that contradicts this worldview, he challenges it, and in the process challenges the patient.

What if the therapist is female? Is modeling a more integrated masculinity then out of the question? The answer is less obvious than at first it might seem. While a female therapist cannot be a male, she can both easily and ably model the kind of integrated masculinity that the violent male patient needs exposure to. Masculinity—from the patient's perspective—is marked by toughness, strength, and fearlessness, all of them qualities that the female therapist can and must manifest if she is to successfully confront and engage with the violent male patient. By doing so, the female therapist can provide an immediate and living example of the *discontinuity* between sex and gender. In so doing, she further undermines the internalized assumptions about gender by which the male patient lives. A tough and fearless female violates those assumptions as much as does a male who has the courage to acknowledge and express vulnerability. So, while a female therapist cannot be a living example of a male living by an alternative code of masculinity, she can both undermine the patient's maladaptive assumptions and also demonstrate by example the kind of unfettered humanness that freedom from gender constraints makes possible.

Sympathy with an Edge

Some therapists are reluctant either to feel or to express sympathy for violent men. Indeed, such sympathy is explicitly barred—at least officially—from some sex offender treatment programs. The implication is that men who have violated others have forsaken the privilege of experiencing sympathy from their treatment providers. While this is not typically made explicit, it is often embedded in the treatment philosophy that only a tough, hard-nosed approach can alter the deeply entrenched behavior of violent men.

It is undeniable that effecting meaningful change in violent men requires hard-nosed psychotherapy. However, if one of the goals of such treatment is to reconnect the patient to his capacity to resonate with his own pain and the pain of other people, then a unidimensional approach of toughness will actively undermine this effort. Violent masculinity is predicated on the splitting off of human capacities that have been culturally defined as feminine. Sympathy and compassion, being rooted in the capacity to resonate with vulnerable emotional states, are routine casualties of this split. To confront such a split man with a unidimensional facade of toughness only serves to reinforce this split. He needs to see and, more importantly, *feel* sympathy from someone who is also—perhaps even simultaneously—capable of genuine toughness. Such experiences tend to occur during very intense, emotional confrontations, and as such provide superb moments for building meaningful changes in the patient.

The strain between sympathy and toughness frequently emerges when the man begins to confront his own victimization experiences. Some therapists view the introduction of such issues as defensive or manipulative; as a deflection by the patient, one aimed at side-stepping his responsibility to acknowledge and change his violent behavior. This is particularly the case when the introduction of such issues precedes any expression of genuine remorse and empathy by the patient. Any therapist who has worked with victims of violence is likely to feel at least somewhat squeamish about listening sympathetically when a perpetrator of such violence implicitly or explicitly describes himself as a victim.

The problem is most perpetrators *were* victims. Most perpetrators victimize others at least in part because they have disconnected themselves from their own pain and vulnerability, and are thereby disconnected from the pain of others. This is a developmental sequence that often can be undone only in the same sequence. That is, they must be helped to confront and experience their own pain and vulnerability as a prerequisite to then finding the capacity to resonate with the pain and vulnerability of others—most importantly, their past and future victims. If the root source of the emotional disconnection is not addressed, it will be difficult if not impossible to resurrect the emotional capacity necessary for empathy. It may feel unjust; it may be very difficult for the therapist; but it is quite likely that genuine remorse and empathy will only come after a perpetrator of violence has been helped and challenged to face his own pain. And that cannot be accomplished without genuine sympathy from the treating therapist.

However, it ought to be sympathy with an edge. Once again, the therapist must be cognizant of what is being modeled. When the perpetrator begins to genuinely experience his own victimization, it is the therapist's job to ensure that there be two victims in the room: the perpetrator and *his* victim. For it is precisely in those moments when he feels some compassion for his own suffering that the perpetrator must be challenged to extend those feelings to the suffering of others, especially those whose suffering is his responsibility.

Psychoeducation about Gender

If a patient describes severe physical beatings he suffered as a child as "normal" discipline—*"I was bad; that's why they had to discipline me"*—most therapists would have little difficulty taking a stand and explicitly confronting the patient's internalization of abuse. How is he ever going to face the painful emotional legacy of these experiences if he cannot first see them as pain-inflicting (i.e., abusive)? The therapist, by validating the experience as abusive, opens the way for the patient to acknowledge his pain.

Though not yet widely perceived, there is a precisely comparable issue when confronting a male patient's internalization of masculinity. If a male patient clamps his jaws, grinds his teeth, hides his pain behind a mask of tense facial muscles, and then erupts in anger—all in the effort to contain his vulnerability—surely the therapist is cast into the same role when confronted with internalized abuse. Only by validating the man's humanity—the utter normality of his vulnerability—can the therapist open the way for the patient to acknowledge his pain. And in validating the man's humanity, the therapist will be directly confronting masculinity, for masculinity is the internalized ideology that has truncated this man's humanity.

Internalized masculinity is equivalent to "truncated humanity," for that is precisely what it is. As such, it can be attacked and critiqued, and the man who labors under its burden can be cajoled and challenged to relinquish its hold on him. Witness the following:

THERAPIST: Your voice is matter-of-fact, but in your face I see fear.
PATIENT: (Face tensing, eyes narrowing in anger.) If there's anyone afraid in this room it should be you.
THERAPIST: You know, trying to make me feel your fear for you won't do you any good. How about I feel my fear and you feel yours?
PATIENT: I never said I was scared.
THERAPIST: Who told you that you weren't allowed to be afraid?
PATIENT: Nobody said I wasn't allowed. I'm just not.
THERAPIST: Nobody told you not to be afraid? How about your father?
PATIENT: (Smiles slightly.) Yeh, my father. He once beat the shit out of me for crying.
THERAPIST: What about other kids? You never got teased for being afraid?
PATIENT: I was never stupid enough to show any fear in front of the other kids. I knew damn well what they'd do to me.
THERAPIST: So then you *were* forced to pretend you were never afraid.
PATIENT: What do you mean "pretend"? I just wasn't afraid!
THERAPIST: Sure you were, just like you were a minute ago when I saw it in your face. We're all afraid. It's part of being human. You've got as much choice about being afraid as you do about breathing.

Through exchanges such as this, a male patient's internalized beliefs about masculinity can be systematically challenged. Often, such challenges are most effective when they consist of a two-pronged approach.

The first prong demonstrates in practical terms the restrictiveness of masculine norms, the ways in which they constrain the patient's choices and limit his ability to adapt to different situations.

The second prong educates the patient about the basic, biological foundations of emotional experience in *human beings*. Such basic lessons in biology can be extremely effective. For one thing, science is both authoritative and typically perceived as a masculine, patriarchal institution. Thus, a scientifically based assault on an aspect of masculine ideology often carries more weight with the masculinized male patient. Further, by explicating the biological basis of emotions such as fear, the therapist implicitly offers the male patient the opportunity to essentially rejoin the human race. The implicit message is, "It's okay to be afraid because all of us humans are and so you can be, too." And finally, there is another implicit message in such psychoeducational challenges. It is that the male patient really has no choice about being vulnerable and feeling fear. Such emotional states are part of the human experience, part of his biological heritage. There is often palpable relief when the male patient finally understands this; the relief from being able to give up the lifelong struggle against his own biological imperatives.

It is easy to underestimate the potential of such psychoeducational strategies and to apply them half-heartedly. A few minutes of explanation will rarely be sufficient. For one thing, it suggests that the therapist himself or herself is only marginally convinced by the evidence. For another, the information is typically far too complicated to be meaningfully assimilated in this way. Depending somewhat on the educational background of the patient, I have combined lengthy and detailed lectures on the neurobiology of emotions—particularly fear—with drawings of the human brain, illustrations from books, and assigned readings matched to the patient's level of understanding. The book, *The Emotional Brain* (LeDoux, 1996), is an excellent resource in preparing the therapist for such psychoeducational efforts.

CREATIVE SUSPENSION OF THE RULES

Violent men were not the typical patient around which the traditions of psychotherapy were designed. Violent men tend not to be terribly verbal nor terribly insightful about either their emotions or their internal psychological states. Therefore, the therapist who treats the violent male patient must be creative and flexible with regard to the traditions and rules of psychotherapy. In essence, the therapist must not be bound or constrained by his or her preconceptions about what constitutes therapy, or by what may be an effective treatment approach. Since this is very much a principle being expounded, and not a technique, the examples to follow must be understood as such, and not by any means as markers that delimit the bounds of creativity that can be applied by the therapist.

Field Trips

Sometimes the therapy office is not the best place to effect therapeutic change. For a male patient who is actively disconnecting himself from painful experiences, sometimes more powerful external cues are needed to help break through that disconnection. When possible, *go get those cues.* Go with him to his childhood neighborhood; to his old school; to the detention center where he was sent as a juvenile. As therapists, we work hard to create a safe environment in our therapy offices. However, at times that safety may be counter-therapeutic, may in fact become another defense the patient can use to keep painful emotional states at bay.

Third Parties

It is often very effective to bring third parties into treatment—whoever may be important to the patient or may provide an impetus to treatment. This must be done with the patient's consent. Spouses and children are obvious candidates, as are the patient's parents. Third parties can powerfully reframe and recontextualize therapy, providing both the patient and the therapist with new vantage points and new insights into the patient's problems.

Documents

Documents represent a nonliving form of third parties. Most therapists are unaware of how much information can be gleaned from a patient's school, psychiatric and medical records, and any other records that might be available, such as those generated by the military and the courts. Such records can and should be obtained only with the patient's consent. Once obtained, they can provide invaluable perspectives for the patient; sometimes validating fragmented memories; sometimes uncovering forgotten but critical moments from his past. For the therapist, such records can be invaluable sources of information and important guides for treatment.

Movies

The media are omnipresent purveyors of cultural myths about masculinity, both reflecting and shaping men's gender ideologies. In the ongoing task of deconstructing and reframing the patient's internalized masculinity, movies can be a powerful tool. Analyzing the patient's film heroes can sometimes be a safe, initial way of analyzing his own internalized gender values. Such analyses can be done in a displaced way, allowing the patient to view aspects of himself more obliquely, and therefore more critically. Movies often provide excellent fodder for such analyses, because they typically portray relatively stereotyped masculine characters who can be easily critiqued.

Videotaping

Videotaping can be a powerful therapeutic tool, both for breaking through defenses and for enabling a patient to see certain characteristics that he might otherwise be impervious to. For example, once the therapist has learned the patient's particular language of body cues—the unconscious behaviors and facial configurations that comprise his nonverbal, emotional expressions—a videotape playback in which this language can be decoded to the patient can be extremely effective. Like psychoeducation, it can have the effect of underscoring for the patient that his emotional system is innate and beyond his control; a part of his human endowment. Internalized masculinity may mute, compress and deflect his emotional expressions, but it cannot alter his basic humanity.

Videotaping sessions in which the patient works with other family members can have a similar effect in revealing to him interpersonal patterns that he would otherwise be too defensive or simply unable to perceive. For example, many violent men tend to be controlling in their interpersonal relationships. Pointing out the number of times he interrupts other family members or the silencing and intimidating effect he has on them may be more effective with the use of videotape, an objective record of interactions he would otherwise dispute.

Videotape feedback such as this can obviously have a shock effect, which accounts for some of its effectiveness in breaking through defenses. Few of us are used to observing ourselves with such clinical detachment, let alone having our behavior microanalyzed. However, videotaping may also work for other reasons. The violent male's intrapersonal and interpersonal disconnection can be conceptualized as being at least partly a consequence of his inability to verbalize—process and integrate—his emotional states. As such, his condition is somewhat analogous to the split-brain patient who, when he sees something with his right hemisphere only, can register the emotional content of a stimulus but cannot transform or communicate his experience verbally. Since the right hemisphere cannot communicate directly to the left hemisphere, it could only transmit the information externally, for example by drawing something that provided sufficient clues for the left hemisphere to guess at the nature of the stimulus. Videotaping similarly provides an external feedback loop, a mechanism that can bypass the apparent breakdown in the internal processing of emotional states.

SUMMARY

What has been presented in this chapter is a decontextualized discussion of particular aspects of psychotherapy with violent men. That is, most violent men receive treatment—when they do—in the context of the criminal justice system, either in programs for batterers or in sex offender treatment programs. Such programs are comprehensive and multimethod in approach. As such, the issues discussed in this chapter would comprise only one or two aspects of a multifaceted treatment program. Put another way, addressing *only* the issues discussed in this chapter would not comprise a viable treatment approach for a violent male patient.

However, there is considerable evidence that the issues discussed in this chapter do comprise an important component of the underlying dynamics of male violence. Among the factors that have been associated with the perpetration of interpersonal violence, few if any come close to the predictive power of childhood abuse, and few have been as consistently documented as hypermasculine gender ideologies. These facts alone suggest that the interacting legacies of childhood abuse and masculine socialization must be actively and creatively targeted in the treatment of the violent male patient.

Finally, some proportion of men who are cajoled or coerced into therapy by their partners have many of the characteristics of the men described in this chapter. These men are often more incipiently than overtly violent. Yet the approaches that have been outlined in this chapter, both theoretical and therapeutic, are likely to be useful in challenging them to some kind of meaningful engagement in a therapeutic process. Like their overtly violent brethren, these men are typically trapped in constraining internalizations of masculinity, and often harbor reservoirs of psychological pain that drive their behavior but that have historically been impervious to conscious confrontation.

REFERENCES

Daly, M., & Wilson, M. (1985). Competitiveness, risk taking, and violence: The young male syndrome. *Ethology and Sociobiology, 6,* 59–73.

Donaldson, S. (1993, December 29). The rape crisis behind bars. *The New York Times,* A22.

Eisenberg, N., & Lennon, R. (1983). Sex differences in empathy and related capacities. *Psychological Bulletin, 94,* 100–131.

Gilligan, J. (1996). *Violence.* New York: Putnam.

Gilmore, D. D. (1990). *Manhood in the making.* New Haven, CT: Yale University Press.

Hopper, J. (1997). *Child abuse and masculine gender socialization: A study of emotional incompetencies associated with perpetration.* Unpublished doctoral dissertation, University of Massachusetts, Boston.

Koss, M. P., Gidycz, C. A., & Wisniewski, N. (1987). The scope of rape: Incidence and prevalence of sexual aggression and victimization in a national sample of higher education students. *Journal of Consulting and Clinical Psychology, 55,* 162–170.

LeDoux, J. (1996). *The emotional brain.* New York: Simon & Schuster.

Levant, R. F. (1990). Psychological services designed for men: A psychoeducational approach. *Psychotherapy, 27,* 309–315.

Lisak, D., Hopper, J., & Song, P. (1996). Factors in the cycle of violence: Gender rigidity and emotional constriction. *Journal of Traumatic Stress, 9,* 721–743.

Lisak, D., & Luster, L. (1994). Educational, occupational and relationship histories of men who were sexually and/or physically abused as children. *Journal of Traumatic Stress, 7,* 507–523.

Lisak, D., & Roth, S. (1990). Motives and psychodynamics of self-reported, unincarcerated rapists. *American Journal of Orthopsychiatry, 60,* 268–280.

Martin, J., Anderson, J., Romans, S., Mullen, P., & O'Shea, M. (1993). Asking about child sexual abuse: Methodological implications of a two stage survey. *Child Abuse & Neglect, 17,* 383–392.

Miller, P. A., & Eisenberg, N. (1988). The relation of empathy to aggressive and externalizing/antisocial behavior. *Psychological Bulletin, 103,* 324–344.

Miller, P. M. (1996). *Psychological distress, abuse histories, and perpetration in college males.* Unpublished master's thesis, University of Massachusetts, Boston.

Russell, D. (1983). The incidence and prevalence of intrafamilial and extrafamilial sexual abuse of female children. *Child Abuse & Neglect, 7,* 133–146.

PART THREE

BROADENING THE SPECTRUM

CHAPTER 11

Treating Anger in
African American Men

Anderson J. Franklin

A NGER EVOLVING from African American men's experiences with
prejudice and discrimination has health and mental health risks.
Moreover, a major aspect of the African American male experience is managing stress which stems from feeling not appropriately validated or respected within society. For many African American men there
is an inner struggle with feeling that genuine talents are invisible to others in society. Personal respect and dignity as a man within the African
American community are often challenged by intolerance and disrespect
from the racism experienced outside of the community. This reinforces
motivation of African American men to embrace validation from within
the African American community, bonding with the "brotherhood",
since expectations for comparable validation in many everyday cross-
racial encounters is lower, racially loaded, and more problematic. Managing inner thoughts and feelings about these differences in validation, and
dealing with racism in society, taxes the ability of African American men
to realize their full potential. This particular circumstance is presented as
a unique psychological challenge for African American men that requires
them to sort out how much their difficulty in personal achievement is a
result of individual responsibility and/or acts of racism. Some excerpts
from a support group session for African American men reveal dimensions of this personal struggle and illustrate the effectiveness of a group
forum as an intervention for anger triggered by perceived racial barriers
and disillusionment in fulfilling gender expectations.

AFRICAN AMERICAN MALE ANGER

Many African American men believe they have much to be angry about. They often place the locus of that anger upon prejudice and discrimination experienced in their lives. Although few African American men are disproportionately preoccupied with these circumstances, many are frustrated and bitter over the persistence of racial slights and treatment governed by prevailing stereotypes.

Expressing and managing anger is often perceived within the African American community as being highly problematic and consequential. For example, racism frequently mistranslates African American men's public expression of assertiveness into aggressive behavior. Furthermore, African American male anger is often fueled by frustration over the difficulty to fulfill gender role expectations because of prejudice and discrimination in the larger society. Racism's specific constraints upon African American men's expression of anger influences their management of that anger. Disentangling these perceived constraints and finding acceptable ways of expressing and managing anger becomes a stressor with personal risks.

Early insight into anger was provided by Grier and Cobbs (1968) from their classic work with African American patients as well as their unique perspective as two African American psychiatrists. Considering the direct and indirect role of prejudice and discrimination, they concluded that African Americans must develop "cultural paranoia" in which the systems affecting their lives are approached with suspicion. African Americans must "cushion . . . against cheating, slander, humiliation, and outright mistreatment by the official representatives of society" (p. 178).

Grier and Cobbs' views on the locus of anger being influenced by the experience of race for African Americans have been underscored by generations of literary voices (Bell, 1992; Boyd & Allen, 1995). Whereas the power of race in the lives of African Americans has been recognized, a comprehensive understanding of its psychological consequences remains wanting.

Hutchinson (1994) represents the contemporary view, growing in acceptance among African Americans, that African American men are so besieged by life stressors that their survival is in jeopardy. He notes that the African American male image is based on "a durable and time-resistant bedrock of myths, half-truths and lies," which puts African American males in the devastating predicament of overcoming a vast array of malevolent implications. Jones (1997) indicates that living with the various forms of discrimination and mistreatment in America from slavery to the present has created unique psychological distress and outcomes for

African Americans and that any theoretical consideration of the African American male personality must take this into account.

Anger as an outgrowth of perceived acts of racism is as idiosyncratic as it is universal. For example, although African American men easily agree on the difficulties in securing job promotions, they differ about the role racism plays. The degree to which people get angry over any particular incident will vary. The African American male's inner vigilance for discerning racial slights and what he believes he should do in response contributes to his style of managing anger. This sixth sense for detecting biased attitudes can also become a psychological burden arising from the stress of additional decision making about how to respond to perceived racism (A. Franklin, 1993).

ANGER AS A RISK FACTOR

The multitude of health and social "at risk indicators" for African American men has serious consequences. For example, African American men have one of the lowest life expectancies due to homicide (Hammond & Yung, 1993), cardiovascular disorders, hypertension, diabetes, and substance abuse (Anderson, 1995; Braithwaite & Taylor, 1992). Approximately 30% of young, African American males are either in jail, on parole, or on probation (Butterfield, 1995; Gibbs, 1988; Taylor, 1995). Many have questionable job skills and functional illiteracy which impedes their ability to get employment, sustain upward mobility, and contribute to their families (Billingsley, 1992; Staples & Johnson, 1993).

Psychologically African American men struggle with lingering stereotypes from the past as well as present misconceptions about them (Gordon, Gordon, & Nembhard, 1995). Conventional wisdom dictates that "you have to work twice as hard in order to get half as much" when competing with Whites, and that African Americans are the "last hired, first fired" (Stone, 1995).

Racial discrimination in the workplace as well as any circumstances perceived as motivated by racism provoke anger responses that increase cardiovascular health risks (Krieger & Sidney, 1996). High blood pressure among African American men has been shown to be related to occupational stressors (James, LaCroix, Kleinbaum, & Strogatz, 1984), as well as to personality traits such as cynicism, hostility, anxiety, and defensiveness (Shapiro, Goldstein, & Jamner, 1996).

These shared beliefs about the impact of racism supported in part by social indicators frame the construction of a psychological reality and life experience that Jones (1997) considers a significant underlying theme. The interpretation and internalization of perceived race-related experiences are important to understanding their behavior and how to work with them.

Invisibility Syndrome

The invisibility syndrome is a conceptual model that explains how the struggle for personal identity among African Americans requires confronting racism and related interpersonal encounters that obscure genuine identity. It is also a model for gauging the degree to which the individual internalizes and reacts to the inherent race and gender stress-related expectations. Chronic frustration, confusion, and disillusionment can result from perceived persistent malevolent cross-race interactions (i.e., activation of the sixth sense) that require resilience, or empowerment/thriving to overcome, or alternatives can lead to serious dysfunctional behaviors (A. Franklin, 1997).

Invisibility is an interpersonal barrier created by feeling that one's talents, abilities, personality, and worth are not valued or seen because of racism. African Americans often experience racism as making them invisible. What reinforces it are encounters, particularly with White men, that lack the acknowledgment and validation essential to preserving personal dignity. Ralph Ellison in his classic novel *Invisible Man* (1952) represents the subjective intricacy of this experience through the encounters and quest for an identity of a nameless narrating African American male protagonist.

Lack of Recognition and Validation

A. Franklin (1993) illustrates the concept of invisibility by the case of Bill who encountered racial slights from the maitre d' in a restaurant, his waiter, and finally from a parade of taxis that did not pick him up after dinner. Contending with feelings of rejection and humiliation, Bill is provoked to throw his body across the hood of the final offending taxi in a fit of anger. No matter how positive Bill's self-regard to that point, he experienced these racial slights as attaching stereotypes to him which, in an attempt, borne of frustration, to preserve his ego-integrity, he reaffirmed.

African Americans are in an invisibility-visibility dilemma that is dynamic, conflictual, selective, and greatly influenced by societal stereotypes, assumptions, and priorities of racism. It is frustrating, provoking, stressful, and breeds confusion and disillusionment. Managing the stress from this interpersonal dilemma taxes resilience.

Microaggression

The array of interracial interactions conveying disregard and creating internal conflicts in African American men often come in the form of slights, called *microaggressions* or *psycho-pollutants* by Chester Pierce (1992). These slights have a cumulative effect in shaping one's view of self in the world. Microaggressions are subtle acts or attitudes experienced as hostile by the recipient and contribute to a pattern of racial slights experienced by that person. They are reminders of social status by their implicit suggestion about unworthiness and self-esteem leveling. They promote defensive thinking and a wariness of future social interactions. Because they occur unpredictably, the individual must remain vigilant and resilient when encountering microaggressions in order to preserve self-dignity.

Microaggressions that result from everyday racism become a part of the intrapsychic structure of African Americans. There is a transient decline in self-esteem and sense of efficacy in each offending encounter, but repeated exposure to such events makes individuals psychologically vulnerable.

Racism, Anger, and Gender Role Expectations

To fulfill societal gender role expectations of provider and protector, African American men must contend with impeding racial barriers, such as disproportionate underemployment and unemployment, as well as racial/gender notions that are disparaging, such as the stereotype of African American men as unreliable.

Pleck (1995) represents masculinity in a gender role strain paradigm in which there exist contradictions and inconsistencies, and despite stern prohibitions, considerable actual violation of gender roles expectations. There can be long-term failure to fulfill male roles, trauma from the gender socialization process, and dysfunction upon discovery that acquired male behavior can be inappropriate for the context (e.g., being a competitive man may be incompatible with being a cooperative partner in a relationship).

In addition to the gender role strain paradigm, formation of the African American male's conception of masculinity is influenced by the unifying theme of racism. Fulfillment of male roles becomes that much more complex for African American men because living within the larger society, conceptions of masculinity have shared and independent attributes with intrinsic conflicts. For example, the same behavior labeled as assertive in White males may be labeled as aggressive when performed by African American men.

Bowman (1992) proposed that socially structured inequalities raised provider role strain for African American husbands and fathers that reduces their psychological well-being and quality of family life. Although prejudice and discrimination form barriers to the achievement of gender role expectations, indigenous ethnic patterns within the African American community may inspire adaptive cultural resources perceived as self-affirming (Majors & Billson, 1992). This might be seen, for example, in the cool but defiant posture of African American youth described by Majors and Billson.

Managing Stress from Invisibility

African American men must deal with thoughts, emotions, and behaviors triggered by what their skin color and physique signify to others. Negative responses to these visible attributes are the source of many conflicts and barriers to success for males, and very often have negative intrapsychic consequences. On the other hand, there are African American men who, in the face of this psychological adversity, develop positive intrapsychic attributes supporting resilience, ego strength, and determination to defy the negative odds.

Many African American men believe that racism compromises their opportunities and contribute to their marginal position in education, employment, and positions of power. They often believe that when they do succeed, their positive contribution results in their race being minimized—their success is seen as an exception. On the other hand, when their behavior is seen as negative, particularly criminal behavior, their race is seen to reinforce stereotypes. Therefore the positive visibility of African American men is experienced as a dilemma, selective, dependent upon the African American community, and at the mercy of societal stereotypes, assumptions, and priorities of racism.

THERAPEUTIC SUPPORT GROUP PROCESS

NEED FOR GROUP

Managing the stress of invisibility—finding clarity and focus from the confusion created by competing racial and gender values for masculinity—is emotionally and psychologically demanding. It can erode belief in gender role expectations, their fulfillment, and self-efficacy. It challenges one's capacity to be resilient and self-empowering in the face of racism.

The therapeutic support group becomes instrumental in restoring perspective through validating and counteracting the life experiences of African American men. Members learn they are not alone; they are encountering circumstances shared by others. Moreover, they acquire insight into how others cope with these issues, internalize emotional reactions to racism, and attempt to resolve them. This becomes particularly important when emotions such as anger and rage are involved, since these feelings are quite common among African American men and are often internalized in self-destructive ways.

As is common with men in general (Levant & Pollack, 1995; Meth & Passick, 1990), most African American men do not talk about personal issues, or share vulnerabilities with each other (Ridley, 1984). African American men will discuss their mutual experiences of being treated negatively because of their skin color, physique, or the public discomfort created by their physical and psychological presence both in society and within the African American community. Such admissions are also part of efforts to distinguish when personal treatment by others is a consequence of being seen as an individual, or motivated from being stereotyped with "all Black men."

The primary goals of the group are:

1. Reducing or managing the stress and feelings associated with negative experiences from being African American and male in society;
2. Achieving clarity in personal life goals;
3. Eliminating or lowering personal barriers to their fulfillment; and
4. Elevating self-efficacy by learning to engage other African American men as a constructive social support and resource.

ORIENTATION AND APPROACH: GROUP THERAPY AS INTERVENTION

Many African American men find their ability to genuinely discuss, ventilate, and resolve their personal issues about the demands and expectations for how to be a man, and African American, inadequate (Cose, 1993; Feagin & Sikes, 1994; A. Franklin, 1992). The therapeutic support group creates a safe environment for African American men to confront personal truths and vulnerabilities, to sort out individual responsibility from acts of racism (Davis, 1984; Sutton, 1996). Most men in the initial group sessions profess feeling uniquely targeted by racism. Subsequent sessions often focus on how each man can handle daily responsibilities in spite of the reality of prejudice. Thus, personal concerns about racism become a presumptive subtext to issues discussed in the group and are acknowledged openly only when there is a need to emphasize its role and influence.

The focus on how racism manipulates their lives becomes a vehicle for the group ultimately examining role competence in other life areas. The deliberate use of commonly shared experiences of being an African American man to bond the group is a clinical device to elevate interest and increase the probability of more lasting engagement of members. This helps generate what Yalom (1985) has observed as important curative factors in group process. It is through discussion of these issues that intrapsychic and personal adjustment issues get confronted. This is different from what takes place in conventional forms of group psychotherapy.

For example, by discussing common experiences of African American men (i.e., being passed by taxi cabs and ignored at restaurants, or tension with police and other authority figures), initial comfort with disclosure in the group is acquired. Sharing mutual indignation about their treatment as an African American man lays the foundation for future exploration of how it effects them personally, makes them feel, and challenges their sense of competence.

These early sessions often allow for venting of anger and frustration while providing personal validation. Participants discover their experiences are not unique. They gain insight into how difficult it is to have genuine disclosure with other African American men. But as comfort and trust level with group members grows, it is inevitably discovered that the risks taken in disclosure are not as consequential as previously imagined. Trust begins to grow at the core of the group process.

Trusting men in this group context facilitates the growth of an alternative model of genuine intimate friendship based on greater self-integrity and interpersonal reliance beyond the "I've got your back" fraternal ethos. Group members become increasingly perceived as a new and different type of African American man: a brother, and friend (A. Franklin, 1997).

GROUP SESSION

The following excerpt from the therapeutic groups for African American men is based on a taped session that has been altered to provide anonymity. The group had been meeting for over a year and had previously raised their frustrations with gender and racial barriers as a major theme in their life.

Composition of the Group

The group was composed of five middle-income African American men, all employed in white collar/professional positions, all but one was college educated, and ranged in age from 25 to 45. Two were married, two were never married, and one was divorced and single. All except one were first-generation, college-educated in their families and were raised in families with limited income.

Most of their extended family members remained with limited income or struggling with their own efforts of upward mobility. Therefore another underlying theme in these men's lives was managing their thoughts and feelings over family expectations of their educational success and how it will lead to career and financial success and family pride. This family history and expectations are typical for many first-generation college educated African Americans and is vital for understanding the psychological stakes in African American men's handling of gender and racial issues properly. It also is another source of African American men's anger.

GROUP SESSION: CONTEXT FOR ANGER EXCERPT

This segment on anger was an outgrowth of the previous week's discussion in the group on how racism affected the men's lives and created confusion in their feelings, thoughts, and behavior. Racism in its mixed expectations for African American men to be men frequently contains the caveat, "Act like men so long as it does not threaten the personal comfort of White society." Acceptable standards of assertive, compliant, subordinate behavior for African American men in schools, workplace, or residential communities remains problematic for many.

Determining their stance on following the covert interpersonal rules—deciding whether "to play the game" by being mindful of the need to maintain in others a personal comfort level—requires a psychic energy that the men find burdensome, frustrating, and upsetting. They wondered whether the pretense was worth the effort and saw how this dilemma of expressing their thoughts and feelings contributed to a persistent inner disgruntlement when encountering racially insensitive people and situations. A source of great personal anguish was the inconsistency between their gut reactions to an incident of racism, what they thought were appropriate responses to maintain their dignity, and how they actually reacted.

For example, the men noted when a racial slight is encountered at work they are confronted with several levels of decision making. If they respond quickly in an assertive manner—irrespective of whether the expression of anger would be considered within a normative range in a business setting—they feel they risk evoking the stereotype image of the threatening, volatile, aggressive African American male. Assertive behavior is consistently at risk for being misinterpreted as aggressive given the public media's socialization and views. Therefore, responding out of anger in their opinion will leave them vulnerable to being linked with a negative racial image.

Further complications arise from slowly transforming values in contemporary society about gender. The women's movement has initiated changes in how men view and fulfill their roles (Levant & Pollack, 1995), but these changes were predicated on situations without a parallel counterpart in the African American community: Orientation to and presumptions of gender inequities are quite different for White women to White men than for African American women to African American men. For example, racism hinders fulfillment of the family provider role for African American men, creating for African American women a greater sharing and independent role (Billingsley, 1992; Bowman, 1992; Staples & Johnson, 1993).

Very often these men, in their moment of anger, are prioritizing a response based upon competing family, community, and societal values about race and gender that preserves their self-respect, dignity, and identity. All of these considerations are not given equal weight since provocative situations pull for habitual ways of responding. Very often, however, reactive behavior is a manifestation of a person's ideological and interpersonal stance on issues of gender and race.

The group discussed the larger issue of personal honesty both with themselves as well as with others. They were concerned that if they were not true to their emotions in interracial encounters involving slights, they would be encouraging a pattern of dishonest behavior. The greatest realm of conflict for the men was not wanting to look bad in handling difficult situations. A source of this conflict was self imposed expectations about how to behave as a man, and particularly as an African American man. Failure generated disappointment and self-directed anger.

Comments centered on being *real* (i.e., honest) with people and the degree to which you could rely on people being real with you. Conversation ensued about how one was expected to conform "in order to get paid" (i.e., rewarded). However, this behavioral pattern was acknowledged to be a two-way street: group members admitted they tended to expect others to be a certain way as well.

A few of the men saw this as a personal shortcoming but felt there were too many situations where African American men had things defined for them and were reluctant to cede one of the few areas in which they had a level of control. Nonetheless, there was also admission that each of them needed to acknowledge their own personal shortcomings and stop making excuses in situations where they should take responsibility.

One group member, Dan, recalled that the previous group discussion about race had helped him finally confront his coworkers about their racial innuendoes and comments in staff meetings after years of passivity. He had previously been immobilized by inner conflicts over if, when, and what to say. His inhibitions to speak up had been causing him as much anger as the emotional sting from his coworkers' comments. After finally expressing his reactions to their racial comments, he was relieved when his coworkers reacted by talking about their various individual experiences of being different (i.e., gender differences, sexual orientation, racial difference).

However positive this experience was for Dan, it only highlighted for another group member, Don, his belief "that you cannot have an honest dialogue with . . . White people . . . You can't trust them or be honest or open to them." In Don's opinion, Dan's coworkers had deflected the intent of Dan's confronting them on their views about race by diverting into a discussion on the general topic of group differences. Don did not see where they had been responsive to Dan's point about their biased views, much less how it made Dan feel, "Wasn't he angry?"

Don was angered by the persistence of biased views and comments, upset with Dan because he took too long to speak up, and upset about how Dan handled it when he finally did, as well as upset with himself for being too judgmental and not supportive enough of Dan in keeping with the spirit of the group's goals.

THERAPIST OBSERVATION ON PROCESS AND CONTENT

This returned the group discussion to the dilemma of not expressing your true feelings when you see racial injustice or insensitivity. Can and should you raise it every time you detect it? Is hiding your upset or anger being dishonest? What psychological price is paid for overcontrolling your emotions at racial indignities for the sake of maintaining everyone's personal comfort, including your own?

One of the key challenges for the therapist in this group is helping the men to understand and distinguish when their personal issues are a product of their own doing, or when it is twisted by society's racism, or both. This dilemma of feeling under siege by racism and determining one's personal stance against it is a prominent psychological theme in the African American experience. Externalizing blame for personal life outcome is easy because of pre-eminence of African American community validation about the locus of racial mistreatment. Engaging and discussing the confusion brought about by this reality and how personal responsibility can be corrupted by it is a major objective of the group process and goal of the intervention.

For a therapist to achieve the competence and wisdom to help African Americans sort out events and tasks of individual personal responsibility from those imposed by circumstances out of one's control requires knowledge of African American history as well as the course of racism in society (e.g., J. Franklin & Moss, 1994; Jones, 1997). It not only provides a vital context for understanding the circumstances of African Americans but also helps determine professional efficacy in formulating clinical intervention.

SESSION EXCERPT ON ANGER

An underlying theme in the reflections of these men was the struggle with racial injustice, coming to grip with its pervasiveness, its longevity, contending with feelings of powerlessness, and finding a response that upholds self-respect and personal dignity. The men felt they had much to be angry about and acknowledged it was unhealthy to hold anger in. But the apprehensions they had in challenging Whites by releasing their anger—and the consequent personal risk—represented the historical and dynamically complicated gender power struggle between White and African American men (Ginzburg, 1962; Kovel, 1970).

The men had strong views and feelings about the effects of channeling their reactions into inappropriate responses, such as "sitting on their anger," on their sense of being African American and a man. Uncertainty about what to do with their indignation forces them to bury their anger "in places I don't even know." This is illustrated in the group's further discussion about tensions created by racial innuendoes. Another group member, Jomo, shares what he struggled with when he encountered what he considered a provocative race coded incident in the workplace.

JOMO: "One of my customers who was obviously very prejudiced when I walked in . . . starts asking me a lot of questions . . . as if I don't know what I am doing when I'm working on a project . . . you know, drilling me . . . asking me personal questions that are inferring some negative things about my ability.

"Now I understand to engage him on any level would open me up to getting really pissed off . . . so on some level . . . [I] tune him out because that's a comfortable way for me to handle that situation . . . to keep working . . . won't bother to interact with him. That's some of my issues!"

THERAPIST OBSERVATION

The issue for Jomo is his dissatisfaction with himself about the way he handles encounters of racial prejudice. Jomo's reflection on his predicament of holding back—often restraining his honesty around White people to protect his job and not have his upset be egregiously misinterpreted by them—is an example of the dilemma of expression for African Americans. There is the need to be true to the feeling and believed appropriate reaction (i.e., what Jomo believes "any man would do in the situation"). But at the same time he exercises caution, citing an array of consequences that may arise from misinterpretation of his intent by persons predisposed to be biased toward African Americans. Being hesitant and conflicted about his response is frustrating for Jomo since he feels he is not being true to himself, the circumstances, or his conception of what he should do as a man, and as an African American. It is in these kind of situations that Jomo feels most powerless and degraded which only angers him further.

A moment of closure for Jomo in the group process and his attempt to restore some personal dignity comes when he relates a belief commonly held among African Americans, "White boys walk around basically like they have the world by the tail . . . like whatever they see could be theirs . . . but for me there is some kind of glass ceiling . . . there's a limit to what I can get out of the situation." Group members concurred by nodding their heads.

THERAPIST FACILITATION OF GROUP PROCESS

When Jomo disclosed his personal conflict in the humiliating situation, the therapist was looking for how the group acknowledged this as a shared experience as well as the degree in which the shared experience converted to support. When the nodding heads of affirmation and Jomo's reflection came to a natural pause, the therapist guided the group into exploring the legitimacy of Jomo's feelings and their own.

The therapist had to balance and strategically determine when introduction of interpretations and interventions were appropriate. This was central to the first goal of making the therapeutic group context safe and assist the men in acquiring comfort with disclosure with greater integrity than in other male group interactions. It is important that the group process avoid inadvertently recreating the dynamics that occur within everyday experiences of invisibility for African Americans. Other group members or even the therapist's behavior appearing judgmental of disclosures can shut down a person's willingness to take a risk to genuinely share in the future. This will encourage them to withdraw into conventional gender facades in communication (e.g., donning the cool, unflappable, have everything under control male image).

Within the theoretical model of the invisibility syndrome, the lack of validation that African American men experience, either in terms of their genuine views of the world or their sense of self, contributes to their lack of racial and gender affirmation and thus their feeling invisible. Receiving concurrence from other African Americans on their perceived treatment—which risked the usual gender expectations of sanctions for showing vulnerability—was helping them to experience and disclose the underlying sentiments and values of their genuine personal identity. The challenge for the therapist was to allow their views to emerge without imposing hasty interpretations or moving the therapeutic process too quickly.

Legitimacy is another key element in the invisibility syndrome model. One of the objectives in this moment of the group process was to delve into how much the men experienced Jomo's problem as exclusively his in spite of nodding heads of affirmation.

It was therefore important for the men to engage in solving the problem by suggesting what Jomo should have done. The therapist monitored and guided suggested solutions by accepting the group members' intent but cautioning the men to not be too judgmental. Each man was asked to reflect on how they would first "*feel* in [Jomo's shoes] and then *think* how they would handle it."

Many African American men find not only a lack of validation for their views, contributing to a sense of feeling invisible, but also a sense that the places in which their views are validated are somehow not hospitable and therefore not the correct place for them to be. The group's validating Jomo's experience, helping him sort out his feelings, and offering emotional support beyond providing task oriented solutions made the group feel like a legitimate place to be, and dynamically integrated acknowledgment and satisfaction into the process. Lack of acknowledgment and satisfaction are other dynamic components of the invisibility syndrome.

The therapist should not discourage the inclination of group members to take charge—to exert competence through demonstrating power with suggestions about handling the situation. This is an important facet of masculinity ideology (if not always constructive and helpful male behavior), and it is not the therapist's place to insist on a conformance to desired contemporary gender role values absent mutual agreement about such need to change. It is helpful to remember that in therapy we treat what is presented and have to deal with the way people actually are.

In order to maintain a level of bonding, the therapist must start with the men's conception of gender role values and behavior. To deprive African American men of this effective tool during the initial therapy process will mimic the defacing and disempowering experiences of everyday racism for them. On the other hand, the therapist must not imprudently indulge members' tendencies to use racism or sexism as excuses for not exercising personal responsibility.

ANGER AT AFRICAN AMERICANS AND POWERLESSNESS

African American men's anger arises not only at injustices from racism alone. The men struggle with sorting out for themselves when to attribute destructive behavior they see or experience in the African American community to racial injustices, or when to attribute it fundamentally to a breakdown of individual personal responsibility.

This dilemma reflects their own struggle with honesty and self-integrity. Can they be fair in the criticism of African Americans as well as themselves? Knowing where to place the blame is confusing and often distressing to them. It forces them to confront their own stereotypes about, their identification with, and what they have contributed to changing circumstances for African Americans. This underlying dynamic theme at this point in the group process acts as a challenge, raising tensions between group members as they state and search for justification of their stance:

HICKS: "... I have rage at both Black and White people if I really let it go. Black folks tend to do more (physical) harm ... than what you get from White folks."

DON: "... a lot of my rage comes from how my [African American] people are now (meaning conditions of African Americans and the way they act) ... and how I come to deal with that.

"You know, we have some decent guys here [in the group] ... and all of us have a certain degree of rage ... well imagine those kids [out in the street] who don't have the moral checks as we do ... you know, ... there are a lot just walking around ready to blow up."

THERAPIST: "A lot of what is at the source of your rage is not only racism and feelings you have about White people but also the feelings over the divisiveness amongst Black folks and what they do to each other.

"You've got a set of anger that's reserved for our own [Black] folks ... you've got a set of anger reserved for White folks. What do we do with all of that?

"I think it's important to understand where the rage comes from ... it's our own anger at ourselves as well as the treatment that we get from White people ... it jams us up!"

Jomo: "Yeah!! Then it goes somewhere! We don't always know where it goes . . . but it goes somewhere.

"I feel like I walk around with rage . . . I stuff it . . . when I find myself doing self destructive things . . . I say to myself, ooOhh! that's where some of that(anger) has gone . . . sometimes we do inflict damage on ourselves.

". . . When I find myself really angry and I stuff it (pause), I've wondered . . . what package did I put that in? . . . I mean, I know I put it somewhere because it didn't just disappear?"

Therapist: "That's a really important observation . . . It should really make everybody think . . . do you know where your anger goes . . . whether it's provoked by racism from White folks or aggravation from Black folks? . . . Do you know what form it comes out in? . . . Do you know how it's wrapped the next time you see it? . . . How well do you know yourself?"

Don: (Reflectively) "Real deep (stuff) huh!!"

DISCUSSION

Comprehending the source of African American men's anger involves recognizing its historic context—how prejudice and discrimination has created an environmental climate of racism that requires African Americans to manage a legacy of stereotypes and mis-attributions about them. It also entails assessing the psychological toll each individual experiences from perceived acts of racism and how such acts lead to the person feeling that their genuine talents and personality are made invisible giving rise to a sense of personal powerlessness.

Moreover, given the reality of racism, a difficult area of personal assessment for African American men is putting the victim mentality into perspective, and genuinely distinguish between how much personal responsibility versus racism is at the source of individual achievements. The etiology of African American men's anger, therefore, is greater than its simple outward or inward manifestations would suggest, and in fact, has an origin far more complex, and rooted in their unique psychological experience of the world.

Therapist Observations about African American Anger

1. African American men's expression of anger can come from a variety of sources, such as feelings of invisibility due to racism and

society's conflicting messages about gender expectations for African American men. These messages present a multiple dilemma for African American men that engenders confusion, disillusionment, and frustration. Typical gender triggers include upholding one's personal ideal as provider and protector. However, there are also racial triggers, such as the values about being appropriately African American; or African American men learning to navigate around racism's dictates in order to fulfill the personal ideal of family provider and protector. A source of great frustration in this dilemma is knowing when and how to be assertive versus aggressive while contending with gender role urges and expectations.

2. The struggle with real or imagined constraints from racism can be anguishing and burdensome for African American men. There is pressure to "be like a man," solve the problem, "to be in control." But the quest for self-efficacy is undermined, if not vigilant and resilient and armed with compensatory skills, by the elusiveness, unpredictability, and persistence of racism.

   This puts African American men at risk for confusion and disillusionment about self-efficacy in their life. An example of how frustration and anger develops is illustrated by the proverbial "slippery slope" phenomenon in which acts of racism pull the rug out from under achievement and personal growth. This undermines confidence and self-efficacy and gives further credence to externalization of reasons for one's status in life while corrupting honesty in ownership of personal responsibility for individual behavior.

3. Gender and racial role values are interdependently determined by society and the African American community. Sorting out the values to subscribe to and then living by them becomes a particular stressor. One dimension of the stress is gender and racial expectations about how men are to seek help and provide support to each other. Very often the contradictions in these expectations work against men assisting each other with the emotional stress and self-doubt about gender role performance.

4. Managing stereotypes and microaggressive racial slights can result in an African American man's invisibility as a genuine person. Trying to have true talents, skills and personality acknowledged becomes a daily quest for finding acceptance and dignity in spite of the persistence of racism. This struggle wears on the emotional well-being of African American men, forcing self-evaluations about tolerance and acceptance of this kind of treatment.

Therapist Observation about the Group Process

The therapeutic support group for African American men has several goals essential to its unique purpose:

1. To be a safe place where (fraternal) trust between African American men can be renewed and transformed so that members may use each other as a resource and a support in the clarification and pursuit of constructive personal life goals.
2. The group is also structured and considered as an alternate peer group and network different from the men's conventional friendships. In this regard the group becomes a new peer gathering place in which efforts at coping with vulnerabilities, self-doubt, and disillusionment are respected.
3. Boundary issues between group members are also allowed to be flexible extending to the development of an out-of-group friendship if desired. This natural inclination is considered important in the transformation of trust between African American men wherein the modeling of new relationship behavior in everyday settings can become a part of the weekly group process.
4. A therapist with an informal interpersonal style with an integrated psychotherapy orientation to group process combined with good personal comfort around African American men will likely be effective in engaging and keeping them in a support group.
5. African American men will respond positively to a group focused upon self-empowerment and achieving personal life goals maintaining self-respect and dignity.

SUMMARY

Working with African American men in group or individual therapy can be effective if the orientation to providing this service is appropriate. Therapist's knowledge about gender and racial issues for African American men is essential. It includes being able to distinguish when masculinity ideology and evolving contemporary male values of African American men are similar to most men, regardless of ethnicity, and when they are distinctively African American. It also involves understanding how society has shaped the meaning of gender values and rules of conduct.

These considerations provide context for also comprehending the complexity of experience, and expression of anger in African American men. Anger in African American men is as much tied to their attempts to sort out personal responsibility in self-efficacy unrelated to racism, as it is tied to their experience of racism. So often anger in African American men is erroneously linked to a perception that a volatile internalized "Black rage" looms percolating beneath the surface. Anger has many sources for African American men as it does for everyone. Utimately confronting and resolving fears, and misconceptions about African American men, combined with a personal comfort level, remains an essential therapist's attribute to work successfully with African American men.

REFERENCES

Anderson, N. B. (Ed.). (1995). Behavioral and sociocultural perspectives on ethnicity and health [Special issue]. *Health Psychology, 14*(7), 589–655.

Bell, D. (1992). *Faces at the bottom of the well: The permanence of racism.* New York: Basic Books.

Billingsley, A. (1992). *Climbing Jacob's ladder: The enduring legacy of African American families.* New York: Simon & Schuster.

Bowman, P. J. (1992). Coping with provider role strain: Adaptive cultural resources among Black husband-fathers. In A. K. H. Burlew, W. C. Banks, H. P. McAdoo, & D. A. Azibo (Eds.), *African American psychology: Theory, research, and practice* (pp. 135–151). Newbury Park, CA: Sage.

Boyd, H., & Allen, R. L. (Eds.). (1995). *Brotherman: The odyssey of Black men in America.* New York: Ballantine Books.

Braithwaite, R. L., & Taylor, S. E. (Eds.). (1992). *Health issues in the Black community.* San Francisco: Jossey-Bass.

Butterfield, F. (1995, October 5). More Blacks in their 20's have trouble with the law. *The New York Times, National Report,* p. A18.

Cose, E. (1993). *The rage of a privileged class.* New York: HarperCollins.

Davis, L. E. (1984). Essential components of group work with Black Americans. *Social Work with Groups, 7*(3), 97–109.

Ellison, R. (1952). *Invisible man.* New York: Random House.

Feagin, J. R., & Sikes, M. P. (1994). *Living with racism: The Black middle-class experience.* Boston: Beacon Press.

Franklin, A. J. (1992, June). Therapy with African American men. *Families in Society: The Journal of Contemporary Human Services,* 350–355.

Franklin, A. J. (1993, July/August). The invisibility syndrome. *Family Therapy Networker,* 32–39.

Franklin, A. J. (1998). Invisibility syndrome in psychotherapy with African American males. In R. L. Jones (Ed.), *African American mental health.* Hampton, VA: Cobb & Henry.

Franklin, A. J. (1997). Importance of friendship issues between African American men in a therapeutic support group. *Journal of African American Men, 3*(1), 29–43.

Franklin, J. H., & Moss, A. A., Jr. (1994). *From slavery to freedom: A history of African Americans* (7th ed.). New York: Knopf.

Gibbs, J. T. (Ed.). (1988). *Young, Black, and male in America: An endangered species.* New York: Auburn House.

Ginzburg, R. (1962). *100 years of lynchings.* New York: Lancer Books.

Gordon, E. T., Gordon, E. W., & Nembhard, J. G. (1995). Social science literature concerning African American men. *Journal of Negro Education, 63*(4), 508–531.

Grier, W. H., & Cobbs, P. M. (1968). *Black rage.* New York: Basic Books.

Hammond, R., & Yung, B. (1993). Psychology's role in the public health response to assaultive violence among young African American men. *American Psychologist, 48*(2), 142–154.

Hutchinson, E. O. (1994). *The assassination of the Black male image.* Los Angeles: Middle Passage Press.

James, S. A., LaCroix, A. Z., Kleinbaum, D. G., & Strogatz, D. S. (1984). John Henryism and blood pressure differences among Black men: 2. The role of occupational stressors. *Journal of Behavioral Medicine, 7*(3), 259–275.

Jones, J. M. (1997). *Prejudice and racism* (2nd ed.). New York: McGraw-Hill.

Kovel, J. (1970). *White racism: A psychohistory.* New York: Vintage Books.

Krieger, N., & Sidney, S. (1996, October). Racial discrimination and blood pressure: The CARDIA study of young Black and White adults. *American Journal of Public Health, 86*(10), 1370–1378.

Levant, R. F., & Pollack, W. S. (Eds.). (1995). *A new psychology of men.* New York: Basic Books.

Majors, R., & Billson, J. M. (1992). *Cool pose: The dilemmas of Black manhood in America.* New York: Lexington Books.

Meth, R. L., & Passick, R. S. (Eds.). (1990). *Men in therapy: The challenge of change.* New York: Guilford Press.

Pierce, C. M. (1992, August). *Racism.* Paper presented at the conference on the Black family in America. Sponsored by the Connecticut Mental Health Center, the Yale University School of Medicine, Department of Psychiatry, and the Yale University Chapter of the Student National Medical Association, New Haven, CT.

Pleck, J. H. (1995). The gender role strain paradigm: An update. In R. F. Levant & W. S. Pollack (Eds.), *A new psychology of men* (pp. 11–32). New York: Basic Books.

Ridley, C. R. (1984). Clinical treatment of the nondisclosing Black client: A therapeutic paradox. *American Psychologist, 39*(11), 1234–1244.

Shapiro, D., Goldstein, I. B., & Jamner, L. D. (1996). Effects of cynical hostility, anger out, anxiety, and defensiveness on ambulatory blood pressure in Black and White college students. *Psychosomatic Medicine, 58,* 354–364.

Staples, R., & Johnson, L. B. (1993). *Black families at the crossroads: Challenges and prospects.* San Francisco: Jossey-Bass.

Stone, A. (1995, February 23). Educated Black women make biggest strides: Good, bad news found in census. *USA Today, The Nation,* p. 8A.

Sutton, A. (1996). African American men in group therapy. In M. Andronico (Ed.), *Men in groups: Insights, interventions, psychoeducational work.* Washington, DC: American Psychological Association.

Taylor, R. L. (Ed.). (1995). *African American youth: Their social and economic status in the United States.* Westport, CT: Praeger.

Yalom, I. D. (1985). *The theory and practice of group psychotherapy* (3rd ed.). New York: Basic Books.

CHAPTER 12

Being Gay and Being Male: Psychotherapy with Gay and Bisexual Men

Steven Schwartzberg and Lawrence G. Rosenberg

ESPITE A lengthy history of injustices perpetrated by mental health practitioners of most every theoretical stripe, gay and bisexual men are no strangers to psychotherapy (Bayer, 1981; Bell & Weinberg, 1978; Garnets, Hancock, Cochran, Goodchilds, & Peplau, 1991). In a survey of clinicians sponsored by the American Psychological Association, nearly all of the approximately 2500 respondents had knowingly worked with at least one gay or lesbian client (Garnets et al., 1991). However, the same study also found that many clinicians provided inadequate or uninformed care, ranging from the blatantly harmful (e.g., attempting to change or interpret a patient's sexual orientation, even when explicitly requested not to do so), to the more subtle and perhaps even unintentional, such as failing to recognize the legitimacy of gay relationships or sidestepping discussions of a sexual content.

Our goal in this chapter is to extend the model of gay–affirmative psychotherapy that has evolved over the past 25 years (e.g., Cabaj & Stein, 1996; Davison, 1976; Gonsiorek, 1985; Garnets & Kimmel, 1993; Isay, 1989, 1996; Isensee, 1992; Marmor, 1980; Silverstein, 1991; Stein & Cohen, 1986) by emphasizing one particular aspect of gay and bisexual men's experience: the interwoven processes of male enculturation and gay identity

formation. Gay men grow up both gay and male, and as such face significant obstacles, but also unique opportunities, in developing a healthy sense
of self. Understanding how these developmental processes interact can
provide a useful conceptual framework for clinical work with gay and bisexual men. More broadly, such a framework is relevant to psychotherapy
with *all* men, given that cultural attitudes about homosexuality are inextricably connected to beliefs about maleness and masculinity (Herek, 1986).[1]

We begin by presenting the case of a four-year psychotherapy with a gay
man, where issues of maleness and self-identity are one part of a more
complex picture. Robert's difficulties with disappointment, depression,
anger, and self-acceptance are one variation of a classic male struggle. The
topics that follow speak both to this specific case and other relevant clinical themes.

CASE STUDY: ROBERT

Robert began psychotherapy with Dr. M. when he was 25, referred by a
friend who feared he might kill himself. The most immediate cause for
Robert's severe depression and desire "to get out of this unfair world" was
the AIDS-related death of John, his lover. For the two years they were together, John had kept his HIV infection secret; only when he could no
longer hide the wasting symptoms of the disease did he tell Robert he was
ill. Hitting Robert just as deeply as this news was the confirmation of his
suspicions that John had been unfaithful during their relationship. Robert
was petrified that he, too, might be HIV-positive. He was relieved to learn
that he was not, but this did little to counter his rage at John's betrayals or
provide solace for his death.

When treatment began, Dr. M. was concerned with the degree to which
Robert's functioning had been disrupted. Early sessions aimed at getting
him back on his feet. Dr. M. provided support and some guidance about returning to work as a paralegal and establishing his own apartment. Once
these immediate concerns were addressed and a sense of crisis had passed,
therapy took a more exploratory tone. Bright, introspective, and very self-
critical, Robert quickly identified a long-standing theme of expectation
and disappointment, in other people and himself (he said he was always
"sabotaging" himself). His grieving process over John was complicated

---

[1] The clinical and developmental issues of gay men overlap with, but also differ from,
those of bisexual men. For the sake of brevity (but at the cost of some specificity), we address both groups together through most of the chapter. Particular issues relevant to bisexual men are discussed in a specific subsection.

by intense anger, which he mostly directed toward himself. John's multiple disloyalties also came to represent the many ways Robert felt he had been mistreated by his family and the world—a mistreatment, he later came to understand, not of outright abuse but of disregard and disapproval for who he was.

Robert began his life in what seemed to be a loving home. His parents were initially delighted to have a son after two daughters. However, as marital tensions worsened in his early childhood, he became the rope in a tug-of-war between an anxious, overprotective mother, given to occasional angry outbursts, and a forceful father, successful at his work but needing to maintain his dominance at home, and prone to burying his sense of inadequacy in beer. Robert learned that approval came from his mother for being "good," and from his father for being "tough." His father did not disguise his disappointment or anger when Robert sided with his mother and sisters in a family conflict.

Robert recalled his first awareness of being gay at around age 5, listening to a friend talk about taking showers with his father. By 7 or 8, he was consciously attracted to other boys, but hid these feelings in confusion. He dreaded gym class, where his teacher publicly ridiculed him for being chubby. He secretly idealized the more athletic boys and wished he was one of them. He enjoyed stereotypically feminine toys, such as his sisters' homemaker set, and evinced no talent or interest for sports. This seemed to further distance his father, who had hoped his son would be a Little League star.

As a young teenager, Robert experimented sexually a few times with other boys. Each brief foray brought excitement but great guilt, and he tried to suppress his homoerotic desires. In high school, he succeeded in appearing "straight" and dated a few girls. Although he achieved some popularity, he always felt fake. In schoolwork, he rarely reached his own perfectionistic standards and suffered depressed and edgy periods. Encouraged by his father, he then enlisted in the army for two years. Ironically, the military environment, which his father had envisioned would make Robert a "real" man, provided fertile ground to start accepting his gayness. He had his first, brief romance with a fellow enlistee.

In the years that followed, Robert had a few failed dating relationships and frequent one-night stands or anonymous sexual encounters. He usually met partners after downing a few drinks at his favorite gay bar. When he met John, Robert found himself falling in love with this masculine and handsome older man. Robert soon moved into John's apartment. His fantasy about having finally found romance overrode his doubts about John's capacity for a monogamous commitment. Robert suspected that John was having sex with other men, but his tentative inquiries about this were always fended off by John's, "Don't be ridiculous." Despite many problems in their relationship, when John died Robert lost not only his partner but what he had assumed was "a dream come true," and he was left disillusioned and embittered.

In his first year of psychotherapy, Robert continually tested the relationship's boundaries. He paid bills late, argued about fees, forgot appointments, and complained how "uncaring" Dr. M. was for always ending sessions at the designated time. Dr. M. tried talking about these behaviors as related to Robert's concerns with expectation and disappointment: Robert had identified this as an important theme, and perhaps he now often felt disappointed in Dr. M.? However, Robert dismissed all such statements as "irrelevant" or "hokey"—therapy was "different than real life," he was paying Dr. M. to help him, and "Why do all you shrinks think you're so important anyway?" Dr. M. believed that the therapeutic relationship was far from "irrelevant." He knew Robert was quite attached to him, but he heard Robert's statements as a need to protect himself from feeling too vulnerable in his dependency, and so backed away from any more direct statements about their relationship.

A change occurred after Robert telephoned Dr. M. late at night, drunk, following a stinging rejection from a potential "trick." Dr. M. managed to suppress his irritation at this inappropriately timed call. Even though it was 2:00 A.M., this was Robert's first overt attempt to reach out to him, and Dr. M. chose to offer the support and reassurance that Robert sought. As they discussed the meaning of this call in the following sessions, for the first time Robert was able to acknowledge Dr. M.'s importance to him. He also came to see that perhaps his earlier behaviors had been a way of testing to see if Dr. M. would abandon or disappoint him, like John and so many others had.

Robert's "testing" behaviors subsided, but he continued to disparage Dr. M. Eventually, he voiced a concern that had bothered him since the start of treatment: He was upset that Dr. M. was not "manly enough." Early on, he had made it clear that he was not sexually attracted to Dr. M., describing instead his "type" as a tall and masculine man, with no hint of femininity. At the time, Dr. M. had said nothing; now, he questioned Robert about his discomfort. In what ways did Robert see him as not manly enough? Could he say what it was about Dr. M.'s lack of manliness that made him react as he did?

Robert responded that "at a gut level" he disliked femininity in men. Dr. M. highlighted the intensity of this reaction, and tied it, gently but firmly, with Robert's ongoing, and mostly disowned, shame about his homosexuality. This led to renewed discussions of Robert's childhood. He had already shared many of the details; he now did so again, but this time with more awareness of long-forgotten pain about growing up a sissy. He discussed his memories of gym class and the many harassments he endured. He reconstructed his early family life with new emotional clarity: his mother's subtle but distinct disapproval when he engaged in feminine play activities; his sadness, confusion, and self-blame as his father incrementally withdrew from him.

Robert's knowledge from the onset of treatment that Dr. M. was gay (he had requested a gay therapist) affected the treatment in several ways. It sometimes made him feel that Dr. M. was on his side in sharing a common oppression. He appreciated Dr. M.'s familiarity with resources in the local gay community. And he assumed that Dr. M.'s own gayness gave him an understanding of his experience that a straight therapist would not have. However, Dr. M.'s orientation was not without its downsides. Even in the large city they lived in, their paths periodically crossed in nontherapy situations (each time leading to a brief discussion of how this affected Robert). Further, as he was eventually able to discuss, the fact that Dr. M. was also gay led to heightened feelings of envy and competition.

These feelings became particularly prominent when Robert learned through an acquaintance that Dr. M. and his long-term partner had recently affirmed their relationship in a commitment ceremony. Robert felt envy, but the knowledge of Dr. M.'s relationship also reconnected him with his own longings to be with a partner. With uncharacteristic empathy, he expressed his admiration for Dr. M. and spoke of his sadness at never having had such a close relationship with another man in his life, including with his father. He despaired that such a relationship might never happen.

These were moving and poignant discussions for both Dr. M. and Robert. Dr. M. addressed Robert's sadness in terms of his childhood, and how his father's disconnection seemed to set the stage for becoming depressed by men's disappointment in him, and his fears of their abandonment. But more importantly, Dr. M. eased his more characteristic therapeutic distance to tell Robert that he was genuinely touched by his expressions of admiration and goodwill, and moved by Robert's sense of longing. He spoke not only of Robert's life, but some of his own, and reflected on what "we" go through, as men, as gay men. He also highlighted the accomplishment of Robert's now being able to risk making himself vulnerable to Dr. M., to another man.

Looking back, Dr. M. saw these sessions, where he and Robert seemed to connect not just as therapist and patient but as two men together, as the transformative crux of the treatment. It had taken much patience and wrangling to get there, but after this juncture therapy took on a new tone. Robert began to redirect his anger away from Dr. M. and more toward those whom he felt had hurt, disappointed, or mistreated him. He seemed to experience an anger mixed with grief, sorrow, and moments of forgiveness. He focused on the people most central in his life: John, for his triple betrayal of infidelity, concealing his HIV status, and death; his father, who had misunderstood and rejected him for not being the son he wanted; and, posing the greatest difficulty, his mother, whose well-meaning but incessant protection inhibited him from discovering that he could truly take care of himself and develop a healthy competitiveness to be ambitious in the world. He also focused on his harsh perfectionism, and the anger he directed toward himself.

As Robert grew more tolerant of himself and others, his self-image shifted from being an inadequate person to being an attractive and strong man, able to get along in life, "just another gay man like the rest of us." In therapy, the volatility of the early relationship had long faded, and Robert now regarded Dr. M. as a "caring and concerned older brother." Near the end of therapy, he embarked on a new relationship. Tony was not the hypermasculine man of his earlier fantasies, but an emotionally available man whom Robert felt he could allow himself to trust. He and Tony met with Dr. M. together a few times to help Robert transfer his understanding of monitoring closeness and distance from the therapy relationship to his partnering relationship. Robert also wanted Dr. M.'s "seal of approval." At the time of termination, Robert felt more satisfied with his life and less depressed.

COMMONALITIES AMONG GAY, BISEXUAL, AND HETEROSEXUAL MEN

Robert, like all males in our culture, whether they are sexually attracted to males, females, or both, grew up influenced by powerful beliefs about how to be a man. All men begin with the experience of being born male,[2] with male anatomy, physiology, and whatever possible male sociobiological inheritance may accrue through evolution (Weinrich, 1987; Wilson,

---

[2] Occasional rare variations and ambiguities in anatomy at birth complicate gender identity as male or female (Money & Ehrhardt, 1972), but these anatomical anomalies are not relevant for the majority of individuals, regardless of sexual orientation. See Burr (1996) or DeCecco and Parker (1995) for reviews of biological theories of male homosexuality, including genetic, hormonal, and biochemical explanations.

1975). Boys are born into the press and privilege of expectations for male-appropriate behavior; they are treated differentially from girls even in infancy (Lewis, Scully, & Condor, 1992).

Through complex familial-societal processes of disidentification with females and identification with males, boys are taught—even pressured—to conform to a masculine style of behavior (e.g., Pollack, 1995). This socialization process, conditioned in manifold ways through explicit and vicarious rewards, punishments, and modeling, encourages particular "male" ways of managing (suppressing) emotion, taking action, and valuing autonomy over dependence or interdependence (Levant & Pollack, 1995). As part of this enculturation, all men are exposed to a constellation of beliefs that include the devaluation of women (sexism), the assumed normalcy or superiority of heterosexuality (heterosexism), and fear, disgust, and hatred of homosexuality (coined *homophobia* by G. Weinberg, 1972). In addition, even as socioeconomic, ethnic, and class differences create harsh inequities among men, many males accept as a birthright the powers and burdens accorded men in our heterosexual patriarchal culture.

Thus, in many gay and bisexual men we see the same psychological strengths that tend to typify heterosexual men, such as an action-oriented coping style, a capacity for logic-based decision making, and the healthy expression of aggression. But we can also see the same difficulties: alexithymia, difficulty compromising one's needs to foster an intimate relationship, rageful aggression, hurtful competition, narcissistic vulnerabilities, and acting out to manage disavowed emotion (Levant & Pollack, 1995). As with heterosexual males' difficulties with women in intimate relationships, two gay men, each with a legacy of male independence and an expectation of doing what he wants, may face particular obstacles in balancing autonomy and intimacy and sustaining romantic relationships (Forstein, 1986; McWhirter & Mattison, 1984).

DIFFERENCES IN SOCIALIZATION AND DEVELOPMENT BETWEEN GAY/BISEXUAL MEN AND HETEROSEXUAL MEN

These similarities go hand-in-hand with important differences between gay and bisexual men and their heterosexual peers. The entrenched existence of bias against homosexuality (e.g., Herek, 1990), the assumed naturalness of heterosexuality (Rich, 1980), and a traditional devaluation of women and femininity, result in a phenomenologically unique developmental and social experience for gay and bisexual men. Like Robert, almost all gay individuals must confront and work through *internalized homophobia* (G. Weinberg, 1972)—the shame-producing attribution to oneself of the homophobic attitudes that saturate, either overtly or by omission, most every stratum of our culture, including what might otherwise be the protective sanctum of family.

An Early Sense of "Differentness"

From as young as age 3 or 4, many boys have some inchoate form of awareness of their erotic inclinations (Savin-Williams, 1998; Stoller, 1968). For boys who later develop a homosexual or bisexual orientation, this awareness often results in feeling "different" (Coleman, 1981–1982; Troiden, 1979). This sense of differentness can powerfully influence a boy's intrapsychic development and interpersonal world, affecting peer relationships and familial dynamics, including father-son, mother-son, sibling, and husband-wife relationships.

This self-perception of differentness may hinge on conscious or preconscious erotic wishes—perhaps soothing or stimulating associations of physical contact with father or other boys, or an erotic reaction to looking at attractive men. Alternatively (or conjointly), it may arise from preferring styles of play, fantasy, and interpersonal interaction that more closely resemble feminine sex-typed behaviors than masculine ones. Nonconforming gender identity and interests characterize many (but not all) boys who later develop an erotic attraction toward males (Bell, Weinberg, & Hammersmith, 1981; Green, 1987; Savin-Williams, 1998).[3]

These boys' discordant experience, due to nonheterosexual erotic inclinations and/or nonmasculine style, can become the foundation of a negative identity, spoiling self-esteem (leading to feeling deviant, sinful, or not good enough), or possibly rupturing a basic sense of selfhood (feeling empty, as having no identity, or not existing). Thus, for example, when a boy with a special affinity for Dorothy in *The Wizard of Oz* realizes that his heartfelt renditions of "Somewhere over the Rainbow" and delight at wearing ruby slippers (mommy's red pumps) are not acceptable to his parents or other boys, the incongruity between others' expectations and his own developing sense of self is apt to leave him isolated and ashamed, and potentially the target of bullying, ostracism, and

---

[3] It is important to distinguish between three distinct concepts: sexual orientation (to whom one is attracted), gender role behavior (acting in a culturally sanctioned masculine or feminine manner), and "core gender identity" (a basic sense of oneself as male or female).

physical, sexual, or emotional abuse. In other words, from a self-psychological perspective, growing up gay in this culture is *inherently injurious*. The routine devaluation, tacit neglect, or frank abuse of this core aspect of self can be a repetitive and pervasive occurrence, and opportunities for the mirroring and idealization essential to healthy selfhood are typically rare or nonexistent (Gonsiorek & Rudolph, 1991).

ADOLESCENCE INTO ADULTHOOD

Given this situation, pubescent boys who become aware of an erotic attraction for males often experience these desires as egodystonic or even repugnant. Growing up in the age of AIDS furthers complicates the meanings attached to homoerotic interests and sexual behavior (Cadwell, Burnham, & Forstein, 1994; Morin, 1988; Schwartzberg, 1996). How is a transition then made from private shame to healthier self-esteem? Many stage models of gay or lesbian identity formation or the coming out process have been proposed (e.g., Cass, 1979; Coleman, 1981–1982; Hanley-Hackenbruck, 1989; Lee, 1977; Minton & McDonald, 1983–1984; Plummer, 1975; Troiden, 1979). These models differ in detail and in their degree of attention to intrapsychic phenomena, but most describe a roughly similar trajectory. A clinician's knowledge about this developmental journey, which typically has no parallel in most mainstream heterosexual lives, provides crucial information regarding appropriate psychotherapeutic expectations, difficulties, and interventions.

Initially, a person often rejects, ignores, or dreads the possibility of a homosexual orientation. Erotic desires or impulses toward other males stay "in the closet." They are compartmentalized, consciously maligned, repressed, or projected. Such defensive strategies may protect the self from what is perceived as too great a threat, but only as they "exact a high psychological price for their maintenance" (Gonsiorek, 1995, p. 30). The psychic suffering of people who remain at this stage can be immense. Internalized homophobia can fester into self-hate, resulting in a range of negative sequelae including depression, substance abuse, and sexual compulsivity (Coleman, 1992). Teenagers struggling with their sexual orientation are at higher risk than their heterosexual peers for drug involvement, homelessness, AIDS, and suicide, with as many as one-third of adolescent suicides related to sexual identity concerns (Gibson, 1989; Martin & Hetrich, 1988; Remafidi, 1989). In its most virulent form, the self-disgust is externalized and becomes the basis for hatred of and violence against gay people (Herek, 1986).

For the person moving forward in the coming-out process, the conflict of self-denial gradually shifts to a period of conscious struggle with accepting a gay or lesbian identity. To degrees that vary markedly, this typically includes sexual and/or romantic experimentation, initiating a process of self-disclosure to others, exploring the gay subculture (tentatively or voraciously), and incrementally recalibrating one's own sense of identity to include sexual orientation. The emergent conflicts of this period may be accompanied by a surge of psychiatric symptomatology, especially around issues of self-disclosure.

Ideally, this struggle then leads to a third stage, characterized by a fuller integration of sexual orientation into a more complete, less fragmented sense of self, concomitant with a significant reduction of internalized homophobia and an increased capacity for intimacy. Often, the gay person finds a new family among gay and lesbian friends and institutions and finds ways to synthesize his gay life with the broader heterosexual world.

Malyon (1982) emphasizes the biphasic nature of gay male development. In order to protect a core and extremely vulnerable aspect of selfhood, the gay adolescent buries his true self and develops an elaborate false self facade. As such, many of the pivotal tasks of adolescence, such as learning to date, integrating sexuality and intimacy, and modulating varying degrees of emotional and interpersonal intensity, go unmet (Malyon, 1982).

Upon coming out and leading a more explicitly gay-identified life—like Robert, a process that often starts in one's late teens or early 20s (Coleman, 1981–1982)—the opportunity arises to explore and develop this hidden true self. However, the young man now faces a marked developmental discontinuity. He lacks the experiential learning that many heterosexuals gained during adolescence, and must address these tasks at a chronological age that does not match his developmental age. Clinically, men in this situation can appear to manifest a range of psychological disorders, including character pathology, given the adolescent or immature nature of their defensive functioning, interpersonal connections, and identity integration. But these phenomena may more accurately reflect normative developmental delay than structural pathology (i.e., they are appropriate for adolescence), and remit with ongoing experience, reparation to the damaged self, and the gradual shedding of long-internalized shame.

OTHER UNIQUE ASPECTS OF GAY
AND BISEXUAL IDENTITIES

Most models of gay identity formation center on undoing the intrinsic psychic damage of internalized homophobia. As such, they parallel other models that describe accepting nonmainstream, oppressed, or stigmatized identities (see Hall, Cross, & Freedle, 1972, on the process of adopting a positive African-American identity). In essence, these are roadmaps for recovering from a sense of deviation. While this is a crucial aspect of the gay male experience, to regard it as the only feature distinguishing heterosexual and homosexual men is to ignore other potentially unique aspects of gay and bisexual men's psychology.

Brown (1988) suggests that three aspects of modern gay life—biculturalism, marginality, and forging new cultural norms—can contribute to an enriched life perspective. Gay people are bicultural in that most grow up in heterosexual families, immersed in heterosexual culture. As with members of other minorities, this dual affiliation allows gay people to be fluent in the ways of at least two cultures—the heterosexual mainstream and the rich, multifaceted subculture of gay male or female life (and often a third culture as well, for gay, lesbian, and bisexual members of ethnic communities). Marginality can be an oppressive burden, but it also allows for potential freedom from repressive social conventions. The opportunity to create new norms speaks to the unprecedented development in Western culture of a large and publicly open gay/lesbian minority. As such, gay men are in the position of needing to create, rather than inherit, self and communal identities.

In contrast to the fear and rejection that many gay men anticipate, coming out can be a liberating, empowering, even celebratory experience. Gay male communities have much less rigid restrictions about expressing affection, emotion, and other traditionally nonmasculine behaviors than the culture at large. Gay men also have great flexibility in styles of expressing sexual behavior, with subcultural norms accommodating styles ranging from monogamy to open relationships to regular, casual trysting.

Gay and bisexual men have long been influential in many aspects of our larger society, present (if not always visible) in every walk of life, and perhaps particularly prominent in cultural arenas such as theater, art, fashion, taste, and styles of humor. Not all cultures are as homophobic as ours (Ford & Beach, 1951; Weinrich & Williams, 1991) and, in contrast to the stigma in our culture, several others accord an esteemed status to men who engage in homoerotic activity or adopt a female-oriented identity. Such persons may be regarded as healers or shamans, or as bearing a special capacity for spirituality or wisdom (Weinrich & Williams, 1991). Often, this esteemed status relates to integrating traits of masculinity and femininity and, by so doing, developing a life perspective unattainable by the society's more conventional members.

SEXUAL ORIENTATION AND MASCULINITY

In our culture, however, it is this same blurring of distinct masculine and feminine identities that fuels the virulence of homophobia. In other words, fear and hatred of gay men may have at its core a terror regarding homosexuality's unconscious equation with femaleness and femininity (Herek, 1986; Pleck, 1981). Male homosexuality, as epitomized by anal penetration, can stir a man's deep fear of emasculation and "getting fucked" (Hocquenghem, 1978). As such it elicits a much sharper phobic response than female homosexuality.

Robert was typical of many gay men: The same dread of femininity that characterizes many heterosexual men is often a key component of gay men's internalized homophobia. Internal conflicts and defensive barriers regarding issues of masculinity and femininity are not unusual. Typically, gay and bisexual men in the early stages of coming out, or those who bear great shame regarding their sexuality, express strong discomfort with effeminate gay men, projecting onto them their own fears of female identification. In psychotherapy with such men, it can be useful to elicit the person's mental fantasy of a gay man. Invariably, the image is that of an effeminate, limp-wristed stereotype, with a verbal response along the lines, "I may be gay, but I don't want to be like that . . ."

Although it typically goes unspoken, a crucial part of gay and bisexual men's self-acceptance involves undergoing a process of redefining what it means to be a man. Some gay men continue to maintain a strong "male" identification, but with new, less restrictive or homophobic criteria for determining manliness. This may even involve regarding being the receptive partner in anal intercourse as the ultimate act of manhood, given the courage and cultural defiance it may take to allow this penetration to occur. Other gay men reject conventional notions of masculinity and instead embrace more of a sense of personhood, integrating aspects of maleness and femaleness.

Conflicts about masculinity and femininity echo at the community level as well. Gay liberationists in the 1960s and early 1970s imagined a future where gay men would be at the vanguard of ushering in a new type of male androgyny and breaking down doctrinaire notions of masculinity (Altman, 1982; Bronski, 1984). However, within a few years, gay male culture took a markedly different turn and instead began glorifying a hypermasculine ethos. Conflicts about masculinity and femininity still abound in gay male life; thus, it is not uncommon for a burly, hypermuscular man to greet another similar looking buddy of his with a hearty, "Girlfriend!"

APPLYING A THEORY OF PRE-OEDIPAL MALE DEVELOPMENT

Theoretically, the increased access to feminine parts of the self that some gay men experience reflects differences in early development. Pollack (1995) theorizes that in culturally normative child-rearing, pre-Oedipal boys are prematurely forced to "dis-identify" with their mother. He argues that this premature separation does not lay the foundation for a healthy adult sense of autonomy (as it is traditionally cast), but instead represents a fundamental, traumatic breach of early connection that leads to later intrapsychic and interpersonal difficulties in men's lives, including "shame-induced defensive autonomy, stoic repression of pain and sadness, and the need to defend against the vulnerability of the interdependent human condition" (p. 31).

Pollack also proposes that boys' subsequent identification with father perpetuates males' internal difficulties with intimacy and emotionality, because fathers typically embody these fundamental traits of disconnection themselves. The initial seed of defensive autonomy may take root with a premature rupture from mother, but it grows to full flower in a world where fathers and most male role models exemplify this style.

To what extent do these ideas apply to gay men? In a manner that parallels heterosexual development, gay boys (like all boys) are encouraged to dis-identify with and disengage from too close a bond with their mothers. However, development may then take a divergent path, particularly for boys whose gender-role identity includes elements of the feminine. These boys may neither dis-identify with their mothers *nor* develop the same kind of identification with their fathers as do other boys.

One might speculate various reasons for this. Perhaps certain boys have a biological predisposition toward female (and hence maternal) identifications (e.g., Green, 1987; Money, 1970). Perhaps gender-atypical boys harbor a sexual longing for father in what amounts to a sort of reverse Oedipal situation, and thus identify with mother unconsciously to fulfill and quell this desire (Isay, 1989). Perhaps fathers, who need to sustain their own masculine and heterosexual identities, consciously or unconsciously make themselves less available to effeminate sons than they would (or do) to sons of a more familiar, and less psychologically threatening, nature. The quiet, sensitive boy, or the one whose temperament or interests are not conventionally masculine, may be singled out and hurt by an angry, insecure father, needing to prove his power and subjugate any hints of nonmasculine or homoerotic behavior in his child. This scenario fits Robert's description of his early family life, where his father's increasing distance matched his disappointment, and likely discomfort, in not raising "a Little League star."

With boys who do not identify with father, mother may re-emerge, or stay constant as, an object of identification. Again, this may be formulated in various ways: perhaps mother, in reaction to father's conscious or unconscious distancing, moves closer to protect her son; or, perhaps gender atypical boys, having a powerful pull toward typically feminine pursuits or identifications, maintain a connection with mother in a less differentiated way than other boys.

This unbroken or reconstituted mother-son connection may give rise to a deeply damaging no-win bind. Father does not serve as a model for identification, even in dis-identification. Mother may serve such a role, but maintaining this connection occurs only in the barbed context of being a "mama's boy," with its yoke of internalized shame and social opprobrium. Further, if mother maintains such a connection primarily because of her anxieties about separation or unmet needs to be loved, admired, or idealized, then significant difficulties with modulating closeness and distance are likely to develop.

Yet maintaining such a bond with mother may also yield psychological benefits. In particular, it may soften the blow of dis-identification that Pollack (1995) theorizes ordinarily causes such harm. By maintaining an ongoing, reconstituted, or less truncated connection with mother, certain boys have the opportunity to develop or recognize an internal familiarity with feminine attributes that other boys and men often lack: an increased comfort and awareness of emotion, heightened interpersonal and relational sensitivity, and a less sexist or misogynistic worldview.

SUBCULTURAL LIFE AND DIVERSITY AMONG GAY AND BISEXUAL MEN

In addition to these unique developmental processes, clinicians working with gay and bisexual men also need to be familiar with subcultural norms and issues of modern gay male life. This includes sensitivity to the range of ways gay communities differ from the dominant heterosexual culture in acceptable sexual styles of sexual behavior, relationship patterns (Forstein, 1986; McWhirter & Mattison, 1984), coping with the ongoing press of homophobia and self-disclosure, the enormous and multilayered effects of AIDS (Schwartzberg, 1996), and even in the unspoken etiquette of day-to-day interactions.

It is also important to bear in mind the heterogeneity of homosexuality: gay and bisexual men constitute a markedly diverse group. Crucial factors of identity and development—family of origin dynamics, a history of trauma or abuse, psychopathology independent of sexual orientation—all play a significant role in shaping individual psychology and appropriate treatment. The clinical literature includes many works addressing specific concerns of gay men and women of many different ethnicities and subcultures (e.g., Chan, 1995; Espin, 1987; Greene, 1994; Icard, 1985–1986; Loiacano, 1989), gay men with a history of sexual abuse (e.g., Hunter, 1990; Lew, 1990; Rosenberg, 1995), and the interplay of sexual orientation and psychopathology (Gonsiorek, 1991).

In fact, it is actually hard to say just who is gay or bisexual and who is not. Many gay men, including Robert, follow a particular pattern: a boy who develops some awareness of his erotic attractions by adolescence, adopts the term gay or bisexual for himself during adolescence or early adulthood, and chooses to label himself as such as an explicit, perhaps central, aspect of his identity. Yet, not all men with homoerotic desires follow this path. Many men who have sex with other men do not call themselves bisexual or gay. Some men who *do* self-identify as gay are not sexually active and may never even have had a sexual encounter with another man. The more behaviorally descriptive terminology, "men who have sex with men," has been adopted by HIV and sex educators to include men whose activity is homoerotic but whose self-definition is not because of the lack of congruity between self-labelled identity, sexual behavior, and erotic desire (Laumann, Gagnon, Michael, & Michaels, 1994).

For some younger persons with the good fortune to grow up in contemporary families or communities that are accepting of gay, lesbian, bisexual, and transgendered persons, the early tribulations of gay identity formation and internalized homophobia may be attenuated, or perhaps even bypassed completely. On the other hand, men who do not accept their attraction to males may throw themselves into a heterosexual life, dating women and getting married in order to maintain an acceptable public face and deny their private inclinations. This may lead to a painfully compartmentalized double life involving clandestine, often anonymous, sexual encounters with men.

The self-esteem of men with homoerotic interests is always vulnerable, regardless of self-definition, degree of "outness," or style of adaption.[4] The "invisible" gay man who appears conventionally heterosexual and

---

[4] de Monteflores (1986) describes various styles of adaptation, or "managing difference," used by lesbians and gay men, as well as other stigmatized groups: assimilation with the mainstream, confronting and asserting one's difference; congregating into ghettoized communities; and celebrating fringe and/or special characteristics that distinguish the subculture from the mainstream.

masculine may endure as much psychic pain as the "visible" gay man, whose mannerisms, speech, or interests lead to social stigma. The "invisible" gay man is falsely esteemed for someone he is not, the "visible" gay man too often degraded for who he truly is.

ISSUES OF RELEVANCE TO BISEXUAL MEN

Bisexual men face some distinct psychological issues that differ from those of gay men (see Fox, 1995, for a detailed review of theoretical and developmental issues of particular relevance to bisexuality). Men choose to self-identify as bisexual for a variety of reasons. Several typologies of bisexuality provide theoretical or descriptive models for this diversity (e.g., Klein, 1993; Ross, 1991; M. Weinberg, Williams, & Pryor, 1994). Some men who label themselves bisexual are in the developmental process of coming out as gay, and eventually adopt a homosexual self-identity. Others derive erotic pleasure from both men and women, either concurrently or sequentially, and are not heading toward a polarized, either-or destination.

Perhaps ironically, bisexual men in psychotherapy may face more clinical bias than gay men. Clinicians may be more apt to pathologize or disbelieve the validity of bisexuality than homosexuality, despite ample data that indicate its existence and nonpathological nature (Fox, 1995). As with homosexuality, studies of bisexual individuals in nonclinical populations indicate no differences in psychological adjustment from heterosexuals (Weinberg et al., 1994). Countertransference issues with bisexual clients may be particularly relevant, with a clinician's internal discomfort with bisexuality and rigid adherence to a more dichotomous, either-or model of sexuality.

Bisexual men often face the additional stressor of lacking the multifaceted community supports that are now available to gay men, particularly in urban areas. Bisexual men may feel as if they are unwelcome in both gay and straight communities. Another unique stressor is developing and maintaining long-term relationships, with bisexual men often facing particular dilemmas in making a long-term intimate commitment to one person.

FURTHER CONSIDERATIONS FOR
THE PSYCHOTHERAPIST

The fundamental tenets of good psychotherapy—empathy, support, nonjudgmentalism, and commitment—obviously apply to treatment with gay and bisexual men. Yet because of the inescapable homophobic and heterosexist biases that permeate our culture, and the likelihood that many clinicians have only limited knowledge about life in the gay community, therapists must also attend to the specific impact of homophobia on all aspects of treatment, including transference and countertransference (American Psychological Association Committee on Lesbian and Gay Concerns, 1991; Cabaj & Stein, 1996; Gonsiorek, 1985; Silverstein, 1991; Stein & Cohen, 1986). Given homophobia's sometimes subtle grip, merely believing that one is open-minded about homosexuality or bisexuality (or sexuality in general) is insufficient preparation.

Many types of errors can further damage gay and bisexual men's wounded selves. For instance, when taking a psychosocial history, therapists might not ask about, and clients might not volunteer, same-gender sexual experiences or fantasies, either because the therapist assumes heterosexual development or is anxious or judgmental about homoerotic desire. Implicitly, the communication is "We don't talk about that here," or "Your kind doesn't exist," thus reinforcing the invisibility and implicit deviance of homosexuality. Therapists who are unresolved about their own sexual feelings may also unconsciously communicate critical messages about the range of acceptable sexual expressions, overtly or by omission.

Or, in assuming that a gay male couple has failed to achieve a mature intimacy because the relationship is not monogamous, a therapist may be misapplying traditional heterosexual values, ignoring research that one key to longevity and happiness for some successful gay male couples is the freedom for one or both partners to be sexual with other men (Forstein, 1986; McWhirter & Mattison, 1984).

Given that more and more gay men and lesbian women are choosing to raise families (and that many gay or bisexual men already have children through more conventional means), homophobic biases about child rearing also need to be examined. Harboring unexamined doubts about the capacity of gay men to raise healthy children can impede a therapist in helping some men accept and act on their natural generative and parenting desires.

Also important is attending to the vicissitudes of the erotic interplay between client and therapist. This is particularly relevant when working with gay or bisexual men, whose sexual impulses may either be denied or exaggerated in the clinician's mind. Regardless of gender or erotic orientation, all clinicians must be aware of the possibility of affectional or erotic attractions traveling from client to therapist and vice versa (Cabaj & Stein, 1996; Pope, Sonne, & Holroyd, 1993; Silverstein, 1991; Stein

& Cohen, 1986). Sometimes, surprises emerge as a therapy relationship develops: a heterosexual male therapist discovers that he has erotic fantasies about a male client, or a female therapist finds that a gay male client expresses attraction for her. These potentially anxiety-arousing and eye-opening erotic events can potentially derail a therapy, either by suppressing exploration or being converted into action (by either therapist or client). This harm can be avoided if clinicians are willing to face and understand the erotic forces at play through their own introspection or supervision, and perhaps, depending on the therapeutic context, judiciously discuss them with the client.

Many gay or bisexual men, like Robert, prefer to work with a therapist of the same sexual orientation, assuming that their experience will be better understood and less negatively judged. Some gay men may only feel comfortable discussing their own internalized homophobia with a gay clinician, fearing that nongay clinicians would misread normative expressions of self-doubt or self-condemnation as, "Maybe you don't really want to be gay." And many gay or bisexual men, particularly in the early stages of coming out, are hungry for appropriate gay role models in a heterosexual and heterosexist world.

The prevalence of misguided and even harmful treatments provided by heterosexual therapists over the decades lends support to gay and bisexual men's wariness of nongay clinicians. Yet it is also true that any thoughtful clinician, who has worked through his or her own discomforts about homosexuality and is well-informed, can offer excellent therapy to gay and bisexual men. Heterosexual therapists may even be able to offer gay and bisexual clients a uniquely reparative opportunity: ameliorating gay men's deeply lodged fears and angers, actual and transferential, toward the heterosexual community. The genuine support and acceptance of homosexuality, conveyed by an openly heterosexual clinician who symbolically represents the dominant culture, can be a powerful healing experience.

SUMMARY

In some fundamental ways, the psychology of maleness transcends the details of sexual orientation. Gay and bisexual men are men, and arrive in adulthood bestowed with the baggage and blessings of our cultural male inheritance. But at the same time, other aspects of identity and development are unique to gay and bisexual men. Some of these differences reflect the developmental trauma and profound narcissistic injury of growing up outside society's permissible norms of masculinity. But gay and bisexual men also have unique opportunities, and perhaps even developmental advantages, in building lives less constricted by social constraints. In this regard, many heterosexual men now struggle with a challenge that gay men have long faced: defining for oneself what it means to be a person, a man, when much of what we learned about manliness does not apply.

Ironically, if culturally normative child rearing *is* inherently damaging for boys, this, too, provides another similarity between homosexual and heterosexual men. Pollack (1995) traces the role of traditional psychological theory in endorsing and perpetuating a pathogenic model of "healthy" male development. Similarly, psychological theory for too long endorsed and perpetuated a pathological model of homosexuality, based in unexamined cultural prejudice but promulgated as scientific truth.

Mental health professionals do more than reflect the culture we live in: We have also accrued the power, tacitly or explicitly, to shape it. How willing we are to forget or disclaim this authority, and how easily we ignore the many social messages we convey in our very private work. But the words of an early gay liberationist are no less apt today than they were 40 years ago, when he railed against the mental health establishment's view of homosexuality as a mental illness, "When psychotherapy attempts to be more than just the key to free the poetry in man then it becomes another tyranny" (Allen cited in Bayer, 1981, p. 77).

REFERENCES

Altman, D. (1982). *The homosexualization of America, the Americanization of the homosexual.* New York: St. Martin's Press.

American Psychological Association Committee on Lesbian Gay Concerns. (1991). *Bias in psychotherapy with lesbians and gay men.* Washington, DC: American Psychological Association.

Bayer, R. (1981). *Homosexuality and American psychiatry: The politics of diagnosis.* New York: Basic Books.

Bell, A. P., & Weinberg, M. S. (1978). *Homosexualities: A study of diversity among men and women.* New York: Simon & Schuster.

Bell, A. P., Weinberg, M. S., & Hammersmith, S. K. (1981). *Sexual preference: Its development in men and women.* Bloomington: Indiana University Press.

Bronski, M. (1984). *Culture clash: The making of gay sensibility.* Boston: South End Press.

Brown, L. S. (1988). *New voices, new visions: Towards a lesbian/gay paradigm for psychology.* Paper presented at the 96th annual convention of the American Psychological Association, Atlanta.

Burr, C. (1996). *A Separate creation: The search for the biological origins of sexual orientation.* New York: Hyperion.

Cabaj, R. J., & Stein, T. S. (1996). *Textbook of homosexuality and mental health.* Washington, DC: American Psychiatric Association Press.

Cadwell, S., Burnham, R., & Forstein, M. (Eds.). (1994). *Therapists on the frontline: Psychotherapy with gay men in the age of AIDS.* Washington, DC: American Psychiatric Association Press.

Cass, V. (1979). Homosexual identity formation. *Journal of Homosexuality, 4*(3), 219–235.

Chan, C. S. (1995). Issues of sexual identity in an ethnic minority: The case of Chinese American lesbians, gay men, and bisexual people. In A. R. D'Augelli & C. J. Patterson (Eds.), *Lesbian, gay, and bisexual identities over the lifespan: Psychological perspectives* (pp. 87–101). New York: Oxford University Press.

Coleman, E. (1981–1982). Developmental stages of the coming out process. *Journal of Homosexuality, 7*(2/3), 31–43.

Coleman, E. (1992). Is your patient suffering from compulsive sexual behavior? *Psychiatric Annals, 22,* 320–325.

Davison, G. C. (1976). Homosexuality: The ethical challenge. *Journal of Consulting and Clinical Psychology, 44,* 157–162.

DeCecco, J. P., & Parker, D. A. (Eds.). (1995). *Sex, cells, and same-sex desire: The biology of sexual preference.* New York: Harrington Park Press.

de Monteflores, C. (1986). Notes on the management of difference. In T. Stein & C. Cohen (Eds.), *Contemporary perspectives on psychotherapy with lesbians and gay men* (pp. 73–101). New York: Plenum Press.

Espin, O. (1987). Issues of identity in the psychology of Latina lesbians: Explorations and challenges. In Boston Lesbians Psychologies Collectives (Eds.), *Lesbian psychologies* (pp. 35–51). Urbana: University of Illinois Press.

Ford, C. S., & Beach, F. A. (1951). *Patterns of sexual behavior.* New York: Harper & Row.

Forstein, M. (1986). Psychodynamic psychotherapy with gay male couples. In T. S. Stein & C. J. Cohen (Eds.), *Contemporary perspectives on psychotherapy with lesbians and gay men* (pp. 103–137). New York: Plenum Press.

Fox, R. C. (1995). Bisexual identities. In A. R. D'Augelli & C. J. Patterson (Eds.), *Lesbian, gay, and bisexual identities over the lifespan: Psychological perspectives.* New York: Oxford University Press.

Garnets, L. A., Hancock, K. A., Cochran, S. D., Goodchilds, J., & Peplau, L. A. (1991). Issues in psychotherapy with lesbians and gay men: A survey of psychologists. *American Psychologist, 46*(9), 964–972.

Garnets, L. A., & Kimmel, D. C. (Eds.). (1993). *Psychological perspectives on lesbian and gay male experiences.* New York: Columbia University Press.

Gibson, P. (1989). Gay male lesbian youth suicide. In *Alcohol, drug abuse, and mental health administration's report of the secretary's task force on youth suicide* (pp. 16–142). Washington, DC: U.S. Government Printing Office.

Gonsiorek, J. C. (Ed.). (1985). *A guide to psychotherapy with gay and lesbian clients.* New York: Harrington Park Press.

Gonsiorek, J. C. (1991). The empirical basis for the demise of the illness model of homosexuality. In J. C. Gonsiorek & J. D. Weinrich (Eds.), *Homosexuality: Research implications for public policy* (pp. 115–136). Newbury Park, CA: Sage.

Gonsiorek, J. C. (1995). Gay male identities: Concepts and issues. In A. R. D'Augelli & C. J. Patterson (Eds.), *Lesbian, gay, and bisexual identities over the lifespan: Psychological perspectives.* New York: Oxford University Press.

Gonsiorek, J. C., & Rudolph, J. R. (1991). Homosexuality identity: Coming out and other developmental events. In J. C. Gonsiorek & J. D. Weinrich (Eds.), *Homosexuality: Research implications for public policy.* Newbury Park, CA: Sage.

Green, R. (1987). *The "sissy boy" syndrome and the development of homosexuality.* New Haven, CT: Yale University Press.

Greene, B. (1994). Ethnic-minority lesbians and gay men: Mental health and treatment issues. *Journal of Consulting and Clinical Psychology, 62,* 243–251.

Hall, W. S., Cross, W. E., & Freedle, R. (1972). Stages in the development of black awareness: An exploratory investigation. In R. L. Jones (Ed.), *Black psychology* (1st ed., p. 440). Harper & Row.

Hanley-Hackenbruck, P. (1989). Psychotherapy and the "coming out" process. *Journal of Gay and Lesbian Psychotherapy, 1*(1), 21–39.

Herek, G. M. (1986). On heterosexual masculinity: Some psychical consequences of the social construction of gender and sexuality. *American Behavioral Scientist, 29,* 563–577.

Herek, G. M. (1990). The context of antigay violence: Notes on cultural and psychological heterosexism. *Journal of Interpersonal Violence, 5,* 316–333.

Hocquenghem, G. (1978). *Homosexual desire.* London: Allison & Busby.

Hunter, M. (Ed.). (1990). *The sexually abused male* (Vols. 1 & 2). Lexington, MA: Lexington Books.

Icard, L. (1985–1986). Black gay men and conflicting social identities: Sexual orientation versus racial identity. *Journal of Social Work and Human Sexuality,* 4(1/2), 83–93.

Isay, R. A. (1989). *Being homosexual: Gay men and their development.* New York: Farrar, Straus and Giroux.

Isay, R. A. (1996). *Becoming gay: The journey to self-acceptance.* New York: Pantheon Books.

Isensee, R. (1992). *Growing up gay in a dysfunctional family.* New York: Prentice-Hall.

Klein, F. (1993). *The bisexual option* (2nd ed.). New York: Harrington Park Press.

Laumann, E. O. , Gagnon, J. H., Michael, R. T., & Michaels, S. (1994). *The social organization of sexuality: Sexual practices in the United States.* Chicago: University of Chicago Press.

Lee, J. A. (1977). Going public: A study into the sociology of homosexual liberation. *Journal of Homosexuality, 3*(1), 49–78.

Levant, R. F., & Pollack, W. S. (Eds.). (1995). *A new psychology of men.* New York: Basic Books.

Lew, M. (1990). *Victims no longer: Men recovering from incest and other sexual child abuse.* New York: HarperCollins.

Lewis, C., Scully, D., & Condor, S. (1992) Sex stereotyping of infants: A re-examination. *Journal of Reproductive and Infant Psychology, 10*(1), 53–61.

Loiacano, D. K. (1989). Gay identity issues among black Americans: Racism, homophobia and the need for validation. *Journal of Counseling and Development, 68,* 21–25.

Malyon, A. K. (1982). Biphasic aspects of homosexual identity formation: Coming out as a second adolescence. *Psychotherapy, 19*(3), 335–340.

Marmor, J. (Ed.). (1980). *Homosexuality: A modern reappraisal.* New York: Basic Books.

Martin, A. D., & Hetrich, E. S. (1988). The stigmatization of the gay and lesbian adolescent. *Journal of Homosexuality, 15,* 163–183.

McWhirter, D., & Mattison, A. (1984). *The male couple.* Englewood Cliffs, NJ: Prentice-Hall.

Minton, H. L., & McDonald, G. J. (1983/1984). Homosexuality identity formation as a developmental process. *Journal of Homosexuality, 9,* 91–104.

Money, J. (1970). Sexual dimorphism and homosexual gender identity. *Psychological Bulletin, 74,* 425–440.

Money, J., & Ehrhardt, A. (1972). *Man, woman, boy, girl.* Baltimore: Johns Hopkins University Press.

Morin, S. F. (1988). AIDS: The challenge to psychology. *American Psychologist, 43,* 838–842.

Pleck, J. H. (1981). *The myth of masculinity.* Cambridge, MA: MIT Press.

Plummer, K. (1975). *Sexual stigma: An interactionist account.* London: Routledge & Kegan Paul.

Pollack, W. S. (1995). Deconstructing dis-identification: Rethinking psychoanalytic concepts of male development. *Psychoanalysis and Psychotherapy, 12*(1), 30–45.

Pope, K. S., Sonne, J. L., & Holroyd, J. (1993). *Sexual feelings in psychotherapy.* Washington, DC: American Psychological Association.

Remafidi, G. (1989). Homosexual youth: A challenge to contemporary society. *Journal of American Medical Association, 258,* 222–225.

Rich, A. (1980). Compulsory heterosexuality and lesbian existence. *Signs: Journal of Women in Culture and Society, 5,* 631–660.

Rosenberg, L. G. (1995, August 13). *Trauma with a difference: Abuse of gay and bisexual males.* Paper presented at Symposium on Male Sexual Trauma Survivor—Gender-Specific Issues at American Psychological Association Convention, New York.

Ross, M. W. (1991). A taxonomy of global behavior. In R. A. P. Tielman, M. Carballo, & A. C. Hendricks (Eds.), *Bisexuality and HIV/AIDS: A global perspective* (pp. 21–26). Buffalo, NY: Prometheus Books.

Savin-Williams, R. C. (1998). *". . . And then I became gay": Young men's stories.* New York: Routledge.

Schwartzberg, S. (1996). *A crisis of meaning: How gay men are making sense of AIDS.* New York: Oxford University Press.

Silverstein, C. (Ed.) (1991). *Gays, lesbians, and their therapists: Studies in psychotherapy.* New York: Norton.

Stein, T. S., & Cohen, C. J. (Eds.). (1986). *Contemporary perspectives on psychotherapy with lesbians and gay men.* New York: Plenum Press.

Stoller, R. J. (1968). *Sex and gender: On the development of masculinity and femininity.* New York: Science House.

Troiden, R. (1979). Becoming homosexual: A model of gay identity acquisition. *Psychiatry, 42*, 362–373.

Weinberg, G. (1972). *Society and the healthy homosexual.* New York: St. Martin's Press.

Weinberg, M. S., Williams, C. J., & Pryor, D. W. (1994). *Dual attraction: Understanding bisexuality.* New York: Oxford University Press.

Weinrich, J. D. (1987). *Sexual landscapes: Why we are what we are; why we love whom we love.* New York: Scribner's.

Weinrich, J. D., & Williams, W. L. (1991). Strange customs, familiar lives: Homosexualities in other cultures. In J. C. Gonsiorek & J. D. Weinrich (Eds.), *Homosexuality: Research implications for public policy.* Newbury Park, CA: Sage.

Wilson, E. O. (1975). *Sociobiology: The new synthesis.* Cambridge, MA: Harvard University Press.

CHAPTER 13

When Women Treat Men: Female Therapists/Male Patients

Marlin S. Potash

STANLEY: I suppose I must be polygamous if I want more than one wife but I don't see why that should be derogatory. I think it's a sign of intelligence. I can reach the most intense state of being and awareness, and in each case it is totally sincere. I feel total fusion and ecstasy with Hilda . . . and with Patricia.

AUGUSTUS: Yes . . . bravo, Cookham.

STANLEY: Intimacy is important, don't you agree?

AUGUSTUS: Absolutely.

STANLEY: Why should I be deprived of her? My closest partner? Simply because a piece of paper says we're divorced?

AUGUSTUS: Bugger the law.

STANLEY: Exactly. My art is being interfered with! I need a dozen homes—that's what I'd like, with me as father in each. That's why men get irritable, they want a change of wife, maybe for just a short time. *(He groans.)* When I think of all the women I might have known!

from Gems, 1997

"Why must a man have only one woman?" laments modern British painter Stanley Spencer in the contemporary play, *Stanley.* If they were honest, he asserts, all men would admit they want more, for "the experience of loving a new woman enriches the old" (Gems, 1997, p. 55).

The women who are objects of this "loving devotion" are idealized, valued for their uniqueness and their role in the man's life. The frustration for Stanley is that women generally don't see things the same way. High-achieving men are not used to problems they cannot solve. In some cases, frustration leads them to therapy, in an attempt to seek relief and solve the problem (which is generally articulated as her displeasure or as his stress) and in my case, there is an additional factor: These men seek therapy with me, a woman therapist.

This chapter illustrates through a case of a man with multiple intimate partners the value-added as well as the conflict-created aspects of a therapeutic alliance in a cross-gender therapist pairing (i.e., when a female clinician treats male patients). I intertwine two major themes:

1. The clinical issues related to a common triad in professionally successful men: the alexithymic, extremely stressed man who confuses sex with intimacy, and
2. The specific treatment issues involved when a woman therapist treats these men.

CONFUSING SEX WITH INTIMACY

Professional success requires excellence in rational, intellectual, solution-oriented thinking, often leading to an overvaluation of these characteristics. Concomitant with this is undervaluation, or even exclusion, of those qualities of emotional life that make for healthier individuals: self-awareness, impulse control, internal motivation, empathy, interpersonal and social competency (Goleman, 1995).

The men I treat initially present themselves as healthy, self-assured, successful and albeit stressed. In New York City in the 1990s, the stress of success is ubiquitous. These highly accomplished investment bankers, media executives, attorneys, and fund managers know how to get to the bottom line, negotiate a deal to their clients' (and their own) benefit, wield power, and make money. It is in some measure the very professional mastery they experience that eventually unnerves them. They often ask, if I've been so successful, why can't I handle the stress better, why are other less competent people moving beyond me, why don't my personal relationships please me more, why am I feeling like this?

ALEXITHYMIA IN MEN

When men enter treatment, they frequently cannot articulate exactly why they've come or even how they are feeling. Recent developments in theory and research document the widespread nature of male alexithymia, that is, the extreme difficulty in experiencing feelings and putting them into words (Balswick, 1982; Brody & Hall, 1993; Eisenberg & Lennon, 1983; Helgeson, 1990; Krystal, 1979; Levant & Kopecky, 1995; Meth & Pasick, 1990; Sifneos, 1991). Mild alexithymia is often considered normative in men, an element of the current male gender role strain (Levant & Kopecky, 1995; Pleck, 1995) which stems in large part from seismic shifts in societal definitions of what it is to be a man or a woman.

Whereas women learn to "grow in connection" (Jordan, Kaplan, Baker, Stiver, & Surrey, 1991), traditional male gender formation rests largely on doing it alone (Levant & Pollack, 1995; Maccoby, 1990; Pleck, 1995; Pollack, 1990). Whereas women have been taught to explore and express emotions, men have traditionally learned to suppress emotions, particularly negative ones (Brody & Hall, 1993). Under such circumstances, the communication differences and difficulties men and women experience are not surprising (Tannen, 1990). What happens to these consciously unfelt, largely unspoken feelings men have? In addition to problems with intimacy and commitment, they often lead to extreme stress reactions.

Hans Selye (1984) defined stress as the nonspecific response of the body to any demand or the rate of wear and tear in the body. Since the initial publication of his seminal *The Stress of Life* in 1954, myriad psychological and physiological diseases have been shown to be correlated with maladaptation to stress: disabling depression, chronic anxiety and unremitting tension or hostility, backache and headache, and cardiovascular dysfunction, to name a few (Goleman, 1995; Helgeson, 1990; Moyers, 1993; Texas Heart Institute, 1996). The behavioral implications of excess stress in men include aggressive and antisocial behavior, and rates of substance abuse higher than women exhibit. Because stress takes such a toll on the body, mind, and interpersonal relationships, men pay an enormous price for their alexithymia and its concomitant stresses (Eisler, 1995; Goldberg, 1976).

Excessive adherence to stereotypic negative masculine characteristics correlates with higher levels of anger, anxiety, and health risk behaviors (Eisler, Skidmore, & Ward, 1988). Male gender role strain has been shown to be a strong predictor of depression in men (Papp, 1997; Sharpe & Heppner, 1991). Current research points to a depression ratio for women and men of approximately 2:1 (Culbertson, 1997). A major NIMH study suggests three explanations for the disparity: biological differences, psychosocial factors, or the fact that men less frequently seek treatment and thereby are not picked up by epidemiological studies (NIMH, D/ART Program, 1987). Because depression is viewed as a largely female psychological ailment and because men may tend to manifest depression differently from women, externalizing rather than internalizing their pain and often discharging distress through action (Real, 1997), physicians frequently underdiagnose depression in men, and under-referring such men for psychological treatment.

Extreme stress reactions and a tendency to somaticize unexpressed emotion eventually lead some men to seek medical attention for what they imagine to be purely physical conditions. Although physicians often overlook psychological symptoms in male patients, a number of cardiologists, neurologists, and internists refer male patients for psychological treatment. In treatment, these men undergo a sort of emotional skills training, motivated by their desire to avoid the eventual outcomes of extreme stress, the breakdown of the body and strained interpersonal relationships at work and at home (Potash, 1990).

THE SEXUAL/EMOTIONAL CONNECTION (OR LACK THEREOF)

Many men confuse sexual intimacy with emotional intimacy. Emotional intimacy requires acknowledging the partner as a person separate from oneself, with needs and feelings of her own (Chodorow, 1978). Relational sex suggests both individuals explore and share emotional vulnerabilities (caring, trusting, showing need) at the same time they are sexually intimate. The promise of merging in erotic, even spiritual bliss within an emotionally intimate relationship is enticing to some. Other men, fearing loss of independence and even identity, run from the possibility of such fusion. In the most extreme cases, establishing any emotional relationship with a sexual partner, and the terror of the dependency and commitment that it engenders, inhibits male erotic desire (Ehrenrich, 1983; Rhodes & Potash, 1988). Since normative male development places such a profound emphasis on differentiation from, and often devaluation of, the female and the feminine, this terror is understandable (Chodorow, 1989; Pollack, 1990).

"Regarding men's interest in sexual variety, I have never seen a study that indicated the contrary" (Zilbergeld, 1992, p. 557). "There seems to be no question but that the human male would be promiscuous in his choice of sexual partners throughout the whole of his life if there were no social restrictions" (Kinsey, Pomeroy, & Martin, 1948). Men who act on this wish for multiple partners, without emotional attachment to the women involved, depersonalize their sexual partners. Mike, a case study described later, talks about monogamy as monotony, and boredom being the emotion to avoid at all costs. Male sexual addicts exhibit these consequences of male gender role strain at its most extreme. Men who feel profoundly powerless and unworthy consider sex their most important need, the fulfilling of which will relieve all personal pain (Carnes, 1992).

The wish for multiple sexual partners makes the possibility of a monogamous relationship which is both sexually and emotionally intimate very difficult. Men's insistent sense of entitlement to sex (Rubin, 1990) and the myth of the omni-available woman (Person, 1986) raise other concerns. Harry, a property rights attorney, explains the differences between men and women in terms of what he calls "bachelor standards" or "mom standards." Bachelors' tolerance for mess, frozen food, and nonrelational sex are much higher than mom's, he asserts. The irony is in this patient's descriptions of the differences between himself and the women he dates: None are *his* mother and few are mothers at all. For Harry, men are bachelors taking care of themselves until a mom comes along to do it better, and all women are mothers-in-waiting, waiting to know and care for men better than men can themselves.

For another case, Ray, sexual intimacy is the only intimacy he understands. His wife's pleas for closeness baffle him since he always wants to make love to her. For many men, sex is split off from feeling. Stan, who loves his wife, visits porno parlors "whenever she gets to me too much. I just always feel relieved after I leave, disgusting as it usually is there."

For others like Dell, sex is a desperate search for feeling. Dell's extramarital affairs began when he learned his wife had cheated on him with her boss. His dependence on her made even the thought of leaving her impossible. He went numb. "These cute young cupcakes who pick me up think I'm such a stud, it makes me feel alive again. And I kind of like getting back at her." Other men, like Roger, experience a brief, albeit powerful emotional release accompanying the physical release of orgasm as "the most incredibly comforting feeling. It's the one time I can ever really let go of control."

Hiding depression in nonrelational sexual activity is common. For many of the male patients I treat, work is the new sex, the place where passion and action meet. When sex is a way to discharge tension, multiple sexual partners often hold out the promise of better sex. John, an executive, likens having multiple sexual partners to dining out, "You just get tired of the same old thing all the time." More may be better, particularly when one is not enough, or at the same time she may be felt to be *too* much.

WHEN MEN SEEK TREATMENT

Men traditionally have difficulty seeking and committing to psychological treatment which requires admission of unresolved problems, exploring uncomfortable feelings, and establishing an intimate but nonsexually active relationship (O'Neil, 1981; Scher, 1990; Scher, Stevens, Good, & Eichenfield, 1987). Limited knowledge of, or even injunctions against feeling or expressing emotions (Dunn, Bretherton, & Munn, 1987; Levant & Kopecky, 1995), the perceived need to dis-identify from female-related traits, including emotions, in order to be a man (Chodorow, 1978; Greenson, 1968; Maccoby, 1990; Pollack, 1990), and experiencing emotional vulnerability as shame (Osherson & Krugman, 1990), loss or impending loss (Cochran & Rabinowitz, 1996), also serve as mitigating factors.

Male patients generally come to me through one of three routes: (a) by referral from a physician specialist, (b) at the request of a female partner, or (c) as a result of a work-related concern. Ira, a 28-year-old stockbroker with three children in parochial school was convinced he was having angina attacks. His cardiologist thought otherwise. The panic he felt about his financial responsibilities and the need to "handle my feelings like a man" (i.e., by making them go away) meant that his only rest was on the Sabbath, a day on which he combined religious observance with meetings with his mistress. By Sunday night, he could neither breathe nor sleep, with no let up until the following Sabbath when the stress dissipated for a few blessed hours. The day his boss warned him he'd be fired if he didn't do more business he called to schedule a psychotherapy appointment to "figure this out, once and for all."

Reluctant Patients

Although men are often reluctant to engage in the emotionally unguarded work of psychotherapy (Shay, 1996) despite their partners' frequent exhortations (Gottman, 1991), I have noticed an increase in men's perceived value of interpersonal skills and longing for true intimate relationships. Male gender role strain, a factor in avoiding psychotherapy, has become an *impetus* to such treatment. Being cut off from one's emotional life, formerly ego-syntonic, is increasingly felt by the men who enter treatment as ego-dystonic. Extreme stress reactions, loss, and depression frequently propel a man into treatment.

Thomas, a 32-year-old financial fund manager, entered treatment when he could no longer tolerate how he felt. He couldn't concentrate at work, couldn't decide which of two women to marry, couldn't stop obsessing about his failure to make the most of the last bull market. As we attacked his alexithymia with homework assignments, depressed feelings became more available. Initially, feeling these emotions raised other resistances: frequent canceled appointments, increased projection. Over time, learning emotional and behavioral skills helped to reduce his stress. And as Papp (1997) describes, when he began to uncover and then to resolve gender role strain issues that made him feel powerless and attacked his self-esteem, his depression lifted.

Ironically, learning the emotional skills in which so many men are stunted can also increase professional and interpersonal success. At the highest level, skills such as team and consensus building, handling one's own and others' distressing emotions, and win-win negotiating are crucial to success (Goleman, 1995). These skills increasingly find favor within the organizations in which these men work (Covey, 1990). This extends the motivation men feel to engage in the hard work of psychotherapy and face their defenses.

ESTABLISHING THE THERAPEUTIC ALLIANCE

The many barriers to treatment, and the extreme stress men generally experience by the time they enter psychotherapy, make it crucial to establish a solid therapeutic alliance as quickly as possible. The men who begin psychotherapeutic treatment are usually problem solvers who want concrete results. They often have no treatment history or understanding of the way treatment works. They do come armed with fears of what therapy will do to them: "turn me into Woody Allen or something, talking about my childhood forever," discover some "deep, dark secret about why it's all my parents' fault," get "all touchy feely," and the great fear that it will be a waste of time. Addressing these concerns with tact, seriousness, alacrity, and a clear contract is essential.

For many men, this is their first encounter with therapy, other than images of psychotherapy from movies, television, and stories they hear. They are familiar with other professionals who charge for their time: attorneys, accountants, and often try to understand treatment in that context. They feel more comfortable knowing the rules and what to expect.

I use a treatment contract to explore expectations and fears. We discuss and agree to fundamental treatment issues including confidentiality, initial goal(s), acceptable behavior for therapist and patient, a timetable for taking stock of progress, and policy matters such as payment schedules, handling of missed appointments (Gans & Counselman, 1996), and length of sessions. The signing of the treatment contract is a concrete, behavioral step toward a crucial balance in psychotherapy: the simultaneous need to establish clear, firm boundaries around appropriate behavior and flexible, considered policies tailored to individual needs and defenses. It also affords a focused introduction to the difficult process of articulating feelings: the meaning of money, the fear of attachment to therapist, talking about rather than acting on sexual feelings in therapy.

Harold entered treatment due to almost unbearable anxiety, a result of his guilt about deceiving his fiancee. His worst fear was that people at work, who adored Dianne, would find out about his many affairs—and that he couldn't bear to go through with the planned marriage. This would cost him a coveted managerial position and eventually his career, or so he feared. May (1977) describes how stress-based anxiety may be interpreted by an individual whose locus of control is external. To the extent that Harold imagined me judging him as negatively as he did himself, we could make no progress. As the therapeutic alliance strengthened and he began to trust that I didn't think he's scum, he began to feel less anxious and more voluble. The treatment breakthrough occurred shortly after he was able to imagine, and empathize with, Diane's feelings: he allowed himself to face his own fears.

REQUIRED THERAPIST ATTRIBUTES WITH MALE PATIENTS

Cochran and Rabinowitz (1996) suggest that effective psychotherapy with men requires the therapist demonstrate four attributes: (a) sensitivity to the male patient's difficulty with therapy itself, (b) explicit empathy for his experiences of loss, (c) direct attention to the existential aspects of these losses, and (d) acknowledgment of positive masculine attributes.

Shay (1996) additionally posits the need to persuasively utilize the therapeutic alliance, know the audience (familiarity with predictable male reactions, including issues of authority, pre-existing beliefs about interactions between men and women, restricted emotionality, resistance to treatment, reluctance to acknowledge difficulties), speak the patient's dialect, and examine countertransference issues around gender.

Special Issues for the Female Therapist Treating Male Patients

In addition to the need for empathy, judgment neutrality, and sensitivity to issues arising out of male gender role strain required of any therapist, the female therapist must be ever-cognizant of the impact of her gender on the development of a therapeutic alliance as well as the unfolding process of treatment. Further, she must address her own countertransference issues so that she is comfortable addressing the transference and psychosocial issues around gender which inevitably color cross-gender treatment.

WOMAN THERAPIST/MALE PATIENT:
CROSS-GENDER TREATMENT

For accomplished professional men, the need to maintain the success facade, in addition to other male gender role strain features discussed previously, makes entering treatment feel even more an admission of weakness. Entering treatment commonly constitutes two firsts: not only the first psychotherapy encounter, but also the first time a man has spoken with anyone about his concerns. The competition, humiliation, and shame that are likely sequelae of the emotionally vulnerable therapeutic situation change when the therapist is a woman.

The tendency of these successful male patients to devalue women lessens the need for competition with them, particularly a woman in a helping profession who does not "count" in the world in which financial success is a scorecard. Perceiving that the woman therapist is not part of his circle, that he will not encounter her in a boardroom or at the golf club, frees the patient from having to preserve the traditional gender role image and all it implies.

The above, as well as other stereotypic expectations of woman's role as nurturer, mother, potential lover can be used to create a safe haven for expression of the male patient's feelings—when the woman therapist sets constant, appropriate limits and can comfortably accept and *utilize* these devaluations, without feeling threatened herself. Appropriately timed, within the collaborative therapeutic context, interpretation of these devaluations can be extremely useful to the patient. The great care that must be exercised by the therapist to establish and maintain appropriate, firm boundaries in this delicate area cannot be overemphasized. Additionally, she must interpret such stereotypic expectations and behaviors routinely and judiciously, as they occur. The female therapist must be prepared for, and capable of handling, the patient's irritation, anger, retrenchment, and denial as they occur.

The dynamic between the female therapist and the male patient can serve as a working model to learn more effective ways to integrate the social, sexual, and the emotional. In the safety of the treatment situation, the male patient can ask questions about what one patient calls "the woman's angle, its anathema" and translate it back into his—often business—terms. Explorations of issues such as competition, control and power, independence and dependency needs, emotional vulnerability, and role expectations take on a more urgent meaning when they are also being played out in transference and countertransference. In therapy, unlike in real life, this man can discuss with this woman all manner of uncomfortable feelings and desires, without fear of reprisal or expectation of sexual activity. Male patients can practice new roles and behaviors in a lower risk environment than real life.

TRANSFERENCE AND COUNTERTRANSFERENCE ISSUES

Male patients bring to, and attempt to act out in, therapy with the woman therapist all the gender role expectations, attitudes, and behaviors they experience in other male-female relationships. Because the therapy relationship is often so new, so different from any other kind of relationship, male patients do not know how to proceed.

Sexualizing the Transference and Boundary Concerns

For many men, there is no model for an intimate professional relationship, that is, one in which there will be no physical intimacy. The transference is invariably sexualized. For example, Ray initially began each therapy session by commenting on how his therapist was dressed and what looks were "hot." After interpretation and discussion ended that behavior by making conscious its purpose, he would periodically end a session with some sexualized compliment, invariably when he felt particularly vulnerable.

The woman therapist must establish and maintain appropriate boundaries, particularly around helping and sexual issues, at the same time as she encourages verbal exploration of uncomfortable intrapsychic, interpersonal, and sexual fantasies, feelings, and thoughts. This requires vigilance because male patients often attempt to catch the therapist off-guard and deprofessionalize the relationship, particularly when feelings are intense.

Johnston and Farber (1996) distinguish between two types of boundaries: logistical (begin/end times, payment issues, scheduling) and conceptual (self-disclosure, theoretical orientation, availability between sessions). Because sexual exploitation of patients "happens before it happens" (R. Simon, 1989) and because of the especial need for safety that male patients require, I advocate strict adherence to conceptual boundaries. Interpretation and discussion of issues arising out of patients' testing inelastic conceptual boundaries can provide periodic necessary reassurance of the safety of the therapeutic alliance (Epstein, Simon, & Kay, 1992), as well as bring to life the very sexual and emotional intimacy issues these patients have come to therapy to deal with.

On the other hand, some intentional degree of elasticity of logistical boundaries can benefit the therapeutic alliance. Male patients generally view occasional willingness to reschedule appointments around business trips, conduct phone sessions when they are out of town, schedule double sessions on a weekend after a big deal concludes, as validation of the importance of their work, and by extension, themselves. Most view the therapist's willingness to be flexible when real life intervenes as an indication of cooperation and mutual good faith, and the outcome is generally a strengthened therapeutic alliance. Care must be exercised that this interpersonal act organized by the patient's subjectivity (Mitchell, 1993) is not a result of some unresolved countertransference distortion.

Countertransference Concerns

The therapist needs to stay attuned concurrently to the issues and feelings, the transference, and the countertransference. To do so, she must be exceedingly open to her own issues and possess great ego strength, comfortable access to id contents, and a distinct super-ego. Continuous exploration of countertransference concerns, including her vulnerability to flattery, enjoyment of flirtation, sexual identity, and so on, is paramount. An effective therapist must become aware of, and resolve any issues relating to, her own biases, psychosexual history, and cultural assumptions. She must also monitor strong feelings that may be engendered in her by the patient or patient-as-representative of some other person or group, including repulsion, fear, anger, hurt, envy, and so forth.

Female Therapist-Male Patient Countertransference Patterns

Carlson (1987) describes three possibilities of particular concern to the woman therapist with a male patient: viewing the patient as son, lover, father. I would add one additional pattern: the patient as sibling: Each pattern has inherent dangers, but also poses certain useful possibilities when appropriately worked through by the therapist.

- Patient as son—The dangers: "acting as mother-caregiver who does not challenge him to grow in significant ways" (Carlson, 1987, p. 48), appropriating responsibility for change. Used constructively, may point to patient's tendency to view women in mothering capacity.
- Patient as lover/husband—The dangers: acting seductively (Carlson, 1987), assuming and re-enacting one's own disappointments, life experiences, and/or wishes. Used constructively: may point to models of mutuality, integration of sexual interest, and emotional attachment.
- Patient as father—The dangers: viewing him as an authority and either deferring to or fighting him (Carlson, 1987). Used constructively: extending respect, according him his wisdom.
- Patient as sibling—The dangers: re-enacting patterns of sibling rivalry/jealousy, caretaking/disregard. Competitive feelings around work and prestige are often a concern. Used constructively: joining to attack a common enemy: the problem. We're in it together.

THERAPEUTIC INTERVENTIONS

Psychological talk is generally off-putting to these patients, particularly initially. As much as possible, I translate concepts into the business language my patients understand. When I can talk about IPOs, the bottom line, negotiating deals, cost-benefit analyses, I not only gain credibility that I understand their world, but also demonstrate appreciation of the area of their lives they're often most invested in: work. Utilizing the common language of business, with which they are appreciably more comfortable than the language of feelings, affords opportunities for the creation of myriad analogies and metaphors for psychological and interpersonal concerns. We get to the feelings by way of their bottom line strengths, working from strengths to tackle areas of relative weakness.

I look for hints of what works at work: "How do you handle it when you're nervous at a presentation?" or "You didn't seem flustered dealing with him that time. What made that different?" My conviction that emotional skills are transferable and assistance in identifying the emotional skills the patient already has, allows us to penetrate dysfunction and increase the emotional vocabulary and range of expressive options in other interpersonal relationships. When patients begin to see things from employees' and business associates' reference frame, the jump to imagining a woman partner's perspective is not so great.

UTILIZING THE TRANSFERENCE TO ENSURE TREATMENT GOALS

The combination of a heterosexual male patient who tends to view women in a nonrelational manner and a female therapist raises myriad transference issues. The patient does in treatment what he does elsewhere. For Mike, in the following case study, the therapist is a smart, psychologically savvy, accomplished, attractive woman of the right age. He issues invitations to parties, tells amusing, flirtatious anecdotes when feelings become too intense to "get you to like me"—strategies he uses with any woman he meets with whom he might have a dalliance. When I interpret this behavior to him, asking him if this is what he does with the women in other areas of his life to whom he feels attracted, his emphatic "Yes!" is an eye-opener to him, and signals the beginning of his realization of the costs of sexualizing relationships in his work life.

For men with multiple intimate partners, it may even be difficult to commit to one therapist. Cal, whose internist alerted me to the fact that he was seeing two therapists simultaneously, was relieved when confronted. A discussion of his "fear of putting all my eggs in one basket" ensued, and he expressed his concerns that "no woman would be smart enough for me. They never are."

TREATMENT STRATEGIES AND TECHNIQUES

I use an eclectic approach, integrating behavioral, cognitive, psychoeducational systems and psychodynamic modalities as appropriate to treatment goals.

A psychoeducational, behavioral approach is generally most effective early in treatment. Ordinarily goal-oriented professional men come with lists of things to be accomplished and initially feel most comfortable with short-term objectives. Since many present with troubling stress-related symptoms, training in stress management techniques offers the kind of concrete solutions these problem solvers favor, as well as providing an example of therapist and patient joining in a mutual undertaking of direct, present concern to the patient. Other short-term goals include interest in learning about emotions—theirs and their partners—identifying deficit areas, and monitoring sexual behaviors.

Studies of the relationship between type of therapist intervention and the level of patient collaboration indicate that a balance of interpretation and supportive interventions, with a minimum of advice and praise, results in better collaboration (Allen et al., 1996). It is not uncommon for patients to ask for advice. It is almost invariably a mistake for the female therapist to provide advice for male patients. Advice is alternately discounted, followed without thought, or found fault with, as in the case of James who demanded a script for handling a telephone encounter with a girlfriend, only to complain when it didn't work as anticipated.

The patient must join in the treatment effort, becoming curious about his own reactions and feelings, increasingly interested in new ways to answer the questions "What should I do?" and "Why am I feeling like this?" The patient who wants the therapist to do all the work, to tell him what to do, is resisting getting to the root of the problem. The skillful therapist empathizes with the wish to have someone else answer the difficult questions, perhaps even poses a number of possible ways to think about the issues, all the while encouraging the patient to face his feelings about not knowing what to do and his nascent sense of how change might benefit him.

Although advice is detrimental, directives are often quite helpful. The benefits of a psychoeducational approach, such as those outlined by Levant (1990, 1997), are myriad. Homework assignments provide an excellent way to extend the therapeutic learning through practice, and often unearth new material and insights. I custom design homework as an experiment, most often in direct response to a current issue of great import to the patient. For instance, for a patient who has just uncovered parental injunctions against erring, and his recurring fear of failure, I suggest he agree to make three relatively risk-free mistakes a day by design, and note situational outcome as well as how he feels. Other directives include generating lists of feeling words, making copies of the list, and checking off feelings as they occur for the patient during the day; or practicing listening to a woman partner's feelings without intervening with repair suggestions, all the while noting any physiological or psychological reactions. Journal keeping is also an invaluable tool.

As appropriate, I prescribe popular movies and books to spur thought, feelings, and provide a common language for discussion of each man's experience: Brooks on the male centerfold syndrome (1995), Goleman (1995) on emotional intelligence, Levant on male alexithymia (Levant & Kopecky, 1995), Moyers on the mind-body connection (1993), Nuernberger on utilizing stress (1996), Phillips' provocative *Monogamy*

(1996), Potash (1990) on hidden agendas, Rhodes and Potash (1988) on men's problems with intimacy, Tannen (1990) on male/female communication, and tantric sex books which meld emotional connection and erotic desire, among others.

Also valuable and frequently overlooked are the use of humor and analogy. Both allow therapist and patient to break out of the literal and the concrete, and explore more complex meaning and feeling concerns. Given the delicate nature of the emotional and sexual issues involved, indirect ways to allow the male patient to save face are invaluable and appreciated. It is often possible to make great leaps in insight with a well-timed story. In the context of a strong alliance with a therapist who is felt to be on his side, many a male patient's well-constructed defenses have crumbled when sharing a joke that is directly to the point. Teaching stories with wise fools for characters, such as the Jewish Helm folk-stories (S. Simon, 1965, 1973) and mystical Sufi tales (Nicholson, 1995; Shah, 1983), humorously explore eternal questions of human nature, life's purpose, and moral meaning. The Sufi story of the Mulla Nasrudin, who searches for his lost key around a lamppost far away from the site where it was lost because there is light there, is a favorite (Shah, 1983, p. 9).

As treatment progresses and trust in the therapist and the process deepens, male patients generally begin asking more provocative questions: How did I get to be like this? Do you think I'll be like my father? Successful attainment of short-term goals contributes to trust in psychotherapeutic outcome and strengthens the therapeutic alliance. This in turn allows for increasing exploration of deeper feelings and attitudes implicated in excessive stress and nonrelational sex. "I see the difference it makes," John said. "Maybe it's worth trying some more." Gently moving from teaching specific techniques to exploring ways to think and building an emotional vocabulary allows for increasing tolerance of emotional distress and patient insight.

In later treatment, it is often necessary to restructure policy matter boundaries. With a strong therapeutic alliance and clear commitment to insight as well as behavioral change, it is possible to allow executives who travel and wish to continue treatment to do so. This frequently requires devising creative, idiosyncratic treatment strategies. I have utilized e-mail, telephone, and on-line therapy, and marathon sessions with great success. When a good working relationship has already been established and patient and therapist have developed a treatment shorthand, such flexibility can deepen the work and integrate it into the everyday life of the patient.

THE CASE OF THE MAN WHO
LOVED TOO MUCH

Most of the men I treat come to me willingly, interested in learning more about their emotional lives. Yet as willing as they may be consciously, most are still defensive, afraid, resistant. Mike is one of these.

Mike came for treatment unable to tolerate his ambivalent feelings any longer. On the one hand, he wanted to divorce his wife of many years and pursue the romantic adventure of his life with his alter-ego love, Ada. On the other hand, he felt enormous guilt about destroying the spouse who had been his helpmate and support for many years. A female work colleague gave him my book, *Cold Feet* (Rhodes & Potash, 1988). He recognized himself and called for an appointment, citing the urgency of his problem. We began work that day.

HISTORY

Mike's history was obtained in bits and pieces over the course of treatment. Men like Mike who present for treatment in great distress feel an urgent need to talk about the problem. Allowing them to do so immediately, and a history taking as we go, helps to forge an alliance.

Mike was raised in a small Northeastern town in a strict, Irish Catholic family. His mother was a schoolteacher turned full-time mother, his father the principal of the local high school and on the board of the local church. The eldest of two, the only son, Mike was the repository of all his father's wishes: to be a good family man, a community leader, a success. Mike loved sports and yearned to see the world; he couldn't wait to leave home. He attended a small local college and then a city law school. He fell in love with the city and began dating for the first time. The emotional, introspective thinker persona that had made him a "loser" in high school made him curiously attractive to smart college girls. His first love, beautiful, smart, creative Harriet, seemed perfect until he realized he envisioned a broader, more exciting life while she wanted to settle down in the suburbs with a family.

Shortly before graduation, he met and married Hope. Hope pursued her professional goals and he worked for a top tier law firm. Then Mike took his first major risk: he accepted an offer of an entry-level job in a high profile public relations firm in New York City, seeing it as his ticket to the exciting life he'd always wanted. He commuted for a year, after which Hope joined him in New York with her own exciting job. Mike's career star kept rising, as he became known for making deals for high-profile athletes. He traveled extensively. He rubbed shoulders with the rich and famous. "I was living the dream: making a living doing the sports I love with a terrific woman who made me a fabulous home."

Smart, accomplished, sophisticated women wanted to be with him. He realized many were interested in him because of what he did and who he knew; and he enjoyed the attentions thoroughly. As time went on, he collected more and more women friends. He listened to their troubles, sent romantic notes, and occasionally had whirlwind romantic interludes. And he went home to Hope: simple, loyal, steady, comfortable, his safe haven. Over the course of 10 years, Mike became increasingly disinterested in sex with Hope. She seemed content, never having liked sex much anyway. When he entered therapy, they had not made love in four years.

Initial Presentation

Mike initiated treatment shortly after his fortieth birthday. He hadn't been sleeping, had lost weight, and felt hopeless. He used the word guilty over a dozen times in the first 20 minutes. He was worried about his job performance slipping—he couldn't concentrate. He earnestly said he was desperate to solve things once and for all, and would do whatever it took. His pleas for help and his torture over his guilt were interspersed with flirtatious asides. He repeatedly looked me up and down, occasionally appraising me when he thought I was looking elsewhere, and stating he hadn't imagined I'd be so . . . (he couldn't finish the sentence).

The Treatment Contract

This was Mike's introduction to psychotherapy. Frequent reiteration of confidentiality rules was beneficial, as he feared for his professional reputation. Even more useful, and new to Mike, was the idea that he could have and discuss *any* feelings toward *any* woman (myself included), secure in the knowledge that there would be no sexual behavior between the two of us, under any circumstances. This became pivotal as treatment progressed and Mike admitted that I was precisely the sort of woman who usually interested him: good at talking about feelings, accomplished, clever, and one who wouldn't let him get away with anything.

Treatment Begins

Initially, treatment focused on Mike's distress over deciding whether or not to divorce his wife. In short order, it became clear to both of us that was the least of his problems. For Mike was a man who loved too much. He loved many, many women. He loved his wife (nonsexually), as well as his alter ego Ada, the "passionate love of my life—she's just like me." But he also loved Dee, an artist with two children in Iowa; Bee, an up and coming journalist; Lee, a famous athlete; Kay a newscaster; and many more. He described them all as friends and indeed they were. Friends with whom he had once, did now, or would have sexual relations, and friends he hoped to keep long after the sexual relationship was over.

The prototypical portrait of the polygamist is the man out of love with his life partner who stumbles, or the man who treats sexual intimacy in nonrelational terms. Mike defied this portrait. Neither did he suffer from some other common male difficulties. He was comfortable with emotional as well as "action" empathy and was not overly angry. He valued emotional communication highly. Indeed, one of the major joys of his relationships with women was "getting into all that psychological, feeling stuff about the relationship. I love it." Yet Mike was dysthymic (often bored, his least favorite feeling), mildly alexithymic (wanting to expand his emotional range and figure out why he feels what he does), and struggling with the interface of sex and intimacy (in particular the dichotomy he felt between security and passion).

He was very concerned that I see him as a good guy who valued women beyond the sexual sphere. Each time he mentioned another woman (there were two main loves, but over time he introduced me to multiple other sexual friends), he made it a point to describe her via her career accomplishments and character. Never did he describe a woman physically. His hope for therapy: I would tell him what to do so he could "finally get all this over with." He asked for the name of a good divorce lawyer—preferably a woman.

The Issues

At our fourth session, it became clear to both of us that Mike was not ready to decide between the security of passionless marriage and the insecurity of the passionate alter-ego lover. I dubbed Mike "The Hedge" (as in hedge his bets). This frank, pithy interpretation both startled and pleased him. I had "gotten it." He thought for a moment, then said, "It's worse than that. At the center, I need to feel secure, that's true. But even more, I need them all to love me. I couldn't bear it if Hope thought I was a louse. Or my father. Or you."

Mike spoke of the adolescence he experienced from 25 to 40, and of his conscious readiness to move on. He spoke of his identification with

Marcello Mastroianni—the bad boy who is always forgiven because he is kind, loving, and means no harm. He spoke of his romanticism and attraction to articulate, professional, emotionally mature women he can really talk with, get intimate with, share himself with.

He began to wonder if his relationships with these terrific women wasn't in some sense an attempt to affirm himself, free himself from the competition he felt in his rarefied work environment and from which he feared falling. Smart women were the perfect combination of safe haven and passionate adventure: challenge, no bullshit or boredom, yet lots of appreciation. One of his many lovely young female assistants, his protege, had this cheerleading advice, "Don't sell yourself short." This admonition proved very important to Mike, for underneath his ostensible professional success was a short, balding, insecure man still trying to prove he was good enough. A son still trying to live up to his father's image, while at the same time trying to burst successfully into a larger, more exciting scene.

TRANSFERENCE AND COUNTERTRANSFERENCE TESTS

Mike asked for, and received, a time change to a 7:00 A.M. therapy hour to accommodate his work schedule. The first time, he brought me coffee and prepared to sweeten it for me, if I liked. My interpretations of his flirtatious, flattering attentions ("Is this the kind of thing you usually do with the women you encounter? I bet they really like it.") were jarring. He began to acknowledge the automatic nature of these attempts to disarm women and win them over. It was also disconcerting to Mike that I was not impressed by his famous connections. He was accustomed to women who wanted to be with him because of these connections and at a loss when they were meaningless to me.

I learned the value of direct, pointed interventions. These generally broke through resistances and pointed out defenses and behaviors so automatic Mike hadn't even considered them. His motivation to change outmoded behavior far outweighed the anxiety and shame he felt. Many times he resisted an interpretation only to come in next time, once even leaving me a message on my answering service, bursting with pleasure in his insight, and eager to learn something new.

THE TURNING POINT

Two years into treatment, Mike moved into his own apartment for the second time. This time, he agreed to take my challenge: for two weeks, he would not have a television, computer, or telephone to distract him from his thoughts and feelings at home. This meant no old movies, no e-mail, and most difficult: no late night phone calls to yet another woman friend to relieve his boredom. During this period, he became ill with flu and canceled our session. When he returned for treatment he described an epiphany, "I realized that it's not so unbearable to be alone. What I really want is a partner who is my best friend and lover. I guess I'm afraid. If I pick just one, what if she leaves me? I also figured out this is two parts. First I have to leave Hope and deal with her not liking me. I can't decide about picking anyone until I see if I can do that. Or maybe I'll just be alone . . ."

Mike subsequently told his parents, left his wife, and is now living alone. Though saddened by her hatred of him, he is comforted by the generous divorce settlement he made. He feels surprisingly little guilt. He has broken off all sexual relationships for the first time in 15 years. He still sees his alter-ego love, and they are discussing the possibility of living together on two coasts. He continues to enjoy fending off the bevy of young women who pursue him. Treatment continues.

ADAM: A MAN WHO LOVED TOO MANY YET NOT ENOUGH

The case of Adam illustrates succinctly the major themes previously delineated in this chapter. A reluctant patient, Adam was aware only of the extreme stress he felt, stress which sometimes interfered with his concentration. He was unaware of his severe alexithymia. Neither did he understand how his history of nonrelational sexual "relationships" gave lie to his professed interest in marrying.

Adam had it all: tall, dark, and handsome, well-educated and traveled, the male heir to a successful third-generation family business that dominated a suburb of a major metropolis. He was an eligible bachelor constantly in demand who averred he wanted only one thing: to meet and marry the woman of his dreams.

And who was dreamgirl? Adam had a long and very specific list: a specific height, with blue eyes, and long, straight blonde hair, intelligent yet somewhat meek, innocent yet admiring of him, and willing to devote her life to him. Over the years, Adam dated and had nonrelational sex with lots of dreamgirls. Somehow each one was found lacking: slightly too tall, a bit too into her career, hair that didn't smell right. The flaws became more pronounced as he became older, and each flaw justified for him his unwillingness (he didn't see it as inability) to commit to this as a full, emotional relationship.

His family suggested Adam seek treatment. Adam himself was becoming concerned, but only with his inability to meet "the right one," with no thought that his difficulties might in some fashion reflect his own inner ambivalence. He was unaware of the dysthymia apparent to me at our first session. He did, however, describe a long list of physical symptoms of depression that had become more pronounced since his thirtieth birthday.

Like many of the men previously described in this chapter, Adam was slow to establish trust. His constricted, stereotypic approach to women extended to his initial assessment of me as a woman, and his behavior in the therapy. Gently, over time, we analyzed his sexualized transference reactions, while I simultaneously monitored the feelings engendered in me by his often demeaning, dismissive, and crude attitude and statements.

I utilized the approach and techniques previously described, including designing and signing a treatment contract, psychoeducational techniques such as generating lists of possible emotions a person might feel (and subsequently noting these on computerized lists as they were experienced), and utilizing his business acumen as a language and methodology to address emotional concerns through analogy.

Therapy progressed slowly, intermittently, and painfully. Adam wondered if I were smart enough to help him. He worried about "how long it would take." He didn't understand the process and what he was "supposed to do or feel." He missed sessions for business travel, market week, feeling "under the gun." He expressed frustration over "not accomplishing anything." Every feeling-related word was hard earned: his marked alexithymia was evidenced in his inability to generate more than five feeling words: horny, angry, sad, frustrated, happy.

After six months of on-and-off therapy, Adam addressed his feelings about me as a woman for the first time and was relieved when I was neither shocked nor won over. Therapy had begun in earnest.

The following session, Adam quietly confessed what he'd vowed he would tell no one: he frequently spent evenings with his perfect dream-girl—a blow-up doll with the proportions and temperament he favored. The marked increase in trust this confession evidenced, along with the lack of horrified response he had feared and his increased openness to interpretation, allowed the therapy to progress in what felt, in contrast to the painstakingly slow first few months, like the speed of light.

The thought of making the transition from having a perfect-doll to being with a good-enough-imperfect-woman partner had been too much for Adam until his epiphany. He had recently broken up with Sarah—beautiful, blonde, blue-eyed, sweet, adoring, and the woman closest to his dreamgirl fantasy—because of a mole on her left cheek. When I confronted Adam with his choice between the perfect inanimate partner and this very slightly imperfect real partner, Adam belatedly and quite painfully began to address his terror of intimacy, which had masqueraded as recurring disappointment in (their) love.

His pride in facing the emotional demons he had previously assiduously avoided buffered him from some of the shame and fear he now felt more consciously. In facing and accepting his emotions, their power over him diminished and his dysthymia lifted. We worked at his understanding layers of feelings, allowing feelings to mutate, and even beginning to feel empathy for the very real women in his life (his employees and family members as well as girlfriends).

We spent hours talking sex: educating him (with books and discussion) about women's bodies and feelings, working to connect his sexual feelings to his newfound emotional self. He read and learned. He felt emotions. The doll disappeared, as did the video cache. The magazines remained, but were used less frequently, and augmented by pictures Sarah had posed for as a birthday gift.

Adam asked Sarah for another chance. They began couples therapy while Adam continued with his individual therapy. A year later they married, and shortly thereafter Adam officially ended therapy. Over the years, he periodically schedules one or two therapy sessions, what he calls "tune-ups to keep me honest."

Adam's case demonstrates multiple themes explored in this chapter. Like many men, Adam entered treatment reluctantly, suffering from the professional male triad described previously. He presented with a severe case of alexithymia, extreme stress, and a repetitive pattern of engaging in serially monogamous, nonrelational sex that defied his stated desire to make a commitment to one woman. The therapeutic alliance developed very slowly, punctuated by many missed sessions. The initial devaluation of the female therapist was slowly replaced by empathy felt from, and growing trust in, the therapist, occasioned in part by flexibility in treatment/session planning, the capacity of the therapist to understand and value his business concerns, and the quickly-perceived usefulness of concrete psychoeducational treatment exercises.

SUMMARY

A female therapist treating alexithymic, stressed men with multiple sexual partners is in the unique position to create a safe, nonthreatening environment in which these patients can explore the psychosocially charged and interrelated issues of emotion, sex, and masculinity.

For men who are reluctant to engage in self-disclosure and psychotherapy, the therapist must exercise particular care in expediting a solid therapeutic alliance. This is most effectively done through a combination of empathy, speaking the patient's language (often business-related), timely interpretation, and identifying clear goals which are frequently reassessed. Initially, a behavioral, psychoeducational approach focusing on stress reconstruction can set the stage for trust that his concerns are taken seriously, the therapist can be trusted, and the process will yield results. A treatment contract, which spells out expectations and appropriate behavior, is also efficacious in this regard.

The very nature of the cross-gender relationship can be a source of both problems and opportunities. Transference and countertransference issues must be addressed continuously and openly, with material unearthed used to address the very issues for which the patient enters treatment. Establishing clear boundaries to acceptable behavior and no boundaries as to what thoughts or feelings are engendered or may be discussed, both recreates a social reality and creates a setting unlike any other. In this forum, the male patient can discuss male-female issues and feelings and explore alternative masculine styles safely.

When the therapist appropriately monitors and takes advantage of the emotional and behavioral particularities of this singular interpersonal situation, she can help the male patient effect behavioral and interpersonal changes congruent with learning and growing toward ever-increasing psychological health.

REFERENCES

Allen, J. G., Coyne, L., Colson, D. B., Horwitz, L., Gabbard, G. O., Frieswyk, S. H., & G. Newson. (1996). Pattern of therapist interventions associated with patient collaboration. *Psychotherapy, 33*(2), 254–261.

Balswick, J. O. (1982). Male inexpressiveness: Psychological and social aspects. In K. Solomon & N. B. Levy (Eds.), *Men in transition: Theory and therapy.* New York: Plenum Press.

Brody, L., & Hall, J. (1993). Gender and emotion. In M. Lewis & J. M. Haviland (Eds.), *Handbook of emotions* (pp. 447–460). New York: Guilford Press.

Brooks, G. R. (1995). *The centerfold syndrome.* San Francisco: Jossey-Bass.

Carlson, N. (1987). Woman therapist: Male patient. In M. Scher, M. Stevens, G. Good, & G. Eichenfield (Eds.), *Handbook of counseling and psychotherapy with men* (pp. 39–50). Newbury Park, CA: Sage.

Carnes, P. (1992). *Out of the shadows: Understanding sexual addiction.* Center City, MN: Hazelden.

Chodorow, N. J. (1978). *The reproduction of mothering.* Berkeley: University of California Press.

Chodorow, N. J. (1989). *Feminism and psychoanalytic theory.* New Haven, CT: Yale University Press.

Cochran, S., & Rabinowitz, F. E. (1996). Men, loss, and psychotherapy. *Psychotherapy, 33*(4), 593–600.

Covey, S. R. (1990). *The seven habits of highly effective people.* New York: Simon & Schuster.

Culbertson, F. M. (1997). Depression and gender: An international review. *American Psychologist, 52*(1), 25–31.

Dunn, J., Bretherton, I., & Munn, P. (1987). Conversations about feeling states between mothers and their children. *Developmental Psychology, 23,* 132–139.

Ehrenrich, B. (1983). *The hearts of men: American dreams and the flight from commitment.* New York: Anchor Press.

Eisenberg, N., & Lennon, R. (1983). Sex differences in empathy and related capacities. *Psychological Bulletin, 100*(3), 309–330.

Eisler, R. M. (1995). The relationship between masculine gender role stress and men's health risk. In R. F. Levant & W. S. Pollack (Eds.), *A new psychology of men* (pp. 207–225). New York: Basic Books.

Eisler, R. M., Skidmore, J. R., & Ward, C. H. (1988). Masculine gender-role stress: Predictor of anger, anxiety and health-risk behaviors. *Journal of Personality Assessment, 52,* 133–141.

Ellis, H. (1936). *Studies in the psychology of sex* (Vols. 1 & 2). New York: Random House.

Epstein, R. S., Simon, R. I., & Kay, G. G. (1992). Assessing boundary violations in psychotherapy: Survey results with the Exploitation Index. *Bulletin of the Menninger Clinic, 56*(2), 150–166.

Fogarty, T. F. (1979). The distancer and the pursuer. *The Family, 7*(1), 11–16.

Gagnon, J. H., & Simon, W. (1973). *Sexual conduct: The social sources of human sexuality.* Chicago: Aldine.

Gans, J. S., & Counselman, E. F. (1996). The missed session: A neglected aspect of psychodynamic psychotherapy. *Psychotherapy, 33*(1), 43–50.

Gems, P. (1997). *Stanley.* London: Nick Hern.

Goldberg, H. (1976). *The hazards of being male.* New York: Nash.

Goleman, D. (1995). *Emotional Intelligence.* New York: Bantam Books.

Good, G. E., Gilbert, L. A., & Scher, M. (1990). Gender aware therapy: A synthesis of feminist therapy and knowledge about gender. *Journal of Counseling and Development, 69,* 17–21.

Gottman, J. (1991). Predicting the longitudinal course of marriage. *Journal of Marital and Family Therapy,* (17), 3–7.

Greenson, R. (1968). Dis-identifying from mother: Its special importance for the boy. *International Journal of Psychoanalysis, 49,* 370–374.

Helgeson, V. S. (1990). The role of masculinity in a prognostic predictor of heart attack severity. *Sex Roles, 22*(11/12), 755–776.

Hornstein, H. (1991). *A night in signing armor: Understanding mens romantic illusions.* New York: Morrow.

Hudson, L., & Jacot, B. (1991). *The way men think: Intellect, intimacy, and the erotic imagination.* New Haven, CT: Yale University Press.

Johnston, S. H., & Farber, B. A. (1996). The maintenance of boundaries in psychotherapeutic practice. *Psychotherapy, 33*(3), 391–402.

Jordan, J. V., Kaplan, A. G., Baker M. J., Stiver, I. P., & Surrey, J. L. (1991). *Women's growth in connection.* New York: Guilford Press.

Kinsey, A. C., Pomeroy, W. B., & Martin, C. E. (1948). *Sexual behavior in the human male.* Philadelphia: Saunders.

Krystal, H. (1979). Alexithymia and psychotherapy. *American Journal of Psychotherapy, 33,* 17–30.

Levant, R. F. (1990). Psychological services designed for men: A psychoeducational approach. *Psychotherapy, 27,* 309–315.

Levant, R. F. (with Kopecky, G.). (1995). *Masculinity reconstructed.* New York: Dutton.

Levant, R. F. (1997). Desperately seeking language: Understanding, assessing, and treatment normative male alexithymia. In W. S. Pollack & R. F. Levant (Eds.), *New psychotherapies for men.* New York: Wiley.

Levant, R. F., & Pollack, W. S. (Eds.). (1995). *A new psychology of men.* New York: Basic Books.

Maccoby, E. E. (1990). Gender and relationships: A developmental account. *American Psychologist, 45,* 513–520.

May, R. (1977). *The meaning of anxiety.* New York: Simon & Schuster.

Meth, R. L., & Pasick, R. S. (1990). *Men in therapy: The challenge of change.* New York: Guilford Press.

Mitchell, S. A. (1993). *Hope and dread in psychoanalysis.* New York: Basic Books.

Moyers, B. (1993). *Healing and the mind.* New York: Doubleday.

National Institute of Mental Health, Depression Awareness, Recognition, and Treatment (D/ART) Program. (1987). *Sex differences in depressive disorders: A review of recent research.* Washington, DC: U.S. Department of Health and Human Services, National Institute of Mental Health.

Nicholson, R. A. (1995). *Tales of mystic meaning.* Oxford, England: One World.

Nuernberger, P. (1996). *The quest for personal power: Transforming stress into strength.* New York: Putnam.

O'Neil, J. M. (1981). Male sex-role conflicts, sexism, and masculinity: Psychological implications for men, women, and the counseling psychologist. *Counseling Psychologist, 9,* 61–80.

Osherson, S., & Krugman, S. (1990). Men, shame, and psychotherapy. *Psychotherapy, 27*(3), 327–339.

Papp, P. (1997, January/February). Listening to the system. *Family Therapy Networker,* 52–58.

Person, E. S. (1986). The omni-available woman and lesbian sex: Two fantasy themes and their relationship to the male developmental experience. In G. I. Fogel, F. M. Lane, & R. S. Liebert (Eds.), *The psychology of men: New psychoanalytic perspectives.* New York: Basic Books.

Phillips, A. (1996). *Monogamy.* New York: Pantheon Books.

Pleck, J. H. (1995). The gender role strain paradigm: An update. In R. F. Levant & W. S. Pollack (Eds.), *A new psychology of men.* New York: Basic Books.

Pleck, J. H., Sonenstein, F. L., & Ku, L. C. (1993). Masculinity ideology: Its impact on adolescent males' heterosexual relationships. *Journal of Social Issues, 49*(3),11–29.

Pollack, W. S. (1990). Men's development and psychotherapy: A psychoanalytic perspective. *Psychotherapy, 27*(3), 316–321.

Pollack, W. S. (1992). Should men treat women? Dilemmas for the male psychotherapist: Psychoanalytic and developmental perspectives. *Ethics and Behavior, 2,* 39–49.

Potash, M. S. (1990). *Hidden agendas: What's really going on in your relationships—in love, at work, in your family.* New York: Dell.

Real, T. (1997). *I don't want to talk about it: Overcoming the secret legacy of male depression.* New York: Scribner.

Rhodes, S., & Potash, M. S. (1988). *Cold feet: Why men don't commit.* New York: Signet.

Rubin, L. (1990). *Erotic wars.* New York: Farrar, Straus and Giroux.

Scher, M. (1990). Effect of gender role incongruities on men's experience as patients in psychotherapy. *Psychotherapy, 27,* 322–326.

Scher, M., Stevens, M., Good, G. E., & Eichenfield, G. A. (Eds.). (1987). *Handbook of counseling and psychotherapy with men.* Newbury Park, CA: Sage.

Selye, H. (1984). *The stress of life.* New York: McGraw Hill.

Shah, I. (1983). *The exploits of the incomparable mulla nasrudin and the subtleties of the mulla nasrudin.* London: Octagon Press.

Sharpe, M. J., & Heppner, P. P. (1991). Gender role, gender role conflict, and psychological well-being in men. *Journal of Counseling Psychology, 38,* 323–330.

Shay, J. J. (1996). Okay, I'm here, but I'm not talking: Psychotherapy with the reluctant male. *Psychotherapy, 33*(3), 503–513.

Sifneos, P. (1991). Affect, emotional conflict, and deficit: An overview. *Psychotherapy and Psychosomatics, 56,* 116–122.

Simon, R. I. (1989). Sexual exploitation of patients: How it begins before it happens. *Psychiatric Annals, 19,* 104–107, 111–112.

Simon, S. (1965). *More wise men of Helm & their merry tales.* West Orange, NJ: Behrman House.

Simon, S. (1973). *The wise men of Helm & their merry tales.* West Orange, NJ: Behrman House.

Tannen, D. (1990). *You just don't understand.* New York: Morrow.

Texas Heart Institute. (1996). *Heart owner's handbook.* New York: Wiley.

Zilbergeld, H. B. (1992). *The new male sexuality.* New York: Bantam Books.

Index

Abandonment trauma/depression, 4, 6, 14, 24, 28, 153–154, 155–156, 158, 164
Abuse, 167, 171, 173, 177, 185, 214, 215
    in childhood, and male violence, 219, 220
Action blunting of empathic recognition, 25, 157
Action disorders, 159
Action empathy, 41, 133, 299
    defined, 41, 133
    vs. emotional empathy, 41
    and emotionality, suppression/channeling of, 41
Adolescence, and homosexual orientation, 267
Advice vs. directives, in therapy, 295
Affective disorders, lifetime prevalence (Table 7.1), 151
African American men, and gender role trauma strain, 38
African American men, treating anger in, 8, 239–258
    anger as risk factor, 241–244
    conclusion, 256–257
    discussion, 254–256
    group therapy, 244–246
        composition of group, 246–247
        goals, 245, 256
        need for group, 244–245
        orientation and approach, 245–246
        process/content, 249–250, 251–253, 256
        session excerpts, 246–253
        therapist observations, 250–251, 254–255, 256
    life experiences contributing to anger, 242–244
    powerlessness, and anger at African Americans, 253–254
Aggressive behavior, predisposition for, 217. See also Violence, male
AIDS, 260, 272

AIM, 46
Alcohol/alcoholism, 62, 65–67, 128, 150
    familial, 167, 173, 174
    and shame, 174
Alcohol/drugs, ruling out (erectile disorder), 198
Alcoholic alexithymia, 164
Alexithymia, normative male, 4, 22, 35–56, 75, 101, 284–285
    case study, 45–51, 52
    and cognitive behavior therapy, 75, 77
    defined, 22, 35
    in disorder of the self, male type, 25, 157
    and emotionality, 41
    in male professional triad, 8, 284–285, 288, 299, 301, 303, 304
    and role socialization process, 37–43
    and sexuality, 201
    treatment program, 46–47
Alliance. See Relationship, therapeutic
Analogy, use of, in therapy, 296
Anger, 14, 24, 27, 63, 69–70, 91, 284
    final common pathway for emotion, 24
Anger in African American men. See African American men, treating anger in
Anger/aggression, overdevelopment of, 133
    consequence of suppression/channeling of emotionality, 42–43
Antidepressants, 150
Anxiety/anxiety disorders, 72–75, 150, 151, 284, 289
    and gender role stress and male erectile disorder, 192–197
    lifetime prevalence (Table 7.1), 151
Athletes, professional, and gender role trauma strain, 38

Attachment, fear of, 102
Attitudes, sexual, 199, 200
Attitudes toward Women Scale, 200
Autobiographical account, as
    homework, in couple therapy, 116
Automatic thinking, 58
Autonomy, 123
    defensive. *See* Defensive autonomy
    need for, 172
Awareness issues, 60, 80. *See also*
    Cognitive behavior therapy

"Big Wheel" (stereotyped male
    ideal/injunction), 22
Biological
    imperatives/predispositions,
    22–25, 59, 150, 156–157, 216–217,
    271
    gender differentiation, 22–25
    toward female identifications, 271
    and violence, 216–217
    vulnerability of males, 156–157
Biologically oriented psychiatrists, 150
Biopsychic constructs, two faulty,
    24–25
"Birth of Superpenis," 196
Bisexual men. *See* Gay and bisexual
    men
Blacks. *See* African American men,
    treating anger in
Blow-up doll, 302
Bodily sensation, experiencing
    emotion as, 42
Books, prescribing (in therapy),
    295–296
Boston University Fatherhood Project,
    44, 48
Boundaries, logistical and conceptual,
    291–292

Cardiac toxicity, stress-based, 164
Catastrophic expectations, 72–75
Change, challenge to, 94–95
Childhood abuse. *See* Abuse
Child-rearing, culturally normative,
    277
Child-rearing, gays/lesbians, and, 275
Cocoon transference, 26
Code of masculinity. *See* Masculinity
Cognitive behavior therapy, 5, 57–82,
    137–138, 173
    and alexithymia, 75
    "awfulizing," 72–75
    basic principles, 58
    case studies, 65–67, 69–70, 75–77

cofounders of, 58
devaluation of women, 70–71
father wound and father hunger,
    77–79
fear of femininity, 71–72
homophobia, 71–72
hypothetical idealized modern
    male, 79–80
intimacy, lack of, 70–71
misogyny and domination, 67–69
"stop and think" method of,
    137–138
viewpoint on male issues, 59–64
Cognitive dimension:
    of emotions (cognitive/affective
        component), 42
    of fear, 72–75
    to unhealthy masculinity, 58
Cognitive schemas, 5
"Communication problems," 98
Communication style, accommodating
    men's (in group therapy), 88
Contra-identification, 18
Counter identification, 18
Countertransference, 108, 188, 290,
    291–293, 300, 304
Couple therapy, 6, 94, 97–126, 303
    case studies ("Betty and Robert
        Marlboro"), 109–121
    dilemmas of, 107–109
    intimate relationships and the
        "Marlboro Man," 100–101
    men and psychotherapy. *See* Men,
        and psychotherapy
    stages in, 117
    summary/implications for
        treatment, 121–123
    theoretical approaches to men's
        intimacy problems, 101–107
Cross-cultural survey, male gender
    role strain, 128
Cross-gender therapist pairing, 283
Curative fantasy, 29

Dark-side behaviors, 57, 128
Death row, case study of prisoner on,
    220–225
"Deep" masculinity workshops, 63
Defenses, immature, 102
Defensive autonomy, 14, 21, 30, 271
Demands *vs.* preferences, 61–62
Depression, 6–7, 147–166
    in case studies, 65, 161–164, 288
    and disorder of the self, male type,
        25, 157

feminized view of, 152–153
forces affecting men, 153–154
and gender, 148–152
and hypertension and heart disease, 153
Major Depressive Disorder—Male Type (suggested new construct), 148, 160
male-based, four styles of, 153
prevalance/incidence, and gender, 147, 148–149, 284–285, 286
summary, 164
theory and treatment, 154–161
underdiagnosis and undertreatment of, in men, 150–152
in women, 68
Diagnostic Interview Schedule (DIS), 152
Differential memory, gender, and depression, 151–152
Directives, *vs.* advice, in therapy, 295
Disconnections, 187
Discontinuity between sex and gender, 229
Dis-identification, 17–18, 19, 102, 155, 157, 271, 272
Disorder of the self, male type (Tables 1.1 and 7.2), 25, 157
Disputation of irrational beliefs, 62–63
Doctor-patient model, *vs.* traditional male role, 176
Domestic violence, 173, 174. *See also* Violence, male
Domination, misogyny and, 67–69
"Dreamgirl," in case, 301

Emotional intimacy, lack of, 70–71. *See also* Intimacy problems, men's
Emotional Response Log, 47, 48
Emotional skills, learning, 288
Emotional socialization ordeal for boys, 38–41
Emotion(s)/emotionality:
  biological foundations of, 232
  components of (three), 42
  experiencing (two ways), 42
  expressing, 23, 137. *See also* Alexithymia, normative male
  psychoeducation about, 231–232
  suppression/channeling of; four consequences, 41–45
Empathic disconnections/disruptions, 7, 14, 155, 219
  and male violence. *See* Violence, male

Empathic psychoanalytic psychotherapy, 3
Erectile disorder. *See* Male erectile disorder
Essentialist views (gender differences and intimate relationships), 103, 106
Expectations, undoing unrealistic (treatment for male erectile disorder), 206–207
"Experience-near," 26, 28, 29, 32, 153
  listening, 153
  psychoanalytic treatment, 28
  understanding, 26
Externalization, 227, 228

Failure/inadequacy (need for revising terminology in sexual matters), 203
False self construction, 24, 157
Family dysfunction, and shame, 173
Family homeostasis, 129
Family interventions, preparing for (men's group therapy), 94
Family systems approach to treating men, 6, 127–144
  vs. all-male group (as initial intervention), 94
  case study, 132–142
  gender role strain and family therapy, 127–132
  male role strain, 132–141
  summary, 142
Fantasy:
  curative/reparative, 29
  sexual, 199
Father/fatherhood:
  case study: "numb expectant father," 5
  Fatherhood Project, Boston University, 44, 48
  father wound and father hunger, 77–79, 159
  influence of, on child development/emotionality, 4, 38, 39, 43, 155
Fear, cognitive dimension of, 72–75
Fear of femininity, 57, 71–72, 79, 89–90
Fear of flying, 74
Fee, discussing (in case), 180–181
Feedback loops, 234–235
Female therapists/male patients, 2, 8, 228–229, 276, 282–307
  alliance, establishing, 288–289
  attributes required with male patients, 289–290

Female therapists/male patients
  (Continued)
  and male violence, 228–229
  and sexuality, 2, 276
  special issues for, 290–296
  transference and
      countertransference issues,
      291–293, 294, 300
Female therapists/male patients, and
  "professional triad" syndrome,
  282–307
  alexithymia, 284. See also
      Alexithymia, normative male
  case studies:
      Adam; "man who loved too many
        yet not enough," 301–303
      Mike; "man who loved too much,"
        286, 297–301
      miscellaneous, 286, 288, 289
  interventions, therapeutic, 293–294
  intimacy, confusing sex with,
      283–287
  men seeking treatment, 287–290
  reluctant patients, 287–288
  sexual/emotional connection (or
      lack thereof), 285–287
  stress, 284
  summary, 304
  treatment strategies and techniques,
      294–296
Femininity:
  androgynous and healthy aspects
      of, 73
  fear of, 57, 71–72, 73, 79, 89–90
  therapy identified with, 89–90, 99,
      107
Feminist perspective, and cognitive
  approach to therapy, 173
Feminist theorists, modern, 155
Field dependence, 173
Field trips (treating male violence),
  233
Flight-fight reactions, 170
Framing men's problems in gender
  context, 88–89. See also Reframing
Funnel system, male emotional, 43

Gay and bisexual men, 8, 38, 179,
  259–281
  adaptation, style of, 273
  adolescence into adulthood, 267–268
  aspects of modern life, 269
  biculturalism, 269
  bisexual men, issues of relevance to,
      274

case study, 260–264
commonalities with heterosexual
  men, 264–265
differences in socialization and
  development, gay/bisexual men
  vs. heterosexual men, 265–268
early sense of "differentness,"
  266–267
forging new cultural norms, 269
and gender role trauma strain, 38
and homophobic ideas about child-
  rearing, 275
marginality, 269
psychotherapy with, 8, 259–281
sexual orientation and masculinity,
  270
subcultural life and diversity,
  272–274
summary, 276–277
theory of pre-Oedipal male
  development, applying, 271–272
and therapist errors, 275
and therapist having same sexual
  orientation, 276
therapists' considerations, 274–276
unique aspects of gay and bisexual
  identities, 268–272
Gay therapists, 179, 263
Gender:
  couple therapy informed by, 94,
      106–107. See also Couple therapy
  psychoeducation about (and
      treating male violence), 230–232
  and psychotherapy, 83–84
  of therapist, in couple therapy, 108,
      115
Gender role(s):
  and family, 142
  male. See Male gender role strain;
      Masculinity
  psychotherapy, 88
  stress, and male erectile disorder.
      See Male erectile disorder
  trauma, 60
"Gender role behavior" vs. "sexual
  orientation" vs. "core gender
  identity," 266
Gender Role Conflict Scale (GRCS),
  200
Gender Role Identity Paradigm, 37,
  194
  vs. Strain Paradigm, 37
Gender Role Strain Paradigm, 6, 22,
  37–38, 51, 58, 142, 194, 243. See also
  Male gender role strain

Generational boundaries, 130, 134, 140
"Give 'em hell" injunction of male code, 22, 42
GRCS. *See* Gender Role Conflict Scale (GRCS)
Grief, 51, 52, 91–92, 158, 164
Group therapy for anger in African American men. *See* African American men, treating anger in
Group therapy for traditional men, 4, 5, 83–96
  anger, bitterness, frustration, 91
  case study, 85–94
  change, challenge to, 94–95
  communication style, accommodating men's, 88
  family interventions, preparing for, 94
  gender and psychotherapy, 83–84
  gender context, framing men's problems in, 88–89
  guilt and grief, 91–92
  hope, instilling, 89–90
  isolation (from other men), addressing men's, 89
  key component in psychotherapy journey of resistant men, 85
  men's aversion to therapy, 84
  noble ascriptions, offering, 87–88
  psychic pain, evoking men's, 91
  self-disclosure, generating participative, 92
  universality, recognizing, 89
  women, countering men's overdependence on, 92–94
Guilt:
  and grief (in men's group therapy), 91–92
  and shame, 168, 169
"Guilty man" *vs.* "tragic man," 158, 159

Healing process, poetic metaphor of, 32
Health risk behaviors, 284
"Heterosexism," 265
Hollow. *See* "Stuffed" (guilt-ridden, self-critical) *vs.* "hollow" (empty, depleted, angry)
Homeostasis, family, 129, 142
Homework assignments, in therapy, 63, 76, 295
Homicide, 1, 241

Homophobia, 58, 71–72, 74–75, 79, 270, 272
  barriers to seeking treatment, 2
  term coined, 265
  and therapist, 275
Homosexuality/homosexual experiences, 188, 199. *See also* Gay and bisexual men
Hope, instilling (men's group therapy), 89–90
Humiliated fury, 170
Humiliation, and shame, 168
Humor, use of (in therapy), 296
Hypothetical idealized modern male, 79–80

Identity, "core gender" *vs.* "sexual orientation" *vs.* "gender role behavior," 266
Impotency:
  criticism of terminology, 201–202
  primary/secondary, 191
  treating. *See* Male erectile disorder
Impulse control disorders, 150
Infants, emotionality/expressiveness, 4, 22–23, 38, 156–157
Integrated masculinity, modeling a more (treating male violence), 228–229
Internalized/internalizing:
  demands, 173
  emotion, 42
  gender role expectations, 60
  homophobia, 265, 268, 273
  masculinity, and "truncated humanity," 231
Interpretation, 295
Intimacy problems, men's, 2, 9, 58, 70–71, 98, 100–107, 140–141, 285–287
  lack of intimacy, 58, 70–71
  relationship problems, 98, 100–101
  sex, confusing intimacy with, 9, 58, 101, 140–141, 285–287
  theoretical approaches to, 101–107
Invisibility syndrome (and African American anger), 8, 242, 252
  managing stress from, 244
"Invisible" gay man, 273, 274
Irrational belief system, 62
Isolation, addressing men's (from other men), 89
I-Thou Relationship, 68

Journal keeping, 295
  Emotional Response Log, 47, 48
  logging, 78–79
Journey, therapy, 5, 85
Judeo-Christian dogma, and sexual
  behavior, 195

Language, learning different
  (treatment for male erectile
  disorder), 201–203
Language of therapy *vs.* language of
  men, 99
Life expectancy, 1
Logging. *See* Journal keeping
"Losers," 92

Madonna and *Whore* dichotomy, 13
Major Depressive Disorder—Male
  Type (suggested new construct),
  148, 160
Male(s), and therapy. *See* Men, and
  psychotherapy
Male code. *See* Masculinity
Male erectile disorder, 7, 191–213
  alcohol/drugs, ruling out, 198
  anxiety and, 192–197
  assessing development of sexuality
    and gender role strain/conflict,
    198–201
  case studies, 203–204, 205, 206–207
  evaluation process, 197–201, 210
  medical factors, ruling out, 197
  overview/introduction/summary,
    191–192, 208–211
  treatment, 197, 201–210
Male gender role *vs.* patient role, 84
Male gender role strain, 6, 22, 37–38,
  51, 58, 59, 142, 194, 243, 286, 287,
  290
Male gender socialization, and male
  violence, 217
Male Role Norms Inventory (MRNI),
  200
Male violence. *See* Violence, male
"Marlboro Man," 6, 100–101
Marriage counseling, 75. *See also*
  Couple therapy
Masculinity:
  code of; need for
    redefining/restructuring, 1, 59,
    80, 105
  dark side of traditional, 57, 128
  ideals off, 21–22, 84, 100
  mandates of manhood, 10 central,
    impossible to attain, 60–61

norms of traditional (seven listed),
  37
vs. psychotherapy, 99–101
and sexual orientation, 270
Masturbation, 15, 199
Medical factors, ruling out (male
  erectile disorder), 197
Medication, 163
Melancholia/melancholic depression,
  147, 158
Memory, differential (gender and
  depression), 151–152
Men, and masculinity. *See* Masculinity
Men, and psychotherapy, 99–101
  African Americans. *See* African
    American men, treating anger in
  aversion to therapy, 2, 84, 176, 287
  depression. *See* Depression
  and female therapists. *See* Female
    therapists/male patients
  gays/bisexuals. *See* Gay and
    bisexual men
  gender and psychotherapy, 83–84
  introduction, 1–10
  sexual dysfunction. *See* Male
    erectile disorder
  shame/trauma. *See* Shame
  treatment modalities. *See* Treatment
    modalities
  violence. *See* Violence, male
Microaggression, 243
Mid-life crises, 159
Misogyny/domination, 58, 67–69
"Mommy track," 22
Money/success, obsession with, 64
Mother:
  ambivalent yearnings toward, 20
  dis-identification, 17–18, 19, 102,
    155, 157, 181, 271, 272
  and emotionality of infants, 38, 39
  influences of, 4, 38, 39
  separation from. *See* Abandonment
    trauma/depression
Motor/behavioral response
  (component of emotions), 42
Mourn/grieve, 147, 158. *See also* Grief
  inability to, 24, 157
Movies:
  prescribing, 295
  use of (treating male violence),
    233–234
MRNI. *See* Male Role Norms Inventory
  (MRNI)
Multiple sex partners. *See* Polygamous
  men

Narcissistic issues, 4, 24, 159, 181
Narcissistic personality disorder, 21, 26, 102, 156
Nature and nurture, 21–25
  biological imperatives, 22–25. *See also* Biological imperatives/predispositions
  gender-bifurcated role socialization, 21–22
Neurophysiological substrate (component of emotions), 42
Neurotic fears, 72
Newborn. *See* Infants, emotionality/expressiveness
New psychoanalytic psychotherapy for men. *See* Psychoanalytic psychotherapy for men
Nonrelational sex, 303. *See also* Intimacy problems, men's; Polygamous men
Normative child-rearing, culturally (inherently damaging for boys), 277
Normative developmental trauma, gender-linked, 19–21, 155
Normatively masculinized male, preconditioned to violence, 218
Normative male alexithymia. *See* Alexithymia, normative male
Normative male socialization pressures. *See* Socialization, male
"No Sissy Stuff" (stereotyped male ideal/injunction), 22

Object relations theory, 25, 157, 172
Oedipal issues, 4, 13–34, 153–154, 185, 271–272. *See also* Psychoanalytic psychotherapy for men
  the Greek myth of Oedipus, 14, 16–17
  and male homosexuality, 271–272
  re-enactment, 185
Over-reliance on women, men's, 123

Pain, psychic, 91–92
Pairing up with mirror-image vulnerabilities, 102
Paradoxes, 98, 104, 156, 225
Parasuicides, 150
Parents, and shame, 170. *See also* Father/fatherhood; Mother
Passive-aggressive behavior, 71
Past relationships/traumas, relative emphasis on, 58, 175

Pathogenic model of "healthy" male development, 277
Patriarchy, side effects of, 68
Peer group(s):
  influence on emotional expressivity, 4, 40–41
  and shame, 170
Penis envy, 18
Perfectionism, 25, 27, 157
Performance (criticism of terminology, sexual matters), 202
Performance anxiety, 201
Playful pleasuring (treatment for male erectile disorder), 208
Polygamous men, 282–283, 285, 299, 304
  prototypical portrait of, 299
Postmodern view of gender, 103–104
Post-traumatic shame, 170–171
Powerlessness, 253–254
Pre-conscious, 58
Preferential thinking, 62
Pride, and shame, 186–187
Professional male triad (alexithymia, stress, sex/intimacy confusion), 303. *See also* Female therapists/male patients, and "professional triad" syndrome
Promiscuity. *See* Polygamous men
Psychic foundations, two faulty, 157
Psychic pain, evoking men's, 91–92
Psychoanalytic psychotherapy for men, 4, 13–34, 101–103
  biological imperatives, 22–25
  case studies, 14–16, 27–32
  disorder of the self, male type (Table 1.1), 25
  gender-bifurcated role socialization, 21–22
  healing process, poetic metaphor of, 32
  for intimacy problems, 101–103. *See also* Intimacy problems, men's
  nature and nurture, 21–25
  normative (gender-linked) developmental trauma, 19–21
  Oedipal issues. *See* Oedipal issues
  theory, 17–19
  treatment, 25–27
Psychodynamic perspective, 175
Psychoeducational therapy, 4, 230–232
  and alexithymia (five-step model), 4. *See also* Alexithymia, normative male

Psychoeducational therapy
(Continued)
about gender (treating male
violence), 230–232
Psychotherapy. See Men, and
psychotherapy
Puberty, 44

Racism, anger, and gender role
expectations, 239–241, 242,
243–244, 254
Rational Emotive Behavior Therapy, 5,
61
Reflective thinking, 62
Reframing, 62, 80, 203–206
framing men's problems in gender
context, 88–89
of gender-rigid images (treatment
for male erectile disorder),
203–206
Relationship, therapeutic, 129,
180–183, 188, 283, 288–289, 296,
303, 304
curative, 175
and treating male violence, 225–226
Relationship problems. See Couple
therapy
Relaxation, responsive (treatment for
male erectile disorder), 207–208
Religion, and sexuality, 75–77, 195
Reparative fantasy, 29
"Report talk" vs. "rapport talk," 100
Repressed feelings, 27
Repression personality, 25, 157
Resistance, 176
to change, in couple therapy, 108
Road rage, 178
Role-play, in therapy, 48
Rubber band syndrome, 43
Rule-governed (families/social
systems), 94

Schemas, cognitive, underlying
unhealthy masculinity, 58
Sealed therapeutic environment,
226–228
Self, disorder of, male type (Tables 1.1
and 7.2), 25, 157
Self-criticism, harsh, 25, 157
Self-defeating behaviors, 62, 78
Self-disclosure:
and homosexuality, 272
participative (in men's group
therapy), 92
Self-mutilation, 196

Self-object, 4, 14, 19, 26, 29
functions of therapist, 4, 29
holding environment, 14
relationships, 19
transference, 26
Separation, 15, 153–154, 155, 156. See
also Abandonment
trauma/depression
premature push for, 155
Sex:
addiction to, 15, 286
boys and, 44, 101
vs. intimacy. See Intimacy problems,
men's
Sexism, 265
Sexual Adjustment Inventory, 200
Sexual dysfunction, 62, 64. See also
Male erectile disorder
arousal disorder, 192
Sexual experiences, 199
Sexual exploitation of patients, 292
Sexual identity concerns, and suicide,
267
Sexuality:
in case studies, 75–77, 177
channeling of caring emotions into,
43–45, 101, 133
as developmental variable waiting
to be nurtured/abused, 196
and gender role strain/conflict, and
male erectile disorder, 198–201
and Judeo-Christian dogma, 195
and masculinity, myths,
misinformation, and unrealistic
expectations, 196
sociocultural abuse of sexuality
model, 195–199
and women, 104
Sexually transmitted diseases, 199
"Sexual orientation" vs. "gender role
behavior" vs. "core gender
identity," 266
Shame, 7, 14, 73, 167–190
case study, 176–189
contemporary theory and research,
171–174
defenses against, 102
defensive function of, 185
dynamics of, 168–171
exercises attacking, 73
and guilt, 14
libidinal vs. aggressive, 173
male gender effects, 171
overview/summary, 167–168
post-traumatic, 170–171

psychodynamic perspective, 175
psychotherapy guided by, 174–175
sensitivity/phobia, 25, 157
and socialization systems, 156
technical issues in treating men, 176
unacknowledged (impact of, on
    psychotherapy process), 27, 154,
    171, 188
Social activism, as part of therapy
    journey, 85
Social construction of intimacy,
    104–106
Social constructivist perspective, 173
Socialization, male:
    and alexithymia, 37–43. *See also*
        Alexithymia, normative male
    emotional socialization "ordeal" for
        boys, 38–41
    gay/bisexual men *vs.* heterosexual
        men, 265–268
    gender-bifurcated role socialization,
        21–22
    and shame, 156, 173
    and violence, 217
Sociocultural abuse of sexuality
    model, 195–199
Split-brain patient, 234
Sports, and development of action
    empathy, 41
Status/success, obsession with, 64
Stereotypes, reinforcing, 244
Stereotypes, widely shared beliefs
    about gender roles, 128
Stoicism, emotional, 41. *See also*
    Alexithymia, normative male
"Stop and think" method of cognitive-
    behavior modification, 137–138
Strain. *See* Male gender role strain
Stress, 42, 46, 164, 244, 284, 285, 303,
    304
    behavioral implications of excess,
        284
    and cardiac toxicity, 164
    defined, 284
    excess, 284, 285, 303
    experiencing emotions as, 42, 46
    gender role, and male erectile
        disorder. *See* Male erectile
        disorder
    from invisibility (African
        Americans), 244
    in professional male triad
        (alexithymia, stress,
        sex/intimacy confusion). *See*
        Female therapists/male

patients, and "professional
    triad" syndrome
Structured clinical interview, for
    assessing development of
    sexuality and gender role
    strain/conflict, 198
"Stuffed" (guilt-ridden, self-critical)
    vs. "hollow" (empty, depleted,
    angry), 147, 148, 158, 159
Substance abuse, 171, 241
    lifetime prevalence (Table 7.1), 151
    vulnerability to, 25, 157
Suicide/suicidality, 1, 2, 150, 171, 260,
    267
    and gay adolescents, 267
Superego, theory of, 158
Supportive intervention, 295
"Sympathy with an edge" (treating
    male violence), 229–230
Systems therapy, 94. *See also* Family
    systems approach to treating men

Task Force on Men's Roles and
    Psychotherapy (APA), 3
Temperament of infants. *See* Infants,
    emotionality/expressiveness
Therapeutic alliance, 129, 180–183,
    188, 283, 288–289, 296, 303, 304
Therapists:
    attributes required with male
        patients, 289–290
    female. *See* Female therapists/male
        patients
    same sexual orientation, 275
Third parties, including (in treating
    male violence), 233
Transactional analysis (TA), 68
Transference, 26, 108, 175, 185,
    187–188, 290, 291–293, 294, 300,
    304
    shame in, 187–188
    utilizing to ensure treatment goals,
        294
Transsexuals, research with, 17
Trauma, 19–21, 38, 58, 60, 155,
    170–171, 175, 219, 220. *See also*
    Abandonment
    trauma/depression; Abuse
    gender role trauma strain, 38
    normative (gender-linked)
        developmental trauma, 19–21,
        155
    past relationships/traumas, relative
        emphasis on, 58, 175
    and shame, 170–171. *See also* Shame

Treatment, psychological. *See* Men, and psychotherapy
Treatment contract, 289, 298
Treatment modalities, 11
  and alexithymia. *See* Alexithymia, normative male
  cognitive behavior therapy. *See* Cognitive behavior therapy
  couple therapy. *See* Couple therapy
  family systems approach. *See* Family systems approach to treating men
  group therapy. *See* Group therapy for traditional men
  psychoanalytic. *See* Psychoanalytic psychotherapy for men
"Truncated humanity," 231
Trust, 31, 121
TS-20, 45

Veterans Administration Hospital, Temple, Texas, 5
Veterans of combat, and gender role trauma strain, 38
Victims, perpetrators as, 230
Videotaping (in treating male violence), 234–235

Vietnam War combat veteran (case study; Luis), 85–95
Violence, male, 7, 214–236
  case study ("resurrecting humanity on death row") 220–225
  documents, use of, in treating, 233
  roots of, 216–220
  summary/conclusion, 235
  treatment of, 225–235
  ubiquity/reality of, 214–216

"Well-sealed pressure cooker," 226–228
Wilson Sexual Fantasy Questionnaire, 200
Women:
  advances/changes, 20th century, 104
  devaluation of, 58, 70–71
  men's attitudes toward, 200
  men's overdependence on, 92–94, 123
Workaholism, 25, 157
World War I trench warfare analogy, male socializaiton, and male violence, 218